CONNECTING YOUNG ADULTS AND LIBRARIES

A How-To-Do-It Manual for Librarians
Third Edition

Patrick Jones
Michele Gorman
Tricia Suellentrop

*HOW-TO-DO-IT MANUALS
FOR LIBRARIANS*

NUMBER 133

NEAL–SCHUMAN PUBLISHERS, INC.
New York, London

Be sure to visit
www.connectingya.com

The companion Web site that accompanies this book offers resources to save you the time and trouble of typing in long URLs.

It will also keep these resources updated.

Published by Neal-Schuman Publishers, Inc.
100 William Street, Suite 2004
New York, NY 10038

Printed and bound in the United States of America.

The paper used in this publication meets the minimum requirements of American National Standard for Informational Sciences—Permanence of Paper for Printed Library Materials, ANSI Z39.48—1992

Library of Congress Cataloging-in-Publication Data

Jones, Patrick, 1961–
    Connecting young adults and libraries : a how-to-do-it manual for librarians / Patrick Jones, Michele Gorman, Tricia Suellentrop.—3rd ed.
p. cm.—(How-to-do-it manuals for librarians ; no. 133) Includes bibliographical references and index.
    ISBN 1-55570-508-1 (alk. paper)
    1. Young adults' libraries—Administration—Handbooks, manuals, etc. 2. Young adults—Books and reading—Handbooks, manuals, etc. I. Gorman, Michele. II. Suellentrop, Tricia, 1970- III. Title. IV. How-to-do-it manuals for libraries ; no. 133.

    Z718.5.J66 2004
    027.62'6—dc22

                                        2004046008

CONTENTS

LIST OF FIGURES AND CORE DOCUMENTS

FIGURES

CORE DOCUMENTS

PREFACE

Wow.

A lot has happened since the publication of the second edition of *Connecting Young Adults and Libraries* in the spring of 1998. I have completed my tour of the country with speaking engagements in Mississippi and Arkansas, thus completing the task of bringing the message of *Connecting Young Adults and Libraries* to all fifty states, not to mention Australia, New Zealand, and several Canadian provinces. Everywhere I go, I meet thousands of people involved in the day-to-day job of serving young adults in schools and public libraries. In these past six years, my work has changed; thanks to the best practices that have been shared with me and the presentations and conferences that have helped me develop my ideas, I am very happy and excited to share those changes with you here.

Young adult librarianship is still very important—and its prominence grows every day. New initiatives, new recognitions, and new formats prove that teens are a major segment of many libraries' users. This new edition touches on these new trends that offer living proof that your services are viable and necessary. Consider the following:

- The creation of the Printz and Alex Awards to recognize the best in young adult literature and in adult books of interest to teens;
- The growing popularity of the teen-friendly graphic novel format;
- The Internet explosion, which brought more teens into libraries than ever before;
- The demand for information literacy programs and the growing need to provide teens with the skills they need to "read" information;
- The "Serving the Underserved" project showing young adult librarians how to train generalists serving teens in libraries;
- The widely (and wildly) accepted Teen Read Week; and

- The Urban Libraries Council's small but very well-funded "Public Libraries as Partners in Youth Development" project providing models and innovative ideas for youth involvement.

And these are just the crest of the wave of innovative teen services sweeping across libraries. There is growing awareness that teen services are about more than paperbacks, youth advisory groups, and programs. The work we do is holistic and helps teens achieve a positive library experience.

What you'll be reading here isn't research, pure theory, or the results of a few successful, well-funded programs from large public library systems (although we include some of those). *Connecting Young Adults and Libraries* brings success stories and proven practices that Librarians Serving Teens (LST) can replicate whether they are "lone rangers" or members of a team in school and public libraries. In addition to these ready-to-go programming ideas and practices, *Connecting Young Adults and Libraries* presents a mind-set—a way of thinking about and serving teens in libraries. This book provides model programs, to-do lists, and books to read, but, in addition, helps you to understand why these things work so you can go out and create new models and methods of service in your own library.

Consistent throughout *Connecting Young Adults and Libraries* is the core message of developing a "YAttitude." It is important to recognize the value of young adults, their right to quality library services, and the passion needed to serve them. For some librarians unfamiliar with or new to YA service, this book may be the start of a conversion. For librarians who already recognize the importance of serving teens, this will be a tool of action—a way of putting your thoughts and commitments to work in ways you had never imagined. This information should help increase your awareness of the needs and wants of YAs, the necessity of YA service, and how libraries and librarians can respond to their communities. The working assumption throughout *Connecting Young Adults and Libraries* is that anyone can connect young adults and libraries once they have adopted the proper attitude and been given the right tools.

This very big book may seem intimidating, but you will discover that it is user-friendly—almost a training workshop in a text. At training workshops, people want two things: to ask questions (the same ones are asked frequently) and to get lists. This book presents answers to the questions you always wanted to ask and puts the answers and information in lists that are easy to read and use. To make sure we are all using the same language, we open the book with a glossary defining over one hundred terms that an LST needs to know.

Just as the second edition of *Connecting* contained about 50 percent new material from the first, this third edition is also loaded with new ideas, examples, and perspectives. It also contains many of the core elements from the first two editions. While the collection section in this book will mention some core titles, the focus is more on trends and larger issues than individual titles. Reinstated in this edition is the valuable programming section, which seems to be the most popular topic for training and listserv discussions. This edition also features a lot more about technology's impact on our teen customers and the need for information literacy. New to this edition are entire chapters on outreach and youth involvement. While these are stand-alone chapters, the idea of involving and reaching out to youth runs like a river through the text.

The first chapter, "Why: The Philosophy Behind Services to Young Adults," looks at the philosophical basis for serving teens in school and public libraries. The "why" is followed by the "who" with Chapter 2, "Who: Understanding the Audience," which looks at the young adult customer and includes plenty of information about what teens want from libraries. Chapter 3, "When/Where: State of the Art YA Services," provides the context by examining the past, exploring ten trends in the present, and looking at the future of connecting young adults and libraries. Customer service—including reference, readers' advisory, and information literacy programs—makes up the bulk of Chapter 4, "Customer Service." If customer service for teens isn't understood and adopted across the library, then the more involved work, like programming and youth involvement, will not be effective.

"Collections" are covered in Chapter 5, beginning with a review of teen reading interests and an overviews of formats and genres. Chapter 6, "Booktalking," focuses on this as one of the key ways to promote teen collections. Chapters 7, "Outreach and Partnerships," 8, "Programming," and 9, "Spaces and Promotion," look at these other methods to power up teens. Chapter 10, "Technology," looks at teens and technology, from building a YA Web page to examining various issues related to Internet use. Youth involvement, which is really a core idea behind all of these services, is examined in Chapter 11, "Youth Involvement." The very nature of all of these services presents LSTs with various "issues," which are presented as discussion questions in the final chapter, "Issues in Young Adult Services." The conclusion reviews some of the core messages about connecting young adults and libraries.

Unlike the other editions of this book, in which documents and forms were included in the chapters, this edition features a separate "Core Documents" section. This should make the documents both more usable (i.e., easier to photocopy) and make the book a little less busy. Following the documents is a bibliography with citations to over five hundred books and articles from inside and outside the library literature related to serving teens. There are no Web sites in the bibliography: instead, visit our Web page at www.connectingya.com to get linked directly to the Web resources that support the ideas in this book.

This third edition of *Connecting Young Adults and Libraries* is a total experience. It isn't meant simply to improve one area of your service—it is meant to change the way you think about your role as a young adult librarian. This book incorporates the recent changes in YA librarianship, but also advocates the basic values, tools, and mindset that will serve this area of service for years to come.

Patrick Jones

ACKNOWLEDGMENTS

The authors would like to thank staff and administration of the Hennepin County (MN) Public Library and the Austin (TX) Public Library for allowing us to use work products in this text. Thanks, also, to Bessie Condos Tichauer of the State Library of California for permission to use information from the Teen Focus Groups for the Young Adult Service Program report, and to Jim Rosinia for use of the "Who Has the Problem?" training exercise. Finally, the authors wish to thank Ken Rasak for his assistance in preparing the bibliography.

PATRICK'S ACKNOWLEDGMENTS

Thanks to the staff of the Hennepin County Library, in particular the Teen Read Month and Teen Links teams, as well as David Lane and Amy McNally of the SWIFT project, and Charles Brown, Gretchen Wronka, Ali Turner, Sarajo Wentling, Ann Melrose, and the entire Outreach department. Thanks to Kelley Worman, Project Coordinator Young Adult Services Institute Fresno County Public Library. Thanks to the usual suspects: Mary Kay Chelton, Erica Klein, Brent Chartier, and Betty Jones.

MICHELE'S ACKNOWLEDGMENTS

This one is for the boys: my brothers, Mark, Michael, and Greg, and my Dad, Robert Gorman. A special thanks also goes out to my boss Jeanette Larson, my research partner Lindsey Schell, my fellow Wired for Youth librarians, the outstanding Carver Library staff, and the amazing teens I have the good fortune to work with everyday. And of course, I would be remiss not to thank my continually supportive and loving triad: Taylor Flores, Holly Hungerford, and Marli Guzzetta.

TRICIA'S ACKNOWLEDGMENTS

Thanks to the staff of the Johnson County Library, especially Jean Hatfield and Kathy McLellan, as well as the "YAACers" who hired me and continue to keep me in line. Thanks to Paula Brehm-Heeger, Sarah Cornish, Denise Leech, Martha Gronniger, Patrick Jones, Jenne Laytham, Kim Patton, Kimberlee Ried, and Shawn Thrasher for helping me become a teen advocate. Thanks to Joyce Suellentrop for all the silly stuff.

INTRODUCTION: THE LANGUAGE OF THE LST (LIBRARIAN SERVING TEENS)

Throughout the text we'll refer, in true librarian fashion, to a plethora of acronyms and jargon. Here is a glossary from the get-go of these shorthand notations that describe and define the core vocabulary for librarians who serve teens (also known as teenagers, young adults, and YAs) in a school or public library. The four most critical are listed first, and another hundred definitions follow in alphabetical order.

- **LST:** a new term we have coined which means "Librarian Serving Teens." While we don't have new numbers since the last national survey of Young Adult (YA) services in public libraries in 1995, we do know from anecdotal evidence that the number of YA librarians in public libraries has increased from 11 percent. Since that time, the membership of YALSA has almost doubled, which indicates an expanded interest in teen services. But even if the number of public libraries with full time YA librarians doubled, that would still mean that less than a quarter of libraries employ a staff member dedicated to reaching that 25 percent of the people who visit public libraries. Yet, as we collected best practices from across the country, it was obvious that some of the best services emerged from people without the title "Young Adult Librarian." The point we want to make by using this term is that any librarian in any library that counts persons ages twelve to eighteen among their patrons is an LST. Some do this full time, while others only do it from 3–6 p.m. across the reference desk. The term "librarian" is also broadly defined to include any library staff member or volunteer. It is also used for school librarians, media specialists, and teacher-librarians who work with students between the ages of twelve and eighteen in a school setting. While school librarians play different roles than public librarians, have different ways of measuring success, and provide different services, they are still LSTs.

- **We:** Patrick, Michele, and Tricia. While each person wrote different parts of the book, the goal is to have the text speak with one voice.

- **YALSA (Young Adult Library Services Association):** a division of the American Library Association, this is the primary professional association for librarians serving teens. The mission of YALSA is to advocate, promote, and strengthen service to young adults as part of the continuum of total library service, and to support those who provide service to this population. Many of the booklists, awards, and projects we'll refer to in the text emerge from the work of this organization and its members.

- **YAttitude:** a "YAttitude" recognizes the value of young adults, their right to quality library services, and the passion needed to serve them. This term was coined in the first edition of *Connecting Young Adults and Libraries*; thus, we think that an LST with a YAttitude is likely to be involved in YALSA, okay? A YAttitude doesn't imply that an LST is "cooler" than other librarians, but merely that they understand the unique information needs of teens, and advocate for others to share a similar understanding. You can't get teen services right unless you understand *why* you are doing it and *who* your audience is. YAttitude is also the name of the YALSA's members-only online newsletter.

In alphabetical order, here are over one hundred other important terms, documents, people, and organizations that we use in the text of this book and we consider essential for LSTs to know to connect young adults and libraries.

- **AASL (American Association of School Librarians):** The mission of this ALA division is to advocate excellence, facilitate change, and develop leaders in the school library media field. About half of all YALSA members are school librarians. The primary document spelling out the AASL agenda is *Information Power.*

- **Adolescence:** the transition from childhood to adulthood; a process during which individuals experience a wide range of events and opportunities for growth and development.

- **Adolescent literacy:** the concern that teens are actively engaged in reading. The most successful adolescent literacy activities are based on the ideas that time spent reading is related to reading skills, academic success, attitudes about reading, and knowledge of the world.

- **ALA (American Library Association):** the largest library association in the world, with more than sixty thousand members. ALA's mission is to promote the highest quality library and information services for public access.

- **ALAN (Assembly on Literature for Adolescents of NCTE):** made up of teachers, authors, librarians, publishers, and others interested in the area of young adult literature.

- **ALAN Review:** official publication of ALAN; contains articles on YA literature and its teaching, interviews with authors, reports on publishing trends, current research on YA literature, and reviews of new books.

- **Alex Awards:** YALSA book selection committee charged with awarding, from the previous year's publications, ten books written for adults that have special appeal to YAs.

- **Aliteracy:** the state of being able to read, but choosing not to pursue reading as a recreational activity.

- **Anime:** a style of animation originating in Japan that is characterized by stark, colorful graphics depicting vibrant characters in action-filled plots, often with fantastic or futuristic themes.

- **ALSC (Association for Library Service to Children):** another ALA division. ALSC consists of over 3,700 members committed to improving and ensuring the future of the nation through exemplary library service to children, their families, and others who work with children.

- **Assets:** the building blocks of adolescence. Assets represent strengths and opportunities in the lives of youth.

- **At-risk youth:** a broad term used to describe teens in trouble. "At-risk youth" often describes a person under the age of twenty-one who is at high risk of becoming (or who has become) a substance abuser, is a victim of abuse, has dropped out of school or does poorly in school, has mental health issues including suicidal tendencies, and/or has committed a violent or criminal act. While some equate "at-risk" with urban or minority youth, all teens are at risk in one way or another. Research tells us that teens without assets are more likely to be at-risk and engage in self-destructive behavior.

- **AUP (Acceptable Use Policy):** an agreement, created by a library and approved by its governing structure, that defines permitted and prohibited Internet use behaviors.

- **Banned Books Week:** a week-long celebration of the freedom to read held during the last week of September. In existence since 1982, this project's sponsors include the American Booksellers Association, the American Society of Journalists and Authors, the National Association of College Stores, and the ALA.

- **Bare Bones:** document created by Mary Kay Chelton and Jim Rosinia to provide basic service tips for public library generalists. The book was jointly published in 1992 by YALSA and the Public Library Association. A second expanded edition, written by Renee Vaillancourt, was published in 2000.

- **BBYA (Best Books for Young Adults):** a YALSA committee charged with the annual creation of a list of significant adult and young adult books. BBYA is one of the most visible of YALSA's various offerings.

- **Big 6:** an information problem-solving approach created by Robert Berkowitz and Michael Eisenberg. The purpose of the Big 6 is to provide students with a framework for thinking about research by following a series of six steps.

- **Blog:** an online diary format growing in popularity among teens

- *Booklist*: an ALA publication that reviews more than 2,500 titles for youth. *Booklist* also publishes a wide variety of feature articles including author interviews, bibliographies, book-related essays by well-known writers, and a selection of columns—including one dedicated to young adult literature. The youth editors for *Booklist* serve as advisors to the YALSA book selection committees.

- **Booktalk:** a paperback blurb as performance. Just as the copy on the back of any YA paperback is designed to entice the teen reader to pick up the book and purchase it, a booktalk is a presentation designed to motivate the teens in the booktalk audience to check out the books being promoted.

- **Broderick, Dorothy:** cofounder, with Mary Kay Chelton, of *Voice of Youth Advocates* (*VOYA*) magazine.

- **Campbell, Patty:** regular columnist for *Horn Book* magazine, editor of a series of books for Scarecrow Press about young adult literature, and an outspoken advocate for "quality" literature for teens.

- **Cart, Michael:** former president of YALSA, winner of the Grolier award, novelist, short story compiler, *Booklist* columnist, editor of *Rush Hour* magazine for older teens, and one of the primary movers creating the Michael Printz Award for young adult literature.

- **Chelton, Mary Kay:** a professor at the library school at Queen's College, one of the cofounders of *VOYA*, editor of three volumes of *Excellence in Library Services to Young Adults*, the coauthor of the first edition of *Bare Bones*, and the leading thinker in the field of library services to teens.

- **CIPA:** Federal-State Joint Board on Universal Service/Children's Internet Protection Act. This law, recently upheld by the United States Supreme Court (Docket No. 96–45), links federal funding for local libraries with filtering software that "protects" children from harmful material while allowing adults the option of having filter removed.

- **Collection development:** the process of selecting (and rejecting) materials to appear in a library's physical and virtual collections. More than just buying new books, collection development is a series of choices based on each library's mission, community, and operating procedures.

- **Developmental assets:** a framework developed by the Search Institute to identify the elements of a strength-based approach to healthy development. This framework identifies forty critical factors for young people's growth and development.
- **Developmental tasks:** the emotional, social, sexual, intellectual, and psychological changes that make up adolescence.
- **Digital divide:** the gap between those who can effectively use new information and communication tools, such as the Internet, and those who cannot.
- **Edgy Fiction:** a mid- to late-1990s trend of young adult fiction that featured mature themes and complex characters—but not happy endings; also called "bleak books."
- **Edwards, Margaret:** the administrator of young adult programs at Enoch Pratt Free Library in Baltimore for over thirty years; wrote the first "manifesto" of YA librarianship. Her name is attached to YALSA's award for lifetime achievement in young adult literature.
- **The Edwards (Margaret) Trust:** a trust that has backed many YALSA projects and awards.
- **Ephebiphobia:** the fear and loathing of teenagers.
- **Excellence in Library Services to Young Adults:** a project that began in 1994 to identify the top programs for YAs in libraries. Funded by the Edwards Trust, this project resulted in three publications edited by Mary Kay Chelton. A fourth edition of the project/book is forthcoming, edited by Renee Vaillancourt.
- **The Fair Garden and the Swarm of Beasts:** a book by Margaret Edwards often considered the "manifesto" of YA Librarianship. It has been updated twice since its original publication in 1974.
- **Focus group:** a technique used in marketing in which one gathers a representative sample of a certain market and by asks questions in a controlled setting to discover the participant's feelings about a certain product or service.
- **Formal learning support:** a role or service response adopted by a public library in which the library offers support to students who are pursuing their education goal through enrollment in a formal program of education or a program of homeschooling.

- **Free Access to Libraries for Minors:** a core ALA document originally adopted in 1972 that is an interpretation/extension of the Library Bill of Rights, which states that any attempt by libraries to deny minors equal access to resources violates the Library Bill of Rights.

- **Freedom to Read:** an important ALA statement that spells out the association's belief that the freedom to read is essential to democracy.

- **GNLIB (Graphic Novels in Libraries):** a listserv that reviews titles, discusses issues, and allows LSTs to share information about graphic novels.

- **Graphic novel:** a broad term used to define a book for teens or adults told in comic book form, in which both text and illustrations tell the story.

- **Grolier award:** ALA annual award presented to a librarian whose contribution to the stimulation and guidance of reading by children and young people exemplifies outstanding achievement in the profession.

- **Guys Read:** a literacy initiative for boys launched by author Jon Scieszka.

- **HC-HY (Healthy Communities-Healthy Youth):** an initiative, based on the Search Institute's framework of developmental assets, that seeks to motivate and equip individuals, organizations, and their leaders to join together in nurturing competent, caring, and responsible adolescents.

- **Hinton, S.E.:** Hinton's *The Outsiders* is considered by many to be the first "modern" teen novel.

- **Homework Center:** not just a physical space, but a public library program that provides homework assistance and/or tutoring to teens after school.

- *Horn Book*: review journal that focuses on literature for youth. While the focus is often on books for children, *Horn Book* does contain Patty Campbell's "Sand in the Oyster," an important and influential column about YA literature.

- **IMLS (Institute of Museum and Library Services):** the federal agency from which much library funding flows.

- **Information literacy:** the ability of any person (in this context, a secondary school student) to be competent in the skills of selecting, retrieving, analyzing, evaluating, synthesizing, creating, and communicating information in all formats.

- *Information Power*: document of AASL (first created in 1988, and then revised in 1998) that provides the framework for work in a school library media center. The book provides the tools for school libraries to fulfill their mission to ensure that students and staff are effective users of ideas and information.

- **IRA (International Reading Association):** association containing the Commission on Adolescent Literacy.

- *JOYS* (*Journal of Youth Services in Libraries*): a publication of ALSC and YALSA. The publication ceased as each organization decided to create their own vehicle for professional communication. YALSA's new journal is called *Young Adult Library Services*.

- *KLIATT*: a bimonthly magazine that publishes reviews of paperback books, hardcover fiction, audio books, and educational software recommended for libraries and classrooms serving YAs.

- **Latchkey:** term used to describe young people who congregate in libraries during the after-school hours because they are not allowed to go home and have few other safe havens.

- **Library Bill of Rights:** core ALA document that advocates for free and fair access to library materials.

- **Library Power:** a multimillion dollar grant-funded AASL initiative that operated in over seven hundred schools and affected over four hundred thousand students. It demonstrated the positive outcomes achieved when librarians build collections, utilize technology, and collaborate with teachers.

- **Lifelong learning:** a common term used by public library' mission statements to describe a library's goal for the self-directed personal growth and development opportunities of their patrons. Lifelong learning is an outgrowth of effective young adult services.

- **LM_NET:** a listserv for library media specialists containing lists, tips, and useful information about serving youth in school media centers.

- **LSTA (Library Services and Technology Act):** the act that provides state library funding. Each state handles these funds differently. Some use a competitive grant process that allows libraries or library systems to get money for a specific project.

- **MacRae, Cathi Dunn:** editor of *Voice of Youth Advocates* and one of the leading voices in the profession for youth involvement.

- **Manga:** the Japanese word for comics. These Japanese comics are often spin-offs of anime. While the popular image of manga is of cartoons like the *Powerpuff Girls*, much of it is actually quite sophisticated, dealing with mature themes.

- **Margaret Edwards Award:** established in 1988, this award honors an author's lifetime achievement for writing books that have been popular over a period of time. The annual award is administered by YALSA and sponsored by *School Library Journal* magazine. It recognizes an author's work in helping adolescents become aware of themselves and in addressing questions about their roles and importance in relationships, society, and the world.

- **Merchandising:** as much a philosophy as it is a practice. Merchandising means arranging library materials in an attractive and eye-catching manner in order to entice users into checking them out. Merchandising grew in libraries out of the "give them what they want" school of collections and the need for libraries to learn from/compete with chain bookstores.

- **NAEP (National Association of Educational Progress):** a government agency that issues "report cards" on student progress in many areas, including reading.

- **NEA (National Education Association):** a group that sponsored a major study of teen reading habits (released 2001) that concluded that teens recognize that turning their attention to the printed page is vital to success in work and life.

- **NCES (National Center for Education Statistics):** federal agency responsible for statistical reports in 1992 and 1995 documenting services to YAs in public libraries.

- **NCTE (National Council of Teachers of English):** a group devoted to improving the teaching and learning of English and the language arts at all levels of education. ALAN is a subgroup dedicated just to young adult literature.

- *New Directions for Library Services to Young Adults*: a document, written by Patrick Jones and edited by Linda Waddle, that represents YALSA's broad philosophical vision. The purpose of the document is to help libraries and their communities develop their teens into healthy, competent, and caring adults.

- **OIF (Office of Intellectual Freedom):** the ALA department charged with implementing ALA policies concerning the concept of intellectual freedom as embodied in the Library Bill of Rights, the Association's basic policy on free access to libraries and library materials.

- **Outcomes:** the effect services (such as library services) have on a person's life. Easy to define, but harder to measure, they are seen as essential.

- **Outcome-based education:** a school curriculum practice that establishes clearly defined learner outcomes based on the premise that all students can be successful learners.

- **Output measures:** a measurement tool used in both school and public libraries to capture quantitative and qualitative data to "prove" the success of services.

- **Outreach:** library services that take place outside of the library setting. Outreach refers to either a community relations function (such as promoting services) or actual service delivery (such as booktalking in a classroom).

- **PAT (Partnerships Advocating for Teens):** a YALSA committee charged with exploring, recommending, initiating, and implementing ways for libraries to work with other organizations that serve youth.

- **PLA (Public Library Association):** a division of ALA with a mission to enhance the development and effectiveness of public library staff and public library services. PLA has been very active in developing tools to plan and evaluate library services, such as *Planning for Results*.

- *Planning for Results*: a PLA document outlining the steps for planning including service responses such as formal education support and lifelong learning. *The New Planning for Results* was published in 2001.

- **PLPYD (Public Libraries as Partners in Youth Development):** an initiative sponsored by the Wallace Reader's Digest Fund that challenged public libraries to work with youth to develop innovative, high-quality educational and cultural enrichment programs for low-income youth during nonschool hours.

- **Popular paperbacks:** a YALSA committee that annually prepares annotated booklists of different genres of interest to teens.

- **Positive youth development:** the process of creating environments that support the social, emotional, spiritual, physical, moral, and cognitive development of young people. Positive youth development addresses the broader developmental needs of youth, in contrast to deficit-based models, which focus on youth problems.

- **Printz Award:** an award for a book that exemplifies literary excellence in young adult literature. It is named for Topeka, Kansas, school librarian Michael L. Printz, who was a longtime active member of YALSA.

- **Problem novel:** the long-dominant genre of realistic fiction written for teens. Early problem novels were characterized by a teen protagonist facing a single social problem (homelessness, abuse, alcoholism, etc.). During the course of the novel, the young person "grew" and overcame the problem. While some of these novels still exist, current fiction is much more focused on the central problems of coming of age in an increasingly complex world.

- **Program:** a library-sponsored activity that takes place outside of the context of reference services and is designed to inform, entertain, or enrich users, as well as promote the use of the library and its collection.

- **Puberty:** the physical change which occurs in young people when the secondary sexual characteristics start to appear. Puberty is usually seen as a physical milestone that marks the beginning of the process of adolescence.

- **PUBYAC:** the Public Library Young Adult and Children's' Services listserv.

- **Quick Picks:** a YALSA committee charged with developing an annual reading list for YAs who, for whatever reason, do not like to read.

- **READ posters:** posters produced by ALA graphics featuring celebrities holding up a favorite book. Many of these have marketed to teens by including sports stars, rappers, musicians, and professional wrestlers.

- **Reluctant readers:** a term used to describe teenagers who do not enjoy reading.

- **Resiliency:** the factors that increase young people's ability to rebound in the face of adversities ranging from poverty, to drug-abusing parents, to dangerous neighborhoods.

- **Search Institute:** a social science research nonprofit that developed the concept of developmental assets. The group's mission is to advance the well-being of youth by generating knowledge and promoting its application.

- *SLJ (School Library Journal)*: a publication whose mission is to serve librarians who work with young people in school and public libraries by providing information needed to manage libraries, from creating high-quality collections to understanding how technology can assist (or hinder) learning.

- **Speculative fiction:** a broad term that encompasses the science fiction, fantasy, and sometimes horror genres, which are all characterized by alternative realities.

- **Student achievement:** the success of students on standardized tests. Often used as a measure of school success, it is also an important factor for LSTs in secondary schools to consider.

- **Student learning:** student learning encompasses the broad process of learning and, similar to student achievement, it is important as measure of success for LSTs in a school setting.

- **SUS (Serving the Underserved):** three seminars offered by YALSA to inform YALSA leaders of techniques to train other staff on serving teens. SUS training sessions have occurred in all fifty states with an estimated 10,000 participants.

- **TAB (Teen Advisory Board):** sometimes known as Young Advisory Group or Teen Advisory Group; a formal group put together by LST to provide assistance into all aspects of planning, developing, implementing, and evaluating library services. While not the only vehicle for youth involvement, this is one of the most successful.

- **TAG (Teen Advisory Group):** see TAB.

- **TAG-L (Teen Advisory Group Listserv):** a topica.com-based discussion forum for the advisors of any public library teen advisory group or board.

- **Teen:** the term preferred by most persons ages twelve through eighteen, based on research inside and outside of the library field.

- **Teen Hoopla:** (now defunct) YALSA's official teen Web site that included not only links of interest to teens, but also numerous opportunities for teens to participate actively in building the content of the site.

- **TRU (Teenage Research Unlimited):** a market research firm headed by Peter Zollo that provides companies with information on how to reach the teen market.

- **TRW (Teen Read Week):** a national YALSA-sponsored literacy initiative aimed at teens, their parents, librarians, educators, booksellers, and other concerned adults. It began in 1998 and has been celebrated the third week in October each year ever since.

- **Tweens:** persons between the ages of eight and twelve who may be served in the public library by children's libraries, but who seek to define themselves as teenagers.

- **ULC (Urban Libraries Council):** an association of public libraries in metropolitan areas and the corporations that serve them. They were the operative body in the late 1990s for work on the role of public libraries in fostering positive youth development.

- **Urban legend:** also known as teenage folklore; stories that the teller will insist happened to someone they knew. The stories, a staple for LST storytellers, are often moral or cautionary tales that sound realistic even up to the end. They almost always end with an ironic or supernatural twist.

- **Vaillancourt, Renee:** author of the second and expanded edition of *Bare Bones*, author of *Managing Young Adult Services* (Neal-Schuman), editor of the fourth edition of *Excellence in Library Services to Young Adults* (forthcoming), editor of *Public Libraries* magazine, and a former YA librarian.

- *VOYA (Voice of Youth Advocates)*: a bimonthly journal owned by Scarecrow Press, addressing librarians, educators, and other professionals who work with YAs. The only magazine devoted exclusively to the informational needs of teenagers, it was founded in 1978 by librarians and renowned intellectual freedom advocates Dorothy M. Broderick and Mary Kay Chelton, and is now edited by Cathi Dunn MacRae.

- **YA (Young Adult):** in the library field, the term that refers to a person ages twelve through eighteen. In the business world, the term refers more to twentysomethings. Generally, "young adult" is the term used in professional settings for this age group, while "teen" is used when interacting with this age group.

- **YALSA-BK:** a listserv from YALSA with the primary purpose of discussing young adult literature.

- **YALSA-L:** a listserv from YALSA with the primary purpose of discussing issues related to serving teens, as well as information about the association.

- **YA-YAAC:** a listserv from YALSA allowing teen library advisory groups and the librarians who coordinate them to share information and ideas.

- *Young Adult Library Services*: the official journal of YALSA that serves as a vehicle for continuing education for librarians serving YAs. The journal also serves as the official record of the organization.

- *Young Adults Deserve the Best*: a document from YALSA, under revision as of this writing, that spells out the competencies needed by LSTs.

- **Youth advocate:** according to *VOYA* founder Dorothy Broderick, "a person who believes in creating the conditions under which young people can make decisions about their own lives."
- **Youth involvement:** the process of moving teens from passive library customers to active contributors; also known as YP.
- **Youth serving organizations:** institutions whose activities are structured to provide a set of procedures, values, and mores that teach and encourage responsible behavior. These organizations include extracurricular, school-based organizations, as well as community organizations such as Boys and Girls clubs, 4-H clubs, church groups, and sports leagues.
- **YP (Youth Participation):** the involvement of teens in responsible action and significant decision-making that affects the design and delivery of library services.
- **Zine:** a relatively low-budget, low-circulation means of self-expression issued independently and usually produced today using desktop publishing and photocopiers; often used by libraries as a YP activity.
- **Zollo, Peter:** the President of Teenage Research Unlimited and author of *Wise Up to Teens: Insight into Marketing and Advertising to Teenagers*. Although not written with libraries in mind, this book is loaded with ideas that libraries can adapt, not just for promoting programs, but also in designing collections, creating teen spaces, writing booktalks, and delivering information services.

1 WHY: THE PHILOSOPHY BEHIND SERVICES TO YOUNG ADULTS

"The library is so very serious. Everyone has a very solemn look. It's depressing. It's very, very depressing to walk into a library."

—a California teen about his library experience

How is that for a start?

This quote illustrates the challenges, and everything that is possible and positive, with serving young adults (YAs) in libraries. Yes, our work is serious, but is it depressing? We want teens to come into libraries and leave with their problems solved and with good feelings. How are we going to turn things around to ensure that the experience of this teenager who participated in a focus group becomes the exception, not the rule? Let's start by laying down one golden rule of young adult library service: always put the customer first.

Most librarians spend all day answering questions, but planning for young adult services is about asking questions. Let's start with these six important questions:

- What do the teens want and need from their library?
- What can your library do in the short term to meet these wants and needs?
- What should your library do in the long term to meet these wants and needs?
- Can your library afford it and is it a priority?
- What obstacles does the library need to overcome?
- How do we know that we have successfully met those wants and needs?

But maybe before we ask those six important questions we should ask these basic questions: Why are we here? Why do libraries exist? Why do we work in libraries? What do we want to achieve?

It is time to step back from the day-to-day, the desk, and the demands of programming, to think about these most basic issues. It is time to form a strong foundation, to reexamine and reaffirm our values, and to refine our role. While libraries have many service responses,

1

they are all aimed at achieving positive outcomes for our patrons. Why do YAs matter? Why should we care?

How to provide all children and adolescents with a solid foundation for life is a pressing social issue in the United States. The evidence that the foundation is fragile appears year after year in newspaper articles and scientific studies that call attention to the challenges and problems facing too many youth. Those of us who work with teens realize, in so many ways, that as a society we are failing to offer our youngest generation the solid footing they need to grow safely and successfully into adulthood. In almost every community, a library in a school or public setting can provide that foundation, if the powers that be make serving teens a priority.

WHAT IS A VISION OF SERVICE FOR CONNECTING YOUNG ADULTS AND LIBRARIES?

In countless workshops, people ask us questions about how to improve services to teens. These are the right questions, but everyone needs to supply his or her own answer to what an improved, quality young adult services program looks like in a school or public library. That vision, of course, is perfectly lined up with the larger institutional vision/mission and will vary by community; but, a vision gives us a place to start, a road to follow, and an objective to achieve.

Throughout this text, we will provide you with the tools and techniques, and introduce the best practices and innovative ideas to turn this

In every agency, a librarian will be dedicated to serving young adults. All library staff who encounter young adults will treat them with respect. Young adults will be working in the library as more than shelvers. They will be volunteering during the summer and during the school year, working for the library on internships, or as community service volunteers. Teens will still use the library for homework and to find materials that lead to increased achievement; but in addition, they will find a broader selection of recreational materials, in particular music, magazines, and an active selection of customer-driven programs. Each library will have a dedicated and appealing young adult space to use when the library is open, as well as a range of outreach services, after-hours services, and Web-based services, which expand the library beyond its normal open hours. Teens will be savvy about using library technology to solve information problems, and will have developed the skills to locate, use, and evaluate information from a wide variety of sources. All of these services will be planned, promoted, and implemented with the assistance of teens serving on formal or informal advisory groups, as well as with community partners. Finally, every young adult will view their library experience as a positive one, and therefore will not only return, but also promote the library to their peers. These positive interactions will contribute to the healthy development of young adults.

Adapted from *New Directions in Library to Young Adults* by Patrick Jones and the Young Adult Library Services Association. ALA Editions, 2003 vision into a reality at your library. Is this really the best vision for your library? It depends upon the unique wants and needs of your teen users. And you will never learn, unless you ask them and allow them the opportunities to work alongside you to effect positive change.

WHAT ARE SIX KEY GOALS FOR REACHING THIS VISION?

If this vision is to become a reality, a process has to happen. Visions flow into missions that flow into goals, and for LSTs (Librarians Serving Teens), youth involvement is the river that runs through it all. Below are six key goals toward which a library, regardless of the size, needs to work. Associated with each of these goals are five practical tasks that most libraries could undertake, many with little expense. We will cover more details on how to do each of these tasks within this book, but start planning, advocating, and building by knowing what you need to do and how to achieve it, one step/task at a time.

GOAL 1

Libraries are committed to providing services that are suitable to the developmental needs of young adults and the principles of positive youth development.

TASKS:

- Remind every one that nowhere in any library mission statement does it read "except for teenagers." Here is another reminder: look at your library's annual report. If there are pictures, no doubt the majority of them are of young people using libraries. That is the message we send to our public: young people matter.

- Organize teens to write e-mails to library/school board members about the importance of library services and the need to keep them a priority. Engage groups of teens already organized (school clubs, faith-based groups, and the like) to lobby for services based upon their needs.

- Plan services and programs not based on the needs of the library, but on the developmental needs of teens.

Then, remind staff and the public about those assets by posting around the library, including staff areas, the list of forty development assets. Send information to board members and others about products from the Search Institute, such as the "150 Ways to Show Kids You Care" poster, the "40 Ways Anyone Can Build Assets" poster, and "Asset-Building Bookmarks" (perfect for libraries). Get serious about adopting the asset framework.

- Be direct with your director, or advocate your principles with your principal. Ask her what she wants the library to do for teens and what resources she is willing to dedicate to make it happen. Good intentions are not good enough. Also, reward your director for any steps taking you closer to realizing the vision.

- Find partners in the community who share a passion for building assets. Just go to the Search Institute Web site and learn about communities involved in asset building (www.search-institute.org/communities/partner.htm). Teach them what libraries can do for teens.

GOAL 2

Libraries employ young adults or certified school library media specialists, and train staff members, volunteers, youth participants, and others to serve young adults.

TASKS:

- Get library staff, from director to shelver, trained in basic young adult skills. Look at the trainers available from YALSA's Serving the Underserved (SUS) project, YAs in your own state, and/or your state youth consultant. There is expertise available; take advantage of it. It is self-defeating for an energetic teen librarian to be working fifty hours a week to get teens to come into the library if they are only then "dissed" by the "Clerk from Hell." We're stereotyping here, but all of us have had plenty of experiences working in libraries with staff members who don't treat teens, and often any patron, with respect.

- Develop a program to recruit and employ teen volunteers through improved communication with school service learning personnel and other entities providing community service volunteers. If you want staff to treat teens well, then get teen volunteers who will present positive images to the staff.

- Develop employment opportunities for YAs that allow for flexibility in scheduling—including internships, work-study programs, and other existing programs.

- Develop funding resources to acquire additional resources for staff, in particular project-based funding with definable outcomes, which provides paid work for young adult themselves.

- Staff must work toward continued improvement to ensure that they meet the competencies established in the "Young Adults Deserve the Best Competencies" document created by YALSA. Hold people accountable for their work with youth. Get managers to write teen customer service objectives into performance reviews. It is hard to fire the wrong people; it is a lot easier to hire the right ones. Educate managers to ask each job candidate, regardless of the level in the organization, behavioral interview questions that will weed out the "kid haters" at the onset.

- Develop young adult librarian positions when staff retires, change in job duties for an existing position, and/or create additional YA positions. Few libraries are adding new positions, but that does not mean that they can't change old ones.

> Research supports a greater quantity and higher quality of service to YAs when a young adult librarian in present.

GOAL 3

Libraries provide for the unique needs of YAs as part of the library's general service responses; for example, readers' advisory, information services, cataloging, circulation, data collection.

TASKS:

- Work with technical services staff to ensure that young adult use of the collection is measured. Make sure not only to count use of YA collection, but use of the entire collection by teens. In all measurement matters, argue for a separate teen report that has the same status as children's and adult services. We can't improve until first we can prove how well we are doing.

- Get involved within the library system, school, or profession to support teen services at all levels. Always ask the question: "Where do teens fit in this?"
- Train staff to understand the unique information needs of teens, and identify the unique skills that your librarians may need to develop, to assist teens with information and a readers' advisory service.
- Increase the library's capacity to serve teens by increasing the awareness of all staff through a presentation on teen services on staff development day, distribution of information about teens and teen services through various library communication vehicles, and through presentations to various library teams.
- Involve teens through formal and informal means to have an effect upon service responses.

GOAL 4

Libraries set aside space(s) for YAs for their use in the library's physical and virtual space. Libraries engage in activities to promote use of these spaces, and to strengthen the information-literacy skills of YAs so they can make best use of these spaces.

TASKS:

- Develop a program to make better use of public library meeting rooms to expand services and programs to young adult customers. Study halls, the "teen time" recreation program, and after school programming and/or tutoring held in the meeting rooms would increase the capacity of the library to serve YAs.
- Realize that the best "space" to provide library services to teens might not be in the library, but rather in their schools and over the Internet. Develop effective outreach services from the public library to schools, particularly in the areas of booktalking that promotes reading and information-literacy instruction. Outreach is an effective and efficient method to provide a high level of service in a short amount of time. It does not require increasing the library's hours; however, you will need to redistribute staff during open and closed hours.

- When planning for new library spaces, involve teens early and often. When developing new library spaces include laptop plug in stations, listening and viewing stations, coffee bars, copying room, a variety of study spaces for individuals and groups, and increased small group-study areas.

- Develop a comprehensive and cooperative plan for information-literacy instruction to ensure that all secondary school students—and their teachers—served by the library understand how to access, use, and evaluate resources via the Internet. Educate teachers on the information resources critical to student achievement, and then provide teachers with resources to educate their students. If you teach them, they will come to your library, via the Net if not in person.

- Build a teen Web page to give teens their own space in your library's online environment. Develop Web pages that support the formal education needs of students. These should include links to library catalogs, databases, and selected quality Internet links in order to increase the efficiency and effectiveness for library staff, teachers, and young adults. Develop Web pages that support the needs of teens for information on current topics, general information, and lifelong learning, in particular in areas of personal interest, such as college and career information. Develop Web pages that support interactivity, such as surveys, polls, and other methods to gather information directly from young adult customers. Develop Web pages that support interactive services, such as e-mail reference, chat based reference, or Instant Message based reference. Organize information on library Web pages so that students can do "one stop" shopping to find the information they need.

Research supports developing library Web pages and content directed to YAs. Involving YAs in the planning, implementation, and evaluation, results in greater success.

GOAL 5

Libraries develop unique collections of resources for YAs and provide plentiful resources and enriching experiences to build and strengthen adolescent literacy skills. Libraries provide remote information and resources needed by YAs for information, education, and recreation needs.

TASKS:

- Develop or support a strong selection of adult titles of interest to teens, particularly in the genres of science fiction, fantasy, and horror. Popular bestsellers as well as classics, both established and contemporary or cult favorites, will meet the reading needs of older teens.

- Develop active collections of print young adult fiction titles in all formats, in particular those that speak to the issues of cultural awareness, those that have been honored as "best" books or award winners, and those that are enjoyable to reluctant readers. Develop active collections of print paperback originals, in particular, series books that meet the recreational reading interest of users. Develop print nonfiction collections within the teen space/area of a public library. These nonfiction collections will focus on popular and informational materials, in particular in the areas of popular culture, health and sexuality, and materials related to college and careers.

- Develop or support nonfiction print collections that support the formal education needs of students, including multiple copies of series books that are in high demand.

- Develop collections that are heavy in non-book items, such as magazines, music CDs, audio books on tape and CD, zines, comic books, videos, DVDs, and computer games.

- Develop methods to involve youth in the collection development process, such as reading interest surveys, participation in magazine and music selection groups, or genre selection committees.

GOAL 6

Libraries utilize the experience and expertise of YAs.

TASKS:

- Develop a program that better uses teen volunteers, through improved training and sharing of knowledge among staff, to ensure meaningful work for young adult volunteers. Work with school counselors to make the library a preferred site for students to do community service projects for school.

- Develop methods to gather teen input, such as formal and informal focus groups, print or online surveys, exit interviews, discussions during class visits, as well as forming a teen advisory council.

- Engage youth to take part in library teams charged with programming, such as Teen Read Week, or service development.

- Engage teens as program providers and active participants in programs that allow them to express themselves creatively.

- Learn about another ALA: Ask / Listen / Answer.

WHAT ARE THE CORE VALUES THAT DRIVE OUR WORK?

In June 1994, the Board of the Young Adult Library Services Association adopted the following vision statement:

> In every library in the nation, quality library services to young adults are provided by a staff that understands and respects the unique informational, educational, and recreational needs of teenagers. Equal access to information, services and materials is recognized as a right not a privilege. Young adults are actively involved in the library decision-making process. The library staff collaborates and cooperates with other youth-serving agencies to provide a holistic community-wide network of activities and services that supports healthy youth development.

A vision statement represents many things to an organization; it is the reservoir from which missions, goals, and objectives flow. It tells everyone what the organization, representing its members working directly with young adults in school and public libraries across the nation, believe to be important. The vision responds to the needs of teens not librarians. The vision provides the foundation on which service responses are built. But mostly, a vision statement is a statement of values. There are many values expressed here, but perhaps the five most important are the values of:

- Respecting unique needs;
- Equal access;
- Youth participation;
- Collaboration; and
- Healthy youth development.

These are also the foundation on which *Connecting Young Adults and Libraries* is based. These values have not changed over much time; they are the values that have always guided librarians working with teenagers. They are values that remain because they work.

> Research, anecdotal evidence, and success stories from the field demonstrate that services planned, implemented, and evaluated based on core values, achieve results.

WHAT DO WE MEAN WHEN WE SPEAK OF THESE CORE VALUES?

- **Respecting unique needs** means recognizing that teens are not adults, and they are not children; they are their own package, but they are also library customers who deserved to be treated with the same respect as every customer. This means realizing that *if*, just *if*, the Internet would have been around when we were fourteen years old, that most of us would be engaging in the very same behaviors that now irritate so many library staff members. This means respecting teen reading choices, rather than to dismiss them with the "At least they are reading something" idiocy. This means that if a teen chooses to use an Internet computer, which has no posted restrictions regarding use, to chat or to play games, then that use is important to them. To say to a teen "We need this computer for something important" is tantamount to telling an adult patron checking out Danielle Steel that we won't be buying those books anymore, because we only spend money on things that are important. This means we accept teen behavior, correct it when necessary, understand and explain it, but don't dismiss it. This means building an atmosphere where teens are respected by the library. Respecting means letting teen tastes and input drive collection development, programming, and space design.

> Youth participation is respect and access in action.

• **Equal access** means, in post-CIPA libraries, being as true to the idea of equal access as allowable by law. It means advocating against censorship from outside community groups and from inside in terms of self-censorship. It means working with partners to share our values in order to gain access to students in their care in schools, youth organizations, or correctional institutions. It means making teens aware of what we do—access is not the same as availability. Databases like *Opposing Viewpoints* might be available to teens, but a failure to promote these in a way that teens understand, is denying access through neglect. This is about policies at the administrative level, procedures at the manager level, but most important of all, it means practice at the staff level. Equal access is as much about attitude as it is about the ALA Bill of Rights.

• **Youth participation** means embracing a new paradigm that doesn't come easy to librarians who, by nature, seek control. This means rather than providing services strictly *to* young adults, the youth development model, coupled with YALSA's leadership, commitment and support of meaningful youth participation, transforms the delivery of services into a collaborative context. This is crucial to the planning process as it requires adults to recognize that YAs can make a positive contribution, and it requires adults to respect the right of YAs to participate in decisions on matters that affect them.

• **Collaboration** is that in addition to collaborating with teens, we join forces with all those around teens who share our values and seek the same positive outcomes for teens. We look at the life of the teen through the connections in their lives: family, school, faith based organizations, other government entities, businesses, youth organizations, and media. Think of the other institutions in your community with a vested interest in raising healthy teens, such as their schools and other organizations. But are those all? Who shares similar missions as the library in the cultural community? In the nontraditional education community? In the business community? In the faith community? In government? How about parks and health and police and fire just to mention a few? How about partnerships with community organizations of all types and sizes? How about partnerships with parents and grandparents? We forge connections with others who reach teens in other parts of their lives. We learn to collaborate successfully by engaging people from all aspects of the community. We agree on outcomes, then work backward in order to achieve them. We take small steps, succeed, and then build upon our successes. We speak the same language—that of healthy youth development—and we learn from each other. We seek to strengthen existing programs and resist the temptation to create new projects to solve problems; instead we collaborate to strengthen our own organization's ability to build assets in young people.

- **Healthy youth development** is exemplified through our profession, showing our constituencies how slogans, such as "Libraries change lives" and "Libraries build communities," actually impact the real world. We have moved from input, to output, and now to outcome. The stimuli are varied, but an overriding motive is to "prove" our value so our public will continue to fund libraries. Our public wants to see what effect we really have; they are wondering if we make kids' lives better.

> Relationships are the key to asset building. As adults encounter kids, we need to learn their names, support them, encourage them, and empower them. We are not talking about social work; we are talking about people work; we are talking about library work. These relationships are not about the payoff for us, but for the teen. For years we have justified youth services to administrators saying "Be nice to them now and these kids will remember us later, when it comes time to vote or pay taxes." That is true, and lets keep that in mind, but be careful not to view youths as merely a means to an end. Teens are the ends.

Libraries don't serve youths because it is good for the library, but because it is good for youths. What is good for youths, it follows, is good for the community. The library is an asset for youths. The more assets they have, the less likely they are to engage in destructive behavior and the more likely they are to thrive, to engage in positive behavior, and to become competent, caring adults.

WHAT ARE THE ELEMENTS OF A SUCCESSFUL PROGRAM OF SERVICE TO YOUNG ADULTS?

One vehicle for tracking these values in action has been the Excellence in Library Services to Young Adults project. ALA Past President Hardy Franklin initiated this program in 1993 to recognize excellence in library service to teenagers. In 1994, and again in 1997 and 1999, the ALA chose library programs serving young adults, from a pool of applications, as examples of outstanding programs for the age group. Another crop of award-winning programs received this recognition in summer 2003. If you look at these programs, you'll see lots of ideas, but there are ten common themes:

- Provides a transition entry and a buffer into adult reading and collections;
- Responds to the school-related demands of YAs;
- Involves cooperation between schools and libraries;
- Encourages reading for personal enrichments and independent learning;
- Models for other staff as an example of service;
- Allows for young adult participation;
- Reaches out to at-risk or special groups of YAs;
- Reacts to social and cultural trends;
- Advocates for free and equal access for YAs; and
- Contributes to the healthy development of YAs.

The one theme that isn't mentioned outright is implied: serving YA works. If you or your administration doesn't believe that, simply refer to the hundreds of examples in this book, which demonstrate when this work gets support, it achieves success. While many of the successes were from grant-funded programs, all work with teens requires support from library administration to succeed.

WHAT ARE THE ESSENTIAL ARGUMENTS FOR SERVING YOUNG ADULTS IN LIBRARIES?

Go back and review the vision at the beginning of this chapter. Then imagine a different scenario. Imagine libraries without respectful staff, without strong collections, and without a concentrated effort to serve teens. What would they look like? Would teens still be using them? Yes. Would there be more discipline problems? Perhaps. If libraries can get by without serving teens, then why bother? If there are no problems with teens, then why make the effort?

One of the foundations of the asset movement is that problem-free is not fully prepared. If teens are to be fully prepared and contribute to, rather than take from, the community, they need to build assets. Again, assets create positive outcomes and positive outcomes create stronger communities. Libraries, thus, create positive outcomes. The ideas and examples in this book provide library staff with the tools to help fully prepare teens. The last edition of *Connecting* presented eighteen reasons to serve those between the ages of twelve and eighteen, while *New Directions* boiled it down to ten reasons. Lets put all of our eggs in one basket, for this one argument trumps all others. Why do we provide quality young adult services in school and public libraries? Because it is our job and it works.

Librarians have many jobs, but one theme that is true of every school and public library is a focus on learning. Libraries are about learning. With teens, learning isn't just done in school with teachers, but outside of the classroom teens are learning to become adults. Adults who pay the taxes, elect the governments, and make up our communities. We serve teens, because libraries are paid to build community.

But how does playing a computer game or reading a series romance contribute to learning? That's not learning, that's playing. Wrong. The young adult doing these things in a school or public library is learning something else, something more important: the value of libraries. They should be learning that libraries are an important part of any school and in every community. Strong communities tend to have strong schools and libraries.

We know this. We know that young people with assets are more likely to contribute to, rather than take from, society. We know the cost to the community of kids without assets—in social services, corrections, and other institutions. We know that libraries can, and do, build assets. Thus, libraries build communities. Assets create positive outcomes and positive outcomes create stronger communities. We serve teens because libraries build community.

Connecting young adults and libraries is not about treating teens as "special," but it is about serving them uniquely; just as services to other market segments of the public library: toddlers, genealogy, seniors, college students, and small business people. Each group of users places different demands upon libraries, reflecting their different needs, based on what each is trying to accomplish. Above all else, teens are trying to accomplish one thing—form an identity. If we believe that libraries are good things for a community, then does it not follow that we want teens, as they are forming this identity, to recognize this value? If we believe libraries have value, then we will want teens to learn through our deeds and action. If we believe that our work has value, then we need to know that it matters. If we believe that libraries should be supported by the community, then we need to show and prove this belief to the community. Communities allocate resources based on what they value.

The same is true within the school or public library—money follows priorities. The allocation of resources hinges on many factors, but one overriding factor is meeting the overall needs of the library. A successful program of service to YAs can be creative, dynamic, and even

> We serve teens, because libraries build community.

When we support student achievement and healthy youth development, we build stronger community.

cutting edge, but it still must support the goals of the larger library or school. If it does not, then the program is at risk for losing support. Allocating resources is the manifestation of priority setting. No library can achieve every aspect of connecting young adults and libraries; this is a vision, not a standard. The only standard for serving YAs is that resources are allocated in a manner that responds to the needs of young adult customers, supports the results of student achievement, and fosters healthy youth development. When LSTs work with teens, they are building community. That's not just theory; the results of case studies of successful services to teens are too clear, too obvious to miss or deny. Why do we serve young adults in libraries? Because it works.

2 WHO: UNDERSTANDING THE AUDIENCE

"If we went into a library, the librarian would look at us like, why are they here. Like we're going to cause trouble or something, like we're being watched."

—*a California teen about his library experience*

It is a normal day at Normal Public Library. It is 10:30 a.m. and story time lets out. Young children run from the story room into the library filling it with noise, no doubt stemming from the excitement of the program. The library staff smile. At 11:30 a.m., a library customer, who just happens to be on the Board of the Library Friends, comes to the desk to place a long list of books on hold. Even though you've shown her many times how to do the holds herself, she insists you do them for her, and all the while, her booming voice supplies commentary on each book. You place the reserves and you smile. At 12:30 p.m. the noise level increases dramatically as the staff talk about where they are going to lunch. Everybody smiles. At 1:30 p.m. an adult walks into the library, sits down at a computer, and then begins loudly talking into a cell phone. The library staff sigh, thinking that coming up with a policy on cell phones would solve the problem. At 2:30 p.m., two seniors are leaving a program you've just had on living wills. They are standing by the front door when one turns to the other and says very loudly: "How did you like that, Chester?" to which Chester replies, "Huh?" and the library staff smile, knowing we've met the information needs of our seniors. At 3:30 p.m., two teenagers walk in, one giggles and the entire staff open a bag of "Shhh," frown, and wonder why can't these teens behave in libraries. We become the stereotypical "librarian action figure" come to life.

Let's examine the unusual treatment given to the teenagers in this story. Why did the librarians feel it was fine to tell the teens how to behave and not the others? As adults we are often uncomfortable and find it embarrassing to approach other adults and tell them how to behave. Perhaps there's a bit of power politics thrown unto the equation. We go out of our way not to offend certain groups of people: story time Moms, the Friends members, the always supportive senior population, or our colleagues. Any action with these special groups might risk negative consequences. Why is telling a teen an easier power trip to take? Are we confident that we can tell them what to do because there are no adults to defend them? Is it easy to shrug and think, "Oh well, even if I reprimand them, what are they going to do about it?

Are there unspoken assumptions underpinning this behavior? One implicit idea revolves around the notion that many YAs don't choose to be in libraries in the first place. They are there because they have to be. They have to come to the library, to find information they aren't interested in, to write a paper they don't want to write, to hand in to a teacher they don't even like, to get a grade in a class they can't stand, so they can graduate from the school that they loathe, so they can get away from their parents, whom they also might just detest. On top of that, they come unprepared, bringing only a notebook or a pen and even sometimes forgetting those basic tools! By far the worst crime committed is that teens come to the library with an attitude. It's the surly attitude of someone being some place they don't want to be. Perhaps it's the bored attitude of someone who doesn't have any other place to go.

Many teens come to us after school out of burden and boredom, not exactly the best motivations for successful relationship.

When they get there, what do they find? Normally, they find an overworked staff without enough resources to do their jobs well. They find staff who are feeling underappreciated and underpaid, feeling overwhelmed in an environment of rapid technological improvement and budget cutting. They don't find people working in libraries who look like them, act like them, or even seem to care about them. And in walks the fourteen-year-old, with everything showing pierced at least once, who would rather be anywhere in the world, but by tomorrow needs a paper on symbolism in the plays of Arthur Miller. He can't figure out how the computer catalog works, but still he and his friends have a good time laughing about it. Fifteen minutes before closing he comes up to the desk and mumbles something that sounds like a reference question. This doesn't sound like a success story in the making.

And worse yet, the teens were laughing. We are sitting at a desk, for some six hours now; we are tired, we are a little burnt out, and when we hear that laughter, face it, we are mostly resentful. While we can redirect inappropriate teen behavior in the short term, we can't really change it—teens will be teens because they have to be. What we can do, which has a long-term pay off for us and teens, is change our own behaviors and attitudes. We can get ourselves a YAttitude that welcomes teens to libraries, rather than just wish they'd go away.

The uniqueness of serving young adults, of course, stems directly from the uniqueness of teenagers as people. Understanding how this uniqueness impacts YAs as library patrons/customers is crucial, because the problems libraries have in serving—and reasons for not serving—YAs often stem from misunderstandings and misinformation. Too often libraries allow the few "problem patron" teens to become the image of how all YAs use or misuse libraries. Many of the behaviors

> Peter Zollo, the president of Teenage Research Unlimited, reminds businesses that the two keys to success in the YA market are acknowledging the importance of teens as consumers and recognizing their uniqueness.

that librarians have always found annoying among YAs—mainly loudness and rudeness—are directly related to the physical and psychological changes taking place in a teen's life. Most things a teen does, or doesn't do in a library, can be explained, understood, and then responded to by first understanding the various developmental stages that make up adolescence.

WHAT ARE THE STAGES OF ADOLESCENCE?

Teens develop at different paces, so not every behavior can be plugged into one slot. Physical development is not always in synch with emotional or psychological development. Teens also differ on when they hit these stages for a variety of factors including, but not limited to, environment, demographics, family history, and national origin. All of those disclaimers aside, there are still some universals. There are three primary stages of adolescent development, each one characterized by different tasks or "milestones." Most of the behaviors that drive us crazy, and make us like, YAs stem from these developmental tasks/milestones. Developmental tasks are those emotional, social, sexual, intellectual, and psychological changes that make up adolescence. For each milestone, we challenge you in your planning for serving teens to develop services responses—collections and programs in particular—that meet these needs.

While certainly one size doesn't fit all, and it is important to respond to teens as individuals not representations of a type, these tasks should guide our work. Older teens might be attracted to youth involvement where they are given adult roles, while younger teens often just want to have fun. Middle teens are curious about the world around them and are gaining interest in ideas, forming skills, asking questions, and setting their values. What all teens have in common is that they are in a process of growth and change.

If you commute to work in a city of any size, then you know all about sitting in traffic on roads under construction. It is one of the most stressful of all activities. The area is messy and disorganized; it makes everyone short tempered because there is only so much patience a person can have. You want to get going, but you are surrounded by the symbol of commuter frustration, the orange cone. You somehow just have to remember that this road construction is a work in progress; when completed, things will look and work much better. That is also what a YA is, a work in progress. A teen is an orange cone.

What are the milestones of early adolescence (11–13)?

- Increases concern about appearance;
- Seeks independence from family;
- Displays rebellious/defiant behaviors;
- Importance of friends increases;
- Peer group dominates, and
- Ego dominates viewing of all issues.

What are the milestones of middle adolescence (14–16)?

- Becomes less self absorbed;
- Makes decisions on own;
- Experiments with self image;
- Takes risks and seeks new experiences;
- Develops sense of values/morality;
- Begins to make lasting relationships;
- Becomes sexually aware;
- Intellectual awareness increases;
- Interests/skills mature; and
- Seeks out "adventures."

What are the milestones of late adolescence (17–18)?

- Views world idealistically;
- Becomes involved with world outside of home/school;
- Sets goals;
- Relationships stabilize;
- Sees adults as "equals;" and
- Seeks to firmly establishes independence.

Adapted from *Adolescence: The Suvival Guide for Parents and Teenages*, by Elizabeth Fenwick. Dorling Kindersley, 1994.

So, if you work with a person who doesn't have a "YAttitude," here is what you need to do. When you observe them saying in a patronizing tone—either these words exactly or something like them—"Why don't you just grow up" to a teen playing a computer game, here is what you do. Put them in your car and drive them to the nearest road construction project. Ask them to pick up one of the orange cones and yell into it, "Why don't you just finish already?" Then ask them how successful that strategy is, and then ask them to rethink their tone with teens. Teens are works in progress and we wish to engage them in libraries, through passive activities like having magazines for them to read, to active ones like involving them in choosing which magazines we purchase; all to help in their process of self-definition. We do this not because it is good of us (although it is), but because it is good for them. We want the orange cones.

HOW DO DEVELOPMENTAL NEEDS RELATE TO LIBRARIES?

While each grouping of milestone is unique, there is some overlap and we would argue four common themes in the lives of all teenagers regardless of race, religion, age, or other factors. The core needs of all teens relate to issues of independence, excitement, identity, and acceptance. For each of these core needs, let's look at how libraries can or have responded.

INDEPENDENCE

From birth, the child learns to depend upon the parents. During the teen years, this basic relationship changes as teens learn to do things on their own. It manifests itself in many ways, but each step is a step from dependence—from the first time staying home alone to the first date; from the first time driving mom's car to buying their own car, the YA tests the waters of independence. One of the big draws of the Internet, in particular e-mail and chatting, is that it allows for a high degree of independence. Akin to achieving independence is learning responsibility, participating in decision-making, and various acts of petty rebellion.

Library responses:

Library cards
Every YA should have their own card so they can check out materials independent of their parents, but also to help them learn responsibility.

Many of the most successful library card campaigns aimed at teens often reward participation, for both teens and teachers, as well as amnesty for previous transgressions.

School and libraries together should wage campaigns to get every YA registered for a card at the beginning of each school year. There are caveats to consider here. Many libraries are struggling with library card issues, such as minors' access to videos and debating confidentiality of records balanced against a parent's "right to know." An increase in YA library cards will create more lost cards, more problems at the circulation desk, and more headaches. But the gain is great; if libraries want YAs to feel welcome, they cannot deny YAs the ability to access materials. With more non-circulation functions in libraries requiring a card, it is vital that YAs not be without access. If a teen doesn't have a card and wants a book that they can't ask mom to check out for them, they are either going to steal it (we lose) or not borrow it (we both lose).

Information literacy instruction

By teaching YAs how to effectively use our resources, we allow them to work independently. Instruction can help YAs learn about the information gathering and evaluating process, develop critical-thinking and decision-making skills, plus teach them time management. For libraries, instruction *is* time-management as it is certainly more efficient to provide YAs with instruction in a controlled setting than give the same instruction in the more frantic over-the-desk routine. In school libraries this is one of the most important, if not *the* most important, role. Similarly, part of the message to teens is that information literacy is time saving for them as well. It's a win-win.

Volunteer programs

Teen volunteer programs give YAs a chance to experience independence and responsibility. It is certainly a contradiction to think that many teens have an excess of time and energy while librarians belabor the fact that there is not enough staff to do things. Training, supervising, and encouraging volunteers take time and effort up-front, but have a huge payoff for the library, and even a better one for the teen engaged either in burning off community service hours or learning, growing, and changing into a healthier person because of the experience.

Advisory groups

Advisory groups provide teens with a forum to learn decision-making skills, to take on new responsibilities, and to participate in different programs and projects. Again, not much research, but plenty of success stories showing why organized and structured youth-participation benefits everyone, but mostly the teens involved.

Music collections

Rap music isn't just popular because of the bass booming tracks. For many white suburban YA youths few things are as "cool" to them as driving around with the volume high and the bass cranked up. In addition, like Elvis, the Beatles, the Sex Pistols, Nirvana, or the Beastie Boys when you were a teenager, listening to rap is wearing your rebellious badge. Music has been a channel for teen rebellion for years. A music collection becomes a prime opportunity to connect with YAs. Allowing YAs to choose the music for a library demonstrates a perfect example of a program with minimal cost and maximum impact on teens. They get to make choices (independence); they get to pick out music (excitement); they get to choose the genres they like (identity); and finally, they get to see their opinions valued (acceptance).

EXCITEMENT

Because everything changes, everything is possible. Teens experience physical changes wrought with emotional changes. The world becomes a more exciting, and scary, place with many more possibilities, opportunities, and dangers. Excitement manifests itself in the abundance of energy, wild enthusiasm, good humor, bad pranks, vandalism, and the desire to sit neither the body nor the mind at rest for too long.

Library responses:

Programming

Programs can offer teens a chance to actively participate rather than react passively. They can generate enthusiasm and channel energy into productive pursuits. Programming may be educational or informational in nature, but it almost always has to be interactive and entertaining. Teens want to act, not just be told.

A YA Area

Not only does it answer their need for independence (their own room), but it also can be the place where exciting things can happen. A better YA area, from most staff's perspective, means YAs will congregate there rather than spreading their potentially disruptive energy through the entire building. This YA area needs materials, comfortable chairs organized so socializing can occur, and a comfortable atmosphere created by posters or other decoration. YA areas belong in school libraries for the very same reason; they are about a library giving teens their own room or area apart from that used by adults.

Magazines

Because the YA attention span is short, magazines are the desired reading materials. In addition, magazines are current, so they talk about

> The model for teen programming isn't that which always creates the best statistics, but rather that which provides the teen participating with the best experience.

what is "hot," and they are full of photos. Magazines present libraries with a simple low-cost bang-for-the-buck opportunity to do something that YAs will view favorably given the interest in periodicals and the importance many YAs place in them.

Games

YA areas should have board games, computer games, and maybe even a video-gaming unit. The library should also sponsor tournaments or groups for role playing games. Games speak to the YA need "to do." Games are social in nature, require mind energy, and are a medium for laughs. Like all of these responses under excitement; however, the drawback is they cause noise. Setting up a computer with games is not going to create a silent area, nor are computers with Internet access that allow teens to visit gaming sites. If you recognize the fact that YAs are excitable and you set up functions to channel that energy, you will have to learn also.

Adjust expectations

You cannot expect a group of YAs full of stored up energy from a day of school to walk into the library and be perfectly still and quiet. Expectations have limits and must be based on circumstance. If these expectations resist flexibility, then an impossible situation is created for both you and the YAs.

IDENTITY

"Who am I?" is the basic YA question. Teens define themselves in many ways; some try to be similar to everyone else, like a thesaurus; some try to be as unique as possible, like a dictionary. Most use a mixture of the two. The search for identity produces even more changes as YAs attempt to say, scream, or whisper this question, "Who am I?" in what they wear, do, and read.

Library responses:

Readers' advisory

What a person reads helps define them. By helping YAs choose materials through matching their interests with the library's collections, you are helping them establish an identity. While we believe that a collection should serve a mass YA audience—many series, comic books, and books about music—there is necessity for balance. The kids not into "what's hot" need materials reflecting their interests, as well; for example, fantasy, science fiction, or the novels of Cynthia Voigt.

Share an interest

Not every thing YAs care about is totally alien to you. A lot of times YAs feel doubts about the things that they like or do not like, especially if it is outside the YA mainstream. For example, if you share an appreciation for classical music and you find a YA that does as well, then encourage that YA. Depending on how well they know you, for some of these YAs you are a role model. Sometimes you will find the kids who are library regulars are having trouble forming an identity; they do not fit in with the other kids and seek refuge at the library. Chances are that by sharing a little of yourself, you have made an impact.

Writer's programs

Offering YAs an opportunity to express themselves creatively is a fantastic way to meet this core need. Through writing, YAs explore themselves. You will be amazed, even shocked, at the things they produce, for many YAs find their "dark side" when they pick up a pen. Taking a writing program a step further and producing a literary magazine e-zine is a low-cost program a library can do that benefits teens, cooperates with teachers, and thus profits the library.

Artist's programs

The benefits gained by a writer's program are the same as when they pick up a paintbrush, or a camera. Working with schools to develop a student art-show to showcase YA expression might even involve more YAs than a writer's program. Art, however, needs to include all the kinds of arts that YAs enjoy and use to define themselves—comics, cartoons, fashion, graffiti, video, collages, computer generated art, Web page design, manga, and even skateboard decoration.

Individualize

Because the YA beast often travels in packs, it is hard to get to know individuals. Some YAs will respond to you immediately, while others might be harder to reach. During a reference interview there really is not time to learn anything, except perhaps a name. But that's a big thing. If you can learn the names of various YAs who frequent your building, then that is a first step to building relations.

By getting to know names, faces, and personalities of even a few YAs, it is more difficult to stereotype and much easier to accept them.

ACCEPTANCE

Because the YA seeks independence, looks for excitement but sometimes only finds trouble, and tries to develop an identity, the last core need is, not surprisingly, acceptance. Because as they are doing all these things, and redefining themselves and their relationships, they are bound to make mistakes. Because they try too hard to develop and carry off a self, it is a fragile thing, under constant attack from outside and inside.

Library responses:

Youth involvement

We show teens we accept them by actively inviting them to participate. We are providing in our volunteer corps, our community service kids, and our youth councils, a sense that their words and work matters. Since many of the kids who are sometimes drawn to these activities are sometimes those shunned by their peers these programs let them get acceptance from not just adults, but provide a vehicle for acceptance from another set of peers.

Positive experience

A YA who comes to the library and finds unfriendly service, no information for schoolwork, and frustrating technology will have a negative library experience. We need to set a tone for all patrons, especially YAs, that the library is a place where they can "win." It is an inviting place people that are helpful and patient. YAs remember those who are rude and take such offenses very personally because they are very self-conscious. A YA's ego is fragile and ranges from bravado to shyness and these extremes make are not easy to endure during a reference interview.

"Deal with it"

YAs will hurl chess pieces across the room and they will rip pictures from magazines. The behavior is unacceptable. That is the needed message, not that they are unacceptable. Correct the behavior and not the person; practice discipline with dignity.

Outreach

There are lots of YAs who may never come into a library, and if they do, they do not get noticed. They are the YAs who do not get into the honor's class, do not write or draw, and do not hang out in front of the building smoking. The only way to meet this large group is to get into the schools or get the schools into our libraries. We need to tell these YAs about what we do and what we have and welcome them.

Meeting special needs

Everyone is accepted; YAs who cannot read are welcomed into the library, along with YAs who do not speak English or cannot speak at all. Those serving YAs need to be always conscious of the fact there is no average YA. If the library cannot cater to everyone, then it needs to be aware of the resources in the community that can assist these teens.

RAP: *Remember* what it is like to be 15. *Accept* that 15-year-olds will always and have always behaved in a certain ways. *Project*—correct the behavior if you must, but imagine it is you as the 15-year-old and imagine how you would want to be treated.

WHAT IS WRONG WITH THESE DAMN KIDS?

Most of the time the conflict in libraries with teens isn't their actions, but our reactions. If we understood better, we would be more respectful of teens. If we were more respectful, we would get that respect returned to us. The environment would be less stressful for staff, more conducive to building assets, and geared toward ensuring that teens have a positive library experience. A positive library experience occurs when YAs find what they need, do not feel frustrated, feel they have been helped not hindered, and want to return. More importantly, they want to come back not just tomorrow, but next year, and for years to come.

Achieving a positive experience is not always easy. Often when teens need to use the library, they cannot find the materials they need or the services they deserve *and* there are even more teens who don't use libraries but could and should; if only libraries saw them as important

TEENS	LIBRARIANS
Concerned with "hip"	Anal retentive detail freaks
Dangerous	Bad hair, ugly shoes
Destructive	Bookworm
Disorganized and chaotic	Bored and boring
Drug-dealing gangsters	Can't multitask
Emotional	Cold and uncaring
Disrespectful	Dull and staid
Full of energy	Judgmental
Internet obsessed	Neutered
Loud and obnoxious	Not interested in teenagers
Not interested in anything printed	Obsessed with quiet
Not interested in libraries	Out of touch with the times
Only care about appearance	Overprotective
Physical/sexual	Read all day
Pressured	Rigid
Rushed	Serious
Smart alecks	Slow people, computers, systems
Travel in packs	Solemn
Unpredictable	Suspicious
Weird looking	Weaklings

Figure 2-1. Teen and librarian stereotypes.

and inviting. They don't see us as inviting or friendly, and we don't see them as adults in the making. Teens do not get the respect they deserve because of too many rehashed stereotypes.

What stereotypes do librarians hold of teens? What stereotypes of librarians do teens hold (see Figure 2-1)?

Are these stereotypes accurate? Well, yes and no. They are based on some knowledge, often limited and often a result of a negative incident. All of the stereotypes of teens match up perfectly with the milestones adolescence; more of the librarian's stereotypes match up just as well with the personality indicators of the Myers-Briggs in which most librarians fall (INTJ). Let's face it, we are a profession of people who doesn't like other people, but we do know what is wrong with them. That's a joke and an exaggeration, but also works because it is based on some truth; often we do act out these stereotypes and become our worst enemies in interacting with teens. Stereotypes are warped perceptions, based on selected truth, that need to be replaced by facts derived not from anecdotal evidence, but actual experiences. In other words, building relationships that build assets probably does more to knock down stereotypes than any other function. Like all relationships, it takes time, involves effort, and requires patience. Knowing the stages of adolescent development and moving behind stereotypes doesn't mean excusing or allowing obviously inappropriate behavior, it means instead understanding it, and redirecting it in a way that is not disrespectful.

HOW DO YOU REDIRECT INAPPROPRIATE BEHAVIOR BY TEENS IN LIBRARIES?

YAs congregate in libraries for a variety of reasons. The most obvious reason is the same reason others do—because they have an information need that the library can meet or they need Internet access. Sometimes this information need is school related, other times not. For younger teens, libraries are a place where they often feel comfortable in a world they are growing more confused about every day. Libraries also serve as an after-school social-center. In many communities, once school is over there are not locations for YAs to gather except their local public libraries. The library is free, easily accessible, and known. It is also an acceptable place for parents to send their YAs; libraries are thought of as safe havens. Libraries are, normally, easy to get to, close to schools or other institutions, and have chairs much more comfortable than those at McDonalds. While some teens do have Internet access at home, many don't, or what they have might be limited by connection speed, parent filters, or time limits.

> Developing realistic expectations of behavior is the first step to solving the YA patron problem.

It is the congregation aspect—the swarm of beasts—that causes the most problems for libraries. In some libraries, it is just a numbers problem. For those libraries located near schools, the crowd that gathers around 2:30 can be intimidating for no other reason than its bulk. This scenario requires leadership, and a single LST cannot be the answer to serving or policing seventy-five YAs at once. The person in charge of the library must set the tone and, with the LST, develop the strategy for all staff. If during this time library staff is merely acting as security guards then, perhaps the better use of library resources would be just to hire one person to police patrons. Security guards are, in many libraries, a necessary evil—YAs want to feel as safe in the library as you do. Yet within that group of seventy-five, many need library help and it makes good sense for people trained to assist customers. Let security handle keeping the peace according to your directions. That is a short-term solution; in the long term, the staff should be working with schools to develop after school programs, working within the community to find recreational alternatives, and finally working within the library to train staff on serving YAs. If a group of seventy-five factory workers, preschoolers, or library school students emerged in the library at one time, there would also be noise and behavior issues, like the YAs.

Teens are in a day-to-day learning process about accepting responsibility. Told what to do as children, they are now facing choices despite not having clear ideas on what the limits are for them. Thus, they test the limits. Confrontations between LSTs and YAs often revolve around this very issue—how much is allowed and who decides. This task explains the contempt YAs hold for adults, especially those connected with institutions like libraries. It explains why some YAs are constantly talking back and challenging. Finally, it should explain why LSTs should always be sure to correct inappropriate behavior in terms of the behavior rather than the person. Remember how you liked criticism when you were learning a new job. Did you want to be attacked and made to feel stupid? Or did you want to learn what was wrong and how to do it better next time? That is what YAs are doing every day, learning a new job that is how to be a person in society. It is on-the-job training with no pull down help screens.

Trying to remember this in the abstract is difficult when confronted with a group of boys cursing loudly in the reference area, or a group of girls shouting in front of the library's front door. In both of those cases, it is clear the behavior is inappropriate because it disrupts others. That of course is the litmus test. What if a class is visiting to work on homework, yet several boys are passing around the *Sports Illustrated* swimsuit issue? While that might be annoying, it is not inappropriate because it does not disrupt others. Or if a group of YAs plop down their textbooks and then proceed to spend three hours in normal library hushed tones—okay with an outburst or two—gossiping rather than

Clearly, when YAs are talking but not disrupting others, the problem is our reactions, not their actions.

doing homework? Well, that is not disruptive either. Or teens who come in, just to use the computers and spend all of their time chatting both verbally with each other and virtually with who knows who; these teens have a window open playing a computer game, another one to check e-mail, and another one to pop-up so it looks like they are doing something "important" in case the librarian walks by? Frequently, the staff appears only to discipline, rather than offer assistance. Thus, the real question with YAs and librarians is getting the correct answer to the question, "Who has the problem?"

How then to deal with the reality of disruptive behavior among YAs? In addition to understanding why YAs behave, some strategies are also in order. These strategies revolve around four R's—relationships, rules, and reactions. The final "r" is basic and more important than the rest—respect. Some librarians just don't like YAs and that is not going to change. No one requires librarians to like the people they serve. The key is respecting YAs as library patrons. Not just characterizing all of them as "loud kids" or the LST's problem, we need to treat them as patrons who demand, require, and deserve our respect. If we don't see them that way, then librarians are the real disruptive element, not the YAs.

RELATIONSHIPS

With YAs

The research on youth development points to building these relationships as *the* key.

It's as if YAs are group animals and it is important to identify the groups and their leaders. Direct your energies toward meeting these leaders—getting to know their names, their likes, and dislikes. You want the leader working with you, not against you. It is much better if the peer groups themselves work to keep things "cool." More than that, there needs to be some other relationship that LSTs establish with YAs other than acting the role of the "quiet police." But what if they saw the LST in a different role? What if they saw an LST as someone who came into their classroom to tell them about library materials, or as someone who helped them learn how to use the library to get their report done? Instead of the quiet cop, they could see an LST as a person who helps them find sites on the Internet or insert graphics into papers they are writing on the library's computer. Then, YAs would define their relationship with the library more personally than if there were no face or name with which to connect.

With staff

No one can do this alone and everyone has to be on board. If you are serious about solving problems, then you cannot have others working against you. All staff, not just whoever bears the brunt of serving YAs, needs information and education about redirecting behavior. It serves no one to have an LST working hard to improve relationships if the clerk at the check-out desk is being rude and insulting. Not everyone on staff can or will be a YA advocate, but then again, everyone must understand that YA's are patrons just like anyone else who walks through the door.

Relationships outside the library

Who else in the community serves YAs? Network with schools, youth groups, churches, human service agencies, and whomever else in your community works with YAs. What about working with businesses that also cater to teens and maybe face some of the same problems? Also, a relationship with the police department is essential. Sometimes YAs— like other patrons—do get out of hand and you might need some help. But, what are your expectations? Do you want the police to just show the badge, or is the library willing to follow through prosecuting patrons who engage in criminal behavior? If disruptive patrons refuse to correct their behavior after reasonable attempts on the part of staff, then it is no longer a library's problem, but a criminal one.

Relationships with a YA

Get to know a YA; you might even like him or her. Once you get to actually know YAs as people, then it becomes harder to stereotype all of them. In addition, you want to nurture a relationship that nurtures YAs to develop responsible behavior. Put the onus on the YAs or YAs behaving inappropriately. Make it their choice and say, "Look, your behavior is inappropriate because it is disrupting others. If you choose to behave this way, then you are choosing to leave. If you wish to stay, then you must be less disruptive; you decide." This is a benefit of youth involvement on any level—it forces us all the move beyond a stereotype and to accept the person.

Relationship with yourself

It is important to be confident within yourself when dealing with YAs. It takes toughness to deal with YAs, even if you understand their actions. If they belittle you, it is just to make them feel bigger because feeling bigger/better is what they are trying to do all the time; self-esteem is a teen's daily concern. Sometimes it seems that many of us working in libraries have the most trouble dealing with teens whom we didn't like when we were teens. Let's accept that might be there, and then move beyond it. Remember, we're the adults.

RULES

Mary K. Chelton's work on this topic makes the point pretty clear that it is not so much teens who are "problem patrons but rather staff who have broken the unwritten rules about fairness and respect, and thus cast the teens as villains when many of us are street level bureaucrats running amok."

Written rules, especially to YAs, are often interpreted as a series of challenges. A simple posted rule like "No gum allowed" seems clear, but YAs could argue for heated minutes with retorts of "It says no gum, not no chewing gum" or "It says nothing about chewing tobacco" and the like. Although we might feel safer with written rules of conduct, unless you allow the YAs to develop themselves, they just seem like trouble waiting to happen. There are, admittedly, lots of valid reasons, some of them legal, for having such rules, so this may not be negotiable. Any written rules of conduct should not, however, be directed only toward YAs. There is much literature regarding problem patrons/situations in libraries; in order to be fair, YAs deserve the same treatment as adults.

Noise versus disruptive behavior

Even without posted rules for using the library, there is one overriding rule and it applies to everyone—if your behavior disrupts others, then that behavior is inappropriate and you must stop it or leave the building. This is a fine line, especially with YAs who tend to become carried away. A small group studying quietly can get very loud very quickly. But are they being consistently disruptive? Probably not, but things just got out of hand for a moment or two. If possible, maintain eye contact, but not the "evil eye," with the perceived leader at the table that might help keep things calm. As mentioned earlier, there is a fine line between perceived appropriate behavior on the Internet and what is truly appropriate. Similarly, a librarian should offer assistance to teens who are perceived as noisy instead of trying to redirect their behavior.

Fair, firm, consistent

You can't treat the honor students differently from the ones that take shop—there is no playing favorites in the YA world. Approaches to YAs must be firm; no snooping around or meekly suggesting, "Gee whiz, can you please not be so loud." Rather, a firm statement that their behavior is inappropriate and cannot continue and/or present YAs with a choice to modify their behavior or leave. This must be as consistent as possible among all staff members. The rules cannot change from day-to-day; it confuses the YAs and creates problems for everyone.

Further, YAs have a sharp sense of injustice. If reprimanded for being loud only to witness a group of the staff talking at a high volume, they will make a stink about it. Basically, "practice what we preach" and the staff should live within the rules they set and enforce. Add another "r"—role model.

Hidden agendas

Librarianship is a female-dominated profession and the job of YA hell-raiser is a male-dominated one. This, too, presents itself as a contradiction. In many libraries it is also a race issue as well; in many public libraries the staff is certainly not a "mirror" of the community it serves. Some additional training from outside our library might help staff handle situations where the problem isn't so much for staff teen issues, but issues related to race. Sometimes the real issue is not YAs, but dealing with diversity of our users.

Enforcing the rules

You can neither threaten to throw YAs out eight or nine times, nor can you just ignore them and hope they go away. If you are going to intervene, then you prepare to follow through with that action. If you follow through, and the behavior continues, then seek assistance in enforcing your decision. If they realize you are all bark and no bite, then YAs might just sit around the table figuring out what to try next.

Crossing the line

We keep track of fines, but we shouldn't carry grudges.

If a particular YA is a constant problem, then don't allow him or her back. If that person is a negative example of a peer leader, then the best thing you might do for all YAs is rid yourself of the disruptive person. Your goal is to ensure a positive environment and present a positive image of YAs to staff. If a disruptive individual later decides they want to return, then let them know that all they have to do is request it. Be sure, to let them know that the library is an accepting, forgiving, and inviting place.

Don't escalate

When enforcing your rules, YAs will often challenge them. They will want to ask you questions or say things like "It is a public library, so I'm allowed here." Sometimes "Y" seems to be the only letter in the alphabet. Without being totally obnoxious, you merely need to restate your position—correct the behavior or leave. Discussions often lead to debates, and debates lead to shouting matches. If they know they can fluster you, YAs will only try harder to do it again; this cycle only breeds nasty scenes in front of other patrons. You probably can't avoid confrontations, but you can derail heated conflict.

Make the first impression a positive one

Often a teen's first encounter with a library staff member is negative, the role of enforcer. Instead, LSTs need to be proactive about greeting, meeting, and developing relationships with the "regulars" who use libraries. Tell them clearly what the expectations are, but also tell them what they can expect of you—assistance, fairness, and respect.

REACTIONS

Don't power trip

One of the reasons librarians have a bad image of YAs is they see us as mean and controlling. Sometimes we think it is "our" library, when really the library belongs to the public, even YAs. This power can also manifest itself in controlling problem-situations. If you abuse your power, then you are setting up a dangerous situation. If you humiliate, embarrass, or humble a YA, that person will remember it, and then in winning you have really lost.

Keep cool

If you lose your cool or become rattled, then YAs get the reaction they wanted and a payoff for their inappropriate behavior. It is hard and it is difficult, but you need to remain relaxed and just let the situation bounce off you. They will test you like they do a new teacher or a substitute.

Not personal

Similarly, these are not personal attacks. If they call you a name, it is because they feel a need to test you or maybe to strike out at you as an authority figure, not you personally. There are certainly limits here—racist, homophobic, sexist, or sexually harassing tirades should not be tolerated from YAs any more than they would be from any other patron.

> Developing realistic expectations is the key; so too, realizing what YAs appreciate most is someone with a sense of humor.

Lighten up

YAs make mistakes because they are YAs learning a job known as life. Most of these mistakes are not the end of the world, or even of the Dewey Decimal system. If we constantly overreact to everything, then real connections are hard to make. All that stress we feel often from YAs is not from them, but from ourselves.

Project/remember

Before we react to a YA, wouldn't it be more productive to take a moment to remember back to being a YA. Recalling the feelings of insecurity and confusion instill sympathy for what YAs endure. Through sympathy and understanding, the relationship between YAs and librarians would be more satisfying and less stressful. Imagine for a moment that you a fifteen again, but something is different; you have Internet access. What would you have done? For many of us, if we had had Internet access as teens we would have printed song lyrics— Springsteen rather than Snoop Dogg—printed pictures, chatted, e-mailed, printed some more lyrics, played games, and had fun. In other words, we'd have done the very same thing that teens do in our libraries every day. So, again, who has the problem?

RESPECT

None of these strategies is foolproof. Like all problem-patron situations, it takes a large dosage of good judgment, timing, and people skills. Despite the contradiction of libraries and YAs, we have some things in common. Our emotional make up is often the same; libraries, like YAs, often feel under-appreciated, and disrespected. It might be hard for some to think YAs deserve respect, but the minute a YA walks through the door they become a library patron who deserves respect. Libraries and YAs might be opposites in many ways, but we share the same ground and should learn to live with each other. More than that, we need to engage in those services that will do more than handle teens, but instead see that they thrive.

WHAT DO YOUNG ADULTS WANT AND NEED FROM LIBRARIES?

If you ask them, they will tell you. The teens involved in the focus groups as part of the Public Library as Partners in Youth Development were asked. These teens, who were all from primarily large urban areas, the target of the project, have a clear vision of a library that has the following characteristics:

- Asks and involves teens in all aspects;
- Appears bright, cheerful, and filled with varied activities;
- Gives teens a place of their own;
- Offers CD-ROM software, word processing, and other info technology;
- Contains collections filled with magazines and new books;
- Provides lots of computers with unfiltered Internet access;
- Keeps multiple copies of books needed for reports;
- Creates music rooms and videos rooms; and
- Offers longer weekend and evening hours; and rethinks fines and other regulations.

If you ask them, they will tell you. The teens involved in the focus groups conducted by the State Library of California have a clear vision of a library that has the following characteristics:

- Feels comfortable, where staff does not view teens with suspicion;
- Creates a place in the library where teens can be themselves;
- Provides access to tutors and homework assistance;
- Expands hours to include late evenings and more weekend hours;
- Employs friendly staff that treat them with respect;
- Improves procedures such as self-check out, no late fees, and easier ways to find information in the library;
- Features a place for teens to talk, listen to music, eat and drink, sit in comfortable furniture, and have access to teen-relevant materials;
- Runs promotional events featuring giveaways, food, and fun teen-relevant activities; and
- Offers materials that are relevant to their lives, help them with school, and are also fun.

But mostly these teens spoke fondly of library reading programs and storytelling that they remembered when they were younger. They wanted to feel the same sense of acceptance as teens that they felt in the library as children. One more thing, they liked being asked for their ideas.

The focus groups from California, of course, reflect the highly diverse nature of that state and its large urban areas. The Urban Library Council's work is also mainly with teens from larger cities; so what do teens in the suburbs need and want from libraries? Research at the Hennepin County Library in suburban Minneapolis shows that—despite difference in geography, demographics, and experiences—what teens want and need from libraries is similar to those who live in the diverse urban areas:

- Younger teens tend to use the library more for recreational pursuits—reading, Internet use. Older teens are more interested in homework support.
- Older teens refrain from using the library because of competition with other activities, and younger teens generally complain about lack of transportation. Both groups also reported they found their information needs met elsewhere, presumably home Internet use.
- Teens would like the library to be open longer hours. During a focus group, one teen commented that, "You are shutting down when I am just getting started."
- Teens also want more study space and more books to support homework, primarily in the smaller libraries.
- Teens are dissatisfied with the music and magazine selections at the library.
- Teens are not interested in programming, youth involvement groups, or after school programs. In many ways, teens have a very traditional view of library services. The unanswered question, however, is *if* the library offered more programming, youth involvement groups, and after school programs, then *would* teens be interested.

> Teens are looking for services that produce positive outcomes in their lives. They want to thrive.

While the quantitative survey data accompanying these small group discussions indicated that only a small portion of teens reported they were unsure what the library offered, the qualitative research found teens neither had a clear understanding of services nor how to best utilize information technology. Teens enjoyed being asked for their opinions and many contributed ideas, such as promoting programs through the check out receipt slips, that benefited the library.

We can infer three things:

- Teens want to have a positive experience in a library.
- Teens want to be treated fairly in a library.
- Teens know that libraries have value and, with changes, could even make more of a difference in their lives.

WHAT DO YOUNG ADULTS NEED IN THEIR LIVES?

The word "thrive" emerges from the literature on youth development, in particular from the Search Institute. Search Institute is an independent nonprofit organization whose mission is to provide leadership, knowledge, and resources to promote healthy children, youth, and communities. The Search Institute has reviewed the research in the field of youth development, as well as conducted their own studies on thousands of adolescents. They concluded that teens require certain positive conditions and experiences in their lives, or what Search has called "developmental assets." The research led the Search Institute to identify forty such assets, twenty external and twenty internal. The external assets are about the relationships available to young people. Internal assets are the values and skills that teens develop to guide themselves. These forty assets are the positive experiences, opportunities, and personal qualities that youth need in order to become responsible, successful, and caring adults. They are the foundation YAs need in order to thrive.

> When you go on a trip, you pack the things you need to make your journey safe, sound, and satisfying. Development assets are the luggage of young adulthood.

Below is a simple chart listing the asset type and name, followed by a definition. The last column shows a library connection: a program, an idea, or a service that libraries could undertake in order to build each asset.

The key conclusion is this, the more assets young people accumulate, the less likely they are to engage in a wide range of risky behaviors and the more likely they are going to engage in positive behaviors. Those positive behaviors include succeeding in school, helping others, and valuing diversity.

Asset Type	Asset Name	Asset Definition	Library Connection
EXTERNAL ASSETS			
Support	Family support	Family life provides high levels of love and support.	Intergenerational programming supports this asset, such as mother/daughter book discussion groups.
	Positive family communication	Young person and his or her parent(s) communicate positively, and young person is willing to seek advice and counsel from parent(s).	Libraries support this asset through workshops for parents of teenagers and by promoting books on parenting teens in the collection.
	Other adult relationships	Young person receives support from three or more non-parent adults.	Library staff can develop strong bonding relationships with teens, either through organized groups or through daily interaction.
	Caring neighborhood	Young person experiences caring neighbors.	Outreach work by library in the community spreads the assets message and helps create a caring neighborhood.
	Caring school climate	School provides a caring, encouraging environment.	Programming at the school media center teaches information literacy skills and demonstrates a caring school climate.
	Parent involvement in schooling	Parent(s) are actively involved in helping young person succeed in school.	Parent technology nights at school or public library provide skills parents need to help their teens succeed in school.
Empowerment	Community appreciates youths	Young person perceives that adults in the community appreciate youths.	Teens are actively involved in library decisions, and are asked for their opinions either formally or informally.

Figure 2-2. Developmental assets: type, name, definition, and connection to the library.

Asset Type	Asset Name	Asset Definition	Library Connection
EXTERNAL ASSETS			
	Youth as resources	Young people are given useful roles in the community.	Teens are used as volunteers, workers, and mentors supporting the library's mission.
	Service to others	Young person serves in the community one hour or more per week.	Year long volunteer programs provide an opportunity for service, from helping the children's librarian with story times to helping the library build its physical and virtual collections.
	Safety	Young person feels safe at home, at school, and in the neighborhood.	Library often acts as the safe haven for teens and provides them with a place to be alone.
Boundaries and Expectations	Family boundaries	Family has clear rules and consequences, and monitors the young person's whereabouts.	Libraries support this asset through workshops for parents of teenagers and by promoting books on parenting teens in the collection.
	School boundaries	School provides clear rules and consequences.	Positive discipline practiced in the library media center supports this asset.
	Neighborhood boundaries	Neighbors take responsibility for monitoring young people's behavior.	Libraries are neighborhood institutions. Through positive discipline and redirecting inappropriate behaviors; librarians play a role in setting boundaries.
	Adult role models	Parent(s) and other adults model positive, responsible behavior.	Librarians can serve as role models for youth, if they allow teens "in."
	Positive peer influence	Young person's best friends model responsible behavior.	Peer programming such as book discussion groups support this asset.

Figure 2-2. Continued

Asset Type	Asset Name	Asset Definition	Library Connection
EXTERNAL ASSETS			
	High expectations	Both parent(s) and teachers encourage the young person to do well.	The school librarian takes an active role in encouraging student achievement, as well as supporting it through a proactive plan of service.
Constructive Use of Time	Creative activities	Young person spends three or more hours per week in lessons or practice in music, theater, or other arts.	Programs that promote creativity such as creative writing programs, talent shows, literacy magazines, zines, book review newsletters, e-zines, and other library sponsored creative expression activities.
	Youth programs	Young person spends three or more hours per week in sports, clubs, or organizations at school and/or in community organizations.	After-school homework-help programs at school and the public library function as a "club," as would a youth participation group.
	Religious community	Young person spends one hour or more per week in activities in a religious institution.	-NA-
	Time at home	Young person is out "with nothing special to do" two or fewer nights per week.	Wide range of after school, evening, and weekend programs established, as well as collections that engage youth.
INTERNAL ASSETS			
Commitment to Learning	Achievement motivation	Young person is motivated to do well in school.	Homework assistance programs involving tutors at the school or public library motivate students to achieve.

Figure 2-2. Continued

Asset Type	Asset Name	Asset Definition	Library Connection
INTERNAL ASSETS			
	School engagement	Young person is actively engaged in learning.	School media specialist involved in designing assignments that provide students with active learning in regard to information literacy.
	Homework	Young person reports doing at least one hour of homework every school day.	Initiate homework assistance programs, as well as collections to support homework; reference services in person, over the phone, and via e-mail assist teens in completing homework.
	Bonding to school	Young person cares about his or her school.	By involving youth in the school media center, as workers or volunteers, this bonding is encouraged.
	Reading for pleasure	Young person reads for pleasure three or more hours per week.	Everything we do: our collections, our programs, our displays, and our readers' advisory work.
Positive Values	Caring	Young person places high value on helping other people.	Youth advisory groups or volunteer programs can involve teens in projects, such as reading to seniors or working with preschoolers, which give them the opportunity to help others.
	Equality and social justice	Young person places high value on promoting equality and reducing hunger and poverty.	Collections and programming illustrate this asset.
	Integrity	Young person acts on convictions and stands up for her or his beliefs.	Youth participation groups encourage the development of this asset.
Figure 2-2. Continued			

Asset Type	Asset Name	Asset Definition	Library Connection
INTERNAL ASSETS			
	Honesty	Young person "tells the truth even when it is not easy."	This value is learned while serving as a teen volunteer or worker.
	Responsibility	Young person accepts and takes personal responsibility.	From participation in after-school programs to daily behavior, libraries help young people learn about responsibility.
	Restraint	Young person believes it is important not to be sexually active or to use alcohol or other drugs.	Collections and programming can speak to this asset.
Social Competencies	Planning and decision making	Young person knows how to plan ahead and make choices.	Youth advisory groups can involve youth in planning programs and services.
	Interpersonal competence	Young person has empathy, sensitivity, and friendship skills.	Youth advisory group, book discussion groups, or other such groups support this asset.
	Cultural competence	Young person has knowledge of and comfort with people of different cultural, racial, and ethnic backgrounds.	Both groups, as well as our collections support this asset. Multicultural programming plays a role here as well.
	Resistance skills	Young person resists negative peer pressure and dangerous situations.	Collections and programs illustrate this asset.
	Peaceful conflict resolution	Young person seeks to resolve conflict nonviolently.	Collections and programs can speak to this asset.
Positive Identity	Personal power	Young person feels he or she has control over "things that happen to me."	Collections and programs illustrate this asset.

Figure 2-2. Continued

Asset Type	Asset Name	Asset Definition	Library Connection
INTERNAL ASSETS			
	Self-esteem	Young person reports having a high self-esteem.	Collections and programs illustrate asset, as can using teen volunteers and/or employing youth workers.
	Sense of purpose	Young person reports that "my life has a purpose."	Collections and programs illustrate this asset, while youth participation provides teens with something of value in their life.
	Positive view of personal future	Young person is optimistic about his or her personal future.	Collections and programs illustrate this asset.
Figure 2-2. Continued			

Other positive behaviors could include maintaining good health, resisting danger, exhibiting leadership, delaying gratification, and overcoming adversity.

The research is clear. Sadly, the research also shows that lots of kids do not have assets. Research reported in the Search Institute's *A Fragile Foundation: the State of Developmental Assets Among Youth* shows that only 38 percent of kids reporting having at least twenty of the forty assets. One of the least reported of all the assets is reading for pleasure; less than a quarter of youth surveyed reported having this asset. While the assets framework is expanding, the research is currently based on young adult students in grades six to twelve.

Great stuff, but what does it have to do with serving youth in school and public libraries? Everything. Putting the library back at the center of the school or community is a strong selling point. Assets give us a way back to the center, a place where home computers, Internet cafés, super bookstores, and school computer labs, have made libraries marginalized. Our quality customer service is something we offer that these other places cannot. What we offer isn't so much our bricks or cliques, but our expertise. Libraries are not really in the information business or the book business, but the people business—connecting people and information.

Relationships are the key to demolishing stereotypes, improving services, and building assets. When staff in libraries start serving young adults as customers and not problems, then relationships will flourish.

Think for a second about libraries. What, at the basic level, do we do? We solve problems and, in doing so, provide our customers with good feelings. That is what a teen wants on their trip to a library; it is what they want out of their life, solutions to problems and good feelings. We do that through relationships; from simple interactions that take place during a reference question to longer commitments like programming or readers' advisory, or just in how we smile at kids every day. When we are in the telephone-reference interview, in the booktalk, or kicking out the rowdies, we need to get to know kids and thus can build relationships with them.

Relationships are the key to asset building. As adults encounter kids, we need to learn their names, support them, encourage them, and empower them. We are not talking about social work, we are talking about people work; we are talking about library work. When we form relationships, we help kids succeed, but also help libraries thrive.

WHAT DO TEENS WANT OUT OF THEIR LIVES?

If we want to understand what teens want and need from libraries, we ought to look at what teens want and need in their lives. Throughout this chapter, we've identified the stages of the teen experience and how we respond, respect, and understand it in the library. But we also must understand what our customers do outside of the library in order to design our services. We do much of this through observation, some through youth involvement, but we accomplish most of it by asking teens. We are, however, not alone.

Libraries don't need to be cool: they just need to have quality services that meet the needs of teen customers.

Teenage Research Unlimited (TRU), led by Peter Zollo, has been the leader in aiding companies market toward teens. While libraries don't have the resources to compete with the "big boys," we can look at what they've learned from Zollo and apply it to the library's agenda. For example, TRU found that the most important feature that makes a brand "cool" is "quality." This finding is a good sign. Libraries, no matter how much technology they acquire, will never be "cool" to the majority of teens. No matter how fancy our "teen zone" is, is there any doubt that most teens in a city still don't visit the library for recreational reasons? We aren't saying that LSTs ought to try and be cool, since most of us are not. It's not about being cool, it's about respecting what makes something "cool" for teens and building on it. So, what makes a product cool for teen isn't about sizzle, it's about steak. Our goal is to ensure the quality of our product, service.

"It's for people my age"; a statement that defines the second most important aspect of a "cool" product according to teens, something libraries have always been about. Libraries try carving out a space, a service, and a collection that is user focused. Doing that with the opinions and involvement of teens merely increases the likelihood that the service will be quality, thus "cool." The problem for libraries, however, is that what is "cool" for a twelve-year-old is not the same as for a seventeen-year-old, and we really aim to serve all ages. If we are to group people by age, we find ourselves confronted with another problem. What does YAs want to be called?

It depends. Zollo found that "young men or women" was most popular followed by "young adults." Fewer than half of people aged 12–19 want to be labeled as "teens" or "teenagers." While there are many reasons for this, in part it deals with the aspirational nature of youth. Driven by lots of factors, the kid who are ages 9–11 want to think of themselves as teens, while most of those over 16, figure they have left that label behind. Thus, teen services in library is normally not for 12- to 18-year-olds, but for those 8–15, while "young adult services" would be for those 16–18. With most libraries lacking even one LST, few have the ability to put equal effort into serving each group.

But Zollo would tell us that age is not the primary "divider" of the teen market. Instead, he writes four types: the conformers (49 percent), the passives (21 percent), the edge (17 percent), and the influencers (13 percent). These groups set teens apart from one another, regardless of age. Conformers are those who respond to trends, and as Zollo would argue, are those who most likely lack self-confidence. Passives are those who pick up trends later and are just less active than other teens. The influencers are the teens that other teens want to be; they are mainstream, popular, and cool. While libraries will never be cool, if these kids can be brought in through programs, outreach, or required school community service, then we stand a good chance of influencing other teens. The final group, the edge, are also kids we see a great deal in libraries, nonconformists who like to break the rules. While we still need to form relationships and move beyond stereotypes, the work of TRU gives us different ways to think about the teen market beyond gender, grade, and demographics.

One of the many contradictions of the teen years is clear in the work of TRU. Namely, the largest percentage of teens can be associated with the "conformers," and the largest complaint teens have about being a teen is "peer pressure." Of particular concern to LSTs is that teens also dislike being trivialized—don't do youth involvement if you don't plan to follow through—and lack of respect. The lack of respect, teens observe, is based on misconceptions about teens. While we've certainly talked about stereotypes and market segments to simplify the discussion, and we've alluded to developmental stages and milestones to highlight the common characteristics, every teen is different. We want teens to identify themselves as readers, lifelong learners, and community members. We help them form this identity when we take the time to understand, listen, and then respond in order to connect young adults and libraries.

3   WHEN/WHERE: STATE-OF-THE-ART YA SERVICES

"Where are the books?" asks Lisa Simpson.
"There are no books," replies the librarian. "We're a high-tech multi-media center for the whole family."

—*from* The Simpsons *(air date 2/8/04)*

The field of YA services is, on the surface, stronger than ever as libraries enter the twenty-first century. A scan of the history of YA services shows how today's state of the art has emerged from an evolution of ideas and activities on both the national and local levels; sometimes progress in great leaps, and other times in lulls. The history of YA services in libraries is an interesting one with a similar waxing and waning cycle that produces two common themes. First, that there is a huge gap between what libraries know they should do and what they actually do. This gap comes from the normal factors that separate library dreams from library reality, but with YAs there seems to be a deeper question underneath, should YAs be treated as a special group? Some libraries have a long history of recognizing YAs as special, while other systems, especially large public library systems, have been unwilling to do so. To classify YAs as a special population is to admit that they need a special service, and that means special staff and collections. YAs are not a group that have extra needs, but have unique needs. They require staff with specialized training and materials.

The second theme, realized in the last few years, is approaching YA services holistically. YA literature, programs, and information literacy aren't enough in themselves, but libraries must be able to avail teens the opportunities to take full advantage and benefit from a full range of library services. If the twentieth-century aim for young adult librarianship was to gain recognition as a real and vital part of the library world, then the profession, as it enters the twenty-first, aims to show that serving YAs in school and public libraries is a real and vital part of creating strong community. Equally as important, for many library directors, is that young adult services are seen as "cutting edge" and part of a library's success. While directors and principals take their cues from their community and their staff, they also look around the field at what other libraries are doing that is producing an effect. The drivers of public

As Zollo tells us and many businesses understand: teens are unique and that uniqueness should be understood, and catered to in service delivery.

47

library work entering the twenty-first century—technology, diversity, and supporting lifelong learning—are the essence of services to teens.

WHAT IS THE HISTORY OF LIBRARY SERVICES FOR YOUNG ADULTS?

The history of services to young adults in public libraries is less than one hundred years old. Like much library work, it is difficult to capture a true snapshot of work in the field; instead, we'll look at the top of the field, in terms of professional associations and publications, as an indicator of the status and state-of-the-art services. The YALSA Web site contains a more detailed history of these associations (www.ala.org/ala/yalsa/aboutyalsab/yalsahistory.htm) and many of the YA literature textbooks are excellent for documenting the history of the literature. Yet, as the great 1980s proto-punk band Gang of Four sang about history, "It's not made by great men," and much of the best work in the field of library services for teenagers is done not on the national level, but on the local level by people who never publish articles, speak at conferences, or write textbooks. We focus on history to give some context to the trends of the present and our predications for the future.

1929	Formation of Young Peoples Reading Roundtable as part of ALA's Children's Library Association.
1937	First YA professional book, *The Public Library and the Adolescent,* published by E. Leyland.
1941	Roundtable becomes part of ALA's Division of Libraries for Children and Young People.
1948–1950	ALA published *Public Library Plans for the Teen Age*. The Roundtable becomes a section of ALA as the Association of Young People's Librarians. Amelia Munson's *An Ample Field* published in 1950.
1958	Association of Young People's Librarians section becomes the Young Adult Services Division (YASD).
1960	ALA issues Young Adult Services in the Public Library from its Committee of Standards for Work with Young Adults.
1968–1969	The magazine *Library Trends* ran an issue entitled "Young Adult Service in the Public Library,"

which provides an excellent overview of the status of YA services entering the 1970s. A year later, Margaret Edwards published *The Fair Garden and the Swarm of Beasts.*

1978–1979 YASD published *Directions for Library Services to Young Adults* to provide the profession with a document to help them plan services. One year later, Libraries Unlimited published *Libraries and Young Adults,* which provided an excellent overview of services as libraries entered the 1980s.

1988 *Library Trends* published another issue dedicated to YAs entitled "Library Services to Youth: Preparing for the Future," which covers various topics from the 1980s, including what the next decade held in store. The same year, the National Center for Education Statistics released a report called *Services and Resources for Young Adults in Public Libraries.* It was the first comprehensive survey of the field telling us that 25% of all public library users are YAs, then documenting how few libraries employ YA librarians, train staff, or even provide basic of services. The statistics quantify the lack of quality in the field.

1994 Under ALA President Hardy Franklin, a triple play of publications were published that parallel the ALA President's Program and a customer service award from the Margaret Edwards foundation. The three publications were *Excellence in Library Services to Young Adults*, a reprint edition of *The Fair Garden and the Swarm of Beasts*, and YALSA's *Beyond Ephebiphobia* join ALA's *Best Books for Young Adults* and Scarecrow's *Hangin' Out at Rocky Creek* for the most prolific year of professional publishing regarding YAs and YA visibility. The Excellence in Library Services to Young Adults Project was started by ALA Past President Hardy Franklin and was funded by the Margaret Alexander Edwards Trust.

1995 Two key documents this year provided LSTs with tools to measure and prove their worth. The first was a revision of a 1992 report that focused on national library usage, which once again showed a heavy demand for services, but few LSTs to provide them. The numbers in the survey, as good as they were, were national in scope and based upon the subjective views of the survey respondents. Later in the year, Virginia Walter produced the indispensable book *Output Measures and More: Planning and Evaluating Public Library Services for Young Adults* that provided librarians with a tool to plan, document, and evaluate their work.

1996   The publication of *Hit List*, though it concerned only books, provided LSTs with another valuable tool to help them through intellectual freedom challenges. By this time, most libraries are Internet connected moving LST from thinking about "How do we get teens in the library?" to "What do we *do* with all these teens?" The Internet also opens up for LSTs new avenues of communication with colleagues.

1997   In addition to the second edition of *Excellence in Library Services for Young Adults*, another key document came out from YALSA entitled *Youth Participation: It Works*. This tool provided philosophical and practical information to get librarians involved with youth. Another YALSA product that made life easier, in particular for smaller libraries, was the listing of Top Ten titles and Quick Picks from Best Books for Young Adults (BBYA). Finally, Teen Hoopla debuted YALSA's Web site with acclaim from librarians and scorn from failed TV talk show host Dr. Laura (Schlessinger).

1998   An amazing year that saw the debut of both the Alex Awards and Teen Read Week. If those projects were not enough, YALSA also rolled out revised competencies for librarians serving youth, while AASL launched *Information Power*, the blueprint for successful school-library media programs. As the twentieth century wound down, most of the tools were in place for LSTs to create dynamic services and teen spaces.

1999   Two major milestones occurred in cooperation with ALA/YALSA. The DeWitt Wallace-Reader's Digest Fund conducted and then reported on a study concerning programs for school-age youth in public libraries. Following up on the survey results, DeWitt Wallace teamed with the Urban Library Council to launch the Public Libraries as Partners in Youth Development project, which provided a select number of large urban libraries with the funding and the philosophy to move away from thinking about services *to* young adults and reconceptualized as services *with* young adults.

2000   The Michael L. Printz Award was established to honor the single best young adult book of the year. When they established this award, the importance of YA literature was recognized; and also, to name this award after the late, great school librarian Michael Printz reminds librarians to connect YAs with books. To help public library generalists do this, YALSA published a revised edition of *Bare Bones*.

2001   YALSA kicked off the new century with internal and external success. Its Strategic Plan provided the organization with a new framework, while the Power Up with Print held at the AASL conference provided the organization with a product to bring the YA message out into the library community.

2002   If you want to know how this explosion in recognition of young adult services and in products from YALSA started, look no further than Linda Waddle, the YALSA deputy director who retired in 2002. In addition to the Printz Award, Teen Read Week, Serving the Underserved, Excellence awards, and a host of other projects, under Waddle's leadership the membership in YALSA exploded, going from 1,787 members to 3,183. One of Waddle's final acts was editing the latest revision of *New Directions for Library Services to Young Adults*. This third edition represents the broad philosophical framework for the association, and thus the profession.

WHERE ARE YOUNG ADULT SERVICES NOW? (TEN TRENDS SHAPING SERVICES IN 2003/2004)

> By focusing on teens, libraries can demonstrate that they have the ability to have a positive impact on the life of young people.

The state of young adult services in 2003/2004 is, considering budget cuts in most libraries, very good. While there are still some large systems that have not dedicated staff to serving teens, many others have come onboard during the late 1990s when budgets were flush. The hope, of course, is these gains can be maintained in a different financial environment. The belief is success breeds success, and few libraries who added a young adult librarian or schools that added an additional secondary school-librarian, would report anything other than "YA works." The idea of "YA works" is important as libraries realize that more and more funders, both public and private, are interested not just in how many books a library checks out, but are just as concerned about what role the library plays in creating a strong community.

Now that we understand from the previous two chapters *why* and *who* we serve, let's look at *what* are ten trends are exploding in the field of YA services in school and public libraries that should provide you with the context for developing your own services. Throughout the text, we'll be talking in detail about *how* to turn these trends into services at your school or public library. The trends are in alphabetic order and represent the overarching ideas driving services to teenagers as we charge into the twenty-first century. What is just as important, however, is realizing that these trends do not stand alone. Most are intertwined with larger societal trends that drive the actions of all institutions involved in the business of positive youth-development.

DIGITAL DIVIDE AND DIVERSITY

Almost one quarter of the patrons of a public library have historically been teens, an argument that advocates of YA library services have used for years. While we have no new studies since a report in 1995, it seems clear that this number has not changed. What is less clear, however, is if this is the same 25 percent of teens; casual observation would tell us it is not. While there has always been the "just hang out" element of teens, for the most part, many teens who have traditionally used libraries came for the purpose of gathering information for homework assignments. The research on teens' use of the Internet shows that many of them use it for informational purposes, and that they use it at home. If those users are now sitting at home doing school research, then who are those 25 percent of teens sitting at our computers? Chances are many of them are ones who don't have home access. Because of poverty or other factors, many teens view the public library not as an informational source, but as a location to access the Internet. This has huge ramifications on every level of service planning, but mostly it touches the missionary desire of all librarians to keep users as "regular" customers—checking out books. The concern is how to move these teens from computer users to library customers; how to get them to learn how to do research; and in many libraries, the real concern is that they should be using the computers for "something important"; that is, not chat, e-mail, games, or lyrics. We believe, however, that this idea of criticizing unconventional computer use poisons the environment of providing high-quality service to teens.

FORMAT EXPLOSION

> In the focus groups from California, the concept that libraries should move beyond the book was consistent.

Much the same, there are many teens finding out about libraries' recreational uses because of the explosion of formats, in particular teenage boys drawn to formats such as computer games, graphic novels, magazines, music CDs, and DVDs. For too long, many libraries have assumed if they purchased the new Richard Peck novel in hardback and had paperback series they were both serving teens' reading and recreational interests. That's never been true, but even less so now when there are so many formats to choose from, and teens have access to them in places other than libraries.

This is probably best represented by the number of libraries that have embraced graphic formats. Why would a school or public library want to collect graphic formats? Take comic books for example. What library would want these in their collection? Here you have a format that is inexpensive, generates circulation, and takes up little space. Who needs that? And it also meets the needs of customers, in particular teen and pre-teen boys. Yes, adults read comics and so do girls of all ages, but the core audience for comics is young males.

What is the pull of comic books for young men in the making? The answers are varied and certainly depend upon circumstances, but much relates back to basic adolescent development. Comic books are just as much fantasy literature as a Harry Potter novel, except these heroes wear capes rather than glasses. Comics are total wish-fulfillment fodder. When a library collects comics, it is showing that it is accepting of teens that have different reading tastes and interests than others. Comics also send a message to poor, reluctant, or new readers that the library is about having a positive experience. If that happens with a Richard Peck novel, that is fine; if it happens with X-Men #207, that is fine as well.

So what is the hold-up? Libraries often view services to teens, which would embrace collecting graphic formats, as "special" and outside of their normal mission. What this demonstrates is radical inconsistency in changing formats because of the changing needs of our customers.

Example: Most public libraries collect large-print books. They collect them primarily to meet the needs of one customer segment, that of seniors. Seniors read large print because changes in their bodies cause eyesight to fail and thus the library responds with a collection of large-print format texts.

Example: Most public libraries collect board books. They collect them primary to meet the needs of toddlers and babies. Toddlers and babies need board books because changes in their bodies cause them to want to hold books, but they are without the developmental skills to not want to rip, and chew, them up, and thus the library responds with the board book format.

Example: Some public libraries collect comic books and other graphic formats to meet the needs of teenagers. Teens like comic books because, as described, the developmental changes occurring in their lives cause them to look for formats that meet those core needs of independence, excitement, identity, and acceptance.

> Collecting comic books is not about doing anything special for teens, it is just doing the same as we do for other customer segments by responding with appropriate formats.

Like so many issues regarding teen services, the crux here is about respect. The stereotype of the comic book reader is largely a negative one: a semiliterate juvenile delinquent who isn't smart enough to read "real books." Like most stereotypes, this runs contrary to fact. Librarians may embrace this stereotype because they themselves were not comic readers, they don't know any comic readers, they don't understand comic readers, and it does not agree with their view of what reading appropriate material is, or should be. It is the same stereotype that kept many libraries on the sidelines during the height of the *Goosebumps* craze; instead of using their hands to place orders and put books in kids' hands, many were wringing them about the "quality" of series books. The research is pretty clear that series readers are "good" readers, they are avid readers, and they will remain lifelong readers because the main thing that young people learn is that reading is a pleasurable experience. When children are learning to read, they learn simply to decode, and then to give words meaning. As adolescents, they are deciding what meaning reading has in their lives. Making reading a positive experience by providing materials to appeal to a broad range of readers, including those who prefer pictures and captions to dense paragraphs of text, should be the primary goal of every library.

As we shift our focus to the outcomes of reading among teenagers and the need to respect the teen experience as a cornerstone to successful young adult service, we realize two things. Firstly, the value comes not from the critics or the value a librarian places upon a particular book or format, but rather what it does for the teen reader. The outcome, the positive experience, is what matters. Secondly, those who believe that the sole purpose of comics is to be a gateway through which kids can pick up quality literature (whatever *that* means—quality literature may be harder to define than a graphic novel) should consider that the "something" they want kids to move beyond is pretty good in and of itself.

INFORMATION LITERACY

This also might be called "de-Googlizing" our users. It is interesting that on one hand, librarians are—correctly—trying to get away from being prescriptive in our services, but in this area, we feel the need to say to our customer, "We know best." Part of it is the missionary and the teacher in many of us, and in particular the school librarian who *is* a teacher first and foremost, but the biggest part of it is that we are concerned with outcomes. We know that teens who learn how to locate, evaluate, and use information will do better in school than those that don't. We know that teens who learn these skills are thus empowered to seek out information on their own. We know that teens who "get it" will find research less frustrating, less time consuming, and while probably rarely enjoyable, at least it won't be as hellish as it could be. We know that by teaching kids these skills we can save them time, and especially when we teach them how to evaluate, maybe just help save their lives. But more than an extreme example is a simple idea, information literacy is youth development in action. When we plan information literacy, we need to remember that we are not developing these programs for young adults because it is good for the library, but rather because these services will make a genuine impact leading to positive outcomes for teens. It does not really matter if these information-literacy activities come through classroom presentations or through one-on-one reference transactions, we teach to empower.

By teaching young adult customers, through formal and informal means, how to access, evaluate, and use information, we are empowering youth. Given the growing research about the "digital divide" in which many youth, especially poor and minority teens, do not gain access to information or skills regarding how to retrieve information, an urban or rural public library must consider this a top priority. Seeking independence is one of the primary tasks that teens undergo as part of the life stage known as adolescence; libraries can help teens by providing them with the skills and knowledge they need to become independent, responsible, and knowledgeable information consumers.

Without being information literate, young adults do not have the skills they need, not just to succeed in school, but also to continue their path to become competent, caring adults. By understanding how to access, evaluate, and use information, young adults become not just better students, but learn a skill that will help them through school, through adolescence, and deep into the adult lives. It is the first step toward lifelong learning; thus, public libraries that have lifelong learning as a focus, need to support or supplement the school library in its quest to make teens information literate.

Information literacy is not library instruction. Much like youth development is a movement toward focusing on prevention rather then intervention; information literacy is focusing on youths learning as a process for solving information problems rather than simply product, or even project, based learning. Information literacy is about teaching teens how to think as much as it is about teaching them how to do. The role of teaching information literacy flows perfectly with the expanded role of school library media specialist, who focuses on the importance of instruction and curriculum planning as opposed to just building the collection. The collection many students are using is not within the four walls of the library, but rather collections that available via the Internet. In a sense, information literacy is teaching YAs the basics of collection development. Just as we choose from the world of "real" materials the best material for students, once we teach teenagers to be information literate, they are using a similar criteria to choose the virtual materials to solve their information problem. Information literacy is youth development in action; we are working *with* the students, not for them. Like youth development, the focus of information literacy is building the assets within young people to help them make better choices. Not surprisingly, the desired outcomes for information-literate students are similar to those found in the youth development movement.

> Information literacy creates healthy youth, which creates a healthy community.

NEW SPACES

The most exciting trend of all is the work being done in libraries large and small to create a welcoming environment for teens. Of all the things that teens treasure in their life, those that have their own room treasure that personal space. That idea has extended to libraries to

The regular "YA Dream Space" articles in *VOYA* have shown libraries large and small how to create a great space for teens.

ensure that teenagers have their own rooms in public libraries. Just as interesting is many school libraries, in particular high school libraries, who are creating YA spaces. While one might argue that an entire school library is meant for teens, most of the books on the shelf serve two masters—the teachers who require them and the students who thus need them. YA areas in school libraries look to what teens want to read, or even listen to. The building programs taking place in many libraries have driven the creation of distinct teen spaces in libraries, no doubt, but old libraries are reorganizing and finding room for teen space. Every library has room for a YA space; they are just spending it on something else. With video collections going away, with more reference multi-volume sets—most anything by Gale comes to mind—going online and thus eliminating the need for a print copy, and with other changes in service requiring less space, there is room for young adult spaces.

OUTCOME MEASUREMENT

The question is no longer how many books do teens check out, but rather, how is their life better because of checking out those books. What actually happens to teens because of their transactions in a library; are they better students? Do they avoid at-risk behavior? Do they become more resilient? How do library services change teen lives for better? Attempting to capture answers to these questions is difficult; it is not work we are used to doing, it is still primarily anecdotal evidence, and it opposes values such as confidentiality. We can infer from national data for our libraries some answers; kids who have assets have better outcomes; thus, can we identify how we build assets? We know that teens who have access to school libraries do better in school, but do our parents and principals know about those outcomes? We know that kids who read, succeed, but can we point to this happening in our own libraries? This takes not only different types of measuring tools, but also a different outlook on our work. More work is being done to help the public sector institutions like libraries draft strategy maps, create balanced scorecards, and quantify the qualitative value of our work.

This is another reason for the big push for real youth-involvement. When we involve teens in libraries, we give them not only an opportunity to contribute, but also to build skills. Some are hard skills, like learning to build a Web page or read a story to younger children, but more are soft skills, such as learning to cooperate, getting along with others, and accepting responsibility. It would be great if libraries could take credit for everything good that happens. A library might have an after school program and during the same time the program takes place, there might be a drop in crimes by and against juveniles. Are the two related? No and yes. No, we can't "prove" that because kids were getting tutored at the library they were not engaging in crime, but we can infer that a tutoring program builds assets and we can prove that assets reduce at-risk behavior. Because we are not researchers, because we respect confidentiality, and because we've never been asked, most LSTs have yet to learn the language of outcomes. By focusing on the quality of a teen's library experience and not just the quantity, we are making a step in the right, and new, direction.

OUTREACH IN THE COMMUNITY

Even while we look for impacts, there is still the pull to make the numbers go up. There are only two ways to increase use of a library, get the people already using your library to use it more, or to get more people to come to the library. Those teens who don't already frequently visit the library are best influenced through outreach programs. Even within outreach programming, there are two primary types of outreach programs. One is about promotion; the other about service delivery. While the promotion part is important and the one most people are comfortable with. A popular promotional program is the summer reading program, which visits schools every May; yet, it is the second type that is perhaps even more important. That type of outreach programming focuses on delivering service directly to users outside of the physical space of the library. While technology is a big part of this, for virtual reference is a type of outreach in some ways, much of it is very low tech. It is about library staff delivering library service by spending time in schools, detention centers, after-school programs, homeless centers, technology centers, and any other place that teens gather. Not just telling these youths what libraries do, but showing them through book discussion groups, programs, and other activities. If it is all about outcomes, then we can rethink outreach. If what matters is the outcome for a teenager, then it does not really matter if the book discussion group takes place in a school or a public library, just that it happens.

PROGRAMMING RETURNS

Programming for teens was the lifeblood of YA services in the 1970s and 1980s, in particular, very traditional events like film nights and game days. But with the technology allowing teens to recreate more and more in their own homes, those types of programs faded away. After struggling for a while, teen programming is back and pulling kids into libraries. The drivers all came together right around the same time. These drivers were media like Teen Read Week that gave libraries a focus for teen programming, after-school programs coming to the

> Outreach programs build on a foundation of collaboration to create a culture of outcomes.

library setting or school-based programs looking for partners, professional publishing giving people ideas and increasing excitement, and the Internet. If the "old job" of programming was to get kids into the library, that is not as necessary in the Internet age; they are there every day. Instead, the question is, since these kids are already in the library, can we provide them with something other than Internet access. The answer in so many libraries is yes.

TEENS AS VOLUNTEERS, INTERNS, PROGRAMMERS, AND THE LIKE

Teen volunteers in libraries are, once again, a related topic. The trend in education to require service learning is one of the primary drivers that is allowing libraries to expand both their services to teens, and their volunteer programs. Librarians are learning that teens who work/volunteer in a library bring with them a set of skills, particularly in regard to technology, that most of us lack. They bring energy, fresh ideas, and sometimes green hair to libraries. If we can let them do more than shelve books, we can take advantage of their enthusiasm and knowledge. Yet, youth involvement must never become youth exploitation; we want them to learn skills and have a positive experience, not just read the shelves and stamp date-due cards.

YOUTH DEVELOPMENT

The mantra of the movement is simple: problem free does not mean fully prepared.

If there is one trend underlying all others, it is how libraries are jumping on the positive youth-development bandwagon. Youth development is a perspective that emphasizes providing services and opportunities to support all young people in developing a sense of competence, usefulness, belonging, and power. Positive youth-development is a process that prepares young people to meet the challenges of adolescence and adulthood through a coordinated, progressive series of activities and experiences that help them to become socially, morally, emotionally, physically, and cognitively competent. Positive youth-development addresses the broader developmental needs of youth, in contrast to deficit-based models that focus solely on youth problems. Youth development is about prevention as opposed to intervention. Youth development has emerged as a vital and vibrant force in the youth field because of this change in perspective, one of seeing young people's journey to adulthood differently. The essential concept of positive youth-development is that a successful transition to adulthood requires more than avoiding drugs, violence, or precocious sexual activity. The promotion of a young person's social, emotional, behavioral, and cognitive development began to be seen as a key to preventing problem behaviors themselves. Prevention is not about stopping something bad, but rather building on strengths.

YOUTH INVOLVEMENT PLUS PROGRAMMING EQUALS SUCCESS

Perhaps one of the biggest trends is combining youth-development philosophy with teen involvement to create a slew of programs in school and public libraries that engage teens not as the audience, but as programmers. The idea is fairly simple, the library provides a forum, and sometimes the training, for teens to practice a skill. An entire book could/should be written about teens who act as program performers. The following are just a few examples from across the country:

- New York: During the summer, the Teen Advisory Groups puts on an original theater production. Teens write, create, promote, and produce a play for younger children.
- Arizona: Teens designed crafts, prepared materials, presented programs, and helped younger kids with craft activities.
- California: The high-school chess club conducted workshops for elementary school students.
- Georgia: Teen magician performed for younger children.
- Georgia: Read to Me Buddies program has teen volunteers who come into the library and then read to small groups.
- Kansas: High school athletes read to kids during Family Literacy Nights using contact Title I teachers.
- Kansas: High schoolers put on a haunted house program for younger children
- North Carolina: Toy library staffed by teens and disabled teens. Teens committed to one evening a week or a weekend day where they cleaned, checked, mended, and processed the toys.
- Ohio: Teen volunteers morphed into a puppet performing troupe (The Puppetteens). They helped prepare scripts, made props, developed scenery, and performed.

Rather than undercutting our professionalism, using teens as programmers demonstrates what our profession is really about—sharing knowledge, empowering young people, and making a stronger community.

• Ohio: Over the summer on a weekly basis teens participated in a drama club in which they picked and then presented a play for younger children.
• Texas: High school students developed a homework club where older students tutored the younger ones.

The overall "big trend" of the information age, driven by technology, is integral to these trends. Calling "technology" a trend is to minimize its importance; quite simply, it has challenged and changed just about every working assumption, and day-to-day reality, of working with youth. The ability for libraries to take advantages of these opportunities will, of course, depend on many factors, including the usual suspects of staff, money, and space. Yet, the most important factor of all is the willingness to place serving YAs as a priority. By doing so, libraries are helping solve today's problems while building an investment for the future. How well libraries respond to each of these trends, each of these challenges, and each of these opportunities, will shape the course of the services to YAs in the future

WHAT IS THE FUTURE OF YOUNG ADULT SERVICES?

As we move further into the age of information, the role of libraries and the services provided for users of all ages will continue to evolve. LSTs know that young people are often on the forefront of cutting edge technology—not only aware of the newest stuff, but often proficient at first touch. These kids have been raised with technology at home, in the classroom, and in the library. Although not all young people have the same level of experience with computers and electronic information, as we move further into the digital age, it will be safe to assume that a majority of teens will have at least a rudimentary knowledge of computers, electronic information, and digital media.

As technology advances and information becomes more widely available in electronic formats, librarians will need to be familiar with digital information in order to help users find what they are looking for. For librarians who work with teens, this will be even more true; one of the things librarians who work with young people know is that your street credit with a teen—that is, your value as a source of information—is only as strong as your knowledge of the things that interest them. Just like being aware of the music they listen to and the books they read, librarians who successfully serve this population will have to be comfortable talking technologically with their teen patrons.

However, no amount of technological advancement in the library will eliminate the need for an LST who can serve as intermediary between teens and technology. This human interface is what sets the library experience apart from a kid doing research on the Internet at home. In the future, as computers become more accessible and the Internet a more congested labyrinth of information, the human interaction between a teen patron and LST will be what helps a library remain more than a repository of information. This interaction contributes to the development of a working relationship between a young person and a librarian, and it is this relationship that will continue to make the library experience an individualized encounter each time a teen walks through the door. Additionally, a relationship founded in the quest for information often breeds trust between the finder and the seeker. With this trust often comes a sense of comfort, an ultimate goal because once a teen is comfortable with you as a source of information, chances are good that he will risk asking you for help with other things, including that all elusive request for reader's advisory—an LST's dream.

While it is safe to say that the future of young adult librarianship is no place for technophobes; a library of the future that provides a space for teens along with quality programming and opportunities for young people to share their voices and their unique experiences on advisory committees and as volunteers will continue to remain a place where information and education collide; thereby, contributing to the development of lifelong library users.

The future of teen services is not just about LSTs knowing computer networks, but becoming equally adept at mastering human networks, both inside and outside of their own organization. While we spoke already, and will again in Chapter 7, about the importance of outreach, which seems to grow in importance as our user base shrinks and thus our nonuser population soars, attention must be paid to the human networks that make up our organizations. We don't just serve teens, but we also advocate for them inside our institutions, outside of them, and make connections with others who can advocate for us.

Youth advocacy means believing in treating youths as first-class citizens in the library world, not poor cousins and not as a marginalized group. Youth advocacy means being a voice with and for youth at all levels of a library organization; ensuring that circulation systems can measure teen use, selecting appropriate furniture, providing information-literacy instruction, and employing programs that increase student learning and achievement. We want to be successful advocates, not marginalized martyrs. Advocacy is a core value, but it is about expanding beyond our core supporters and finding others in the library and community who share our vision and core values. True youth advocates engage allies, share resources and successes, and create a stronger community for kids.

> It is with good reason that the most important publication in our field is called *Voice of Youth Advocates,* for it reminds us that our role isn't just to serve teens, but to be advocates for them in our libraries and communities.

4 CUSTOMER SERVICE

"They're [librarians] hired to help you and they don't. I think that's the main reason I don't go there no more."
—*a California teen about his library experience*

"Everybody who works there [the library] looks so bored."
—*a California teen about his library experience*

The California State Library commissioned a research company to conduct qualitative research to learn what teens did and did not like about public libraries in the state. Twenty-nine focus groups were conducted throughout the state in May and June 2001. Many of those included in the focus groups self-reported as nonusers of public libraries. The groups were put together to get a mix of age, gender, and ethnic backgrounds. The results were the same across the board, from San Diego to Sacramento and all parts in between. Despite the diversity of experiences and locations, teens across the country all told a very similar story; librarians and libraries don't "get it." This, sadly, backs up our own stories; we've all worked in libraries where staff demonstrate that they don't get it, and produce quotes like the one above. This also backs up the working assumption of YALSA's SUS project; to take people who understand and respect teens and put them out into the field to train others on the best ways to provide quality—remember, quality is cool—services to teenagers.

Some working in the field oppose the SUS approach, believing that the underlying message is "We, the young adult librarians, are really the only people who understand teens." This is a serious misreading and misunderstanding of the SUS approach. The idea is not that LSTs are "cooler," but, just as genealogists better understand the needs of genealogy customers, so do many LSTs better understand the customer service needs of their customers. Rather than a negative reading, we believe this approach comes from the research about the lack of LSTs working in libraries, the lack of continuing education on YA services to most librarians—before the SUS project—and, as the results from the focus groups held in California tell us, the frequent lack of quality customer service for teens in many libraries.

> You can't jump directly to library services *with* teens getting a place at the table until library staff and administration acknowledge that teens, and their behaviors, need to be respected.

> Customer service takes place not in a vacuum, but in context.

By customer service, we don't just mean one-on-one interaction at the information desk, although that is a big part of it. Customer service means everything we do that touches a customer; how we design our services, lay out our buildings, create signs, organize our collections, and prioritize our resources. The information transaction is the most visible, but hardly the only customer service interaction. Also, what customer service means to a school librarian is very different from those LST working in a public library. School librarians provide service by teaching teens; public librarians normally provide service by doing for teens. Also, school librarians have many customers other than students—administration, other teachers, and even parents also act as customers. Public librarians who engage in any outreach are also involved in serving other customers. For example, an outreach program to teens in a correctional facility means serving both the teens, but also, the staff at the facility.

HOW DO TEENS DESCRIBE CUSTOMER SERVICE AT LIBRARIES?

Let's use some more quotations from the California focus group participants to tell the story of how teens get the short end of the customer service stick at public libraries:

- "If we went into a library, the librarian would look at us like, why are they here. Like we're going to cause trouble or something, like we're being watched."
- "Some of the librarians don't even care about you. Libraries at school, they are nice. But outside, they are kind of rude and they don't really care."
- "If I ever go when I need a book, I'm scared to ask them where it is, because I don't want them to think I'm stupid."
- "When you ask them how to find something, they'll just tell you to go over there."
- "I don't think it's so much the age (of the librarian); it's the way they speak to you. The point is that a person needs to know how to communicate with people no matter what age they are. They're supposed to help you and that's what they are there for, but they don't take it like that."
- "Some librarians just don't like you. They pick on you, especially us teens."

• "The library is so very serious. Everyone has a very solemn look. It's depressing. It's very, very depressing to walk into a library."

Quite an ugly picture of how teens view libraries. Just because they said it, does it mean it is true? It doesn't matter what is true. What matters is the perception that these things are true. What matters is that teens shop with their feet, and many of the focus group participants preferred researching at home, or finding books at Barnes & Noble, than visiting a library. Libraries, pre-Internet and pre-book superstore could give lip service to the idea of customer service. It is easy to do when you have a monopoly on the information business. But now, teens have other choices, and the voices from California clearly tell us we have not given them a compelling reason or positive experience to attract them to our business.

The results in California were similar to those of libraries involved in the Public Library as Partners in Youth Development Project. While teens may use libraries, it doesn't seem like they connect with the staff, or, even more importantly, believe the library staff wants to connect with them. In California, the conclusions of the focus groups, related to customer service, were the following:

- Teens didn't see either value or convenience in using a public library;
- Libraries made teens feel uncomfortable, unlike a bookstore;
- Teen believed that the library staff views them with suspicion;
- Teens used libraries primarily for homework;
- Libraries needed to be more user-friendly; and
- Library staff needed to become more user-friendly.

In general, teens, in this study, felt disenfranchised from the public library. If so, how do we develop a customer model to reconnect young adults and libraries?

WHAT IS GOOD ABOUT CUSTOMER SERVICE TO TEENS?

We start by looking at what we are doing right, at least in the perceptions of teens participating in the California focus groups. While teens easily described what they didn't like and had lots of ideas on how to make things better, they also did have plenty of positive comments. Let's catch ourselves doing things right, and then promote these six things that teens think are positive about their library experiences.

- **Displays.** This certainly confirms what teens often tell us on reading interest surveys: make the materials attractive. This also reflects a common theme that teens want libraries to be more like the bookstores were they feel comfortable. In a survey of teens in suburban Hennepin County (See Figure 4-1), displays where the number one answer when asked what libraries could do more to promote reading.
- **Computers and Internet access.** This again backs up what teens report in other surveys and opinion polls; it's not so much about how they use libraries, but how they do their homework. The issue for libraries is how to manage these often limited resources. There are plenty of choices that limit by time, by content (no e-

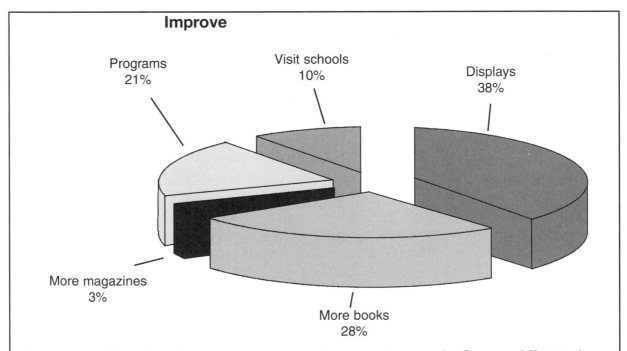

Figure 4-1. Results of survey conducted by the Hennepin County Library in 2001 on areas teens suggest libraries improve. Librarians could promote and improve these elements to increase teens' positive views of the library.

mail and no chat), or by function (homework only). In addition to access, teens want fast computers, good graphics, and free printing. The customer service negatives are the opposite; libraries have old, slow computers that don't allow for graphics and they charge for printing. The fact is that Internet access, not programs or books, is the number one draw for most teens to most libraries.

- **Homework.** Teens recognize that libraries can still be a place to do homework, in particular if there are both quiet places to study/read, as well as areas for group work. For all the push that LSTs do programming, teen involvement, and booktalking, many teens still see libraries offering very traditional services. The issue for many libraries is rather than extending help finding information for homework, to help students actually do homework by setting up a tutoring program. Some libraries purchase rights to www.tutor.com, a Web-based tutoring program, while others, often through grant funding, set up full access homework assistance centers. One of the best practices for youth involvement is to engage high school or college students looking to earn community service credits, for National Honor Society or other groups, to assist in tutoring teens and children. This is a wonderful example of a service that seems free but really isn't, as the costs of recruiting, training, and scheduling volunteers can be very labor intensive. Many libraries get around this by merely providing space, resources, and Internet access for already organized groups to do tutoring in the library.

- **Free.** Not counting fines and printing costs, in terms of out-of-pocket expenses, libraries are free. Is this something we stress enough in outreach work? Do we not have teens inquire about renting DVDs, as opposed to borrowing them? Some of this is perhaps related to cultural background, as many of our new immigrant users are from countries that lack free public libraries. Much like a library card, which we just assume everyone knows about, we assume something as basic as the free library is known to all.

- **Quiet.** Much of our training goes into issues such as redirecting behavior, creating realistic expectations for behavior, and managing large and often loud groups of teens who congregate in libraries after school. All of that said, many teens are looking for a quiet place to study as they lack such a place at home. Providing quiet study rooms, headphones for use on the computers, and end-of-the-term study halls in unused meeting room space are ways that we can meet the needs of these teens while not seeming like the "librarian action figure" stereotype.

As a profession, we are much better at finding answers than portraying our friendly nature.

- **Helpful staff.** While rude staff was a common answer in what made for a negative library experience, some teens—although not as many—did talk about helpful staff. Helpful is a catchall word that means many things; but perhaps, most of all, it indicates that teens believe the person across the desk acts helpful. All those small things you don't learn in library school, but do learn by working in retail, such as smiling, making eye contact, offering assistance, being friendly, and the like. Yes, we're information professionals, but that's not really how people, especially teens, view us. They view us as someone who is going to help them.

There are plenty of things we do right in libraries with teens, but that doesn't mean that there are not areas in which we can improve, or that everyone on the staff knows how to do things right. But is doing it right good enough any more? With so many options available to teens to gather information, find books, and attend programs, don't we have to go one step more? How do we create raving fans and make our services better? How do we shift our focus from what is good for the library to what is best for the user?

WHAT IS THE IDEAL CUSTOMER FOCUSED LIBRARY SERVICE FOR TEENAGERS?

A series of questions posed during these focus groups was aimed at getting teens to describe an ideal library. Later, we'll talk about teen spaces in particular, but let's look at larger library issues that impact customer service. Teens want and expect libraries to emulate the retail experience; they want a high tech experience, but mostly they want a positive customer service experience where they enter with a problem (I need a book; I need to do research; I need to access my e-mail) and leave with a solution delivered by a staff member that is above all else "friendly." They also desire the following:

- A checkout system like the one at Blockbuster;
- A handheld device that locates books on the shelf;
- An area that has supplies like paper, pencils, and glue sticks;
- Areas for private computer use or group study;
- Communication with the library through the computer;
- Better computer programs to search for books; or better yet, one place to search everything the library has (what we call broadcasting searching);
- A book synopsis on the computer with staff recommendations so you have a better idea what the book is about;
- A drive-through to pick up and drop off books;
- Having a free day where you can return past due books without a charge;
- Longer time using computers;
- No late fees—probably the number one complaint;
- Open longer hours; and
- The fastest Internet connections and computers.

Are these things possible? Of course, each one is possible. If we don't choose to make these improvements in libraries, it is because we have not made them a priority. It is because we are spending the money on something else. Namely, library staff. Every library's biggest expenditures are always staff. Teens, of course, have clear ideas on what would make an ideal LST.

WHAT IS THE IDEAL LIBRARIAN TO TEENS?

When California teens were describing teen-friendly staff in libraries, they thought the ideal would be staff that is the following:

- Friendly, knowledgeable, and helpful;
- Treats everyone with respect;

- Is younger, or at least that the staff is of various ages; and
- Has customer-service skills.

The next question then is what customer service skills mean in the context of helping teens in libraries. It means the same as helping any other customer in a library, only a little different. This difference is understanding that even more than hard core reference skills, having the soft skill to treat teens with respect.

It is also through a YA's one-on-one interaction with the library—either through the choice of materials or getting reference assistance—they will determine their level of satisfaction. What then makes for excellent service for YAs? While not directly related to customer service, it is also interesting what teen marketing guru Peter Zollo found to be the top "rules for advertisers" for attracting YAs.

- Use humor/be funny.
- Be honest.
- Be clear with a message.
- Be original.
- Don't try so hard to be cool.
- Use great music that fits.

While not all these elements—librarians rarely use great music that fits—are relevant many of the other advertising techniques are also personality traits for providing service—using humor, being clear, being honest.

So what would the perfect LST look like?

- "Approachable," because no matter how many other skills you have, if a YA does not feel as if you want to help, if your body language or maybe even the layout of the reference desk configuration says "stay out," then the other skills will not be utilized.
- "Knowledge of YAs" is important as LSTs feel that to serve this user group knowing something about them helps.
- "Nonjudgmental" attitudes towards YAs are closely related. Training sessions where teen or twenty-something employees participate will almost always rank as the most important quality.

Zollo reported that most YAs feel that adults assume they are going to cause trouble and don't treat them with the same amount of respect, dignity, and patience as they treat others.

- "Respectful" attitudes are just as important. It is very hard to say what respect looks like, but it is very easy to recognize someone acting disrespectful.
- "Sense of humor" shouldn't be overlooked, but sadly can't be trained. Nor is there a wit implant surgery. A better term here might be "sense of perspective." Instinctively, most LSTs realize that Zollo is on target and feel that a sense of humor is probably most important. Important because not only will most YAs appreciate it, but it also dispels numerous negative stereotypes about librarians.

Other than knowledge of the customer, it is interesting that all of the most important traits in serving YAs are "soft skills." More than that, they are as much personality traits as they are work attributes. Maybe the real key to working with teens isn't what we learn in library school, but what we learn in life about treating other people.

WHAT SKILLS DOES A LIBRARIAN NEED TO WORK WITH TEENS?

That said, there are certainly other skills, both hard and soft, that a librarian needs to do a good job working with teens over an information desk, such as being:

- Adaptive,
- Advocate,
- Articulate,
- Collaborative,
- Competitive,
- Creative,
- Emphatic,
- Energetic,
- Enthusiastic,
- Forgiving,
- Know YA literature and YA reading interests,
- Know YA pop psychology,
- Knowledge of computers,

- Listener,
- Patient,
- Persistent,
- Pleasant and friendly,
- Problem solver,
- Promoter,
- Rule breaker/risk taker,
- Teacher,
- Understanding, and
- Youth involver.

All of these traits could be summed up simply—whatever skills it takes to ensure that every teen has a positive library experience. Also, these skills complement each other. You can't be great in involving youths if you are not patient. It does no good to be great with computers but not be pleasant and friendly with teens.

Every reference transaction is about solving a problem: "I need three books on this," or "I need to find who did this," or "Can I find this article?" The second part we all know—everyone wants to leave with good feelings. With YAs this is vital, since teenagers are emotional beings. They are stars in their own movies and a reference transaction is just another scene. They can come out feeling good about themselves because they solved their problem and someone treated them with the courtesy and respect they deserve *or* they can exit the scene still with their problem and feeling bad, normally about themselves. Those are not customers we have won for life.

WHAT DOES IDEAL REFERENCE SERVICE TO YOUNG ADULTS LOOK LIKE?

We have bricks (what teens want) and we have mortar (what LSTs need to do), so lets build a house of reference. If these are candidates for what a quality LST should look like, then how would that translate to an overall program of quality service? Drawing on YALSA's vision, the measurement of a quality YA service relates to how well it does the following:

- Responds to YAs;
- Respects YAs as individuals;

- Readies YAs as they move from being children to adults;
- Reaches out to the community;
- Reaches in to involve everyone on the staff;
- Reacts to changes;
- Involves youth in the library;
- Resists efforts to restrict access;
- Advocates for youth, in particular for equal treatment; and
- Creates raving fans.

The idea of raving fans was the basis for the book *Do It Right: Best Practices for Serving Young Adults in School and Public Libraries* and is taken from business guru Kenneth Blanchard. The raving fan customer-service relationship is one that goes far beyond the product. If you don't listen to your customer's thoughts to learn his or her needs and desires, you fail to give the person what he or she needs as a product because you simply don't know what that need really is. Further, you reject him or her as a person. By not listening not to the teen, you're saying his or her thoughts have no value. The results from California indicate that libraries are not creating raving fans.

How then to construct information services which provide teens with a positive experience? Let's present a possible model (QUICK) based on what we believe that teen customers value.

- **Quality:** We did some research called "buyer beware," looking at the customer service provided teens in one large urban library. The experiment used a checklist of both "good" and "bad" customer-service/reference behaviors. Eight teens were hired to "secret shop" this library. They were given reference questions to ask in person, over the phone, and via e-mail. The secret shoppers were asked to check which behaviors were demonstrated by the LST providing the customer service as well as to report back the answers they were given to the reference questions. The same questions were also asked by adults in person, on the phone, and via e-mail. The thesis, of course, was that the teens would receive worse service than the adults. That was not the case. Instead, *no one* got good service at this library; but even worse, about one-third of the answers were wrong. Thus, the first part of this model is quality. We pledge to get the answer right 100 percent of the time, not 66 percent. Part of that is knowing where to look, but just as important is knowing how to ask the question and being energetic enough to do the work. It was noted that a question was wrong whenever the library staff member didn't get up from their seat and put the item in the teen's hand. There is a lot of literature about promoting the quality of reference, though sadly, less literature about measuring, and even less literature about case studies of libraries that took measurement seriously and held librarians accountable. Retail establishments use secret shoppers on a regular basis and there is no reason that libraries should not adopt this same proven technique of measuring, and then improving, customer service. Remember, quality is cool.

- **User focused:** We need to rethink everything we do in terms of what is best for the user, not what is easiest for staff, what causes the least amount of headaches, or what makes the clerical staff happy. The implications of this focus are enormous and run through everything we do: How we design our buildings, signage, how we staff our desk; but mostly, how we approach our work. Of course, the best way to be user focused is to know what the user wants; youth involvement strikes again, but so does understanding the user.

- **Inviting:** Staff's invitational attitudes are a vision of reference service for teens. Inviting is more than approachable; it is an attitude that is eager to invite teens to use libraries, have a positive experience, and return. Inviting information-service finds users where they are: in the stacks or on the computers or any place in between, and then offers assistance. Remember the quote from the teen about feeling stupid asking for help. Many just are not going to ask unless we approach them in an inviting manner, and they will respond if we are interested, even enthusiastic, about supplying assistance.

- **Convenient:** This is a logical extension of a user-centered approach. We offer reference one-on-one in the library, but also through every other way that technology and cost will allow: e-mail, chat, phone, and consider whatever technology presents itself to become more convenient.

A constant complaint from teens about libraries is we are not convenient or easy to use.

- **Knowledge sharing:** We'll go into detail later about organized, formal information-literacy instruction, but a vision of reference service for teens must also include the idea that we are open to every opportunity to empower teens to work on their own. Any transaction in a public library, for example, should now include an offer for the teen to learn more through classes, tutorials, or through practice. If we share our knowledge with users, then they can use libraries when we are not there, which given budget cuts, is going to become a necessity.

Finally, services need to be as the mnemonic device spells out: quick. Teens have always had little patience, and, if possible, even less in the Internet age. We must adapt or be left behind.

WHAT ARE THE ELEMENTS OF SUCCESS OF YA REFERENCE SERVICE?

If reference for teens embraces these values of quality, user focus, inviting, convenient, knowledge sharing, and quickness, then what does that look like at the desk? Let's translate these values into actions or elements of success.

- Always let YA customers know what good service they are getting. This is more than knowledge sharing; this is making sure that teens understand the nature of our work, but also how that work revolves around them. This is not just about information service; this is more about marketing. This is not flyers or posters, but real one-on-one customer building. And not just the new or "special stuff"; the majority of teens we believe have no idea about even our core services. Surveys and focus groups of teens in several large library systems found that teens don't know they can renew books, ask e-mail reference questions, access databases, interlibrary loan, or even reserve books online. Think in your own life about being at a dinner party or family gathering, then sharing a story about some strange telephone reference question, only to have someone be amazed that libraries offer such services. Putting out a flyer on a new chat reference service doesn't mean

Every transaction with a teen should end with an offer to do one more thing; offer to provide one more service now or in the future.

teens will understand what good in-person services we offer when we have not done a good job with teens who visit, and don't visit libraries.

- Always offer short-term follow up ("Come back if this doesn't help.") and long term ("See me again when you have another paper due."). If building assets is about relationship building, then we need to rethink the reference transaction as a relationship. Sometimes it lasts thirty seconds, sometimes three minutes, and sometimes longer. Regardless, the onus is on library staff to invite the teen customer to continue the relationship: a business card, a bookmark with the library's phone number, or whatever other collateral can serve to underscore the most basic points like, "Thanks for coming, please come back." And we do this not only for teen customers —by the way, tell them to tell their friends—but also for ourselves. Most of us don't get raises or even recognition for the good service we give kids, so lets start asking for something better: real success stories from teens about the impact of our services. When kids tell you they are working on a paper, invite them to tell you the results of your work. When they check out a book, invite them to tell you if they liked it. It is not research, but getting teens to tell these stories starts to build an anecdotal wave of evidence documenting our effect upon creating positive outcomes.

- Always find a way to say yes, always find a way to agree, and whenever possible demonstrate your competence. The kids in California are most disgusted with the number of rules libraries impose, all of them about limits and saying no. While every institution needs policies to function, we should be bound to appreciate results from our teen customers more than anything else. Look for ways to say yes in everything we do: In signs that tell teens what they can do at a library rather than the laundry list of prohibitions to making sure reference questions are, within limits of common sense, answered with the affirmative. There might be a "but" or "however," but answering a question with a negative, to teens, shuts down the conversation.

- Always show YAs you are knowledgeable—most act impressed rather than intimidated by your knowledge.

And by the same token, don't be afraid; ask teens to show you the stuff that they know. Whether it is how to do something on a computer, to a shared pop-culture obsession, to, more than likely, common reading interests, teens are interested in what the adults in their life know.

• Always be sensitive to a teen's sense of space—in terms of eye contact, body language, and other nonverbal cues. There are two sub rules here. First, never take the mouse or keyboard away from a teenager working on the computer; you always have to let them drive. When you drive, it sends the nonverbal message that they are not competent, and besides, they are less likely to learn whatever it is you want to show or teach them. Second, never ever say, "Well, if you would have come in earlier" to any customer, let alone a teen. They know that; you don't need to remind them. Help them first, and then tell them that you will help them even more if they visit again, if they provide you with more time to do so.

• Always listen, learn, and then ask open-ended questions. Many librarians complain about not getting information from teachers about assignments; simply by listening to teens ask us information requests, we can learn a great deal. We should be careful never to ask "why" a teen is requesting information Why? Because it is none of our business and that knowledge in and of itself doesn't really help us do our jobs. When the teens volunteers that it is assignment related, use that opening. Gather information: what school, who is the teacher, and when is it due? Build Web pages, create pathfinders and mail them to the teachers, and, most of all, consider the collection development applications—teachers don't change their assignment; more kids will be in next year looking for the same stuff at the same time.

• Always be prepared to do triage reference—working with several YAs at one time. Just as teens are great multitaskers, those of us doing reference with them, must have that ability as well. Getting teens started, inviting them to work with each other, and being visible by offering follow-up assistance are keys to successful triage reference. But just as important is prevention. If we are greeting teens when they show up or engaging them soon after they sit down at a computer, we are allowing them to use our services before they get frustrated with an open-ended Google search. Information-literacy instruction is the best prevention of all.

- Always be empathetic, relaxed, and maintain a sense of humor. You were a teenager once. Remember that experience, accept that teens behave a certain way, and then project that it is a fifteen-year-old version of you standing on the other side of that desk. This rule is simply the golden rule in work clothes.

- Always reward the YA customer through encouragement, positive reinforcement, politeness, kindness, and by saying "yes." The research on positive reinforcement of teenagers is pretty amazing; simply saying thank you to teens so unaccustomed to getting that from adults outside of their family is monumental. Just imagine what services for teens would look like, and what problems would be avoided, if every library staff member simply took the time to sincerely thank teenagers for visiting libraries.

- Always think of every reference transaction as a moment of truth; the success or failure of it will perhaps determine if your YA customer is coming back again. This is now truer than ever as teens do have other options in their lives than visiting school or public libraries. If we want to create users for life, then we need to make an impact. We need to prove our value every day, in every way, that libraries matter. We do that by simply projecting to teens the knowledge that they matter to us.

We must be proactive in our work to combat the problem of YAs who won't approach a reference desk at all. Some don't ask for help because they want do to it for themselves, while others think they should do it themselves. Then there is plain old fear—unsure of what or whom to ask, so it is easier not to bother. Whatever the reason, it is safe to say that there is a large percentage of YAs who use libraries without seeking assistance.

Reference service for YAs requires all the same skills and techniques used with other patrons. In particular with YAs, the developmental tasks play a huge role. The self-consciousness of YAs is a major barrier; after all, a reference question is admission of not knowing a particular element. By utilizing the techniques of customer service, by adopting a proactive posture, and by integrating a customer-centered/problem-solving focus, reference services for YAs will create raving fans. But more than that, YA reference can create winning staffs. Just as good as the outcomes of positive customer service that solves problems and creates good feelings, it also is rewarding for the providers of that service.

WHAT ARE THE BEST METHODS FOR DOING READERS' ADVISORY WORK WITH TEENS?

Much research has told us the bad news that librarians are often not where YAs turn to get advice on what to read. Because they don't ask us, we don't do it enough. Because we don't do it enough, we can't or don't keep up on the literature that YAs require. Because we don't know, we often give bad advice. Also because there are so few LSTs, probably most library staff are not reading YA books. Because we don't read it, we don't feel comfortable recommending titles. Finally, given lack of training and lack of information, too many fall back on prejudices about what YAs should read as opposed to what they want to read. That's a harsh statement, but it is reflective of the need to move toward a customer-centered base of service—their needs become our needs.

We need to determine how readers will respond to any given book. We do that by learning what they have responded to in the past. For all the rules below, one trumps all. The most important question to ask teens is not "Why did you like a book?"—perhaps teens don't often analyze deeply what they have read. Instead, ask them to tell you about the book. In doing so, they will tell you what they like and what they responded to. Once you can understand their preferences, then the work begins by connecting readers to another book that will provide a similar experience. If this is the first rule of teen readers' advisory, then others include:

- **Don't wait for them**. Many YAs do want help but just won't ask for it. They are inhibited by bad experiences or, maybe, just plain shyness, so you need to go find them when they are browsing in the stacks. Also, know those stacks; especially with older teens, is probably are not going to be in the adult section.

- **Be creative.** For non-readers, or teens whose only experiences reading are the books assigned and despised in school, asking about reading response isn't going to work. So, ask about movie or TV shows—anything that will give you an idea on what interests this YA.

- **Develop your own core collection**. Either on paper or in your mind sit down with some of the tools and develop a core list of authors and/or titles. Learn the names of at least three mystery authors you can always recommend; three historical authors; and so on.

- **Narrow the categories through questions**. Ask if they care if it's a boy or girl? Younger or older? Scary or funny? Fat or thin? First person or third person? Hardback or paperback? Rural or urban? Even if you can't recommend certain books, at least help the person develop an idea of what they are looking for, and then maybe together you will find something.

- **Eliminate what they don't like**. A lot of YAs are inarticulate when it comes to telling you the books they like, but can easily list all the things they don't like in a book—"fat" and "boring" are common answers.

- **Use the books**. If you have discovered something they have read before, find it and examine it. Most paperback publishers include "If you liked this book, then try…" ads right in the books. It is the cheap way out. Related, you can quickly scan book spines for books by the same publisher. It is not the best way, but you might stumble on something.

- **Be smart**. If the person hasn't expressed a real interest in reading and has told you they have a book report due tomorrow, then set *Moby Dick* aside.

- **Be aware.** You need to be very sensitive to how the person is reacting to you. If they are quiet, then you should stay low key.

- **Know what not to say.** Assertions to avoid include, "I loved (gush gush gush) this book," or "I loved this book in school," or "My son/daughter loved this book," or "They use this in many schools," or "Teachers often recommend this book," or "Everyone should read it." Since many teens are, by nature and design, adult and authority contrarians, an endorsement from teachers or parents isn't a selling point, and in fact, might even be a negative recommendation.

There is nothing wrong with asking if they want a "thin one," but just make sure you and the teen understand that thin doesn't always mean easy.

- **Find a fit**. If possible you always want to avoid stereotyping, but often a YA's clothing, hair, and manner does say something about their identity and possibly their reading tastes. In other words, consider suggesting *Weetzie Bat* to anyone who wears a Mohawk. But at the same time be careful of stereotyping and handing a person of color any book by an African American author. Let them "open the door" and then be ready with a fit.

- **Aim higher rather than lower**. You will immediately lose whatever minimal credibility you have by suggesting a book that is below the YA's reading level or tastes. As a rule figure most YAs want to read about kids one to two years older. Thus, your high school juniors/seniors want recommendations out of the adult collection, not "YA kid stuff."

- **No advice can be best advice**. If you cannot really peg the kid or nothing "in" comes to mind, then just admit it. Remember many YAs get turned off because they get bad advice rather than no advice at all. The worst thing you can do is recommend the wrong book. If you just can't get a good read, suggest several titles rather than just one, and leave the teen alone to decide.

- **Recommend without request**. Sometimes a person browsing is doing just that, and they don't want or need help. This time. If you see they have tucked away a particular title, then jot down some titles for next time.

- **Recommend by special request**. Develop a reading relationship with teens through book groups, advisory councils, or over the desk. Over time you may become their own personal (live) Amazon.com.

- **Recommend by parent's request**. Many times it is mom who has come in to pick up something for her nonreading son hoping to find that the one book that will hook him. For such an occasion, every YA area should have a copy of "Quick Picks" easily accessible, for staff and patrons. If the YA is there with the parent, as with the reference interview, you want to try to isolate the YA from the parent long enough to gather information without commentary. You want to find what the YA wants to read not what the parent thinks they should read.

Amazon remains the simple, most amazing free-space that allows readers to connect with other readers.

- **Use tools**. The professional literature is loaded with tools recommending books because they are "best," "the in-thing," or "like another book." While it is impossible to purchase all of these tools, at least one needs to be bought for every library serving young adults. The best of them, like Novelist, are subscription databases.

- **Use conversation**. Approach YAs you know are avid readers and get input from them about their likes and dislikes in literature. Listen in on conversations in the stacks, ask opinions, and gather information from readers. Always ask teens what they are reading and get them to tell you the story.

- **Use statistics**. Do periodic checks about what YA titles have holds and are circulating the most; then buy more copies, because those titles might just be examples of the big ones.

- **Learn the big ones**. In addition to your personal core collection, you should also choose a personal favorite —the book you would recommend to almost any YA. The big ones actually might be several titles instead— one for boys, one for girls for middle, junior, and senior high.

For all the Luddites who still condemn technology, for teens, the Internet is as much a complement to reading as it is competition. Amazon is the model for library readers' advisory service. We can't duplicate the technology, but we can adopt the ideas of being proactive, about linking readers with readers, and about giving readers a vehicle to respond to books.

IS CUSTOMER SERVICE WITH TEENS REALLY THAT BAD?

All these elements of success about reference and readers' advisory are necessary because the perception, among many youth advocates, is that front line staff still doesn't "get it." Consider this scenario, originally created by Jim Rosinia for *Bare Bones*, which we've added to and updated:

Here is the setting. It is 5:45 p.m., fifteen minutes before closing after a busy Saturday. At the reference desk is seated the librarian (L), who has been on desk all day answering one demanding reference question after another. She feels as if she has been slowly nibbled to death by ducks. She is taking the lull to read a professional journal. Meanwhile at a nearby computer terminal, a young adult patron (P) has been using the computer, unsuccessfully, for the past thirty minutes; thus, the librarian has been listening to an incessant beeping sound for some time when finally she says:

L: That's not a toy.

P: I'm using it.

L: Well, it sounds to me like you are just playing with it. Why don't you take a seat and get to work?

P: (Walks toward her.) Um, so like, where are the scary books?

L: (Sigh.) The library does not house a collection of scary books. Do you mean horror novels?

P: Yes, like Stephen King, like that.

L: Well (sigh), as you should know by now, works of fiction are shelved alphabetically by the last name of the author. These materials are located in the last few ranges of shelving which follows the end of the nonfiction area.

P: Whatever. (Leaves, then comes back.) I couldn't find anything.

L: Stephen King writes fiction, right?

P: I think so.

L: Do you know what letter his last name begins with?

P: K.

L: Well (sigh), then they should be in fiction under K, which is where I just sent you to look. (Sigh—turns to keyboard). Are you looking for a particular book by King?

P: No, I have read all of his.

L: (Sigh.) Well, then what is it you need? I have people waiting on the phone.

P: I want a book like his. Aren't all the horror books together?

L: No, as I've told you, fiction is shelved alphabetically by author unless it is a story collection, then it may be shelved by the editor or the title or in the 800s.

P: I just need a scary book.

L: Then look under the names of other authors. Don't you know the names of any other authors?

P: No.

L: Well, there are some bibliographies of horror literature housed in the reference area at the call number R809.092. You should check there.

P: Bibliography? I don't need a book about his life; I just gotta have a book he wrote for tomorrow.

L: No, not a biography, a bibliography; a collection of citations grouped by subject. (Sigh.) Wait a minute. Is this for school or for yourself?

P: No, it's for this stupid assignment in junior English.

L: In that case, you should read Bram Stoker, Henry James, Edgar Allen Poe, or one of the classic writers in the genre, rather than trash like Stephen King.

P: We had to read a story by that Poe guy in class. I didn't get into it all; it was so boring and there were no monsters or vampires. We can read anything, so do you have a book written by somebody who is alive now?

L: Well (sigh), does it have to be horror?

P: It doesn't have to be, that is just what I signed up for. Don't you have any ideas?

L: Just a moment. (Stands, walks out to a table.) Listen up. There are too many of you at this table and there is far too much talking going on here. You should get to work. This is a library and you must be quiet. If I have to warn you again, I will call the police. (Returns, and sits back down.) (Sigh.) Still don't know the name of a book you want? I can't look it up in the computer unless you know the name.

P: But I don't know any other authors!

L: Well, (sigh), then, you will just have to go looking through that paperback fiction collection in the children's area. It is just past the charge desk.

P: Where?

L: (Points.) Past the circulation desk.

P: Where?

L: (Points again, puts head back in magazine, raises voice.) Over there.

P: Oh, you mean the front desk. (Leaves, returns with a copy of *Rosemary's Baby*.) Hey, I found this one, it sounds neat. The lady lives with all these Satan worshipers.

L: (Interrupts.) Good. We are closing so you need to check that out now.

P: But I need to a find a book about devil worship.

L: Didn't you just find one?

P: I need two books for tomorrow one story and another one about my subject.

L: So you need a nonfiction work on demonology in addition to contemporary imaginative work from the horror genre?

P: I have no idea what you just said.

L: Well go look at 974 and be quick about it!

P: (Leaves; returns.) There is nothing there.

L: Well, we just don't have enough books for all you students. Don't you have a school library? All the books must be in circulation or on a hold list.

P: What?

L: They're all out.

P: Don't you have anything else?

L: Well (sigh), I have these reference books behind the desk you can use them here and I need ID. And we turn off the copy machine five minutes before closing. You must have exact change.

P: (Starts behind desk.) So I take these home. (Picks up a book.)

L: (Rips out of his hands.) No! These are reference books. They are noncirculating for use in the library only!

P: What am I gonna do?

L: Those are the rules. Next time, you should come in earlier.

P: Forget it.

This scenario is a case study in how not to do reference. It is taking every positive trait and turning it on its head. Rather than solving the teen's information problem, the librarian is compounding the problem. The teen is neither leaving with good feelings, nor could one imagine the librarian in this scenario feeling positive about her work. If this book is loaded with to-do lists, consider this scenario for the do-not list. The following is a list of the qualities that the librarian in the previous example portrayed:

- Immobile;
- Intrusive;
- Jargon-filled;
- Lacking perspective;
- Preaching;
- Rude;
- Unapproachable;
- Uninformed; and
- Uninterested.

> Don't just mentor youth; mentor adults to work better with youth.

It does no good whatsoever for a library to employ a high energy and highly effective YA librarian only to have other staff commit these cardinal sins. Other than trying to do everything themselves, and burning out, thus helping no one, LSTs have three separate paths to pursue to improve customers service in libraries. Two involve training: training our users to become information literate and thus not dependent on libraries; and second, to train staff about teens and customer services so they "get it." The third involves acting as role model, mentor, and coach for other staff. While classroom training and online tutorials are fine, the literature on tutoring is robust, demonstrating that the best practices are handed down more through informal one-on-one relationships than training manuals, even how-to-do-it manuals.

HOW DO WE TRAIN TEENS TO BECOME INFORMATION LITERATE?

It is the responsibility of all professionals whose jobs fall under the teaching umbrella, including classroom teachers, school library media specialists, and public librarians who serve young people, to help contribute to the development of information-literate young people. At its core, information literacy is the ability to "read" information, or to problem solve by learning how to locate, evaluate, and effectively utilize information. It can also be broken down into the following subcategories:

- visual literacy (the ability to see and understand images);
- media literacy (the ability to access, evaluate, use, and create media in a variety of forms);
- computer literacy (the familiarity with computers and the ability to use hardware and software for a specific outcome); and
- network literacy (the ability to access and use information from a networked setting, for example, the Internet).

Information literacy is not library instruction. Much like youth development is a movement toward focusing on prevention rather than intervention; information literacy is focusing on youth learning as a process for solving information problems rather than simply product or even project based learning. Information literacy is youth development in action; we are working with the students, not for them.

An information-literate teen knows how to do the following:

- Determine an informational need;
- Construct a strategy to locate the information;
- Locate the desired information;
- Evaluate both the information and the source of the information;
- Organize and apply the information; and
- Adhere to ethical practices in the use of this information.

WHY IS INFORMATION LITERACY SO IMPORTANT?

If "old-school" library instruction, in the world of card catalogs and the *Readers' Guide* was important, then teaching information literacy skills in the age of the Internet is vital. Both the Internet and information technology have dramatically changed the way YAs use libraries, for better and for worse. For the better, we actually find a lot of teens who are excited about research, excited about all the different formats where they may find information, and even excited that much of this work can be done sitting in their bedrooms. But with that excitement comes frustration, as there is so much information so readily available, and all of it seemingly useful. This is where your job comes in, providing not only the tools, but also the skills young people need to complete their research. These skills, including problem solving and the ability to locate, evaluate, and use the information, are similar to a student's ability to write a paragraph or solve a mathematical equation, in that, they are skills that must be learned. Like youth development, the focus of information literacy is building the assets within young people to help them make better choices. Therefore, as an information professional who works with young people, it is your responsibility to recognize the importance of information literacy and to make it a priority to not only provide the tools, but to teach teens how to use these tools in order to become creative, critical, and engaged problem solvers.

WHAT IS THE GOAL OF INFORMATION LITERACY AND WHY SHOULD PUBLIC LIBRARIES CARE?

The ultimate goal of information literacy instruction is to ensure that YAs leave high school able to participate fully in the learning community. Not surprisingly, the desired outcomes for information-literate students are similar to those found in the youth development movement. According to "Information Literacy Standards for Student Learning" developed by AASL (American Association of School Libraries), students who are information literate can "become independent, ethical, lifelong learners who achieve personal satisfaction and who contribute responsibly and productively to the learning community and to society as a whole." In short, information literacy creates healthy youth, which, in turn, creates a healthy community.

Although the role of teaching information literacy runs parallel with the expanded role of the school librarian—focusing on the importance of instruction and curriculum planning in addition to building the collection—public librarians do play a part in helping young people develop information literacy skills. As an LST in a public library, a large part of your job is to build a comprehensive collection of print and electronic materials that not only meet the educational needs of young people, but also meet the recreational needs of this audience. However, your job goes far beyond just supplying these resources. Whether we are talking about books, online databases, or the Internet, it is your job to make these resources user-friendly so that teens know where to go to find the answers they need. It is up to you teach teens to not only ask the right questions, but to seek out answers on their own so that they can do that in the school library, public library, or at home on the Internet. The widespread availability of the Internet has changed how we provide services to young people, allowing us to provide informational tools at the click of a button. The sheer amount of information that can be found on the Internet requires savvy search skills, and once we teach teenagers how to be information literate, they can then successfully choose the virtual materials to solve their information problem. Information literacy can easily be considered the first step toward lifelong learning; thus, public libraries, which have lifelong learning as focus, need to support or supplement the school library in its quest to make teens information literate.

HOW DO WE TRAIN TEENS TO BECOME INFORMATION LITERATE?

"Teach, don't tell" is a good motto for librarians who have made it a priority to help young people become information literate.

First, you need to teach a young person to be self-reliant, to seek out the answer to a question on his or her own. In this day and age, immediate gratification is the norm. Unfortunately, librarians often perpetuate this idea, serving up an answer without considering the developmental needs of the young patron. Too often, it is easier to give an answer than to walk a teen through the steps of evaluating his or her need. In order for you to contribute to a young person's ability to think analytically, logically, and creatively about hisor her need, you might need to step back and allow the teen to think for him or herself; all the while recognizing that thinking independently can be a frustrating experience for a teen, especially one who has spent a large portion of his or her life being told what to do and how to do it by parents and teachers. With regard to the development of information-literacy skills, a reference transaction between a teen and an LST needs to be more than a series of questions followed by a series of answers.

HOW DO I TEACH A TEEN TO EVALUATE A WEB SITE?

Network literacy, or the ability to use the Internet to locate quality information, requires education. Although teens today are often computer savvy, being comfortable with technology does not equate to being information literate. Like teaching a student to read or to write, teaching information literacy is a process. In addition to teaching young people how to search for material, you need to teach them how to evaluate accurately the material that they find. This is especially important when it comes to information on the World Wide Web, as the Internet is a free-for-all publishing venue where anyone can post information, regardless of accuracy or validity. In order for a teen to evaluate successfully the content of a particular Web site, he or she needs to know what questions to ask. The following series of questions can serve as a foundation for this evaluation.

In order to answer, "Does this Web site have author credibility?" the student needs to ask certain questions:

- Who is the author of this Web site?
- Is the author's contact information provided somewhere on the site?
- Is this author affiliated with an organization or institution?
- Does the author's organization or affiliation bias the content of the Web site?
- What are the author's credentials? Does the author have experience/education in the topic(s) covered on the site?

In order to answer, "Does this Web site contain accurate, reliable, and up-to-date information?" the student needs to ask other questions.

- Does the content on the site appear to be fact or opinion?
- Can all of the information on the site be verified by another source?
- Does this site contain primary or secondary material?
- Do all of the links work?
- Is there a date listed for when this site was created? How about a date for when it was last updated?

It is also important to teach young people to determine the type of Web site they are looking at, as this often defines the overall goal of each site, whether it is to teach, to sell, to inform, to support, or to entertain. Something as simple as teaching a student to be cognizant of a URL's ending (for example, dot-com, dot-org, dot-gov, dot-edu, and dot-mil) as a key to a Web site's mission is one easy step toward helping young people become more information literate with regard to the Internet. Types of Web sites include: educational (Educator Astronaut Site, http://edspace.nasa.gov), promotional/marketing (Fubu, www.fubu.com), informational (The *TV Guide*, www.tvguide.com), news (*The New York Times*, www.nytimes.com), advocacy (Greenpeace, www.greenpeace .org), entertainment (*Entertainment Weekly*, www.ew.com), and personal (writer Neil Gaiman's Web site, www.neilgaiman.com).

OUTSIDE A CLASSROOM ENVIRONMENT, HOW CAN I STRUCTURE INFORMATION LITERACY PROGRAMMING?

All LSTs have access to one of the best tools for teaching information literacy at your fingertips—the Internet. The Internet is a great tool upon which to base either a structured, yet entertaining, class or an unstructured, one-on-one lesson that can be tailored to fit an individual teen's interest. Whether you are incorporating the Internet into a formal class or an informal session, the most important thing to remember is that every interaction is a "teachable moment," or an opportunity to help a teen navigate and make sense of the hodgepodge of valuable information and useless data available on the Net. However, before you set out to make information literacy a goal, remember that young people are more apt to learn something if they can do so in the context of a real-life experience; for example, if you want a teen to learn how to live within a budget, give him an allowance and let him make the decisions about how and when to spend his money.

In the National Library Power Program initiated by the DeWitt Wallace-Reader's Digest Fund, researchers found that students who were focused on task-directed research problems were more likely to emerge with good information-literacy skills than those who were learning library skills out of context. In other words, teens that have an opportunity to apply their searching skills to a real-life situation have greater success retaining the skills necessary to find an informational solution to their problem. To apply this logic to information literacy, you need to incorporate a real-life application into your library programs for teens, such as the following:

- You see a teen searching the Web for information about Dragonball Z. This might be a good time to slide up and ask him if he knows about the official Dragonball Z site, compared to all those fan sites he is currently searching. Help him determine exactly what he is looking for. If he is looking for a TV schedule, then explain how the official Dragonball Z Web site would be the best place to find that information. If he were looking for an image gallery of fan art, then a fan site would most likely be the best source of information.

- You see a teen "building" his or her dream sneakers on www.nike.com. This might be a good time to wander by and ask him or her how much it would cost to purchase these sneakers. Is that more or less than the retail price? Use this opportunity to teach a teen how to compare the price of the sneakers purchased directly from the manufacturer to the price of the sneakers that can be purchased from a local retail chain, via their Web site. What about comparing the price of those retail sneakers online to what you can actually find in the Sunday newspaper advertisement? Again, this can be done by taking a minute, going and getting the Sunday newspaper, and flipping through the ads until you find one that includes sneakers.

- You plan to purchase headphones for your library's technology center. In order to help you spend the least amount of money for the best product, have the teens in your library conduct an online price comparison for some of the major retail stores around you.

- You want to include a list of links on your library's Web site about Hanukkah, or Kwanzaa, or Christmas. This is a great opportunity to have the teens help you select informational Web sites that offer accurate, age-appropriate information about these holidays.

- A student is working on a subject-related research project. This is probably a good time to help him or her distinguish between an authoritative Web site, and a marketing, promotional, or personal Web site. For example, a young person is working on a project about his home state of Arizona, and he or she is browsing the Web looking for factual information on someone's personal vacation Web site, or the home page of a local Arizona travel agency. This is a great opportunity to explain the difference between an authoritative site that can provide factual information—such as the official state guide from the government or the local vacation guide from the chamber of commerce or the tourist board—and Mom & Pop's Web site talking about their summer vacation to the Grand Canyon.

- A student is working on an opposing viewpoints presentation. This is a great opportunity to talk about a Web site's validity, author bias, and the best place to get the most relevant information on a subject. For example, if a student is working on a paper that presents both sides of the abortion controversy. He or she needs to be aware that the there are two kinds of sites: 1. Those whose sole interest is to persuade the reader either for, or against, abortion. 2. Those that provide both the pros and cons of abortion, without bias toward either option. He or she also needs to know that it is possible to get additional information about a topic such as abortion, especially court cases, and non-biased supplemental information, from reference databases such as the Opposing Viewpoints Resource Center, CQ Researcher, and LexisNexis, in addition to the Internet.

Information is all around you, and as a librarian, information is your specialty. If you work with young people, use your knowledge. Be aware of the role you can play in the development of information-literate preteens and teens, and remember that every interaction you have with a young person can easily translate into a teaching opportunity.

HOW DO WE TRAIN TEACHERS TO HELP US DEVELOP INFORMATION LITERATE TEENS?

One only has to read through Information Power from AASL and the accompanying documents to realize the fundamental importance of the necessary partnership between the LST working in a school setting and that school's faculty. The very first goal of Information Power is "to provide intellectual access to information through learning activities that are integrated into the curriculum and that help all students achieve information literacy by developing effective cognitive strategies for selecting, retrieving, analyzing, evaluating, synthesizing, creating, and communicating information in all formats and in all content areas of the curriculum." But is that enough? While the Internet looks the same to a teen at school as it does in a public library, and the skills taught at school can be carried over, there is one key difference—access to databases. While many schools do provide access to databases for students, often the number is limited and access is only through the school, not from home. Thus, the public library has an important role to play in teaching students how to use the unique resources while complementing the conceptual curriculum of the school LST. And, of course, every public library has the staff to teach every teen? Right? Wrong.

The Hennepin County Library developed a grant funded project in order to expand the number of students gaining information about the public library resources while understanding that the library could not directly teach thousands of students. The SWIFT (Student Web Instruction For Teachers) project is a pilot partnership between Hennepin County Library and area middle and high schools dedicated to improving online research skills among students and teachers. Through classroom visits and staff development workshops, the SWIFT Project teaches students and teachers to use Hennepin County Library's online resources, such as Teen Links to access databases, selected Web sites, and the library catalog. SWIFT works to promote information literacy by teaching students and teachers how to effectively locate and evaluate Internet sources on a specific topic. For students, the goals of SWIFT are to learn how to access and use online research tools via the HCL Teen Links Web site, how efficiently to locate and evaluate Internet sources for research on a specific topic, and how to cite online resources correctly. For teachers, the goals are similar with the addition of learning how to efficiently incorporate the above skills into specific units of instruction.

During its first year in operation, the SWIFT project provided training for students, teachers, and media specialists at over a dozen area schools. Training sessions have been held for students in conjunction with specific research projects. Students, however, are the secondary focus of SWIFT: the goal is to teach those that teach. Thus, most of the effort from SWIFT has been put into workshops held for teachers during school staff development workshops. As a short term grant funded project, another focus of the SWIFT project is to increase the library's capacity for information literacy by creating systems that will enable librarians to efficiently locate resources for classroom visits and trainings.

The SWIFT project develops and distributes curricular materials and resources for area middle schools and high schools. These materials and resources include an interactive tutorial created for the high school classroom, a public Web page for teachers and media specialists that contains printable curricular tools, contact information, descriptions of trainings and services, subject-specific pathfinders and training outlines for use in the classroom, and classroom handouts on Web site evaluation and Internet searching. The SWIFT project complements and supplements the information-literacy work of certified

The SWIFT project received numerous teacher comments:

- "A good tool for me to help and teach kids."
- "A great site for discriminating between all the different Web sites."
- "Dying to apply this in teaching."
- "I want to use this in advisory and hand out the pamphlet on Teen Links."
- "I will go to this Web site more often—easy to use. I will use it with my students and help them get a card on line."
- "I will now be able to assist students in finding information."
- "I will use this info to set up informational classroom presentations on Web searching."
- "'Teen Book Reviews' are helpful for recommendations for students."
- "The information can now be passed on to the students."

school librarians by providing teachers with access to more resources as well as underscoring the LST's information-literacy agenda.

The work of the SWIFT program is designed to complement, not compete, with work being done in the school libraries. All of the initial contacts are made through the school librarian, and often the school librarian will participate in the presentation. The fact is that many public libraries have bigger budgets, or are tied into state-wide resource sharing agreements, that allow for more access to more databases. The SWIFT project realizes that no LST has time to teach every teen on the best ways to locate, retrieve, and evaluate information; instead, the SWIFT project acts on the idea of teaching those who will teach others.

HOW DO WE TRAIN OTHER STAFF TO PROVIDE QUALITY CUSTOMER SERVICE TO TEENS?

SUS was born out of the recognition that the number of young adult librarians wasn't about to increase, so instead let's make everyone working with teens in a library trained in core ideas. The continued frustration and constant complaining of some staff members when dealing with YAs should normally alert someone to the fact that something is amiss. We become frustrated with things we don't understand, that we don't know how to deal with, and that scares us a little. That means there's a problem regarding knowledge, skills, and attitudes. Deficiencies in any of these areas negatively impacts YA services and thus demand fixing; they demonstrate a need for training. But if there is a need for training, what are the needs within training? What needs to be learned? Setting clear and measurable learning-objectives directly tied to these needs will increase the quality of training. Likewise, by recognizing the unique traits of the adult learner, there are elements of success that can improve quality. Finally, training should not just be a lecture; instead, by using active learning-exercises, training not only has a better chance of "sticking," it is also more interesting, enjoyable, and memorable.

Even if the statistics are not up-to-date and things are looking up; it seems that the truth of the NCES survey of 1995 still holds true in many libraries: many public library users are YAs and few public librarians are YA librarians. This void is filled with training. While there are staff who will never learn to work well with YAs—the classic kid haters—many would like to, but just don't have the tools. Books like this, as well as documents like *Bare Bones* are trying to be those tools. The problem, of course, is twofold. First, to use this book serves as self-training and indicates self-motivating behavior. Second, everyone learns best by reading. Some people learn better by doing, some by seeing. Some learn better alone, some in small groups, others only in large groups. Regardless, training is a key to improving YA services—training everyone in the building on the who, what, when, where, why, and how of serving YAs. If you're giving 1 percent more, then someone else delivering 1 percent less doesn't balance it out—certainly not for the YA who gets less.

The goals of YA training workshops will be different considering the time allotted, but primarily on the needs of the hosting organization such as a library. A generic training session might cover, in brief or in depth, the core of YA services generalists need to know. The table of contents of this book is a pretty good outline. The first of two methods of transforming work behaviors is changing people's goals, or convincing them their current strategies won't allow them to reach their goals. If the librarian's goal is simply to be less frustrated, then the answer isn't in expecting YAs to change their behavior, but rather librarians changing their goals. The other method is reached by providing skills, knowledge, and a YAttitude. This will allow a change in strategies for serving YAs. If the library's overall goal is to be a provider of quality service, then the negative strategy of not serving YAs will deter them from their goal.

Yet, the key to effective training isn't teaching, but learning. Learning happens when a concept, an aptitude, or a body of knowledge is understood, assimilated, and mastered by the learner. Trainers need to try to get themselves into the heads of the learners—if I were them, what would I need to know and how would be the best way to learn it. That is why we often use the genealogist example. When trying to think if there were a training called "connecting genealogists and libraries," what type of information would change our attitude toward members of this strange subculture. Defining who drives the training is one of the big differences between training adults and teaching youths. It is not the teacher's, but the learner's agenda that matters most. The assumption, perhaps naïve, is everyone who works in a library wants to be an LST— they want to do a good job. They want to get better at helping teens have a positive library experience.

CONCLUSION

One of the teenagers involved in the California focus group offered an interesting insight on why libraries need to do a better job of connecting young adults and libraries. He said, "I don't want my kids to grow up not knowing what I didn't know about libraries." For this teen, it seems that he never discovered all the ways in which libraries could have added value to his life. We do this through our customer service which speaks not only to technology and tips from latest business trends, but getting back to basics. We do this by speaking to the core needs of the teen customer. Customer service for teens will succeed when it provides teens with opportunities of independence, excitement, identity, and acceptance.

5 COLLECTIONS

"The stuff I want is always checked out, or too hard to find. Like music, there's never any good music to listen to, unless you like polkas."

—*a teenager in a focus group in Minnesota*

> We like YA lit too, but we believe that the majority of library use by YAs has very little to do with YA literature.

Collection development isn't about buying books; it's about resource allocation. The decision to create a vital graphic novel collection isn't a random choice; it results from a series of choices that LSTs make on both macro and micro level, about collections. Those decisions are based on the library's priorities, space considerations, and the reading interests of teens. Although not as prevalent as it was in the past, there are still many who correlate teen services with young adult collections, and young collections with YA literature. This chapter, while it *cannot* stress YA literature more, provides information on other materials used by YAs. One reason for pushing aside YA literature is that there have been so many other sources that address it, such as the standard text in most YA literature courses.

During any given day, the percentage of an LST's time spent dealing with YA literature is minimal; a lot more time will be spent fielding questions for research papers, answering inquiries for homework, and enforcing discipline than it will be noting the literary merits of the latest novel with a starred review in *Booklist.* That is the literature that library school students study and librarians put on BBYA (Best Books for Young Adults), but it is primarily not what YAs read. YA popular materials are that glut of mass-market paperbacks found in bookstores and libraries as well. There are also YA products that we and YAs recognize instantly—series romances, thrillers, and the like—that sell primarily because they bear a certain brand name and Zollo's research repeatedly points out the importance of branding in the YA market. The printed materials most often used by YAs are information sources such as books, articles, and the like are often used for recreational reasons, but also read as a means to an end. Further, perhaps the most popular YA items in libraries are often not even books. Many more YAs want the new hip-hop CD, information off the Internet, a gaming CD-ROM, or a wrestling DVD than the new "best book."

So, the greatest of all questions is, what is a young adult collection in a library? Is it all of these things, or some of these items? Is it both fiction and nonfiction? Does it meet just recreational needs, or do materials also speak to the recreational and informational needs of teens? And what about formats? Teen areas in public libraries, and school libraries, are all different based upon the resources allocated. There is no best young adult collection; instead, there are a series of choices for LSTs, with support from their administrators, to make about what materials. In this chapter, we'll lay out the choices available to LSTs to create an exciting collection for teens.

WHAT ARE THE BEST BOOKS FOR TEENAGERS?

Deciding the best books for teenagers is a topic the interests many LSTs and library school students. It is the basic collection-development decision, yet the statement itself is loaded with questions. Why books? Couldn't the best reading experience be a magazine? What does best mean? Does it mean highest quality or most popular, or something with a little of each? What does teenager mean? Does it mean books written for teens or books read by teens? Does it mean twelve-year-olds or eighteen-year-olds? What are the best books for teenagers? It all depends on who is asking the questions and what kind of answers they are looking for.

The answer to this, like most collection-development questions begins at your library, not in the editorial offices of *Booklist* or at a BBYA meeting. These end-of-year lists produced by YALSA committees and review magazines represent the best books in one year for the young adult audience as chosen by a group of informed observers. That may or may not indicate that they are the best books for the YAs in your library, for the customers you serve, or want to serve. While YALSA's Quick Picks list gets the closest to listing books by perceived popularity, the function of these lists is to name the best books, almost always is defined by quality. Moreover, none of these lists name best books for their audience; they name the best "new" books for an audience.

Collection development isn't just about buying new books; it is about developing a collection that mixes new titles with older ones. It is about weeding and maintaining, not just ordering everything on BBYA or ordering just the "hot" series. Since many youth collections, in particular those aimed at teens, weigh more heavily on the side of collecting items based on real customer popularity than pure literary quality, the most important lists that LSTs need to consult each year come perhaps not from journals or committees, but from our own IT departments or circulation systems. The BBYA and other lists tell us what others think are the books we need to buy; these homegrown lists from our circulation system allow teens to tell us the books they read, need, and even steal.

At the end of every year, but probably more often than that, LSTs need to obtain reports on collection use, including the following:

- The items with the most circulation (raw numbers);
- The items with the highest turnover rate (ratio of circulation to number of copies);
- The items with the most reserves;
- The items with the highest ratio of reserves to copies owned;
- The items which are reported lost or damaged or long overdue; and
- The items which are reported missing (which often means "stolen").

We need information to manage our collection and must push for systems that produce the data we need to do our jobs.

If possible, these lists should be by collection—teen items—and by customers—checked out by teens. Not every circulation system can generate reports by user type or birthday, but since so much of teen circulation does *not* come from the young adult area, it is vital that LSTs work with the IT department to gather this data while at the same time not compromising privacy rights or setting up parameters that make limiting access easy. If these lists can't be produced by your circulation system, then perhaps LSTs need to get themselves involved in work teams that look at migration or automation issues.

We serve teen customers, not young adult collections.

Yet, even with that report, we only get half the story since we might only learn about those items classed "YA" that are missing. But that doesn't represent the collection used by teens. A real teen collection has to be a collection for young adults, not a collection of young adult books or a collection in the YA area. It is not just a matter of semantics, but a shift in thinking about who drives collection development and the role, especially in a public library, of the LST. Developing a collection is customer focused; it does not matter to the teen where the book is located, just that the library owns it. In most libraries, this is much easier said than done. Collection budgets are broken down by materials, not customers. Some library systems won't shelve a book like *The Hobbit* or a biography of Tupac in more than one part of the collection. If you are an LST, your goal can't be just to develop a young adult collection, but to make sure that adult and children's collections contain those items that teens want and need.

WHAT ARE THE READING INTERESTS OF TEENS?

The first rule of developing any collection is to know the audience. The chapter on collection development in the second edition of *Connecting Young Adults and Libraries* began with a review of the available research about the reading habits of teenagers. Several studies were reviewed with the following themes emerging:

- Girls are the primary YA readers;
- Periodicals are the most popular format;
- Young adults interested in "pure" YA literature decreases with age;
- Although surveys vary, horror is the most popular genre, then mystery, and then true stories. Historical fiction is almost always rated as the least popular;
- Science fiction and fantasy both have a consistent following of 10 percent of all YA readers;
- Paperbacks are the preferred format for books; and
- The majority of readers prefer fiction, then nonfiction, and then graphic formats.

The research reviewed consisted of studies primarily conducted between 1992–1996. Studies about reading interests during the early years were reviewed in the first edition of *Connecting Young Adults and Libraries* documented similar findings. While many of these "facts" hold true in 2003/2004, there is perhaps one truth that becomes even more apparent; young adult literature is not synonymous with the reading interests of teens.

Perhaps nothing demonstrates the wide scope of teen reading interests better than a series of recent surveys asking teens about their favorite books. One recent survey was conducted in Teen Hoopla as part of the Teen Read Week in the fall of 2000. Teens were asked to answer the question "What's the best book you have read this year so far?" Lets break down this list by broad types:

Nonfiction (4 titles)	*Book of Mormon, Concrete Wave: The History of Skateboarding, Chicken Soup for the Teenage Soul, Yoga for Teens*
Adult titles (4 titles)	*The Green Mile, The Hobbit, Of Mice and Men, Ender's Game*

Figure 5-1. Results of survey conducted at Teen Hoopla, part of Teen Read Week in the fall of 2000 on the best books read that year.

Newbery winners/ books for children/ young teens (7 titles)	*Shiloh*, *Holes*, *Hatchet* (and sequels: *Brian's Return* and *Brian's Winter*), *Number the Stars*, and the *Harry Potter* series by J.K. Rowling
"Pure" Young adult (5 titles)	*Outsiders*, *Something Upstairs*, *Tears of a Tiger*, *On the Devil's Court*, and *Dawn Rochelle* by Lurlene McDaniel

Figure 5-1. Continued.

In 2001, YALSA teamed up with SmartGirl (www.smartgirl.org) to do a reading interest survey, one of the questions was "What's the best book you've read this year?" The top fifteen answers broken down are:

Nonfiction (4 titles)	*Chicken Soup for the Soul* books, *A Child Called It*, *The Odyssey*, and *The Bible*
Adult titles (5 titles)	*Left Behind* series, *Ender's Game*, *Sloppy Firsts*, *The Hobbit*, and *The Lord of the Rings* trilogy
Newbery winners/ books for children/ young teens (5 titles)	*The Giver, Holes*, Redwall series, *Where the Red Fern Grows*, and *Watsons Go To Birmingham*
"Pure" Young adult (1 title)	*The Outsiders*

Figure 5-2. Results of survey conducted by YALSA and SmartGirl in the fall of 2001 on the best books read that year.

An isolated phenomenon? In the fall of 2001, the Hennepin County Library in suburban Minneapolis conducted a reading interest survey and asked, "What was the best book that you read last year?" The top ten choices, broken down, are:

Nonfiction (1 title)	*Chicken Soup for the Teenage Soul*
Adult (3 titles)	*Ender's Game* by Orson Scott Card, *To Kill a Mockingbird* by Harper Lee, *The Hobbit* by J.R.R. Tolkien
Newbery/younger teen (3 titles)	*The Skin I'm In* by Sharon Flake, *Harry Potter and the Sorcerer's Stone* by J.K. Rowling, and *Holes* by Louis Sachar
Pure young adult (3 titles)	*The Princess Diaries* by Meg Cabot, *The Face on the Milk Carton* by Caroline Cooney, and *The Golden Compass* by Philip Pullman

Figure 5-3. Results of survey conducted by the Hennepin County Library in the fall of 2001 on the best books read in the previous year.

These reading interest surveys document two central premises of building a teen collection: that a collection for young adults is not just young adult novels, and much of the reading done by young adults is not limited to books checked out of the young adult area.

So what do young adults like to read? Let's examine the results of several recent reading-interest surveys. Few of these would pass the muster of science, but they are attempts to gather information from teens about reading interests. We'll focus on the questions that were asked and some of the most interesting findings that might help us answer, but not locally, what are the best books for teens. In particular, we'll look at how boys, who, according to studies, read less and therefore score lower in standardized reading tests, view reading and suggest some ways to combat the reading gender gap.

STUDY #1:

The survey took place in October 2001 as part of YALSA's Teen Read Week celebration with SmartGirl as a partner. 2,809 people responded, of which over 61 percent were girls and more than 37 percent were boys; their average age was fourteen years old. The key findings related to reading interests and habits are shown in Figure 5-4:

Full results of the YALSA Smart Girl survey can be found at www.smartgirl.org/speakout/archives/trw/trw2001.html.

Which of the following do you read most often?	Girls	Boys	Total
Newspapers	4%	6%	5%
Books for pleasure	41%	23%	43%
Fashion/beauty magazines	17%	0%	11%
Schoolbooks	10%	9%	9%
Comics	2%	4%	3%
Sports/automotive/hunting magazines	3%	30%	13%
News magazines	0%	1%	4%
Video magazines	0%	9%	4%
Music/entertainment magazines	6%	4%	5%
Puzzle magazines	1%	0%	1%
Online reading	2%	3%	3%
Computer manuals	0%	1%	1%
The writing on packages	2%	3%	2%
Miscellaneous magazines	10%	6%	9%
All of the above	2%	1%	2%
None of these	1%	2%	1%

Figure 5-4. Results of survey conducted by YALSA and SmartGirl in the fall of 2001 regarding what's read most often.

Books for pleasure was the number one answer with 43 percent, which should be no surprise. Books were put into one category, while magazines were divided up by subject like fashion, car, and sports. Magazines, if the categorical percentages are added up, equal 47 percent of the favored literature.

Which of these statements describe how often you read?	Girls	Boys	Total
I read constantly for my own personal satisfaction.	35%	17%	28%
I don't have much time to read for pleasure, but I like to when I get the chance.	41%	40%	41%
I only read what I'm supposed to for school.	13%	24%	17%
I basically don't read books much at all.	5%	9%	5%
No answer.	6%	10%	7%

Figure 5-5. Results of survey conducted by YALSA and SmartGirl in the fall of 2001 on how often the teens read.

Girls tend to read something; boys tend to read about something.

The implications here might suggest that teens have more time to read certain formats, like magazines, than books. The most interesting result here was the gender gap that found girls tend to read for pleasure, while boys tend to read for information.

Why do you read?	Frequency	Percentage
No Answer	246	8.8%
Because my parents encourage me to	103	3.7%
Just for the fun of it	1149	40.9%
Because I get bored	348	12.4%
Because I have to for school	543	19.3%
To learn new things on my own	276	9.8%
I really don't read much	144	5.1%

Figure 5-6. Results of survey conducted by YALSA and SmartGirl in the fall of 2001 on why the teens read.

There was no gender distinction, but the highest response of 40 percent came from of teens who read mainly for themselves, and the lowest response of 3.7 percent from teens who said their parents encourage them. This does not mean, however, that parents do not have a role in enabling reading, especially for boys. All of reading research from schools tells us that access to reading materials is very important, and one of the mantras of the early literacy movement is to create a print rich environment. Adults who want boys to read more should just "seed" the house/library with magazines and nonfiction on topics boys are interested in; create easy access, and they will find the boys reading.

If you don't read much or don't like reading, why?	Girls	Boys	Total*
No time/too busy	41.4%	29.8%	36.1%
Boring/not fun	29.3%	39.3%	33.7%
Can't get into the stories	6.3%	7.7%	6.9%
Boys are more interesting	.2%	NA	.1%
Like other activities better	7.8%	11.1%	9.2%
Too much school work	5.5%	1.4%	3.7%
Makes me tired/causes headaches	1.9%	2.5%	2.2%
I'm not good at it	2.6%	4.3%	3.4%
Video games/television more interesting	1.8%	2.3%	2.0%
Books are too long	1.2%	.9%	1.1%
Friends make fun of me	.4%	0%	.2%
Other	1.9%	.9%	1.5%

Figure 5-7. Results of survey conducted by YALSA and SmartGirl in the fall of 2001 on why the teens don't like reading or don't read much.

This table confirms the earlier results that a lack of time was the top answer for not reading, regardless of gender. Interesting though, is that *no* boys answered that they didn't read because of friends making fun of them. Magazines, with their appeal to short attention spans, and lots of nonfiction, with its appeal to those who want to look at pictures or read short snippets of information, can be read in less time that most fiction.

Not including for school, how much do you read?	Girls	Boys	Total
Outside of school assignments, I don't read at all	6%	9%	7%
Under one book per month	12%	17%	14%
One book per month	16%	17%	17%
2-3 books per month	22%	20%	21%
3-5 books per month	13%	10%	12%
5-10 books per month	10%	7%	9%
10-20 books per month	7%	2%	5%
More than 20 books per month	6%	4%	5%

Figure 5-8. Results of survey conducted by YALSA and SmartGirl in the fall of 2001 on how much teens read outside of school.

Most teens reported reading two to three books a month, and there were few gender differences. The gender gap emerged in the avid readers with more girls reading over three books a month. Conversely, those teen boys who are readers often read large science fiction and fantasy novels. Some boys want longer books for the challenge of it.

STUDY #2:

A survey of three hundred teens was conducted during the fall of 2001 at the Hennepin County Library in suburban Minneapolis. The gender difference was overwhelmingly—84 percent girls and 16 percent boys. The survey was delivered primarily through schools, as well as having an online component.

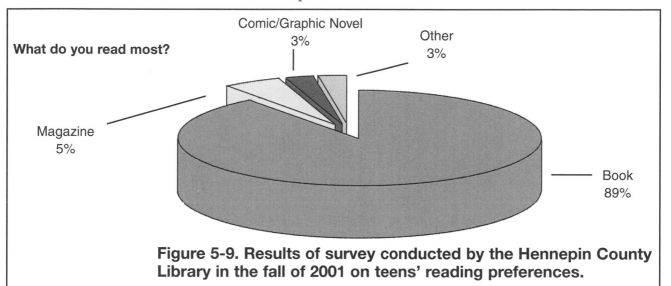

What do you read most?

Comic/Graphic Novel
3%

Other
3%

Magazine
5%

Book
89%

Figure 5-9. Results of survey conducted by the Hennepin County Library in the fall of 2001 on teens' reading preferences.

And what a difference it was with teens in the suburbs of Minneapolis reporting a dominating preference for book reading (80%) and little interest in magazines (5%).

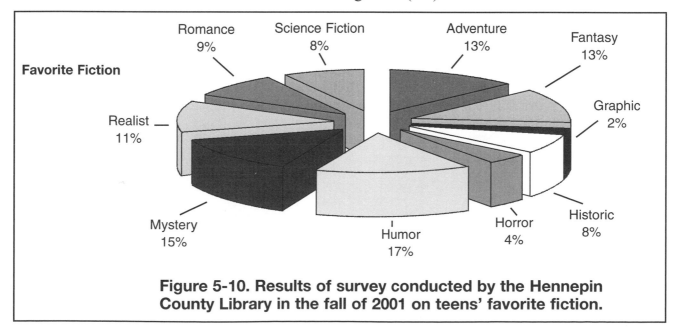

Favorite Fiction

Romance
9%

Science Fiction
8%

Adventure
13%

Fantasy
13%

Graphic
2%

Realist
11%

Historic
8%

Mystery
15%

Humor
17%

Horror
4%

Figure 5-10. Results of survey conducted by the Hennepin County Library in the fall of 2001 on teens' favorite fiction.

The answers in this survey were varied, yet humor was the top choice. An interesting question that follows is, does this represent what teens *do* read or what they would like to read?

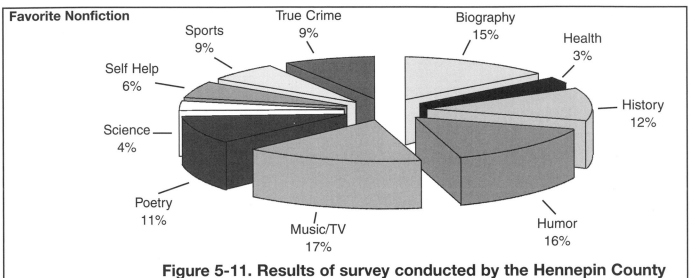

Favorite Nonfiction

Figure 5-11. Results of survey conducted by the Hennepin County Library in the fall of 2001 on teens' favorite nonfiction.

The subjects here are not surprising, with the exception of self-help, which is a big market for teen nonfiction, aimed above all at girls. True-crime nonfiction had little following, and humor still ranked high on preference.

STUDY #3:

Five hundred and eighty young adults in Fresno County, California were surveyed in 2001. Gender difference was 57.6 percent female and

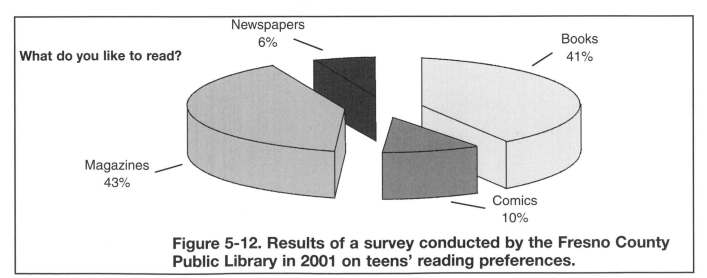

What do you like to read?

Figure 5-12. Results of a survey conducted by the Fresno County Public Library in 2001 on teens' reading preferences.

42.4 percent male. As a county system that also has branches into the inner city, as well as a central library, the Fresno County survey presents a diverse look at teen reading interests The participants were mainly older teens.

Results here are much different than Hennepin County, with a significantly smaller number of users noting that books are their favorite reading material.

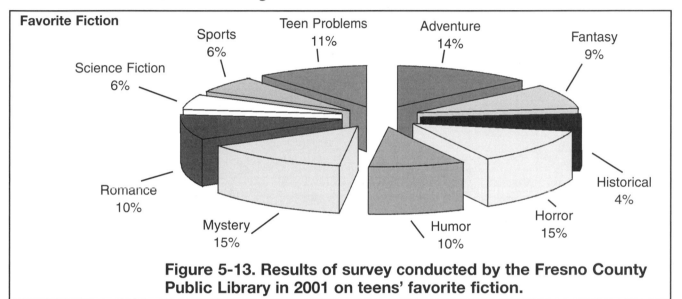

Favorite Fiction

Sports 6%
Teen Problems 11%
Adventure 14%
Fantasy 9%
Science Fiction 6%
Romance 10%
Mystery 15%
Humor 10%
Horror 15%
Historical 4%

Figure 5-13. Results of survey conducted by the Fresno County Public Library in 2001 on teens' favorite fiction.

There are few strong preferences, as Fresno readers seem to have a wide variety of interests, although not much support for science fiction and sports, which may be related to the majority of survey respondents being female.

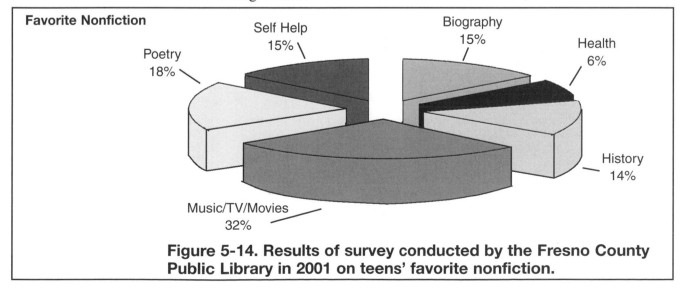

Favorite Nonfiction

Self Help 15%
Biography 15%
Poetry 18%
Health 6%
History 14%
Music/TV/Movies 32%

Figure 5-14. Results of survey conducted by the Fresno County Public Library in 2001 on teens' favorite nonfiction.

These results again support that perhaps libraries should look at collection development that complements mass media.

These reading interest surveys represent a snapshot of teen reading in the United States. While there are many differences, there are some clear common-elements in all surveys. Are these the same reading interest of your teens? You'll never know unless you ask them.

WHAT ARE READING INTERESTS OF BOYS?

Almost any LST who has visited a secondary school classroom or booktalk session could tell the tale about the student, often a male, who will defiantly and proudly announce to the librarian that he doesn't read. Chances are that this response is mainly for show, to mark turf and to challenge authority; chances are that these boys do read; but not the stack of novels the booktalking librarian no doubt has in front of her. ("Her" is the correct pronoun to use as the overwhelming majority of LSTs are female.) Instead, that male is probably reading newspapers (comics, sports and entertainment), magazines (same list as newspapers, but add video gaming magazines), graphic novels or collected comics, and maybe even heavily illustrated nonfiction. Thus, the boy at the booktalk session saying he doesn't read might simply be saying that he doesn't read what libraries offer.

Most young adult sections in public libraries are filled with fiction; there is little recreational nonfiction. If there is recreational nonfiction, it is more than likely self-help, health-related, about teen issues, or pop star biographies. There might be magazines, but the chances are that they are aimed more at girls than boys. Comic books are more than likely not there, and graphic novels, if collected, are not featured. There probably isn't a newspaper lying around. Boys who venture into the YA area will find shelves so jammed that they won't have a catchy cover grab their interest and it is doubtful if anything but new books—which no doubt are all fiction—will be on display. Given these choices, the teen boy, especially a younger one, will opt for something safe like a series—boys like brands—only to get the message from a teacher, parent, or maybe even a librarian that the book is okay because "at least they are reading something." What the boy is getting is, given the choices available, maybe the best by his own standards, not by a librarian or committee. His best book is one that will provide him with information or entertainment. It is one he will read.

Michael Smith's book, *Reading Don't Fix No Chevys*, reviews a dozen major findings of research done regarding boys—not just teens—and reading:

- Boys don't comprehend narrative (fiction) as well as girls;
- Boys have much less interest in leisure reading than girls;
- Boys are more inclined to read informational texts;
- Boys are more inclined to read magazine and newspaper articles;
- Boys are more inclined to read comic books and graphic novels than girls;
- Boys like to read about hobbies, sports, and things they do or want to do;
- Boys tend to enjoy escapism and humor;
- Some groups of boys are passionate about science fiction or fantasy;
- The appearance of a book and cover is important to boys;
- Few boys entering school call themselves "nonreaders," but by high school, over one half do;
- Boys tend to think they are bad readers; and
- If reading is perceived as feminized, then boys will go to great lengths to avoid it.

HOW DO YOU SELECT THE BEST BOOKS FOR TEENAGERS?

These reading surveys show that while there is some continuity in the reading interests of teens across gender, grades, and even over time, young adult readers are difficult to stereotype. They read all genres and read both young adult books and adult books they find of interest. The unpredictability of the teen reader presents those developing collections with their greatest challenges, opportunities, and rewards.

Active involvement from teenagers is the best opportunity for developing productive collections, as with other aspects of connecting teens and the library previously mentioned in this book. Libraries should look for methods to engage teens in the collection-development process. One library in Ohio, for example, involved teens in the paperback-book selection process. The LST took a vendor catalog of new paperbacks and copied pages, handed them out, and then ordered based on the suggestions of the teens. An LST in New York knew she needed to develop a collection of manga, but was at a loss. She found a group of teens who knew the genre, and allowed them, with guidance, to select materials for the library. A school library in Texas had a school's science-fiction club do the selection. The LST copied pages from *VOYA*'s spectacular speculative fiction review section and handed them out at a meeting. The LST then said, "We can only afford five," which both allowed teens to make suggestions (all which were taken), but also to learn a little bit about difficult a process that collection development is. Some libraries make collection development easier by having teens help with weeding—actually pulling the books, not just developing weeding reports. They also looked at books in bad condition or that they would never think of reading. Many libraries involve teens in monthly sessions of choosing music, or doing surveys—sometimes with prizes—when it comes time to order new magazines. This isn't giving up your professionalism, instead, it is proving it.

> By empowering teens, you are creating more powerful services, building better collections, and more importantly, building relationships.

WHAT KIND OF TEEN COLLECTION DO YOU WANT TO BUILD?

A YA section is usually small enough that over a short period of time transforming it to meet someone's particular vision is viable. What is your vision? That vision will be influenced by several factors:

- Library's total collection-development philosophy;
- Quality and quantity of school library collections;

- Budget, space and staff available;
- Reading interests of YAs in your community;
- Your own professional values;
- What needs that collection should meet; and
- The roles the library has chosen for itself.

Despite, or maybe because of, your "vision" for the collection, you need to set priorities; because, doing it all is not possible. A "balanced collection," most think, is desirable; however, if you really want to set priorities and concentrate efforts, funds, and space on certain areas, the collection will be out of balance. The whole battle about collection balance (popularity vs. quality; breadth vs. depth) involves the basic philosophy of your library. Let's first look at some collection-development choices, emphasizing YAs. It seems in doing so we will discover we need to answer the same question we have already dealt with repeatedly: what is quality?

- **Demand vs. quality?** The oldest debate needs to be settled first. Do you buy series paperbacks? Do you buy multiple copies? Given money to buy only one book and a choice between a popular book and a quality one, which one would you choose?

- **Circulation vs. standards?** A related question is, "Does the library have a 'responsibility' to provide YAs with materials of only high literary quality?" Follow-up: which is easier to quantify on an annual report, an increase in circulation or literary standards being upheld? How do you measure a book's "value" to the collection? Is "will it move" the only selection criteria? Will a book's appearance on a "best books" list merit its purchase and/or place on the shelf?

- **Permanency vs. immediacy?** What should the turnover rate be in a YA collection? Should you choose stocking it with long lasting hardbacks that will last decades and create a permanent YA collection, or should you choose to fill it with books that meet immediate reading interests but, due to paperback format, will not survive two years? Obviously there needs to be mix, but given the fact that most YA areas are small and so are most YA budgets, our guess is even if teens did not prefer the paperback format, librarians would.

- **Recreational vs. educational vs. information vs. cultural?** This choice ties back to the roles which libraries choose. This decision also hinges on the strength of the school library collections. Does the adult/reference department buy sufficient copies of materials needed by YAs? What type, if any, YA nonfiction is in the YA area?

- **Professional vs. careful?** Another old debate concerns professional values, personal opinions, and community standards. The bottom line: do you buy YA materials that you and most adults object to, but YAs would love? Do you respond to your customers—YAs—or to supporters in the community? Do you buy rap music? Would you buy a professional wrestling magazine, a skateboarding magazine, or a tattoo magazine? Do you buy Zane or Stephen King for the YA collection? Do you collect books for gay/lesbian teens?

- **Librarian vs. book buyer?** If your focus is popular reading, then have you forsaken your "professionalism" to become a glorified Border's book buyer? A group of YAs could probably select a more responsive collection than many librarians charged with developing YA collections. What parts of YA book selection take some degree of professional judgment? Is the best selector the person who selects the most titles that end up on a "best books" list or the one who selects all the YA best sellers?

- **Customers vs. collections?** Actually, this is the big question. Believe it or not even schlock masters want quality in YA collections, it is just that we would measure quality differently. A customer service centered process puts the customer first. What is one way to measure satisfaction in customers? Circulation of materials. A focus more on traditional quality seems more input- or material-based. For many YAs, paperbacks and popular fiction met their recreational and even emotional reading needs. For many, but not for all. Part of a quality collection, admittedly, is diversity. An all graphic novel collection would be popular, but you would also be not serving many of customers if you had nothing else. One LST totally stopped buying hardbacks for the branch libraries and putt the money into magazines. The circulation soared and everyone was happy, except of course, those kids that didn't read that format and liked new YA literature that came out in hardback. It was certainly a smaller group than those who read magazines, but focusing on one group of readers was unsatisfactory. Part of the problem about improving any service is that there are probably some customers who won't think it is an improvement.

Why are series books popular? Why do series belong in libraries? Series books meet the needs of teen readers.

- **Quality vs. popularity?** Here's the scenario: it is near the end of your fiscal year and you have dollars, literally just a few dollars, available to spend on books for young adults. On your desk, you have an open BWI monthly catalog and the latest issue of *Booklist*. You have $14.95 to spend; you can buy one of these hardback offerings, or several of the paperbacks. Some of the paperbacks are not just reprints of hardbacks, but rather originals, and most of them parts of a series. Where is that money going to go? Yet, rather than a choice of where to spend this $14.95, it's a choice of quality vs. popularity. Thus, deciding to buy paperback series is really the result of a series of choices which you have already made about how to develop your collection. Perhaps the teenager reading any kind of literature is, in effect, quality. Perhaps series fiction provides teenagers with the type of reading experience they want at a particular time of their lives, and once that time in their life has passed, they will move on to something else. It's not because they want to move to "quality" literature, but because series reading no longer meets their emotional or recreational needs.

- **Reading vs. reading something?** The choices YA librarians are making about series and other popular materials are, therefore, similar to those that adult librarians make as well—it's not, "Do we buy Danielle Steel," but rather "How many copies?" We wring our hands as we "soil" our shelves with this "trash," for we feel that we have a "higher mission" to save people from their own "bad" reading habits. Or sometimes that line of thinking overshadows the argument that, "Well, at least they are reading something." The problem with that attitude is it tells the readers that that "something" is really what lacks value and, thus, the subtle message we transmit is *they* lack value. It sets up a caste system of reading; it is insulting, absurd, and counterproductive. The only bad reading choice is the one many YAs make, not to read at all. The best thing libraries can do to influence that choice is provide materials that a YA would want to read. The best type of material for YAs to read are materials that meet their needs, have proven popular, have peer approval, and lead them to reading something else, if only another book exactly like the one they just finished.

These are just some of the questions an LST might face when making collection decisions. We write "might," because the sad fact is that many large public library systems do not allow LSTs to make any of these choices. Instead, the choices are made for them. Centralized selection is counterproductive to building a teen-responsive collection. It doesn't allow for differences in communities, in readers, and in the vast skills most LSTs posses. When we were routing journals, perhaps centralized selection made some sense, but we don't do that anymore. You can still centralize acquisition without centralizing selection. The notion that someone sitting in an office with no interaction with teens can build a quality collection is pure fiction. In this book, we don't want to load you down with titles that we think you "must buy," because we don't know what is right for the teens using your library. Along the way, we will suggest some titles here as examples or best bets, but these are merely suggestions. We don't work with your teens, you do.

HOW DO I START BUILDING A COLLECTION FOR TEENS?

We often build or assess a collection by the titles and authors we recognize; they have a reputation, whether good or bad. Teens also asses and judge books, but they generally use a different set of criteria—the story and the cover. The cover may get them to pick it up but the story will make them read it. There is a core collection or a core set of authors that one would expect to find in any YA collection, such as Chris Crutcher, Walter Dean Myers, and Sarah Dessen. There are different ways to go about building your collection—the author/title route or the genre/list route. The author/title route may include comfortable authors that write many different titles and titles that may cross over genres. If you have a grasp of several YA authors there are a variety of books that are at your fingertips to recommend to teens. The genre/list route may seem like a narrow focus at first but in the end you may end up with a better collection because you are looking at each genre individually so it gets the attention it deserves.

You may also want to take a hard look at your juvenile and adult collections; if your library has always been without a YA collection there may be titles that have been purchased over the years that would fit in your YA collection. This may help you gather a collection without spending any money but give you immediate results. Topics and formats such as biographies, magazines, music, videos, science fiction, and recreational and informational nonfiction could all be culled from the juvenile and adult collection. By pulling out certain titles that have teen appeal, you give older titles a new audience. *Into the Wild,* by Jon Krakauer, for example, is typically classified as an adult biography, but has high school appeal and may be lost in the adult biography section. *Big Book of Optical Illusions,* by Al Seckel, *Enders Game,* by Orson Scott Card, *A Child Called It,* by Dave Pelzer, and *The Art of Hand Reading,* by Lori Reid, are all titles that have teen appeal but are typically found in the adult collection. Also, Garfield comics, Holocaust survivor stories, *Phineas Gage: A Gruesome But True Story About Brain Science,* titles of the "Alice" books, by Phyllis Reynolds Naylor, as Alice hits high school, poetry, and *Left For Dead: A Young Man's Search For Justice For The USS Indianapolis,* by Peter Nelson, may be titles that can make the move to your YA collection from the juvenile collection. You may have to negotiate liberating those titles from the juvenile and adult collections but it can be a great start. Which route you decide to take in building your YA collection may depend on your budget, purchasing cycle, as well as your library's philosophy, service response, and partnership with other departments to make sure the informational and educational needs of the teens in your area are met.

FICTION

Teens are using your fiction collection for recreational reading, but also for required reading for school; so be sure that you have done your research and included titles that show up on reading lists for the area high schools. One LST regularly collects donated copies of "classics" that are on the high school required reading lists. Those donations are available for teens that need a classic at the last minute, after everyone else in their class has been to the library, and all the copies of *To Kill a Mockingbird* are checked out. Since these are donations, copies now become available, but these donated books have not been added to the collections, are not cataloged, incur no expense in processing, and customers experience good customer service. Not every title with teen appeal can be located in the young adult collection. There are physical limitations and some titles that have teen appeal are located in the adult collection; often, depending on your community, that is the best place for that title. As LSTs, a comprehensive knowledge of other collections within your library can be very beneficial. You can serve the teens in your community better and spend money wisely. Because of how libraries often determine their collection budgets, you may have to partner with the adult-fiction selector to make sure that certain titles appear in your library no matter who is purchasing them. Be aware of teen programming that goes on as well as any special library initiatives, such as "United We Read" or "One City, One Book."

The "one book idea" assumes that there is one book that everyone will enjoy reading. That's a unrealistic idea, as teens vary in their reading tastes. Some will read only certain authors, only certain genres, while other teens, normally the 14- to 15-years-olds, will read numerous subjects, often choosing books by the cover or the title. While teens may choose books for different reasons, what they get out of fiction may not vary much.

If you look at the books that stand up to the test of time with teens (*The Outsiders* and *Ender's Game*), or those that suddenly become wildly popular, most will meet many of the emotional needs teens are looking for in fiction. With many teens, fiction isn't just about escaping; instead it's about making a connection with characters who share similar feelings. These characters may be aliens, or wizards, or everyday normal teens, the best young adult fiction is not always that which paints through language the most beautiful pictures, but rather that which presents teens with a mirror in which they see their own lives reflected in the novel.

If you take a survey of what teens enjoy reading, there are a few genres that zoom right to the top of the list; these are what you should be buying. And, there are some that fall to the bottom of the list; don't ignore those completely. They are probably required reading, so some poor soul is going to need one on Sunday night; lend him a hand and buy the short and really good ones.

> There are primary emotional needs that teens meet when reading fiction, which you can meet if you:
>
> - Reassure them they are normal—physically, mentally, emotionally, and socially;
> - Present opportunities for emotional independence from adults;
> - Show how to resolve problems;
> - Allow to experience success;
> - Picture satisfying relationships;
> - Provide help establishing roles;
> - Support development of socially responsible behaviors;
> - Help them work out personal philosophy; and
> - Furnish opportunities for emotional engagement, pleasure and relaxation.

- **Adventure.** This is a great example of a genre where the subject matter itself might not be the most important thing in the book. *The Maze,* by Will Hobbs, is high adventure. In it, Rick Walker breaks out of a juvenile detention center and stows away in a truck heading for Utah's canyon country. He ends up reluctantly becoming part of a legitimate condor reintroduction project, evades the authorities, and encounters some unwanted attention around the project. But the two best parts of the story are the relationship between Rick and Lon Peregrino and the connection with the Greek myth of Icarus and Daedalus.

Divide your fantasy and science-fiction collections. It will help teens find what they want quicker, and it will also help your adult staff who may not read science fiction or fantasy. Help your teen customers with more accuracy.

- **Fantasy**. These readers, like science-fiction readers, can be vocal in asking for what they want—the next one in the series. So we tend to hear from them more than the fifteen-year-old girl who likes romances by Sarah Dessen. They are just as interested in the information about where the next book is, but somehow fantasy readers have learned to speak up. These fictitious worlds like Pern and Discworld are places teens triumph over evil and learn about courage, bravery, honesty, and all that other stuff they are supposed to learn to be better adults. It is almost the equivalent of traveling to a different country as a foreign-exchange student. While you learn about the country you are visiting, you also learn plenty about yourself.

- **Historical Fiction**. Historical fiction is almost always ranked as the least popular genre; although, it is the genre most mentioned on lists of good books for teens. This is one of those genres that adults enjoy, but most teens are not clamoring for it, because it gets so much attention from the teacher types. Teens do not see historical fiction as exciting or interesting. Money must be spent on it because of its value in researching assignments, but use your money wisely. Cover the milestones in history but keep the rest current—that which would probably not be considered historical fiction by you and your friends. The 1970s now count as historical fiction and soon the 1980s will, as well. Go for the short and exciting if you can swing it.

- **Horror.** This is the genre parents love to hate; but, if you think of popular adult TV shows, at the top of the list are true-crime mysteries that have their share of blood and decaying bodies. Teens love to be scared and freaked-out; and if it is *Goosebumps* or Dean Koontz that does it for them, we need to buy it. The lack of true YA horror books is one challenge that we face; they often deal with the supernatural, paranormal, and are bloody, but not true horror. For most tenth graders searching for horror, Christopher Pike is going to fall very short.

- **Humor**. This is the genre that adults seem to want more of probably to counter the horror their teens are craving. But funny is tricky; funny movies for teens don't translate well into books because most of the time there is a visual need for the laugh. There are many titles that don't overflow with funny scenes in every chapter; but there are plenty of YA books that have good humor in them. *Speak,* by Laurie Anderson, has some very funny moments that only someone in high school can truly appreciate. Chris Lynch's *Extreme Elvin* combines some painful experiences with a few classic conversations. *The Ear, the Eye, and the Arm,* by Nancy Farmer, portrays the future with some humorous observations. Humor seems silly and a little painful at times, like when you got dumped or your best friend moved away; but, as with adults, the reading tastes of teens change and, after reading a few titles from one genre, they will move on to the next.

- **Inspirational fiction.** In many libraries, the most popular series read by teens is the *Left Behind* series, while the most popular series aimed directly at youth is the *Left Behind for Kids* series. There is a huge interest among teens in things spiritual, and often it is reflected in their reading interests. A few years ago there were numerous mainstream teen publishers doing series with a Christian fiction theme, as well as series related to angels.

- **Movie and TV.** A benefit of the entertainment industry conglomerates is that every big movie comes as part of a package deal. The package includes soundtracks, posters, T-shirts, countless other merchandise, and a rerelease of the book associated with the movie. These books are gobbled up by YAs who either want to relive the experience of the movie, or the movie was rated "R" and they couldn't go and see it.

- **Multicultural literature.** As more children of recent immigrants hit their adult years, we have seen an explosion in multicultural literature. This reflects their experiences but also the incredible diversity in teens today. A recent example is *A Step From Heaven,* which depicts the common experience of immigrating to the United States with high hopes, no matter your background. In this book, teens also learn a little about Korean culture.

- **Mystery.** Stock your shelves with the scariest titles you can find, because scary is always in demand. Hair-raising is one thing, but don't overlook the good who-dun-it story with a twist. Just as mystery programs in the adult sections of libraries are popular, teens crave both a familiar plot line and a good challenge. Once they graduate from mysteries by Joan Lowery Nixon, we need to have more challenging titles waiting like *The Killer's Cousin,* by Nancy Werlin, or the short story collection *Cat in Glass,* by Nancy Etchemendy. Most adults feel comfortable redirecting a high schooler to Patricia Cornwell or John Sanford, but these adults are missing some great stories mostly because they aren't familiar with the YA titles.

• **Realistic fiction.** You will hear this referred to as the "problem novel," but that is selling it short. These are the stories in which teens find characters in the everyday situations they too are experiencing. These situations may seem like a challenge, obstacle, or issue to the teen; but if an adult begins to call every teenage situation a "problem," of course teens will begin to look at their lives as problems. Reading about issues like friendship, sexual experience, betrayal, religion, violence, and school, encourages teens to consider how they would react in similar situations. It does not mean that every teen who reads *Cut,* by Patricia McCormick, will begin to cut themselves and follow the path that Callie took. It could mean that a teen who is cutting himself or herself may see a different way or an explanation offered in the story. You can be assured that in most realistic fiction the problem is resolved, the teen protagonist learns from the situation, and things, in general, get better; although better may not be what the teen protagonist expected. Realistic fiction offers teen readers options and consolations instill feelings that they are not the only person experiencing a particular moment of embarrassment or confusion. Reading about such problems may help them understand the situation from another perspective. These effects aren't too far from the reasons why adults read novels that deal with tough situations such as *The Lovely Bones,* by Alice Sebold, or a variety of the Oprah Book Club selections.

• **Romance.** This is the emotional category that is probably the easiest to match with teens. Just as they are experiencing highs and lows, they are interested in the trials and tribulations of other teens that may not have the bad skin condition or the overprotective parents they find themselves with. You could pick up ten YA novels and find a romance in the story in at least four of them. Romance, while maybe not a major theme, is a topic that runs through many YA books. Romance titles for teens vary from the mild first-crush to the full-blown bad relationship that is going too far, too fast. Teen romance novels with more than a hint of sex is a recent trend in YA literature. The *Gossip Girls* series, the breakthrough novel *Sloppy Firsts*, and the comedic romantic musings in the books by Louise Rennison are some of the works that illustrate this trend.

- **Science fiction.** Science fiction and fantasy both have a consistent following of nearly 10 percent of all YA readers. Again do yourself a favor and separate science fiction from fantasy. These genres are not the same and while devoted readers know the difference, library staff may not at first. Your teen customers will be much better served from a divided collection; even a sticker on the spine, at the very least, will go a long way in their minds. It will be clear that your library knows the difference and puts equal importance on both, which translates into placing importance on the reader.

- **Short story collections.** This subgenre has blossomed in the past five years, and thankfully so. There are now collections that touch every possible genre and topic that a teen experiences. They fulfill assignments for teens who need to read a short story. These collections give teens experience with the literary devices used in short stories, adding the bonus of a teen protagonist and covering teen issues. Teens can connect with both of the characters and issues and then move onto higher-level short stories. They give teachers, counselors, and parents a tool with which to introduce discussion topics. They can also act as the catalyst for various creative writing exercises.

- **Sports.** These stories are not only about who wins the game, but they also do a good job of incorporating the struggles that every athlete faces—balancing their studies with responsibilities at home and sports. Expectations of parents, coaches, and other teens from the teen athlete often come to the forefront in these stories as well as using sports as a vehicle to explore prejudice, honesty, and pressure. Chris Crutcher, Will Weaver, John Ritter, James Bennett, and Carl Deuker are all known authors in this genre.

• **Trauma**. This genre seems like a cross between realistic fiction and romance; and the works of these authors, like Lurlene McDaniel, have as much trauma as drama. The disease-of-the-week might strike a family member, or a friend, or the narrators themselves. With YAs so full of life, the preoccupation with death is easy to explain and hard to ignore when choosing books.

• **Urban fiction.** As the influence of hip-hop on teen popular culture and fashion cannot be overstated, YA literature has yet to produce a great hip-hop novel. The works of Walter Dean Myers come close, but really lack true street credibility for older teens. Mostly, it is adult authors, like Sister Souljah's *The Coldest Winter Ever* or Omar Tyree's often-banned *Flyy Girl,* which most African American teens enjoy. Gary Soto's works like *Buried Onions* and *Petty Crimes* provide a glimpse into Latino teens living for the city, as does Victor Martinez's award-winning *Parrot in the Oven.*

SERIES FICTION

For every adult who hopes they never see another *Buffy the Vampire Slayer, Fear Street,* or *Mary-Kate & Ashley Sweet 16* book, there is one word for them—"Relax." Seriously, you must relax. Almost everyone goes through a time when they read series fiction, bad things will not happen to teens that read series fiction. In fact good things will happen; all of the research supports the value of reading series fiction.

The appeal of series fiction for teens is varied, but generally, they appreciate the following:

• Enjoy reading, and this enjoyment will lead to more reading and more times than not reading a variety of genres while they find the subjects that interest them;

• Develop relationships with familiar characters and thus develop and practice empathy;

• Take comfort in predictable endings because their lives are not predictable. Might we mention Danielle

Steele, Mary Higgins Clark, or Stuart Woods? We may not associate those authors with series fiction but their books do have many similarities to series fiction and no one is discouraging adults from reading those authors;

• Work out a variety of situations through the characters they already know;

• Pick up on various points of interest in the stories, such as setting, character development and vocabulary because of the familiarity with the plot and its predictability;

• Achieve something. Series fiction allows readers who are struggling with their reading to progress, keep reading, and become more confident with each success;

• Get more of what they want (horror/romance) without the hassle of asking adults and getting redirected to something they didn't want (mystery/historical fiction) in the first place; and

• Move on to other genres and books cranky adults think are "appropriate."

CLASSICS

One definition of a classic might be any book a YA would reasonably expect to find in any library; again that covers a lot of ground.

The term classic means different things to different people. One definition is a book that is "never hot but never cold." Any book for which there is and can always be a demand qualifies as a classic. For titles that fit this definition, you will have to check periodically because they have a way of disappearing.

The popular idea of a classic is those with a capital C: Dickens, the Brontës, and others. These are books that are taught in school, often read by YAs out of necessity rather than choice, and were primarily written before any teen's great-grandparents were even born. You might want to consider getting these in Permabound editions, so you don't constantly have to repurchase them. The primary audience for classics is often a person who knows exactly what book he or she wants to read so format doesn't matter. Because of that, don't waste valuable display space; put them on a bottom shelf near the back of the YA area.

But another kind of classic is just as important, and it's not handed down from teacher to student from one generation of teens to the next. They don't always make our lists, but they do make several trips around a group of YAs who end up marking the pages. Some of these make BBYA, while others escape attention. These titles represent books that YAs will be looking, but rarely asking, for in a library collection. All will be popular; almost all present selection vs. censorship questions. Most of these types of titles obtained that cult status by being controversial (e.g. *Go Ask Alice*, *Fight Club*, and *Coldest Winter Ever*).

Perhaps though, the most popular classics among teens are all by the same author—the late great Mr. Cliff. For every copy of *Moby Dick*, you should have a Cliffs Notes book as well. Some libraries have refused to stock Cliffs Notes, but then there are always Barron's and Monarch's notes.

NONFICTION—RECREATIONAL AND INFORMATIONAL

Some libraries ignore YA nonfiction altogether, or they shelve it with their adult collection. Their rationale is if teens need nonfiction for homework, then they will find more sources if YA nonfiction is housed with the adult collection. That may be true; a teen doing a report on the Holocaust may find more sources in the adult collection. But you are assuming that teens are only using nonfiction for educational purposes. This is not true. Teens use nonfiction for recreational, informational, educational, and reference pursuits.

Don't assume that fiction is the only type of book that will provide pleasure reading; it just isn't so. Teens are developing special interests and will read whatever comes their way if it pertains to their passions. The best of these are found not in reviews from library professional journals, but by visiting bookstores in person and online. The real "pop" stuff might never get reviewed and may be found at a local magazine vendor. Specific titles that reflect these special interests may come and go, but there are some topics that continue to have long-term teen appeal.

Not all learning that teens do is related to school. They do homework, but they also do lifework. Teen bodies and lives are constantly changing so naturally they need information on what is, or is not, happening to them and what will be happening. Combine a desire for independence, lack of confidence, and embarrassment, and you get teens who need information but probably won't ask for it. These books may not have high circulation but they will get the highest marks for creative shelving and the information they find might just save the life of a teen.

While titles change, the following are subjects that seem, year after year, of interest to teens who explore subjects outside of a school assignment as they develop their personal cultures and becoming lifelong learners.

Just as there emotional needs are met through fiction, nonfiction speaks to many teens.
- They are fascinated with facts.
- They are developing special interests.
- They are developing intellectual curiosity.
- They have short attention spans.
- They want to look at pictures/visuals.
- They view nonfiction as socially acceptable.
- They find "fiction" difficult.
- They like real-life stories, such as personal narratives.
- They are reluctant readers.
- Nonfiction is relevant to their lives.
- Nonfiction inspires lifelong learning.

For specific titles in many of these areas, see *A Core Collection for Young Adults,* by Patrick Jones, Patricia Taylor, and Kirsten Edwards (Neal-Schuman, 2003).

000	Symbols and signs		Cheerleading		Drawing
	UFOs		Study guides for the		Comic book illustration
	Unexplained		GED, SAT, and ACT.		Drawing manga/anime
	Web page building		College admissions,		History of comics
	Computer languages		scholarships, and		Photography
	World Records		directories		Music and musicians
100	Philosophy		Death customs		Movies and movie
	Witchcraft/Wicca		Fashion		stars
	Parapsychology		Urban legends		TV shows
	Astrology	400	Sign language		Professional sports
	Handwriting analysis		Slang dictionaries		Professional wrestling
	Palm reading		Rhyming dictionaries		Martial arts
	Dreams	500	Math puzzles		Skateboarding/snow-
	Self-help		Codes		boarding
	Eastern philosophy		Animals		Sports card collecting
200	Mythology	600	Inventions		NASCAR
	Angels		Sex	800	Poetry
	Eastern religions		Teen health		Collected writings of
	Islam		Suicide		teens
300	Teen studies		Eating disorders		Humor
	Relationships		Mental health		Jokes
	Gay/Lesbian/Bisexual/		Depression		Book about fantasy,
	Transgender issues		Substance abuse		science fiction, and
	Spies		Yoga/Tai Chi		horror
	Careers		Vegetarianism		Haiku
	Civil rights		Teen pregnancy	900	Survival tales
	Legal rights		Bicycles		Names
	Armed Forces study		Cars		Biographies
	guides		Motorcycles		Ancient Egypt
	Child abuse, home-		Pet care		Medieval studies/King
	lessness, drug		Cooking		Arthur
	addiction, and first-		Babysitting		Holocaust survival
	person narratives		Make-up/grooming/		tales
	Dating violence		beauty		Vietnam War
	Adoption		Strength training		Sixties culture
	True crime	700	Graphic novels		9-11 terrorist attack
	Gangs		Calligraphy		against the United
	School success		Origami		States

Figure 5-15. Popular teen reading in each Dewey subject group.

Be prepared to weed and update your nonfiction section regularly. This section, unlike fiction, loses it popularity quickly. This is also a great place to involve teens; they may have a better sense of what is "in" or "out" than you do, so have them help with the weeding and selection of your nonfiction section.

NONFICTION—EDUCATIONAL AND REFERENCE

> Despite the tremendous amount of information available via electronic means, providing books for students will remain a central role of libraries for some time to come.

Librarians didn't need another study from the Pew Foundation to tell us what we have been observing since 1996: a majority of students who have Internet access will use that first and foremost to do research on any topic, even if the Net is not the "best" place to gather information. The problem, of course, is that a student who looks for information on abortion using Google is not going to find the same quality or organized quantity of information as a book would provide. Further, the time spent looking for such information would probably be greater than if they had read a series book on the topic. Also, some teachers will resist technology and still require only book sources, so there is still a demand for printed academic information.

Students do not do research primarily by thoroughly reading books, but by gathering information from a variety of sources. The genius of most of the YA nonfiction book series is how they organize that information, how they gather material from other sources, and how they present that information in an easy to read text, complemented by graphics. Often, when students are looking for material for argumentative papers or a speech, we'll show them *Opposing Viewpoints* in print—or the fab online version—and say, jokingly, "Here's the report." But it is not a joke; because, like teen fiction series, *Opposing Viewpoints* and other YA nonfiction series succeed because they give students not just what they want, but also what they need.

Currency is the watchword here. New topics become "hot"—who was writing about terrorism five years ago? Who is writing papers on solar energy now?—while others become almost classic in their constant popularity. Collecting materials for term papers involves a choice about collection scope and balance. Given funds to purchase ten books on the topic of abortion, how best is the money spent? On ten different titles on the subject or ten copies of the same? Each approach has problems because of how many YAs do research; if there are ten titles on a subject available, one YA can take out everything. If you buy ten copies of the same title, then ten YAs get a book, but only one title.

But again, what would be the best book to buy ten copies? In libraries without YA librarians determining what might be the best one to buy, the problem is compounded. Coupled with shrinking materials budgets and staffing shortages, librarians are finding it difficult to do

REASONS TO BUY NONFICTION SERIES:

* **Kids like them.** They are easy to use, well organized, timely, about "exactly" the topic they are researching, and thin—less than 200 pages.
* **They fill a collection need.** Every collection needs books on "hot topics." Just as paperback series support the need for recreational reading, these support the need for educational materials.
* **They save time.** If you find a series you like, put it on standing order. If you find a really good series, buy multiple copies: that saves time and money.

We would propose the following criteria when looking at series nonfiction:

* **Readability.** Are the books easy to read? Is the author's style clear, concise and understandable?
* **Facts/opinions.** Are the books unbiased? Does the author present both sides, including labeling facts and opinions? Are the facts accurate?
* **Organization.** Are the books easy to use? Do they contain detailed table of contents, indexes and glossaries? If there's no index, how will a reader access the information?
* **Format.** Are the books approachable? Is the format appropriate for young adults? Are charts, graphs and/or photos used? What about margins?
* **Photographs.** Do the books have photos? Do they add to the text? Are they captioned? Are they of good quality? Are they color or black/white?
* **Documentation.** Are the books well documented? Are all statements, statistics, etc., tied to sources?
* **Timely.** Are the books current? Do books in the series get updated? How often and to what extent?
* **Short.** Are the books under 200 pages? Are the chapters short/easy to photocopy?
* **Reluctant readers.** Could a nonreader use them? Is the vocabulary simple?
* **The back pages.** Do the books have addresses for more information? Up-to-date bibliographies? Lists of 800 numbers or Web sites?

collection development to buy books kids need. More now that ever, publishers are turning to series nonfiction, flooding the market with series after series. Series nonfiction presents librarians with brand names they can trust to provide good information in easy-to-use formats that meet young adult homework-assignment needs. While older students often need more in-depth material, younger teens are the perfect market for nonfiction educational series.

It is odd that we devote the most pages in review journals and give honors to the books that youths probably read the least. Many titles on those lists are "should" reads—books librarians think of as high quality that YAs should read. Others are "gonna" books; a David Eddings fan doesn't need to see his latest book on a list to want to read it. Yet, most books on those lists are "wanna" books—books that kids look for when they "wanna" read a good book. Nonfiction series represent the "hafta"; the books kids need when they have to do homework.

Reference books are a separate area. Much of the professional literature concerns books that never leave the library and, with the increased use of technology, are even used less and less. Thus, we'll talk more about reference in the section on technology, for that seems to be where many reference books are headed. While there are still some reference books we need in print, others, like *Gale's* fab *Decades* series, are moving to online subscription services. Deciding where reference dollars are spent, print vs. electronic, is a discussion that goes far beyond just the LST. But from the LST viewpoint, one of the primary ways in which we can serve more teens would be to offer services on their schedules (24/7 using technology) and not ours (reference books only available when the library is open and normally only by obtaining help for library staff). If information is empowering, then let's make sure to empower our teen users by providing them direct and easy access to reference materials through the Web.

PERIODICALS

Magazines are a great draw to your YA section; they can provide the visual flash and current pop-power that your books, no matter how new, do not provide. In recent years magazines typically aimed at adults have spun off teen versions—*Cosmo Girl*, *Elle Girl*, *Teen People,* and *Teen Vogue*. If this isn't an example of teen power what is? Media moguls clearly see the power, potential dollars, and market for these magazines. Teens read magazines and libraries should provide them. There are as many reasons why teens are drawn to magazines as there are teen magazines.

- **Current.** The only quicker information source is the Internet; magazines spot and drop trends before most book publishers.
- **Visual.** Use good pictures and lots of them.
- **Focus on special interests.** Who could resist a whole magazine devoted to your favorite thing? The library may never buy a book on your skateboarding idol, but he or she will be featured in an article in several skateboarding magazines.
- **Speed.** Teens can get a lot of information in a short amount of time, works with their busy schedules, perfect for those who can't or don't sit still–unlike books.
- **Cool factor.** No one gets laughed at for reading a magazine.
- **Availability.** Magazines are sold everywhere and are generally inexpensive.
- **Decoration potential.** They give useful tips on decorating lockers, bedrooms, and anywhere else a teen could be creative.

- **Reading level.** The variety of ways information is packaged appeals to teens on all reading levels and those who don't consider themselves readers.

If you have given a reading survey recently the results confirm that teens want, and are reading, magazines. Several reasons become immediately evident when we think about why magazines are so valuable to the library.

- **High circulation.** If you allow your magazines to circulate, they will often circulate more than any suggestion from the "Best Books for Young Adults." They will go until they drop, rip, or are mangled.

- **Word of mouth.** This benefit has two parts. First, teens that read the magazines will tell other teens who aren't reading; therefore, increase the number of readers. Second, you will get instant feedback to titles that are popular when teens come to the library and ask if the latest copy of any given title has come in yet.

- **Free posters.** These add decoration and color to the YA area; and they also make nice giveaways.

- **Marketing.** Magazines also are a great way to market your library; teens will come read them if they know you have them. Magazine displays are visual magnets; they draw teens to a central area and, while there, teens see what other materials are there for them to use.

- **Reach "nonreaders."** Most reluctant readers say that "nothing interests them" as the reason they don't read. With special interest magazines you can reach these teens as well as teens at a lower reading level.

> If a teen magazine is around and in one piece after a year, then it is not the right magazine—teen magazines and comic books should be weeding themselves with use.

There are, however, some drawbacks to magazines. The time and effort required to circulate and claim lost titles can be a hassle. They are popular so they often walk out the door, while things that get stolen can be a testament to "on target" selections, it is also an unwise way to spend your budget. Introducing a system in which someone must exchange a library card or some other form of identification for the magazine they desire to read, would decrease the amount of items stolen. Magazines fall apart. YA magazines fall apart, just like any given children's or adult's magazine. With almost everything else in the library that we select or collect, we try to keep it around and in good condition long enough to serve its purpose. With five circulations, a magazine has served its purpose; five circulations are often more than some YA fiction titles get in a year.

> Allowing magazine circulation is another step away from professional values and toward customer values.

Magazines should be used and circulated. Policies restricting magazines circulation need to be readdressed. Like card catalogs, those policies seem a relic of a different time. We didn't circulate magazines because we needed to hold them for reference and most teen magazines have no reference value. Those that do can now generally be found online via a subscription database..

The best way to select which magazines your library should collect is to involve teens. See what magazines they have access to at their schools and try not to duplicate them; this only aids your budget. Browse the grocery store and local bookstore and observe the magazines teens are buying. Chances are you might find these are the top-forty most popular titles that are used for pure recreation and information. Many of these are magazines for the adult market, but

TITLE	TOPIC	AGES	TITLE	TOPIC	AGES
1. *Animerica*	Japanese animation	14+	22. *Slam*	Sports (basketball)	12+
2. *Black Beat*	Music (rap)	12+	23. *Slap*	Sports (skateboarding)	12+
3. *Bop*	Fanzine	12–14	24. *Source*	Music (rap)	14+
4. *Computer Gaming World*	Computer games	12+	25. *Spin*	Music (general)	14+
5. *Cosmo Girl*	Girl's magazine	12+	26. *Sports Illustrated*	Sports	12+
6. *Electronic Gaming Monthly*	Computer games	12+	27. *Starlog*	Science fiction	12+
7. *Elle Girl*	Girl's magazines	12+	28. *Teen en Español*	General interest (Hispanic)	14+
8. *Entertainment Weekly*	Entertainment (general)	14+	29. *Teen Ink*	Teens' writings	12+
9. *ESPN*	Sports (general)	14+	30. *Teen People*	General interest	12+
10. *Girl's Life*	Girl's magazine	8–12	31. *Teen Vogue*	Girl's magazine	12+
11. *Glamour*	Women's magazine	14+	32. *Thrasher*	Sports (skateboarding)	14+
12. *Hot Rod*	Automobiles	14+	33. *Transworld Stance*	Sports (extreme)	12+
13. *J-14*	Fanzine	12+	34. *Urban Latino*	Latino	14+
14. *Jet*	African American	12+	35. *Vibe*	Music (rap)	14+
15. *Latina*	Latino women	14+	36. *Weekly World News*	Tabloid	14+
16. *Low Rider*	Automobiles	14+	37. *Word Up*	Music (rap)	12+
17. *Mad*	Humor	12+	38. *WWE*	Sports (pro wrestling)	12+
18. *Nickelodeon*	Humor	8–12	39. *XXL*	Music (rap)	14+
19. *Rolling Stone*	Music (general)	14+	40. *YM*	Girl's magazine	12+
20. *Seventeen*	Girl's magazine	12+			
21. *Sister to Sister*	Girls magazines (African American)	12+			

Figure 5-16. Top forty most popular magazine titles for pure recreation and information.

have huge teen appeal. While there can certainly be a debate whether a magazine like *Spin*, which has ads for smokes and booze in it, belongs in a teen area, it certainly does belong in a public library. With the curriculum focus of school libraries, the only way to justify subscriptions to most of these magazines is that they provide "reading motivation" since there is little reference value to *Seventeen*, *WWE*, or *Weekly World News*.

This list is by no means all inclusive. There are plenty of adult magazines, local zines and freebies, and even daily newspapers that teens are interested in reading. For a library that really wants to reach teens, in particular have something to show nonusers, the quickest and cheapest way isn't through programming or promotion, but rather by developing a circulating magazine collection based heavily on teen opinion.

GRAPHIC NOVELS

> More than a fad, graphic novels are a format whose time has come in a library serving young people.

To the surprise of many library patrons, teachers, administrators, and even a few disappointed young people, a "graphic" novel is not one that contains explicit content, but a book-length story published in a comic-book style. But wait. If you rolled your eyes at the thought of comics filled with "Zap!" and "Kapow!" taking up space in your school, then you are in for a pleasant surprise. In the past two decades, the comic-publishing industry has been redefined, producing award-winning, creative works that have as much literary merit as they do artistic credence. These graphic novels are filled with complex characters, well-developed story lines, literary devices like foreshadowing, imagery, and allusion, and artwork that can leave you breathless. Today's graphic novels are like a third cousin, once removed, from their distant dime-store comics kin that were widely popular in the 1950s. Today, graphic novels are being embraced by librarians around the country for their ability to pull in new audiences of readers, both those who have been reluctant to enter the library and those who are simply reluctant to read. An emerging format for a new generation of visually-literate young people, graphic novels often appeal to teens' predilection to a more visual medium, transcending apathy and the lack of "coolness" sometimes associate with reading.

So why should I include graphic novels in my library's young adult collection?

Obviously, they are popular and they will circulate. Additionally, it is important for LSTs to realize the appeal of this format. There are several possible reasons for collecting graphic novels in your library.

- Graphic novels offer fast-paced action, conflict, and heroic endeavors. This can appeal to boys who like all of these facets in entertainment, but can't seem to find them in the pages of a straight narrative.
- Visual Learners are able to connect with graphic novels in a way that they cannot with text-only books.
- Graphic novels help young readers develop strong language skills including reading comprehension and vocabulary development.
- Graphic novels often address current, relevant, and often complex social issues such as nonconformity and prejudice. They also address themes that are important to young adults including coming-of-age, social injustice, personal triumph over adversity, and personal growth.
- Graphic novels often stimulate readers to explore other genres of literature including fantasy, science fiction, historical fiction, and realistic fiction as well as nonfiction and mythology.
- Many fans of graphic novels become avid book readers.
- Graphic novels are good for the young person who reads English as a second language or who reads on a lower reading level than his or her peers because the simple sentences and visual clues allow the reader to comprehend some, if not all, of the story.

So, in addition to the most important reason, which is that a lot of teens enjoy reading comics and graphic novels, there are plenty of youth-development reasons as well.

Is the graphic novel a genre?

No. The most important thing to remember is that a graphic novel is a format, not a genre. Like audio books, DVDs, and paperbacks, the graphic novel format is an umbrella under which all genres could fall, including the traditional genres like realistic fiction, mystery, romance, western, historical fiction, science fiction, horror, and fantasy. In addition, graphic novels can also fall under a few other categories, or genres.

- **Superhero.** Typified by costumed characters with extraordinary abilities, the superhero genre is often the first genre associated with the term "comic book."

- **Nonfiction.** Like any format, the nonfiction genre of graphic novels is diverse, running the gamut from an autobiography, historical timeline, presentations of scientific theory, and poetry.
- **Graphic (or comic) journalism.** Although titles in this genre could fall under the nonfiction category, what sets them apart is that they often combine a first-person account, told in a narrative style, with images to help tell a tale. Stories that fall under this genre often have a historical significance, documenting civil unrest, war, genocide, and human nature at its best and worst.

What is manga, and is it a genre that falls under the graphic novel umbrella?

The term "manga" is Japanese for "comics," although that is a very simplified definition of a very complex format. And yes, manga is its own format. Like the term "graphic novel," "manga" is an umbrella term under which all genres such as romance, science fiction, historical fiction, and the like reside. Manga is typified by characters with large eyes, most often published in black and white, and increasingly printed in the Japanese fashion—reading right to left. A manga manuscript is usually created by one person, where one individual does both the writing and the art. In addition, manga is series-oriented; a one-volume publication is rare. Some of the critically-acclaimed series and their creators include *Astro Boy* and *Metropolis,* by Osamu Tezuka, and *Ranma 1/2* and *Inu-Yasha,* by Rumiko Takahashi.

Who are some of the more renowned authors and illustrators of graphic novels?

Like any format, there are hundreds of well-known writers who pen graphic novels. In addition, the comic publishing industry is overflowing with artists who often work as a team to complete the "illustrations" for graphic novels. Although some creators do serve as both the writer and the illustrator like *Bone,* by Jeff Smith, it is more common to see a graphic novel created by a writer/illustrator twosome like *The Murder Mysteries,* by writer Neil Gaiman and illustrator P. Craig Russell, or as a collaborative project with a writer, a penciller, an inker, a letterer, and sometimes a colorist, like *Meridian: Flying Solo,* by writer Barbara Kesel, penciled Joshua Middleton, inker Dexter Vines, and colorist Michael Atiyeh. Some of the most well-known writers and illustrators of graphic novels, beside those listed above include Jessica Abel, Brian Michael Bendis, Daniel Clowes, Mark Crilley, Will Eisner, Warren Ellis, Garth Ennis, Jaime Hernandez, Frank Millar, Tony Millionaire, Alan Moore, Terry Moore, Joe Sacco, Eric Shanower, Art Spiegelman, Osamu Tezuka, Chris Ware, and Judd Winick.

What other graphic formats might appeal to teen readers?

There is a number of formats that might be of interest to teens that fall under the graphic umbrella, including graphic nonfiction, comic books, and picture books.

- **Graphic nonfiction.** Although books that can be classified as graphic nonfiction generally fall under the umbrella term of "graphic novels" they are not novels. Graphic nonfiction covers a range of subjects with just as much diversity in content as in artistic style and intended audience, such as poetry, biographies, and historical timelines. The graphic nonfiction titles below have been selected to demonstrate this variety.
  - *Last Day in Vietnam: A Memory,* by Will Eisner
  - *The Cartoon Guide to the Environment,* by Larry Gonick and Alice Outwater
  - *Cartoon History of the Universe Volume I: From the Big Bang to Alexander the Great, Volume II: From the Springtime of China to the Fall of Rome,* and *Volume III: From the Rise of Arabia to the Renaissance,* by Larry Gonick
  - *Clan Apis,* by Jay Hosler
  - *Fax From Sarajevo: A Story of Survival,* by Joe Kubert
  - *Still I Rise: A Cartoon History of African Americans,* by Roland Owen Laird, Jr., Taneshia Nash Laird, Elihu "Adofo" Bey
  - *Barefoot Gen, Volume 1: A Cartoon Story of Hiroshima,* by Keiji Nakazawa
  - *Dignifying Science: Stories About Women Scientists,* by Jim Ottaviani.
  - *To Afghanistan and Back: A Graphic Travelogue,* by Ted Rall

- *Safe Area Gorazde: The War in Eastern Bosnia 1992-1995,* by Joe Sacco
- *The Complete Maus: A Survivor's Tale: My Father Bleeds History/Here My Troubles Began,* by Art Spiegelman
- *Pedro and Me: Friendship, Loss, and What I Learned,* by Judd Winick

- **Comic books.** Not to be confused with a book-length graphic novel, a comic book is a thirty-two page, staple bound, serialized comic that is available monthly, bimonthly, or quarterly. Comic books are considered periodicals, and can be purchased as part of a periodicals standing order. However, because most comic publishers—with the exception of DC, Marvel, and Archie—do not offer direct subscriptions for individual series, most major library subscription agents do not carry comic books. There are companies—Diamond Comic Distributors, Mile High Comics, and Midtown Comics—that specialize in providing comic book subscriptions, and most of these agents are willing to work with libraries. If you choose not to work with a subscription agent, you can always purchase issues separately at a local comic bookstore, or set up an account with this comic retailer.

- **Comics on DVD.** Due to the ephemeral nature of comic books and the negative cost/benefit differential inherent in the effort to catalog them, libraries that collect comic books generally do not circulate them, but have them available for in-library reading as part of a separate browsing collection. However, there is a new product on the market that could make comic books available for circulation—Comics on DVD. These audiovisual comics, available for approximately $10.00 per DVD, include original comic book art, enlarged word balloons, voiceovers reading the text, and accompanying musical scores. Although major comic publishers are considering this format as an option, only Marvel and CrossGen currently have comics on DVD available.

- **Picture books for teens.** Picture books, like graphic novels, are a format. Picture books differ from graphic novels in that picture book illustrations are one part of a full-page narrative, while the illustrations in graphic novels correspond directly to the text in each panel. Also, picture books are generally shorter than graphic novels but longer than comic books. The picture book format also covers a range of genres including science fiction, nonfiction, realistic fiction, mystery, horror, poetry, historical fiction, and the like. In spite of what most people in the library profession think about picture books, all books with thirty-two pages that contain pictures are not intended for young children. In fact, there are quite a few picture books that would be completely out of place mixed in with the easy readers, as their thematic content and language are intended for an older audience. The following list of picture books easily fit under the graphic umbrella, incorporating both images and text in such a way that they are both visually and intellectually appealing to teens.

- *Palindromania,* by Jon Agee
- *Life Doesn't Frighten Me,* by Maya Angelou, illustrated by Jean Michel Basquiat
- *Zoom/Re-Zoom/Minus (-) Equals (=) Plus (+),* by Istvan Banyai
- *Animalia/The Water Hole,* by Graeme Base
- *Smoky Night,* by Eve Bunting, illustrated by David Diaz
- *The Wolves in the Walls/The Day I Swapped My Dad for 2 Goldfish,* by Neil Gaiman, illustrated by Dave McKean
- *Black and White,* by David Macaulay
- *Who's Got Game? The Ant or the Grasshopper?* by Toni Morrison
- *Little Lit,* edited by Art Spiegelman
- *Jumanji/The Mysteries of Harris Burdick,* by Chris Van Allsburg
- *Sector 7/Tuesday,* by David Weisner

For much more information on graphic formats, and how to use them successfully in school and public libraries, see Michele Gorman's book *Getting Graphic! Using Graphic Novels to Promote Literacy with Preteens and Teens,* from Linworth Publishing.

AUDIOVISUAL FORMATS

Growing up in an exceedingly visual world, where multiple television sets per household are the norm and computers and the Internet are as often used for educational instruction as entertainment, it is no surprise that preteens and teens gravitate toward audiovisual materials in the library. In addition to books, library collections today generally include music, movies, audiobooks, and sometimes computer games or video games. From CDs and DVDs to videotapes and cassette tapes, library collections today are not your mama's library collection. According to a recent *Library Journal* research survey, the circulation of audiovisual materials has grown more than 32 percent in the last three years, with an average annual budget increase of 28.8 percent for movies, both video and DVD), 28.5 percent for audiobooks, both on cassette and CD, and 17.3 percent for music CDs. These numbers reflect what most of those who work in libraries know—audiovisual materials circulate, and, therefore, is it justifiable to budget for these materials in order to meet the growing requests of library patrons. Those of us who work with teens know that, like magazines, audiovisual materials are often a catalyst to get teens in the door of a library. Although some teens do have disposable income, some do not. In the public library, a teen does not need a credit card to check out a movie. All he or she needs is a library card, available free for anyone who fills out an application. This is the beauty of the public library, and this is what makes us such a valuable resource for all teens, but especially those with empty pockets.

Is it really that important to have an audiovisual section for teens at my library?

Yes. Public libraries are repositories of educational materials *and* cultural materials, in other words, a home to books *and* music *and* movies. One of the most unique things about libraries, especially for teens, is that we offer services and materials for free. In addition to books, we circulate movies and music to anyone, regardless of their age or socioeconomic class. It is not our responsibility to compete with Blockbuster or the Virgin Record Megastore. It is our place to meet the needs of our patrons—including making leisure materials such as the latest movies and the most popular music and video games available to the public—in addition to instructional and educational videos and audiobooks. Our goal is to be responsive to our customers' needs, and to do this we need to be open to the idea of collecting materials that serve both educational and recreational purposes.

Why do teens like the audiovisual formats?

For the same reason they like the Internet and television. Teens today are a visual generation, immersed in a multimedia culture that is both fast-paced and immediate. Music, movies, audiobooks, computer games, and video games are also a lot of fun, which greatly contributes to their popularity among teens. As adults, we struggle to provide teens with materials that somehow contribute to education; it can be easy for us to overlook the value of these formats in the face of such "frivolity." However, providing teens' access to movies, music, books on tape, and games is just as much a part of our job as helping young people connect with books because all of the above our sources of information. It is respecting their development needs and it is remembering our own teen years.

Why should my library indulge pop culture?

The answer to this question is philosophical: pop culture is a real-world reflection of the world in which you, and your teen patrons, reside. Pop idols today are the music icons of tomorrow, and just as you cannot imagine a well-rounded, diverse public library collection without the greatest hits of the Beatles or an Elvis CD, libraries with collections that serve teens should include the music they listen to, including rap, hip-hop, and top-forty music. Outkast today is no more or less important than Ella Fitzgerald was in her day. In the 1920s and 1930s, people thought jazz was the demoralization of human civilization. Today, adults say the same thing about punk and rap music. In the present, it can be difficult to see a body of music as culturally significant; however, history has shown that music has the ability to define a generation. Teens are participating in the development of culture as it evolves. Therefore, teens are entwined in what will become known as the defining music of a generation, in the same way Elvis and the Beatles did for the Baby Boomer generation and their parents. To not exclude hip-hop, rap, or pop music, is the same as saying we shouldn't have jazz music in our collections. It is up to us, as professional librarians, to extend our cultural cache, to acknowledge the younger generation's musical tastes, and to purchase music they want to listen to in order to acknowledge their rightful place in the library community.

What do I need to know about music for teens?

There is a lot to know, and it changes daily. With CDs, MP3s, dot-wav files, the new and now legal music downloading services, music these days is seemingly as complex as teenagers themselves. Music is as defining for young people as it has always been; it is just that N'Sync and B2K have replaced the Beatles and the Jackson Five. Music can be an escape. Music can also be a shared language for young people, providing a foundation upon which to form alliances.

While no particular genre encompasses the musical tastes of all teens everywhere, there are a few genres that are pervasive among young listeners.

Music today is as powerful as it has always been, but sometimes we, as adults, forget that just because we don't like the music, it is no less valuable as a medium.

- **Contemporary Christian.** The contemporary Christian (CC) genre of music has reappropriated the sound of popular music with Christian-themed lyrics. A diverse genre with a shared premise of Christianity, CC runs the gamut of style from pop to punk as praise and worship. Well-known artists in this category include Third Day, Point of Grace, Michael W. Smith, Jars of Clay, DC Talk, Rebecca St. James, Audio Adrenaline, and Creed.

- **New (or popular) country.** County music has always been more than a sound. For a majority of listeners, including teens, it is a way of life that often portrays a lifestyle about which people are still nostalgic—a simple, self-made, family-oriented, small-town, living-off-the-land, way of life. The use of technology is what often distinguishes the sound of old country and new country. New, or popular, country is more influenced by the evolution of preexisting instruments, the introduction of new instruments, and the influence of other genres, pop culture and musical technology. Some of the most popular artists of new (or popular) country include Faith Hill, Alan Jackson, Toby Keith, Tim McGraw, Jo Dee Messina, Rascal Flatts, LeAnn Rimes, Shania Twain, and the Dixie Chicks.

- **Americana/alternative country.** The term "Americana" is synonymous with alternative country and usually refers to music created by country bands that play traditional country but bend the rules slightly. Alternative country artists do not usually conform to Nashville's hit-making traditions, but instead work outside of the country industry's spotlight, frequently intertwining musical traditions with singer/songwriter and rock-and-roll aesthetics. The biggest difference between traditional country and this genre is the rock influence; Americana is really more of a hybrid of classic country and rock and roll. In fact, a lot of the artists in this category are often played on both country and pop/rock stations. Well-known artists in this genre include Ryan Adams, Billy Bragg, Patty Griffin, Gillian Welch, and Whiskeytown.

- **Electronica/Techno.** A uniquely American genre, electronica/techno developed in Detroit in the early 1990s and has spread worldwide in the past ten years. Considered an urban genre, the idea behind this style is very simple—it is generally music created through electronic machines such as synthesizers, turntables and samplers, not live instruments. This is a new and evolving genre that it is often hard to put one name on it; a lot of people who work with this genre refer to themselves as DJs, because they are working with turntables. The term "electronica" refers to dance music, like the Chemical Brothers, Prodigy, and Ministry of Sound, often heard in clubs and raves; however, this genre has also grown to include more ambient compositions by acts like Massive Attack, William Orbit, and John Digweed.

- **Heavy metal/punk.** Angry, rebellious, loud, and subversive, heavy metal and punk are fast paced and aggressive styles of music. Heavy metal is characterized by excessive electric guitar (with whammy bars), drums, and over the top vocalizations; repetitive chords, mumbled lyrics, and a rally call of anarchy characterize punk music. After taking a hiatus in the 1990s while Grunge became the subversive music of choice, heavy metal resurfaced in the new millennium with a more industrial sound. Older heavy metal includes the likes of Kiss, Metallica, and Motley Crüe. Older punk includes acts like the Sex Pistols and the Ramones. Newer heavy metal artists include Stained, Tool, the Def Tones, Korn, and Linkin Park; while newer punk artists include Green Day, Good Charlotte, and Blink 182.

- **Independent/alternative.** It is important to note that alternative music and independent music are not necessarily interchangeable terms. Originally, in the 1990s, alternative, or alt/rock, was a label given to music that was unlike the majority of music on the popular charts. Independent, or indie, music was music produced on a label that is not corporate—not affiliated with the five big music labels that monopolize the music industry: BMI, BMG, Universal, Sony, and Time Warner. The rise of independent and alternative music happened with the emergence of digital recording technology, which allowed people to create their own product; the rise of the Internet allowed artists to market their own product. Recently, alternative has become an umbrella term for describing new rock music.

- **Indie rock.** Independent rock is simply music created by rock groups or artists that do not conform to the mainstream trends and who publish on independent labels like Righteous Babe Records, Subpop, Kill Rockstars, and Saddle Crick. Indie rock artists the include the White Stripes, the Dandy Warhols, Bright Eyes, Slater Kinney, and Ani DiFranco.

- **Pop/rock.** Pop, or popular, music is perhaps the most widely marketed contemporary musical genre and thus appears to be the most popular, or at least the most pervasive, among the American public, especially teens. The pop/rock genre of music is constantly changing, due in large part to the short-lived nature of fads that define popular culture. Some of the leading pop/rock artists include Coldplay, Pink, Britney Spears, Justin Timberlake, Christina Aguilera, and Kid Rock.

- **Rap/hip-hop.** Rap is basically a spoken-word style of music that is dominated by percussion and often accompanied by turntables. Hip-hop is similar music with a different vocal style. Although rap started out mostly in urban areas, it quickly spread to the white suburbs due in part largely to the aggressive, hard, sexually explicit, and status-oriented lyrics. More than any other genre of music, rap addresses a social struggle. Artists in this genre include Run DMC, LL Cool J, the Sugar Hill Gang, the late Tupac Shakur, Nas, Lil' Kim, and Eminem. Gangsta/hard-core rap was an early form of this genre, sung by gangsters commenting about life in American inner cities and epitomized by artists including Dr. Dre, Snoop Dogg, and Eazy-E. Hip-hop, which is sometimes considered a descendant of disco, really emerged as a dominant form in the 1980s, and is a little less abrasive and more emotionally vulnerable than rap music. Some of the most well known hip-hop artists include TLC, Destiny's Child, Beyoncé, Bow Wow, B2K, Ashanti, Jennifer Lopez, Usher, and Mary J. Blige.

No one expects that you listen to, or even like, the music your teen customers listen to, but you should respect it, its influence, and its importance.

Confused? You should be. Recall images of your parents shaking their head over Elvis, the Beatles, the Doors, or whomever was unpopular in your house when you were growing up.

Where can I find out what music to purchase for this audience?

You do not have to listen to Top-40 music or program your car radio to the local hip-hop station to keep abreast of the music to which young people are listening. You work with your best source of information—the teens themselves. Ask them what they like, and make it a point to purchase the preferences they mention. You can also check out various Web sites dedicated to the newest, hippest stuff out there. "All Music" is a great site (www.allmusic.com), as are the online sites for the most popular cable television music channels, including MTV (www.mtv.com), VH1 (www.vh1.com), and BET (www.bet.com). You can also read the leading music magazines, like *Rolling Stone* (www.rollingstone.com), *Spin* (www.spin.com), *Billboard* (www.billboard.com), and *Blender* (www.blender.com), for ideas about what music is currently topping the charts. To find out more about the music produced by independent labels, you can read *CMJ* (*College Music Journal*) *New Music Monthly*, which comes with a CD of new, independently produced, music each month; or check out their Web site at www.cmjmusic.com. You can also visit a music store and spend some time browsing; perhaps taking your teen advisory group with you on a "field trip," so that they have an opportunity to provide direct opinions about the collection you are building for them and their friends.

What are MP3-CDs? And will this format one day replace CDs as the preferred format for music?

An MP3, short for MPEG audio layer 3, is an audio-compression format where digital files have been compressed to a very small size while still retaining their sound quality. An MP3-CD is a compact disc that holds MP3s. The wonderful thing about this format is a digital file can be shrunk to 1/10 the original size, allowing for more information to be stored on one compact disc. While it is theoretically possible for MP3-CDs to replace traditional CDs in the future as the primary format for music, it is unlikely to happen anytime soon, because developers have still not figured out how to improve the quality of music on this format so that it is comparable to CDs. However, it is highly likely that a large number of audiobooks in the near future will be sold as MP3-CDs because a voice is easier to compress than music. Therefore, an audio version of a book in this format, which allows up to forty-eight hours worth of playback per disc, is more practical and would take up less space than an audiobook on CD, which can only hold seventy to eighty minutes worth of playback per disc.

MOVIES

The teenage years are a time of identity development where young adults often struggle with themselves, their peers, and society as a whole. Movies created for a teen audience often address these struggles, both realistically and idealistically, with comedy, dark humor, sarcasm, and drama. Teen coming-of-age movies that aim to be representative of their young adult audience address things like relationships, sexual identity, body image, and popularity; and, while the movies are not real, a teen can spend two hours watching characters like them, or someone they know, deal with the same issues that they deal with in their real lives. Movies, like books, can be a great escape from reality. The difference is that majority of teens watch movies for fun and recreation. The inclusion of popular movies in a library's collection will not only make the library a "cooler" place for teens to frequent, it will make us more teen-service oriented and teen-consumer responsive, which is what really matters. In addition, there is always a chance that the presence of popular movies in the teen area will have a ripple effect on library services, whereby increased library traffic in general will increase general print circulation, computer use, and reference.

I want to include movies in my library's teen section, but I'm not sure what titles are appropriate for this age group?

The great thing about movies is that the rating system created and carried out by the Motion Picture Association of America (MPAA) takes the guesswork and subjectivity out of evaluating movies and assigning each a rating according to the age appropriateness of content. For the most part, some G, PG and PG-13 movies will be appropriate for a teen movie section in your library, depending on your community. "G" stands for general audience, and movies that have received this rating contain no adult-themed content, profanity, nudity, sex, or violence, and are considered appropriate for audience members of all ages. "PG" stands for parental guidance suggested, and movies that have received this rating may include some profanity, violence, or brief nudity. No drug use appears in a PG movie. "PG-13" stands for parents strongly cautioned, and movies with this rating may contain subject matter that is inappropriate for viewers under thirteen, including violence, nudity, sensuality, language, or other content that is more explicit than in a PG movie, but less than what a viewer might see in a movie that has received the restricted R rating.

How can I find out what current and "classic" movies are popular with teens?

Again, ask them. Ask your teen advisory board for feedback. Put a survey on your YA Web page asking teens to select their top-ten favorite

For more information about movie ratings, visit the MPAA Web site at www.mpaa.org. To search for a rating of a specific title, visit the MPAA database title at www.mpaa.org/movieratings/search/index.htm.

Check the "Teen Movies" Web site (www.teenmovies.org) for some great information specifically about teens and their movie preferences.

movies from a drop down box of fifty titles selected by your teen advisory board. Here you can read movie reviews written by teens and get movie trivia for contests, icebreakers, and the like. There is also a place for teens to vote about their favorite current movies on the big screen. For an LST, this is a great place to begin making a list of titles to purchase as soon as they are released to the video store. Also, see the list below of film favorites that are usually a hit with teens.

Austin Powers: The Spy Who Shagged Me (1999, PG-13)
Bring It On (2000, PG-13)
Charlie's Angels (2000, PG-13)
Clueless (1995, PG-13)
Daredevil (2003, PG-13)
Drumline (2000, PG-13)
Dude, Where's My Car? (2000, PG-13)
The Fast and the Furious (2001, PG-13)
Holes (2003, PG)
The Lord of the Rings: The Fellowship of the Ring (2001, PG-13)
Men in Black (1997, PG-13)
Monty Python and the Holy Grail (1974, no rating)
Pirates of the Caribbean: The Curse of the Black Pearl (2003, PG-13)
Princess Mononoke (1997, PG-13)
She's All That (1999, PG-13)
Spider-Man (2002, PG-13)
Spirited Away (2001, PG)
Star Wars, Episode 1: The Phantom Menace (1999, PG)
Uptown Girls (2003, PG-13)
X-Men (2000, PG-13)

Figure 5-17. Favorite movies of the Net generation.

Should I just purchase popular, recent movies for my teen library collection, or other videos that may appeal to this audience?

A collection of popular materials will circulate with teens. While this is important, it is also equally as important that libraries provide videos that a teen might not be able to get anywhere else, including instructional videos on teen-oriented subjects like martial arts, snowboarding, and backpacking through Europe on $40 a day, along with educational videos like those that address teen pregnancy, violence in the schools, drug addiction, and legal rights. It is not that any library can compete with a local retail store with regard to keeping the newest, hottest videos on the shelves. That's not the library's job, and we shouldn't aspire to be a movie store. We should aspire to be a well-rounded collection of educational and recreational videos for teens by including movies that they'll come in looking for, and videos that they might find interesting once they start browsing the shelves. You could even go so far as to include professional wrestling videos/DVDs as well.

Should I purchase videocassettes or DVDs?

The answer to this depends on your budget for audiovisual materials and the community in which your library resides. Similar to the shift in audio format from audiocassette to CD in the past few years, there has been a shift from VHS to DVD as well. However, the shift to DVD has been slower because most people still have a VCR in the home, in addition to a DVD Player. Due to budget constraints, most librarians do not have the option of purchasing titles in dual formats; therefore, they must select the one format that best suits the needs of the community. For example, in multilingual communities, DVDs would be most beneficial because of their multi-language capabilities, usually accommodating up to seven-language tracks. For hearing impaired patrons, most DVDs also have a closed-caption option.

Can I show movies in my library if we have them in our collection?

Well this depends on whether or not a movie purchased by your library comes with a public performance site license. This also depends on whether or not your library has purchased a blanket Public Performance Site License from an outside source. A Public Performance Site License, available from Movie Licensing USA (www.movielic.com), is a site-based license that allows a library to exhibit in a public setting movies that have been licensed for "Home Use Only." This license is not that expensive and it can be a great asset when developing programs for teens, such as a summer movie series or thematic movie festivals such as "Superheroes on the Big Screen" or "Classics You'd Rather Watch than Read."

AUDIOBOOKS

Fifteen years ago people doubted whether or not audiobooks would ever make their way off the library shelves and into the homes of listeners; now it seems that audio books are a booming business. In the past, librarians have had apprehensions of whether audiobooks would be accepted and used by teens. Those fears have largely been put to rest by librarians and teachers who have seen and written about students who have experienced major changes in attitude about audiobooks.

This format has not only changed teens' stances about reading, but about the library and how the library really does have something for everyone.

Like any other nontraditional format, audiobooks have their fair share of skeptics. However, librarians who work with teens know that sometimes it takes a nontraditional format coupled with traditional library services—meeting the needs of the patron and providing an appropriate vehicle for information—that contribute to both a positive library and literary experience for a teen. Like some adults, some teens would rather listen to a book than read it. Learning styles differ widely in people, and again, teens are not different; some readers are more visually literate and some are auditory learners. Teens are often on the go and audiobooks can be an excellent form of mobile entertainment, especially in the car or on a long bus ride to or from school.

Even still, there are many parents, teachers, and even colleagues who feel like audiobooks are not "real" books. If you are wondering if this format is a viable and legitimate method of "reading" a book, know that researchers, classroom teachers, and librarians throughout the country have seen, firsthand, the effect audiobooks can have on reluctant readers, less-proficient readers, readers of English as a second language, and even capable readers who have had limited exposure to good-reading models. Audiobooks often act as a scaffold, helping limited proficiency-readers increase both their comprehension and oration skills, while allowing struggling readers to engage in positive reading experiences.

Why should I collect audiobooks for teens?

- Young people who have had limited experience listening to English often listen to books on tape while reading along with a text to hear how punctuation is used in inflection.
- Listening to audiobooks often helps readers improve their own reading fluency, or the ability to enunciate while reading aloud without breaking a narrative by stopping mid-sentence.
- Audiobooks contribute to both vocabulary development and extension, allowing listeners to hear new words and then use context clues to assign meaning.
- Audiobooks encourage active listening and critical thinking, contributing greatly to a reader's listening-comprehension skills; skills that are much needed in the real world but rarely taught in the school.

- Audiobooks can capture a character's dialect in a way that is not possible in print, granting a student the opportunity to "read" a book as the author intended.
- Literary devices such as satire and irony often translate better orally than on the page, allowing a listener to experience the material within the context of the writer's intent.
- Classic authors such as Shakespeare and Homer created their works to be heard and not read. Audiobooks provide this authentic literary experience and allow listeners to focus more on hearing the story than on deciphering the text.
- Finally, and most importantly, an audiobook has a rightful place in the library for both educational and recreational purposes; because, just like a print book, an audiobook is capable of pulling a reader into the story and providing a literary experience.

Should I buy audiobooks on cassettes, CDs, or MP3-CDs?

Similar to the answer about films on VHS or DVD, whether you select audiobooks on cassette tape, CD, or MP3-CD will depend greatly on your annual budget for audiobooks. Some libraries will be able to purchase multiple copies of one title in all three formats to meet the various needs and format preferences of their patrons. Other libraries will have to make a decision about what format best suits the needs of their community. In addition to your budget, here are a few things to keep in mind when selecting the appropriate format for your library and teen patrons.

- Most new cars produced today come standard with a CD player, and no longer include a cassette player.
- Teens who generally listen to music on the go, listen to either portable CD players or MP3-CD players.
- Very few teens own a portable cassette player today. If your library purchases a mix of audiobooks on both CDs and MP3-CDs, both can be listened to on a computer's CD-ROM drive and on some multiple format support players.
- Although audiobooks on cassette and CD are approximately the same price, books on MP3-CDs

are generally significantly cheaper. For example, *1984* by George Orwell costs approximately $35 on tape, $40 on CD, and $15 on MP3-CD.

• Books on cassette tape take up the most storage room, followed by CDs, and then MP3-CDs. For example, Orwell's *1984* is read on seven tapes, nine CDs, and one MP3-CD. One MP3-CD can hold approximately 1,300 minutes, or 22 hours, of audio.

COMPUTER GAMES/VIDEO GAMES

Teens play video games. They play them at home, on handhelds, in cars, on buses, in restaurants, in class, at school, and yes, at the library. This is no revelation for anyone who works with teens. This is certainly no surprise for any LST who works in a library that provides Internet access. Like it or not, gaming is a large part of the "Net Generation" culture. You can either fight this by refusing to allow teens to play computer games in the library and, as a result, lose the opportunity to develop meaningful relationships with these teens, or you can accept it, embrace it, and begin working to develop a relationship with the teens that frequent your library. You can use the computer and video games as a gateway to this age demographic.

A brief history of gaming

The computer and video game industry has grown exponentially since the late 1970s, beginning with the Atari's introduction of Pong, and soon after Space Invaders, as the first home video game system. During this time some basic computer games surfaced, as either text-only games or games with limited text and very simple graphics. By the mid-1980s, personal computers—like the Commodore 64 and the Apple—infiltrated homes across America, and more advanced computer games began to rival game consoles like the Nintendo Entertainment System. By the early to mid-1990s, several gaming consoles, including the improved Nintendo 64, the Sony PlayStation, and the Sega Saturn, became more widely available because of decreased prices. Around this time computer games, or games played on a PC like Myst and Dune, were becoming more popular.

In the next decade, rapid advancements in technology and high-user demand skyrocketed the gaming industry. By the dawn of 2000, both computer games and video games were more popular than ever, with children and teenagers playing games on consoles including Sony's

PlayStation 2, Microsoft's X-Box, Sega's Dreamcast, and Nintendo's Game Cube, playing CD-ROM games on the computer, and getting more involved in playing Internet-based games that allow for players to interact via the Web. Today, gaming is a billion-dollar industry. Although the term "computer game" is often used interchangeably with the term "video game," a video game is usually played on a game console connected to a television while a computer game is a game played on a PC. Internet-based computer games are played on a PC, but they require the player to have an Internet connection.

Do video games have any educational value?

Yes. If this answer surprises you then you probably have either never played a video game or not played since the early days of video development. In the beginning, video games were very task oriented whereby kids were preoccupied with what was happening on the screen and gave little or no thought to the background story or the characters. In these early games like Atari's Frogger or Nintendo's Super Mario Brothers, there was very little text on the screen, the story had little or no plot, and the player had to fill in the back-story by reading the booklet that usually came with the game. As video games have evolved, they have become more literary. Today, the narrative is absorbed into the game through interspersed text segments as well as textual and audio dialogue between characters. Unlike older video games, today's games require players to be active participants in the story; and, something you might not have ever considered, today's advanced computer games contain major elements of literature, including plot, setting, conflict, and resolution. To draw another parallel between reading and playing a video game, character development is a driving force for gamers, allowing players to develop the same sense of character loyalty that readers often experience with their favorite book characters.

I want video games in the teen section of my library, but should the teens be able to check them out?

To circulate or not to circulate—that is the question. Like with many questions in this chapter, the answer to this one is situation specific and will depend greatly on your library policy and budget. Some libraries do not purchase any video games or computer games for circulation, but have certain computer games on CD-ROM—like Rollercoaster Tycoon or The Age of Mythology—available for patron use within the library. Some libraries have a gaming console—like PlayStation or X-Box—in house, and allow patrons to checkout video games—like Lara Croft Tomb Raider or Tony Hawk's Pro Skater—that can then be played in house only.

Some libraries circulate both computer games on CD-ROM and video games either for free or for a fee. There is no set method for circulating or not circulating this format. While there is no doubt that computer games and video games will circulate in just about any library where they are made available, the question is usually whether or not they will return. There is no standard answer for this question, but it appears that libraries that circulate this format have deemed it valuable enough to educate their patrons on the importance of returning materials and then have budgeted accordingly for lost item replacement costs.

The rating system, created and carried out by the Entertainment and Software Ratings Board (ESRB), has two parts, in which each game is assigned a rating symbol and content descriptors.

EC: Early Childhood
Game content is suitable for players three-years of age and up and contains no inappropriate material.

E: Everyone
Game content is suitable for players six-years of age and up and may contain minimal violence, slapstick humor, and/or crude language.

T: Teen
Game content is suitable for players thirteen-years of age and up and may contain some violent content, adult language, and/or suggestive themes.

M: Mature
Game content is suitable for players seventeen-years of age and up and may contain mature sexual themes, intense violence and strong language.

AO: Adults Only
Game content is suitable for adult players and may contain graphic depictions of violence and/or sex. Games that receive this rating are not intended for players under eighteen-years of age.

RP: Rating Pending
Game has been submitted to the ESRB and is awaiting a final rating.

The content descriptions provide a more in-depth detail of what each game contains. It allows the ESRB to give more information to purchasers about the expectations in a given game, including level of violence, references to drugs, tobacco, alcohol, sexual content, level of gore, realism of violence, blood, etc. For more information about content descriptors, visit the ESRB Web site: http://www.esrb.org.

WHAT ARE THE BEST SELECTION TOOLS FOR CREATING A TEEN COLLECTION?

The dilemma facing the LST is that our selection processes are driven by selection tools/review journals, while the majority of materials mentioned above are rarely reviewed. There are no library-review sources for teen magazines, popular music, DVDs, comic books, or computer games. Some of these items may have reviews, but they are not in our literature and they may be done more by consumers than professionals.

Thus, the first step in YA collection development is realizing that even our best selection tools offer but a slim selection of the materials that best belong in an active, customer-driven teen collection.

That said, there are the big "four" review journals for teen materials.

- *Booklist*. Their reviews include YA notes at the bottom of titles that have teen appeal for educational and pleasure reading. The real plus in *Booklist,* aside from lots of subject lists, is that YAs are not the primary interest. Instead, by reviewing primarily for the public-library market, this provides the LST, especially those working in high schools, with the best information about new adult books with teen appeal. *Booklist* also does the best job of reviewing reference books, and as an ALA journal, is normally the first print journal to publish the various YALSA lists.

- *KLIATT.* Publishes reviews of paperback books, hard-cover adolescent-fiction, audiobooks, and educational software recommended for libraries and classrooms serving YAs—published bimonthly. *Kliatt,* which only used to cover paperbacks and audio books, is very electronic in its choice of what to review, but seems very strong in materials which support formal education support.

- *School Library Journal.* In addition to the regular reviews, the Nonfiction Booktalker and Graphic Novel Roundup are two *SLJ* sections of interest to LSTs. Of all the big four, it has the best Web site with the most giveaway content. Under new editors entering the twenty-first century, the journal seems to be getting back more to its roots and focusing on all schools, not just secondary schools, which is of interest to LSTs. Of great interest, however, are the sections on technology, in particular articles and columns by Walter Minkel.

- *VOYA. Voice of Youth Advocates* is a great source for fiction, nonfiction, and graphic novels; they also do genre lists throughout the year that are invaluable because most of their reviewers are practicing teen librarians, and increasingly there are more teen reviews. *VOYA* does the best job of reviewing science fiction and fantasy, small press and Christian publishers, and professional materials. Through regular columns, it provides fantastic information on graphic novels, teen series, as well as a "best list" in each of its six issues. Trying to serve teens without subscribing to *VOYA* is like trying to build a house without a hammer. It can be done, but it is not going to be easy, or pretty.

In addition to these four, there are two journals from the education community that LSTs with a focus on literature and/or working with teachers need to know.

- *ALAN Review.* The Assembly on Literature for Adolescents publishes the *ALAN Review* three times each year (fall, winter, and spring) with a current circulation of 2,500. The journal contains articles on YA literature and the teaching of YA literature, interviews with authors, reports on publishing trends, current research on YA literature, a section of reviews of new books, and ALAN membership news. The review section is on "clip and file" index cards, but the reviews are often much more in-depth than those found in library journals. Many of the journal are articles from academics about arcane topics in YA literature, but there are enough practical articles to satisfy most LSTs.

- *Voices from the Middle.* ALAN is a division of NCTE, as are those who comprise *Voices from the Middle,* which focuses, as the title implies, on literature for the middle grades. While there are articles regarding teaching young adult literature, there are also reviews, columns, and lists.

One of the best places to learn about new teen fiction is the YALSA-BK LISTSERV where librarians, and often authors, review, discuss, and debate books, and the issues surrounding them. For graphic novels, the GN-LIB is the best LISTSERV with a library focus.

The purpose of all of these journals is to review materials objectively for librarians and teachers. Jobber catalogs are designed to hype, and they are just as important as journals that review. While there are numerous book jobbers out there, Book Wholesalers, Inc. (BWI) is one the of the best for teen materials and graphic novels. That's also a disadvantage since BWI neither carries information on adult fiction and nonfiction with teen appeal, nor do they focus on homework support. Which jobber you use, however, depends upon your library's contracts. While you probably can't make that decision, you should, and can, advocate for the jobbers which do concern themselves with teen materials.

The problem with all of these tools, however, is they are all from the view of adults; although VOYA does have some teen reviewers. In addition to whatever vehicles you've chosen to add teen involvement into the collection mix, there is always Amazon. While the professional reviewers in the teen section are among the best in the field, it is the authentic teen reaction, rants, and reviews of titles that LSTs need to read on a regular basis. Amazon is probably the only free source to get bibliographic information on certain types of materials, such as books with game codes. Don't bookmark the teen page; you should make it your start page on your browser.

The purpose of any collection is to fulfill the wants and needs of a particular library's users. While every library may have different protocol for this mission, the customer is the bottom line. The challenge of serving YAs, of course, is that those wants and needs are innumerable, varied, and changing. Developing any collection for YAs is trying to hit a moving target. A teen collection can't be all classics, nor can it be all paperback collections. Can a book be great if no one reads it? Can a book be great if no one wants to read it again because they forget it five minutes after finishing it? If there is a common theme that runs through our ideas on collection development, it is about selecting that which helps teens do their job. These are books that evoke emotional responses among teen readers through the year—core needs create a core collection.

HOW DO I MAINTAIN MY YA COLLECTION?

- **Weed.** It is safe to say that even libraries with separate YA collections do not have the luxury of space. Constant weeding is necessary, but not only for space considerations. First, if a teen is browsing the nonfiction area in the 780s and happens upon an M.C. Hammer biography or a book about the Backstreet Boys, that sends a pretty clear message about your collection. Second, weeding is one of the best ways to increase circulation. For example, by doing a big weed in your hardback area you have now freed up space to display at the end of the bookcases and YAs get the chance to see the book covers. Third, if possible, consider temporary weeding. That is, prune down the collection to a couple copies of core titles and series and store the rest until you need them in the summer. If not, then either you are forced to have an area overflowing and overstuffed with titles or you weed them; these are not books you don't want, they are simply ones you don't have room for. Sure, storage is a problem, but find a box or two and an area in the basement or on top of a cabinet.

- **Buy the Printz winners and the honor books.** While these books are not always the most popular, LSTs should support this award. These books also support the readers who want to be challenged.

- **Consider all of the books which are selected for Best Books and Quick Picks.** Buy those which make both of these lists. For small libraries, these lists are both way too long, but for the past few years a "top ten" list of titles which received the most votes has been compiled.

- **Consider all the books reviewed in *VOYA*.** Focus your attention on those that received a four or a five in either popularity or quality; buy those which are perfect tens. Each year *VOYA* puts together this list of perfect tens which represent the best of the best.

- **Buy any book which is listed as the year's best teen seller on Amazon.** In many cases these may not always be a piece of YA literature. Also consider those books which are listed as the year's best by Amazon's editors.

- **Consider any book listed in the various *VOYA* "best lists."** Also consider the other YALSA lists like the Alex Awards or popular paperbacks; *buy* those by authors or subjects with a strong track record.

- **Look at circulation reports.** Buy another copy of anything that is getting heavy, heavy use, and look at lost-books reports. Buy and replace core titles often.

- **Look at YALSA-BK.** Follow the discussions of titles, and learn which titles librarians who post are praising.

- **Look closely at the monthly catalogs of vendors.** Consider Book Wholesalers to find the paperback reprint edition of titles that are, as of this writing, only available in hardback

- **Ask teens continuously about their preferences.** Survey, open up your Web page to teen reviews, do book discussion groups, conduct exit interviews, conduct an annual favorite book poll, and listen. Ask teens the question—what they are reading—and then *buy* the answer.

COLLECTION DEVELOPMENT CONCERNS

According to Judy Druse from Washburn University, primary reasons some teens prefer adult books are:

- The plots are more complex and dramatize adult conflicts, issues, and themes.

- Many adult books feature young adult characters and address the developmental tasks of adolescents going to college, entering the job market, or working through the first year of marriage.

- The adult books have been spotlighted by the media or recommended by popular media personalities.

- The peer network has recommended a title and/or friends in college have mentioned them.

- In science fiction, fantasy, and horror genres, few books are published as YA novels.

- YAs are interested in nonfiction biographies, autobiographies, celebrity books, true stories of people living lives of action, adventure, and unusual human experiences.

- YAs want nonfiction that digs more deeply into subjects of interest than YA books do.

- Some favorite young adult authors also write books for the adult market.

If building an active YA collection were not challenge enough, librarians also face a series of special concerns. Some of these are large societal problems, while others are specific to libraries. Later in Chapter 12, we will address many of these concerns, but let's examine four key issues—reaching rampant readers, reaching reluctant readers, reaching incarcerated readers, and reaching readers who only want the best—that consistently arise doing teen collection-development work.

REACHING RAMPANT READERS

The seventh graders who were initially excited by teen romance series, might be coming to you by eighth grade for more serious romances. Eventually by tenth or eleventh grade the materials in the YA section will no longer be of interest to these rampant readers. Finding materials for this group is often difficult because, although their reading tastes, interest, and abilities have matured, many of the adult books might be developmentally inappropriate. If we are to serve these readers, let's first understand why they might prefer Charles Dickens or Eric Jerome Dickey to Lois Duncan.

Teens also like books for three simple reasons: sex, drugs, and violence. It is naïve to assume that a sixteen-year-old hasn't seen one R-rated movie in their lives, and even the "edgiest" of teen novels are still purely PG-13. While most of the review journals do a good job of informing LSTs about new adult books for teens, it is the Alex awards from YALSA where they get beyond the bestsellers and find adult books with unique teen appeal.

REACHING RELUCTANT READERS

This is normally a boy who wants the book on tape if possible, or if not available, then wants a "thin one." If we are going to understand how to "turn" reluctant readers into willing ones, let's understand first the obstacles.

- **Association with failure.** Does anyone like to do something they are not good at? Of course not, and that is perhaps the most important thing to understand about reluctant readers. For numerous reasons, many of which have been well documented in the recent research, plenty of teens don't have good reading skills. By making them read books in school that they can't read, we are setting them up for failure. For teens who are literate, but not in English, this is just as much an obstacle. Many libraries report great success with audio books with new English language learners.

• **Lack of time and energy.** For boys, it might be the opposite; they have too much energy to sit still long enough to read. This is a factor facing most teen readers; their schedules and secreting hormones don't always allow time or focus for reading. If these are obstacles, then nonfiction, graphic novels, and magazines are all formats which certainly knock down those walls.

• **Negative peer pressure.** A teenage boy "caught" with a big, fat novel in some peer circle is made fun of by others, but the same boy caught with a music magazine, a book of Tupac's poetry, or a Jackie Collins novel will not be heckled. The latter boy is asked to share. The issue is more that developmental, teens will reject certain books merely because adults want them to read them.

• **Not stimulated by ideas.** Novels are about many things, but most deal with themes that require some thought and reflection. Disregarding whether we like or dislike a book, and accepting that it is a piece of literature that the teen might like is a viewpoint we should take when working with reluctant readers. Books that produce responses from teens might be best, especially in this culture that is both media heavy and saturated with computer games.

• **No history of reading or reading encouragement at home.** Many nonreading teens come from homes of nonreaders. Sometimes, for the same reason outlined here, or sometimes because parents are too busy working two jobs to dive into a good book. Again, this is the opposite of the upbringing and daily lives of many LSTs. A number of us learned the value of books and reading from our parents; it is assumed and understood. It is part of our culture; but in many homes, for many reasons, books are an alien form.

• **Can't find the good books to read.** Dr. Kylee Beers, one of the primary people looking at alliterate teens—those who can read, but choose not to—tells a great

Reluctant readers sometimes just want the action; this was the great success of *Goosebumps* years ago. The characters in these novels didn't have time to learn and grow, Stine says; they were too busy running for their lives.

story about middle-school teens visiting a school library. All the kids, except a few boys of course, took books every week. When she asked the boys why they didn't pick a title from all the good books available, one said, "But which are the good ones?" While for a reader, a library full of books is a paradise; for a non-reader, a library full of books is a minefield. Dr. Beers proposes the "good book box," where LSTs could help teens narrow their choices. Some LSTs take the same notion with displays called "teen picks." Nonreaders need guidance in finding a book that won't turn out to be for them, yet another bad experience.

• **Not a priority.** Admit it. In high school, once you got a car, how much reading did you do? If you played sports, how many novels did you knock off during the season? You went to school all day, participated in an after school activity, and then went to work at McDonalds for another five hours. Do you think you would still have the energy—and reading does take energy—to knock off a novel? Now, add to that the choices available to today's teens; it is not just deciding to read or watch one of three network channels, but making a decision between reading a book and hundreds of cable channels, piles of video games, and the time-sucking hole that is the Internet.

• **Reluctant readers are not stupid.** They are kids who do not choose to read. Treating them like dummies is just as counterproductive as pushing Jane Austen down their throats. Because they are reluctant to read, they will need encouragement from adults, in addition to materials that encourage them. Not pushing, but real encouragement matched with materials that will help make reading a positive experience.

Reluctant-reader titles take many shapes and sizes. Books like Walter Dean Myers' 300-page *Fallen Angels* have appeared on the Quick Picks list, but so have wordless picture books. In general, fiction books for reluctant readers will do the following:

• Have a hook to get the reader's attention immediately;
• Move at a fast pace with only a few characters;
• Have a single point of view and few flashbacks or subplots;

- Deal with real-life situations and high interest topics;
- Have an emotional impact and are gripping and memorable;
- Use short sentences and paragraphs and nonchallenging vocabulary;
- Have attractive covers, wide margins, and easy-to-read type face; and
- Weigh in at less than 200 pages.

Nonfiction will meet many of this criteria, but also will do the following:

- Contain diverse illustrations to complement the text;
- Adopt of magazine-style layout approach; and
- Contain first person narrative and real-life experience.

One powerful tool has been YALSA's Quick Picks committee. The evolution of the committee has been interesting. It started as the "Hi Lo" committee; meaning high interest, low vocabulary group who found the Fry reading level for each book and listed titles for librarians to use with nonreaders. In the 1980s the committee changed its name to the Recommended Books for the Reluctant YA Reader committee and further evolved placing more emphasis on the high-interest aspect and less on low vocabulary. In the 1990s the committee changed names once again to the Quick Picks committee, thereby reflecting a change in the committee's intended reading audience. Its annotated list targeted YAs. YAs then got involved in the selection process, and the committee had moved away from looking at the number of words in a paragraph to looking at titles that would hook reluctant readers.

Librarians, of course, are not on the real front line in this area—reading and English teachers deal daily with such students. The professional literature in education overflows with articles about methods of instruction, motivation, and encouragement. For librarians, reaching the reluctant reader takes rethinking some attitudes and developing methods to reach this audience. The escalator theory states that the only real reading is book reading. This theory falls in line with our mission, and even a thin book is acceptable for a reluctant reader.

REACHING INCARCERATED READERS

In a recent survey conducted by the Young Adult Library Services Association and the SmartGirl Web site (www.SmartGirl.org) about teens and reading, the majority of survey respondents (72%) reported that they like to read for pleasure when they have time. One might

Teens in the correctional systems have much time to read. This group of teens provides libraries with unique opportunities to do outreach.

therefore conclude that not having enough time is a major obstacle to teens reading heavily. The hectic schedule of teen life coupled with the plethora of recreational choices often leaves little time for reading. But there is one group of teens who have a very rigid schedule and few choices—teens in correctional facilities.

But while teens in corrections have time for reading, many of them lack skills. Speaking at the 2003 American Library Association conference, Vibeke Lehmann, the Library Services Coordinator for the Wisconsin Department of Corrections, noted that 40 percent of prison inmates in the United States are illiterate. The cycle is easy to see and hard to stop. People who end up in prison often became engaged in illegal acts as teens. While there are hundreds of reasons, it is clear that many became engaged in crime because they were not engaged in school. Again, a hundred reasons, but many don't engage in school because they don't do well. They don't do well because they can't read well. They can't read well because they never learned, didn't have positive early literacy experiences, were not raised in print-rich environments, and never learned the value in reading for educational reasons, let alone as a recreational activity.

Yet, teens in corrections do value recreational reading. If they have access to reading materials that meet their interests and are on their reading level, they will read them. Meeting those interests is not as easy it sounds. While there are clear guidelines for library services for youth in corrections that embrace intellectual freedom, there is the reality of working with the correctional system. Any person in a correctional facility is deprived of certain liberties. So, a teen in corrections finds the facility acting "in loco parentis" and determining which materials are appropriate to be read.

Naomi Angier, Juvenile Justice Outreach Librarian at the Multnomah Library in Portland (OR) spoke about this issue at ALA as well, noting that censorship is a big problem when working with juvenile detention centers. In her work, she set up a review committee with the detention center staff, pulled the most controversial materials— street life novels by Donald Goines and Iceberg Slim—out of the collection, and has instituted an age policy. By doing so, she has build up trust with the correctional staff and the review committee only meets now if they have a specific book to discuss.

The Multnomah County example is instructive. In order to provide all teen inmates with access to a wide variety of materials, the library had to prevent access to a few very specific materials for some residents. It is a compromise, but then most partnerships which libraries undertake require accommodations to the rules and culture of the partner. Multnomah County's approach is rare, as few other libraries serving correctional facilities have formal policies or procedures in place to

Twenty of the most popular books or subjects with teens in corrections are:

1. *Always Running,* by Luis Rodriguez
2. *Angry Blond,* by Eminem
3. *Autobiography of Malcolm X,* by Malcolm X and Alex Haley
4. *Babylon Boyz,* by Jess Mowry
5. Books on calligraphy or origami
6. *Boondocks,* comics by Aaron McGruder
7. *Coldest Winter Ever,* by Sister Souljah
8. *Fallen Angels,* by Walter Dean Myers
9. *Flyy Girl,* by Omar Tyree
10. *Imani All Mine,* by Connie Porter
11. *Monster,* by Walter Dean Myers
12. *No Disrespect,* by Sister Souljah
13. Novels by African-American Authors Eric Jerome Dickey or E. Lynn Harris
14. Novels by Jackie Collins, Sidney Sheldon, Stephen King, and Dean Koontz
15. *Push,* by Sapphire
16. *Rose that Grew from Concrete,* by Tupac Shakur (poetry)
17. *Simpsons,* comics by Matt Groening
18. *Spawn, Blade, Akira,* and *X-Men* graphic novels
19. *Tupac Shakur,* by Vibe Magazine
20. *Who Will Cry for the Little Boy,* by Antwone Fisher

provide library and corrections staff with a forum to solve issues related to materials.

If libraries want to partner with correctional facilities, then they must agree to support the goals and objectives of that institution.

Despite those limitations, reading and reading promotion can thrive within juvenile correctional institutions. In addition to supplying books and magazines, many libraries promote reading in correctional settings using similar techniques as they would in a school setting, such as:

- Booktalking,
- Book discussion group,
- Book review programs,
- Creative writing workshops,
- Guidance programs,
- Poetry slams,
- Read Alouds,
- Readers Theater, and
- Storytelling.

In addition, many teens in corrections are parents, and libraries should be assertive about early literacy programs, such as Born to Read, which teach these young parents about the importance of reading to their children.

Despite obstacles that are inherent to working in the correctional setting, there are plenty of books that teens will find of interest. Reading levels vary widely, as do interests.

Our top-twenty list (to the left) contains by no means the only books of interest to young men and women in the correctional system, but they do represent a selection of the most popular. Interestingly, there are few young adult problem novels, perhaps because the problems faced by fictional protagonists often pale in comparison to the hard real lives of teen offenders.

When working with teens in corrections, libraries have ample opportunities to demonstrate the value of reading. But to what end? What is our real motive? The core work of librarians isn't about books, but about building assets in young people. Reading for pleasure is one of the forty assets that kids need to succeed. While incarcerated, librarians want teens such as the one quoted below, to discover that:

> "Never knew reading could be so fun. When I was out, I never did read a book. But now that you showed me how fun it can be, I'm going to read every book I can, not just 'cause of you. But because I really like reading and like to learn new things. Things I never knew."

REACHING THE READERS WHO ONLY WANT THE BEST

The Printz is meant to be like a teen Newbery award designed to honor the best book regardless of popularity or accessibility.

The Michael L. Printz award is an award for a book that exemplifies literary excellence in young adult literature. The award is new and was not introduced without some controversy. Should there even be such an award? What constitutes excellence; and for that matter, what constitutes young adult literature? To help answer these questions, the YALSA committee, which established the award, developed criteria for eligibility and selection. The book must have been designated by its publisher as being either a young adult book or one published for the age range that YALSA defines as young adult—12 through 18. Thus, adult books are not eligible. The book can be fiction, nonfiction, poetry, or an anthology. Books published previously in another country are eligible. There is really only one criterion for selection—literary quality.

While any book award is bound to have those from the field that disagree with which title wins, the Printz Award committees have done a pretty good job so far selecting the best works from among the hundreds of books that come before them. So far, the winners and honor books are:

2003 Winner	Chambers, Aiden	*Postcards from the Edge*
2003 Honor	Farmer, Nancy	*The House of the Scorpion*
2003 Honor	Gantos, Jack	*Hole in My Life*
2003 Honor	Freymann-Weyr, Garret	*My Heartbeat*
2002 Winner	Na, Ha	*A Step from Heaven*
2002 Honor	Dickinson, Peter	*The Ropemaker*
2002 Honor	Lynch, Chris	*Free Will*
2002 Honor	Wolff, Virginia Euwer	*True Believer*
2002 Honor	Greenberg, Jan	*Heart to Heart: New Poems Inspired by Twentieth-Century American Art*
2001 Winner	Almond, David	*Kit's Wilderness*
2001 Honor	Coman, Carolyn	*Many Stones*
2001 Honor	Plum-Ucci, Carol	*Body of Christopher Creed*
2001 Honor	Rennison, Louise	*Angus, Thongs, and Full Frontal Snogging*
2001 Honor	Trueman, Terry	*Stuck in Neutral*
2000 Winner	Myers, Walter Dean	*Monster*
2000 Honor	Almond, David	*Skellig*
2000 Honor	Anderson, Laurie Halse	*Speak*
2000 Honor	Wittlinger, Ellen	*Hard Love*

Figure 5-18. Winners and honors of the Printz Award.

This is a fine list of books, but also a short one. It represents only the best of the best since the year 2000, but young adult literature has been around since the mid-1960s. While those who are concerned with young adult literature eagerly each year await the answer to the question of which book would win the Printz Award, yet another question lingered: "What if?" What if there had been a Printz award five or ten or even twenty years ago, then what book would have been named the winner?

It is a question that we asked for help in answering. In February 2001, we e-mailed a ballot to 125 people with knowledge of young adult literature. We (and YA librarian Sarah Cornish) asked each person to select for each year their pick of what book would have won the Printz Award since 1978. We started with the first year of VOYA and went up through the last year before the Printz award was developed. It was easy for the 1996-1999 BBYA list years as we used the top-ten BBYA lists. For the years before the 1996 list, we selected ten titles from the BBYA list. We used BBYA as our foundation, working under the assumption that the Printz book for every year would, or should, be a BBYA. In 2002, one of the Printz books was not a BBYA book, but we believe that the BBYA list is so comprehensive, and involves both a committee and teen input, that it is highly unlikely that the best YA book of the year would go unrecognized by BBYA. Also, not using the BBYA would have also been a logistical nightmare. We looked at several factors such as reputation of the book and author over time, other awards the book has won, the impact of the book on how people read, wrote, and/or reviewed YA literature, and the placement of the book on the various rankings produced by YALSA.

Below is the ballot; the book which received the most votes and won the Retro Mock Printz is in all caps. While this is not a YA literature text book, this is a nice initial reading list for teens and LSTs who want only the best of the best.

CONCLUSION

So, are these titles of the best books for teens? Earlier we wrote about the importance of collecting materials that address the basic needs of YAs, whereby core needs create a core collection. A collection full of fiction, nonfiction, magazines, video games, DVDs, and music that explores or celebrates an adolescent's journey, while at the same time addressing the issues of independence, excitement, identity, and acceptance, will be both accepted by teen library users and promoted by teens to their peers. Good collection development is not only about allocating our resources, but also about giving teens a plethora of good reasons to allocate their most valuable resource—time—to a school or public library.

	TITLE	AUTHOR LAST	AUTHOR FIRST
1999	*Rules of the Road*	Bauer	Joan
1999	*Corpses, Coffins, and Crypts*	Coleman	Penny
1999	*Love Among the Walnuts*	Ferris	Jean
1999	*Whirligig*	Fleischman	Paul
1999	*My Louisiana Sky*	Holt	Kimberly Willis
1999	*No Pretty Pictures: a Child of War*	Lobel	Anita
1999	*Soldier's Heart*	Paulsen	Gary
1999	*Harry Potter and the Sorcerer's Stone*	Rowling	J.K.
1999	*HOLES*	SACHER	LOUIS
1999	*If You Come Softly*	Woodson	Jacqueline
1998	*Growing Up in Coal Country*	Bartoletti	Susan
1998	*Seamstress*	Bernstein	Sara
1998	*TANGERINE*	BLOOR	EDWARD
1998	*Tenderness*	Cormier	Robert
1998	*Out of the Dust*	Hesse	Karen
1998	*Blood and Chocolate*	Klause	Annette Curtis
1998	*Ella Enchanted*	Levine	Gail Carson
1998	*When She Was Good*	Mazer	Norma Fox
1998	*Swallowing Stones*	McDonald	Joyce
1998	*Subtle Knife*	Pullman	Philip
1997	*A Girl Named Disaster*	Farmer	Nancy
1997	*Who Killed Mr. Chippendale?*	Glenn	Mel
1997	*Far North*	Hobbs	Will
1997	*Rebels Against Slavery*	McKissack	Patricia
1997	*One More River to Cross*	Myers	Walter Dean
1997	*Slam*	Myers	Walter Dean
1997	*Sabriel*	Nix	Garth
1997	*Golden Compass*	Pullman	Philip
1997	*RATS SAW GOD*	THOMAS	ROB
1997	*Wrestling Strubridge*	Wallace	Rick
1996	*We Are Witnesses*	Boas	Jacob
1996	*In the Middle of the Night*	Cormier	Robert
1996	*IRONMAN*	CRUTCHER	CHRIS
1996	*Watsons Go to Birmingham*	Curtis	Christopher Paul
1996	*The Midwife's Apprentice*	Cushman	Karen
1996	*Othello*	Lester	Julius
1996	*Tomorrow When the War Began*	Marsden	John
1996	*The War of Jenkins' Ear*	Morpurgo	Michael
1996	*An Island Like You*	Ortis Cofer	Judith

Figure 5-19. Results from Retro Mock Printz ballot (Winners are in all caps.)

	TITLE	AUTHOR LAST	AUTHOR FIRST
1996	*Like Sisters on the Homefront*	Williams-Garcia	Rita
1995	*Am I Blue*	Bauer	Marion
1995	*Driver's Ed*	Cooney	Caroline
1995	*CATHERINE CALLED BIRDY*	CUSHMAN	KAREN
1995	*The Ear, the Eye, and the Arm*	Farmer	Nancy
1995	*Kids at Work*	Freedman	Russell
1995	*Deliver Us From Evie*	Kerr	M.E.
1995	*Spite Fences*	Krisher	Trudy
1995	*Earthshine*	Nelson	Theresa
1995	*The Ramsay Scallop*	Temple	Frances
1995	*I Hadn't Meant to Tell You This*	Woodson	Jacqueline
1994	*Crazy Lady*	Conley	Jane
1994	*Staying Fat for Sarah Brynes*	Crutcher	Chris
1994	*Bull Run*	Fleischman	Paul
1994	*Eleanor Roosevelt*	Freedman	Russell
1994	*Uncle Vampire*	Grant	Cynthia
1994	*Toning the Sweep*	Johnson	Angela
1994	*THE GIVER*	LOWRY	LOIS
1994	*Harris and Me*	Paulsen	Gary
1994	*Freak the Mighty*	Philbrick	Rodman
1994	*Make Lemonade*	Wolff	Virginia Euwer
1993	*Blue Heron*	Avi	
1993	*Ajeemah and His Son*	Berry	James
1993	*Tunes for Bears to Dance To*	Cormier	Robert
1993	*IF ROCK AND ROLL WERE A MACHINE*	DAVIS	TERRY
1993	*Sojourner Truth*	McKissack	Patrica
1993	*Where the Broken Heart Still Beats*	Meyer	Carolyn
1993	*Somewhere in the Darkness*	Myers	Walter Dean
1993	*Missing May*	Rylant	Cynthia
1993	*Briar Rose*	Yolen	Jane
1993	*Pigman and Me*	Zindel	Paul
1992	*Nothing But the Truth*	Avi	
1992	*WE ALL FALL DOWN*	CORMIER	ROBERT
1992	*Athletic Shorts*	Crutcher	Chris
1992	*Wright Brothers*	Freedman	Russell
1992	*Girl with the White Flag*	Higa	Tomika
1992	*Downriver*	Hobbs	Will
1992	*Man from the Other Side*	Orlev	Uri

Figure 5-19. Continued

	TITLE	AUTHOR LAST	AUTHOR FIRST
1992	*Lyddie*	Patterson	Katherine
1992	*Wolf By the Ears*	Rinaldi	Ann
1992	*Mozart Season*	Wolff	Virginia Euwer
1991	*True Confessions of Charlotte Doyle*	Avi	
1991	*Beyond the Myth*	Brooks	Polly
1991	*Across the Grain*	Ferris	Jean
1991	*Franklin Delano Roosevelt*	Freedman	Russell
1991	*THE SILVER KISS*	KLAUSE	ANNETTE CURTIS
1991	*Woodsong*	Paulsen	Gary
1991	*Tiger in the Well*	Pullman	Philip
1991	*Maniac Magee*	Spinelli	Jerry
1991	*On Fortune's Wheel*	Voigt	Cynthia
1991	*Dealing with Dragons*	Wrede	Patricia
1990	*WEETZIE BAT*	BLOCK	FRANCESCA
1990	*Up Country*	Carter	Alden
1990	*Celine*	Cole	Brooks
1990	*Chinese Handcuffs*	Crutcher	Chris
1990	*On the Devil's Court*	Deuker	Carl
1990	*Eva*	Dickinson	Peter
1990	*Phoenix Rising*	Grant	Cynthia
1990	*Wrestling with Honor*	Klass	David
1990	*So Much to Tell You*	Marsden	John
1990	*Shabanu: Daughter of the Wind*	Staples	Suzanne
1989	No list due to change in naming lists		
1988	*Girl from Yamhill: A Memoir*	Cleary	Beverly
1988	*Fade*	Cormer	Robert
1988	*Lincoln*	Freedman	Russell
1988	*American Sports Poem*	Knudson	R.R.
1988	*Arizona Kid*	Koertge	Ron
1988	*Memory*	Mahy	Margaret
1988	*Silver*	Mazer	Norma Fox
1988	*Outlaws of Sherwood*	McKinley	Robin
1988	*FALLEN ANGELS*	MYERS	WALTER DEAN
1988	*Scorpions*	Myers	Walter Dean
1987	*Permanent Connections*	Bridges	Sue Ellen
1987	*Shelia's Dying*	Carter	Alden
1987	*GOATS*	COLE	BROCK

Figure 5-19. Continued

	TITLE	AUTHOR LAST	AUTHOR FIRST
1987	*Crazy Horse Electric Game*	Crutcher	Chris
1987	*Redwall*	Jacques	Brian
1987	*Fell*	Kerr	M.E.
1987	*After the Rain*	Mazer	Norma Fox
1987	*The Year Without Michael*	Pfeffer	Susan Beth
1987	*The Ruby in the Smoke*	Pullman	Philip
1987	*Nell's Quilt*	Terris	Susan
1986	*Midnight Hour Encores*	Brooks	Bruce
1986	*Stotan*	Crutcher	Chris
1986	*Necessary Parties*	Dana	Barbara
1986	*Howl's Moving Castle*	Jones	Diane Wynne
1986	*Night Kites*	Kerr	M.E.
1986	*Catalog of the Universe*	Mahy	Margaret
1986	*The Keeper*	Naylor	Phyllis Reynolds
1986	*After the Dancing Days*	Rostkowski	Margaret
1986	*Fine White Dust*	Rylant	Cynthia
1986	*IZZY, WILLY-NILLY*	VOIGT	CYNTHIA
1985	*MOVES MAKE THE MAN*	BROOKS	BRUCE
1985	*Prairie Songs*	Conrad	Pam
1985	*Pocket Poems*	Janeczko	Paul
1985	*I Stay Near You*	Kerr	M.E.
1985	*Hero and the Crown*	McKinley	Robin
1985	*In Summer Light*	Oneal	Zibby
1985	*Remembering the Good Times*	Peck	Richard
1985	*Woman Who Loved Reindeer*	Pierce	Meredith Anne
1985	*Dead Birds Singing*	Talbert	Marc
1985	*Runner*	Voigt	Cynthia
1984	*Beggar Queen*	Alexander	Lloyd
1984	*Place to Come Back To*	Bond	Nancy
1984	*One-Eyed Cat*	Fox	Paula
1984	*Sixteen*	Gallo	Don
1984	*Prank*	Lasky	Kathryn
1984	*Changeover*	Mahy	Margaret
1984	*Tracker*	Paulsen	Gary
1984	*INTERSTELLAR PIG*	SLEATOR	WILLIAM
1984	*Center Line*	Sweeney	Joyce
1984	*Heart's Blood*	Yolen	Jane
1983	*Dance on My Grave*	Chambers	Aiden

Figure 5-19. Continued

	TITLE	AUTHOR LAST	AUTHOR FIRST
1983	*Bumblebee Flies Anyway*	Cormier	Robert
1983	*RUNNING LOOSE*	CRUTCHER	CHRIS
1983	*Voyage*	Geras	Adele
1983	*Red as Blood*	Lee	Tanith
1983	*What's Happening to My Body Book Girls*	Madaras	Lynda
1983	*I Will Call it Georgie's Blues*	Newton	Suzanne
1983	*Earth's Seed*	Sargent	Pamela
1983	*Solitary Blue*	Voigt	Cynthia
1983	*Bigger Book of Lydia*	Willey	Margaret
1982	*ANNIE ON MY MIND*	GARDEN	NANCY
1982	*Class Dismissed*	Glenn	Mel
1982	*Sweet Whispers Brother Rush*	Hamilton	Virginia
1982	*This Strange New Feeling*	Lester	Julius
1982	*Good Night, Mr. Tom*	Magorian	Michelle
1982	*Blue Sword*	McKinley	Robin
1982	*The Darkangel*	Pierce	Meredith Anne
1982	*Marked by Fire*	Thomas	Joyce Carol
1982	*Homecoming*	Voigt	Cynthia
1982	*Dragon's Blood*	Yolen	Jane
1981	*Westmark*	Alexander	Lloyd
1981	*Changing Bodies, Changing Lives*	Bell	Ruth
1981	*Tiger Eyes*	Blume	Judy
1981	*Notes from Another Life*	Bridgers	Sue Ellen
1981	*Rainbow Jordan*	Childress	Alice
1981	*Another Heaven, Another Earth*	Hoover	H.M.
1981	*Ace Hits the Big Time*	Murphy	Barbara
1981	*Hoops*	Myers	Walter Dean
1981	*Friends Till the End*	Strasser	Todd
1981	*LET THE CIRCLE BE UNBROKEN*	TAYLOR	MILDRED
1980	*High and Outside*	Due	Linnea
1980	*Leaving*	Hall	Lynn
1980	*Quartsize Trip*	Hogan	William
1980	*Beginning Place*	LeGuin	Ursula
1980	*The Truth Trap*	Miller	Frances
1980	*Language of Goldfish*	Oneal	Zibby
1980	*JACOB HAVE I LOVED*	PATTERSON	KATHERINE
1980	*About David*	Pfeffer	Susan Beth
1980	*Far From Home*	Sebestyn	Ouida
1980	*Pigman's Legacy*	Zindel	Paul

Figure 5-19. Continued

	TITLE	AUTHOR LAST	AUTHOR FIRST
1979	*All Together Now*	Bridgers	Sue Ellen
1979	*AFTER THE FIRST DEATH*	CORMER	ROBERT
1979	*Vision Quest*	Davis	Terry
1979	*Disappearance*	Guy	Rosa
1979	*Tex*	Hinton	S.E.
1979	*Last Mission*	Mazer	Harry
1979	*Up in Seth's Room*	Mazer	Norma Fox
1979	*Motel of the Mysteries*	McCaulay	David
1979	*New Teenage Body Book*	McCoy	Kathy
1979	*Words by Hearts*	Sebestyn	Ouida
1978	*Bel Ria*	Burnford	Sheila
1978	*Killing Mr. Griffin*	Duncan	Lois
1978	*Edith Jackson*	Guy	Rosa
1978	*GENTLEHANDS*	KERR	M.E.
1978	*Fragments of Isabella*	Leitner	Isabella
1978	*Best Little Girl in the World*	Levenkron	Steven
1978	*War on Villa Street*	Mazer	Harry
1978	*Beauty*	McKinley	Robin
1978	*Father Figure*	Peck	Richard
1978	*Happy Endings Are All Alike*	Scoppetone	Sandra

Figure 5-19. Continued

6 BOOKTALKING

"It's really cool how you tell us a little about the books. It gets me interested in reading. I normally only read magazines, but you make all the books sound good."

—*a booktalk evaluation*

Even the best collections need to be promoted to let teens know the collection exists and that it is filled with good material. One of the best ways actively to promote a collection is through word of mouth: words in the form of a booktalk coming out of the mouth of a librarian visiting a classroom or other group setting. While booktalks do take place informally, this chapter answers the basic questions about formal booktalking—a time- and research-tested method of connecting young adults and libraries.

WHAT IS A BOOKTALK?

> The cardinal rule of booktalking is simple: don't tell, sell.

A booktalk is a paperback blurb as performance. Just as the copy on the back of any YA paperback is designed to entice the teen reader to pick up the book and purchase it, a booktalk is a presentation designed to motivate the teens in the booktalk audience to check out the books being promoted. A booktalk is *not* a read-aloud, a review, or a literary criticism of a book; instead, it is a performance—sometimes written, but most often ad-libbed—to excite the audience into reading the book. It is not a summary; it is a sales pitch.

Booktalks sell reading as an activity. You are trying to persuade, convince, and even manipulate this audience in order to sell a product. Since that is the case, use some of the most effective advertising techniques that appeal to teens: have a sense of humor, be direct, and don't preach. You don't have to be a Nike commercial, but you should be aware of what YAs respond to in advertising.

WHO IS THE AUDIENCE FOR BOOKTALKING?

The key to booktalking is similar to that of readers' advisory: finding books to which readers will respond.

The young adult audience is a tough crowd. Very few young adults would cheer upon learning that someone from the library is coming in to talk about books. Often, LSTs are asked to visit "reading classes," which tend to be the nonreading classes—teens who have reading problems or issues and who may lack the motivation or the skills to read well or often. Sometimes, the situation is exactly the opposite, and is asked to present a booktalk to a high school honors English class in which students are reading the great works of Western literature rather than the latest teen coming-of-age novel. Normally, the audience is somewhere in between, and the students have a wide range of reading interests, levels, and experience. The common denominator is that they are teenagers; thus booktalks must always consider the developmental and emotional needs of teens. Books don't always have to be YA novels, but they should speak to the interests and needs of teenagers. Look for the four core goals of adolescence—acceptance, independence, identity, and excitement—in the books you choose for booktalks. Keep in mind that the needs of high school students differ from those of junior high or middle school students.

Teens, however, are not the only audience of booktalks; in public library settings, the first audience is often the library manager who must find someone to be "on the desk" while an LST is off booktalking. When staff is short, how can they spare you? In the school setting, if the school librarian is in the classroom booktalking, who is minding the store? How can you justify time spent away from the desk to present and prepare even one booktalk presentation, let alone an entire day visiting classrooms to booktalk?

WHAT ARE THE TOP TEN JUSTIFICATIONS FOR BOOKTALKING?

1. **Booktalking increases circulation.** There is research that proves it, and there is the anecdotal evidence of just about every booktalker on the planet. Booktalking works. The advertised books fly off the shelves, garner reserves, and, as word of mouth spreads, remain popular long after the presentation.

Booktalking increases customer service credibility.

If the goal of a library is to increase circulation, booktalking meets that goal.

2. **Booktalking promotes the library as a place of recreation for YAs.** With the concern that books, reading, and libraries are no longer "relevant" to YAs, booktalking reminds teens that there is more to libraries than just the Internet. In this way, booktalking should be counted as programming, since the goals are very much the same.

3. **Booktalking allows the LST to work with schools and to get his or her face seen by students.** This certainly has advantages for all other aspects of YA work—programming and readers' advisory in particular. For the school librarian, it allows the students to see them in another light—not merely as someone writing passes or enforcing discipline, but as a source of presenting information and entertainment.

4. **Booktalking promotes YA collections efficiently—especially when the booktalk supports a school assignment for outside reading.** Rather than having thirty students come to the library at different times and getting different levels of service and expertise when finding a book to read for school, one booktalk session levels the playing field and provides the students with the information they need. It makes sense; it is more efficient to have one LST present to thirty students once, rather than have those thirty students asking, "What's good to read" over the desk—if they bother to come to the library at all.

5. **Booktalking provides LSTs with the opportunity to use their creative talents for the good of the library.** No one got into this profession to sign up people for computers. Many people working in libraries, in particular those working with youth, have that creative urge that needs to be flexed for the good of the library, as well as for the LST's morale. Booktalking provides LSTs with the opportunity to share their creativity with customers, coworkers, and managers.

6. **LSTs reach more YAs in one day of booktalking than they will probably see over a week's time.**

How many high school students, not counting those who are home schooled or homeless, will you see if you are at one desk from 10:00 to 2:00 during the school week? Zero. How many would you see if you spent one day visiting every classroom of just the ninth grade? Of course, it depends on the size of the school and the number of classes, but let's say three hundred. Okay, now which number is larger: zero or three hundred?

7. **Booktalking is one of the few library activities whose primary audience is the nonuser.** There are two ways to increase circulation: to motivate current users to check out more materials or to create new users. Booktalking can accomplish both tasks. While many in the audience may know you and the books you are talking about, chances are there are just as many who have not a clue. There is no doubt that booktalking reaches nonusers, but just as important, booktalking shows library users new possibilities. Lots of teen library users have functional and specific reasons for coming to the library: to get a certain book, to check their e-mail, to wait for a ride. Booktalking does in the classroom what we don't have the time or the opportunity to do with these functional users: show them the bigger picture. While booktalking is limited by how many titles you can cover in a fifty-minute class period, what is not limited by the time available is the message: there's a lot of good stuff in the library beyond that computer screen.

8. **Booktalking is the most effective method actively to motivate reading.** Booktalking presents the library as an active force promoting reading in the community rather than a passive warehouse of books and a free Internet café. Is there any parent, teacher, or library manager who believes that we shouldn't promote reading to our teens? Of course not.

9. **Booktalking increases the audience's awareness of the library.** The first step toward getting people moving toward an action is to increase their awareness. The booktalking visit is a vehicle to promote everything LSTs do for teens. Booktalking visits must always include the basics: information on how to get a library card, library

hours and location, fines, upcoming programs, and homework help.

10. **Booktalking builds relationships.** Relationships with teachers can be used to promote programs, create collaborative assignments, or share information. Booktalking builds relationships between LSTs, but most importantly, it can build relationships with YAs. Before and after booktalks, it is a given that some teens, often the ones who are readers, will come up to speak with you. Are these kids you've seen in your library before? Probably, but have you, between reference questions and paper jams, had a chance to listen to them talk about books they've read? Doubtful. When taking or asking questions during the presentation, you are building relationships; but most of all, the booktalk is a performance of the role of a friend recommending a good book. One of the keys to successful teen services is building relationships, and booktalking provides LSTs with a unique opportunity to do this in the classroom, where the discussion is about books, not bytes.

WHAT ARE THE MODELS FOR BOOKTALKING?

- **Paperback blurbs.** The blurbs on the back of paperback books are a wonderful model for booktalking: all sizzle, no steak. They are written with one purpose: to sell the book. While perhaps a little shorter than most booktalks, the key questions are there: Who are the characters? What is the conflict? Why should the reader care?

- **Movie preview or trailer.** Another fine model is the movie preview or trailer. Again, you see the main character, get a sense of the theme or mood of the work, and often witness a sneak preview at some of the best scenes or lines. It's short, powerful, and designed to sell the product.

- **Pop music single.** Pop music also serves as a model. A classic radio single is catchy, and it rarely clocks in at over four minutes. There is often a hook or memorable part and repetition of the title of the song. The best singles always speak to some common yet intense human emotion.

- **Joke.** A joke is a good model for booktalk construction. A joke has enough details to get people interested—yet not so many as to bore them—and ends with a punch line.

Booktalking builds nicely on most LSTs' experiences as storytellers. The main thing is to evoke a sense of performance. This does not mean you must become an entertainer, but you should recognize that the booktalk situation—a person standing in front of the room with an audience before them—is a performance setting. This doesn't mean you must be theatrical or dramatic, but it does mean you should understand some basic concepts of performance—the most important of which is to know and respect your audience. It is about them, not you.

WHAT ARE THE RULES OF BOOKTALKING?

The rules of booktalking are fairly well established. Beginners to the craft should be very careful to abide by them; seasoned vets know which ones can be bent or broken.

Of all of the established rules for giving a booktalk, perhaps none is more important than "have realistic expectations." Some teens will be more than happy to show interest, ask questions, and check out books, while others will merely look on with bored indifference. The research is on your side: booktalking works; it may not always work and it may not work for every student, but it will motivate teens to read.

There are rules, and then there is the prime directive—remember your audience. When you are writing, attempt to visualize not only yourself giving the talk (that will help with performance), but also your audience. As you plan a ten-minute booktalk summarizing every key scene in the book, can you visualize your audience sitting in rapt attention?

HOW DO YOU WRITE A BOOKTALK?

The most critical part of booktalking is selecting material. This requires knowledge not only of your collection, but also of the interests of your

---

Don't

1. booktalk books you have not read;
2. booktalk books you did not like/would not recommend;
3. gush;
4. give away the ending/the secret/the surprise;
5. give a book review;
6. label by gender/race/other;
7. oversell;
8. read aloud unless it is absolutely necessary;
9. talk about sex/drugs/violence without clearing it with the teacher;
10. booktalk books you don't have in multiple copies;
11. be boring to yourself;
12. start booktalks with booktalks.

Do

1. bring books with you/check them out;
2. memorize talks and have cheat sheets;
3. vary the themes/types of talks;
4. keep good records of visits;
5. be prepared to ad-lib and interact;
6. vary length of talks;
7. start strong and end strong;
8. have realistic expectations;
9. be organized, cool, and confident;
10. relax and enjoy;
11. measure success;
12. learn from mistakes.

readers. All the tools and techniques used to build a collection should be taken into account. There are plenty of published sources available on booktalking in print and on the Web to serve as models, but eventually you will need to start fresh.

The books you select to booktalk will certainly vary based on the teacher's needs, the reading levels of the audience, as well as your reading interests. You may choose to booktalk only new books, but if they are in hardback, that might limit access greatly. You may choose books on a theme or subject, but like a story time, it is creating a presentation, not just having a great theme, that results in the best outcome for the audience. It's best to strike a balance between fiction and nonfiction, between serious books and funny ones, between popular authors and less-known writers, between classics and contemporary works, and between books you like and those you love.

After choosing books, it is time to start writing the talks. Some people write down every word, while others merely read the book and sketch some notes. Some people start with the blurb as the framework and then fill in more details, while others take extensive notes as they are reading the book. Most people read the book all the way through, but some read just as many pages as necessary. Some people, especially when booktalking nonfiction titles and graphic novels, scan illustrations and project them, while others stay as low-tech as possible. There are endless numbers of ways to prepare, to write, and to present. But the bottom line remains the same: don't tell, sell.

> Like all things, booktalks need to be customer-focused and the reading interests of the teens, not the teacher or LST, drives the selection of material.

WHAT ARE THE MOST COMMON TYPES OF BOOKTALKS?

- **Mood.** The goal here is to convey to the audience the general "mood" of the book. This works best with scary books, and reading from the text is part of this technique. But setting the mood can work equally well with genres such as humor, for example. To set the mood, you can use props, dialogue from the book, or lighting. For the most part, a mood-based talk aims to share the experience of reading the book with the audience. This works well with senior high students who might be more appreciative of an author's language. Why summarize Maya Angelou when you can let the power of her words do the work?

- **Plot:** This is the most common—and seemingly the easiest—technique. Hit the high points of the story, just as if you were telling a friend about a book or movie. With a booktalk, the hard part is to know when to shut up. If you tell too much, few will want to read the book because you've told everything, including the ending; if you tell too little, the audience won't become interested. If there is a failing with most book talkers, it is to include too much plot, too many characters, and too much action. You have to keep it simple so the audience can track your words, form the images, and still want to hear more. Finding the right stopping point in a book's plot is what makes booktalking more art than science.

- **Character.** The preferred method for many booktalkers is to present the booktalk in first person. As many teen novels are told in the first person, this really allows the audience to experience the "voice" of the book. It also introduces a character that teens might want to get to know more about. Some booktalkers who do this go all out, using costumes and accents, while others will merely read from the text. Presenting in first person can be tricky and sometimes confusing to the audience, but when it works, it is very effective. It will only work, however, if you are comfortable with these techniques. If you are not, teens will see through it and reject it.

- **Scene.** Rather than telling the entire plot, going into details about all the characters, or reading a great deal to set the mood, this type of talk presents a part to stand for the whole. This technique works well with thrillers or adventure novels. The key is to find one scene to share that really captures the essence of the book. You'll need to give some background to the story, but like some movie trailers, one exciting or comic or scary scene can be enough to give the audience a taste.

Nonfiction booktalks—in particular, biography and history—could use any of these techniques. A "scene" talk for a self-help book might involve doing one of the quizzes. For a poetry book, you might consider reading one or more poems. While there are variations from the four forms—plot, form, character, and scene—they do represent the frame on which most booktalks are built.

HOW DO YOU START A BOOKTALK?

- **With a character.** Use a quotation or description, but in the first sentence of your booktalk, give the audience a good (or bad, depending) first impression of the character. If you use a quotation, do it with a different tone of voice. This gets attention and announces that something is different about this book.
- **With a question.** A question forces the audience to pay attention because they want to answer it.
- **With an action.** Share something that a character does that is dramatic and attention-grabbing: an act of violence, daring, or even stupidity.
- **With a shared experience.** Open with something in the book that the audience has probably felt, done, or said. Again, your first sentence might best be a question.
- **With a shocker.** Many books have shocking incidents. Rather than building up to them, use them as a point of departure. It is the cheap way to build excitement, but it works.

WHAT GOES IN THE MIDDLE OF A BOOKTALK?

The middle is the hardest part to create. Many people write the first and last sentence before anything else. In this middle section you want to:

- **Keep it simple.** Use short declarative sentences, mostly.
- **Follow a narrative.** Go from point to point without detours.
- **Keep to a few characters.** The more you throw out, the less you have to get confused and the less your audience will be baffled by.
- **Repeat things.** In information-literacy instruction, you always repeat what you want people to remember; the same is true of booktalking. Work in the book's key

phrases (the title, perhaps) a couple of times, or use whatever "tag line" you devise.

- **Watch words.** A booktalk is not the time for a vocabulary lesson. Make sure the words, images, and allusions are appropriate your audience and their grade level.

- **Read sparingly.** Your task is to sell the book, not to recite it. Reading takes your eyes off your audience and your audience's eyes off you. And do you really want to take your eyes off a class of seventh graders for long?

- **Watch timelines.** You don't want to cover three years' time in one talk. The book's time frame will help determine this, but events should not happen that far apart.

- **Watch your watch.** movie trailers and pop songs last about two to four minutes. Any booktalk over four minutes should be pretty special.

- **If in doubt, leave it out.**

> The average booktalk should be between two and four minutes. Any less time, and it is hard to get in the sizzle; much more, and you've given away too much steak.

Most booktalk presentations are timed to last a class period. Allowing time for asking and answering questions, handing out materials, taking attendance, and allowing for teens to look over the books, most booktalk presentations last around thirty minutes. Within those thirty minutes, some people could do ten to fifteen separate booktalks, while others might opt for greater coverage of a smaller number of books. Like a band putting together a set, there should be some mix in timing.

HOW DO YOU END A BOOKTALK?

Many booktalks end with the title of the book, which acts as the punch line. The idea is that the last line should be memorable—and what is the one thing you want all the YAs to remember more than title? But you shouldn't force a booktalk to an awkward conclusion just to work in the title, and doing it every time probably borders on compulsive and annoying. The rule is simple: end with whatever it takes to get at least one teen in the audience to say "I want to read that!"

HOW DO YOU TURN BOOKTALKS INTO PERFORMANCE?

Paperback publishers are great with hooks and taglines—you can find them on the cover or in big letters on the back of the book. The hook is what keeps you interested in the book and the thing that answers the question, "why should I want to read this book?" Your best models are paperback back cover blurbs. They introduce the character, describe the conflict, outline the emotions, and ask a question that reading the book will answer.

Booktalks can have hooks in the same way. Just as a hook is makes each book different and memorable, each booktalk can have a different spin. Sometimes the hook will come naturally out of the book, while other times it takes more creativity to develop the hook. At first, you may be so concerned with remembering all of the character's names that you don't want to think about adding anything to your talk. But after a while, especially after booktalking the same titles a few times, you will notice what types of things work with an audience. Using hooks ensures that you sell, as well as tell.

WHAT ARE HOOKS ON WHICH TO HANG A BOOKTALK?

- **Audience participation.** Look for ways to get your audience involved. Have them answer questions. Include sound effects. Repeat "tag lines." Do your booktalk as part of a larger presentation. Overall, remember to let teens participate in booktalks, as in all things.

- **Diary.** Obviously, many YA novels come in diary format, and that authentic voice can be a real selling point and a great read-aloud opportunity.

- **Empathy.** Almost every writer of teen fiction is aiming to build a character that young readers can relate to and care about. Present in second person, or talk about the character's emotions with the teens sitting in front of you. If they can understand the character's plight and start to care a little about the character, then they will care about reading the entire book.

- **Experience.** Lead into a talk by relating a personal experience, or better yet, do a short booktalk pretending the events that happened to the character actually happened to you.

- **First sentence/one sentence.** Some books have such well-crafted, dramatic, and spellbinding first sentences that a discussion of those sentences could be the center of a booktalk.

- **Your own gimmicks.** Maybe your gimmick is magic or riding a unicycle. Use what works for you. Part of getting booktalks "through" is getting yourself across as someone your audience will want to listen to for a class period.

- **Gross-out.** Younger teens in particular enjoy a gross-out. From the adventure novels of Gary Paulsen, to the pulp horror fiction of Stephen King, to photos found in many a book about mummies, there are plenty of opportunities to turn the stomach of teen listeners.

- **Headlines.** Just as the TV show *Law and Order* talks about being "ripped from the headlines," there are plenty of young adult titles, both fiction and nonfiction, that mirror current events. Make the connection obvious, and use it.

- **Heat.** Many books have good guys and bad guys. In your talk, discuss all the terrible things the bad guys have done, especially to the sympathetic good guy. This will, as they say in professional wrestling circles, "draw heat" and make your audience want the good guy to get revenge.

- **Kiss and tell.** YAs are interested in sex. Talk with the teacher first to get an idea of how much (if any) freedom you have to discuss sexual content. Even then, you will want to allude to the sexual aspects of a book rather than playing kiss and tell.

- **Know a secret.** Is there any more intriguing question to most teenagers than "do you want to know a secret?" Since many teen novels are built around this simple premise of a character hiding a dark secret, this is almost a foolproof way to structure a booktalk. Tell a little about the characters, hint at the secret, get ready to reveal it, and then stop.

- **Link.** Link a book with a current movie, or link a popular fiction title with a nonfiction title. Link a book that students have read in class with one you are booktalking. Look to connect pieces of the teen world with the literature written for them. This works really well with graphic novels based on TV shows or novels that have been made into movies.

- **Next line.** This, the easiest hook of all, works best with scene-based talks. Set the scene, build the action, and then just as a character is about to do or say something, stop, pause, and then hold up the cover of the book.

- **Pantomime.** Adding a little bit of movement every now and then will make talks more entertaining for the audience and for you—just remember not to go overboard.

- **Props.** Show materials from the book. This works well with first-person talks.

- **Repetition.** Repetition of phrases like the title or the tagline is vital to making sure the audience gets hooked on the book. Plus, repetition adds rhythm to the talk.

- **Sound effects.** From knocking on the door to imitating the sound of a beating heart, let sounds rather than words carry key parts of the booktalk.

- **Unifying experience.** Get everyone thinking about the same thing by asking questions about something almost everyone should have in common.

- **Vocabulary.** Begin a talk by asking the audience to define certain words. Repeat these words throughout the talk, then come back to them at the end.

- **Xerox.** If you were booktalking *Scavenger Hunt* by Christopher Pike, you might choose to photocopy and distribute the pages with the list of things on the hunt. Other books which have short, easy-to-read documents (letters and comics, for example) would work, as well.

Adding hooks such as these, as well as those you develop, will help ensure that a booktalk presentation is something more than an LST standing in front of the room describing a bunch of books.

Just as not everyone can be successful in information literacy, it takes some special talents to be a good booktalker. Every booktalker,

---

If the book is the steak, and a booktalk is the sizzle, then hooks are the spice: they kick it up a notch.

like every storyteller or reference librarian, has a different "style." Style can be copied, but it can't be taught. However, techniques for book-talking can be learned. Often people will see someone else booktalk and say "I couldn't do that," which is exactly the case; no two people could, would, or should booktalk exactly alike. What hooks do is add to your toolkit proven methods for constructing a talk.

After accepting that booktalking, like storytelling, is a performance and admitting that you want to influence your audience, you will begin to handle your booktalks differently. You will learn to perform rather than recite your talks, and you will learn your own performance style. The style you choose will be the one best suited to get your point across. Gushing over a book is not getting your point across, nor is it "getting you through." Getting through means becoming accepted by your audience as someone who will entertain them, someone they will want to have visit them again in their classroom, and as someone they will want to visit in the library. By arousing the audience's curiosity; by using sound, movement, repetition, and other hooks; by creating empathy for characters; and by evoking emotions, all while entertaining them with a lively presentation, you will succeed.

WHAT ARE THE ELEMENTS OF BOOKTALKING SUCCESS?

- **Know the crowd; don't be too proud or too loud.** The teacher needs to tell you as much as possible about the classes you will be visiting. You don't want to go into a class of lower-level readers and present books they can't read, nor do you want to visit a group of students with high reading levels or sophisticated tastes and do series mysteries.

- **Speak to feeling, not lofty ceilings.** What will grab most YAs about a book are the emotions. Being ego-oriented as YAs are, they will be looking for characters like themselves in your booktalks, not elements of style or literary devices. The group may have a variety of different reading levels and interests, but YAs share certain emotional similarities.

- **Don't just speak out, seek out.** Involve the audience as often as possible. In a performance setting, an involved audience gives energy back to the performer.

If other peers are involved, the audience is more likely to become interested in the booktalk.

- **If you want a reaction, create an action.** The worst thing during a booktalk is total silence. You don't know if you are getting through, and they are not giving you any clues. If you want your audience to react, you need to create situations for them to react to. Let the books do the work: tell the one-liners in funny books if you want to hear laughter, or read the graphic descriptions of horror in Stephen King books to get a groan.

- **Use your style, not cards from a file.** When you write your talk, you probably will not have a hook in it right away. Only through practice and experience will you move from file cards to re-creating the talk as something to be performed rather than read.

- **Think stage, not printed page.** Again, write your booktalk, but think about adding movement. Think about adding sounds or props as you write. Challenge yourself by working one of the hooks into a talk already in your file.

- **Be yourself, lose yourself.** You have to be yourself when you speak in front of a group. YAs in particular will pick up on any falseness in your presentation. Don't load down your talk with slang or attempts to be something you are not. As a performer, you will notice a change. For some it is gradual, for others it is a very dramatic change and part of developing a performing style.

- **No matter what you try, answer the question why.** Hooks are gimmicks, and like most gimmicks, they only go so far. You can never get away from the central point—providing a group of YAs with the reasons why they should take their precious time to read a certain book.

- **Remember needs, not just deeds.** When deciding which books to booktalk, focus on what is really happening in the book—the "journey" the teen protagonist is experiencing—rather than just the "plot" or the action. Chances are the characters are grappling with issues or feelings like independence, acceptance, identity, and excitement. Those are the real selling points.

HOW DO YOU PUT TOGETHER AN ENTIRE BOOKTALK PRESENTATION?

To ensure successful booktalks, most booktalkers develop formal or informal policies for visiting classroom visits. Some LSTs ask that all booktalks be scheduled at least two weeks in advance, that they must last the length of one period, and that teachers must stay in the room (and not read the newspaper). Some booktalkers don't mind doing all six or seven class periods in one day, while others won't do that many in a row. However, combining classes might mean that different grades and reading levels are in the same room. The best setting is the classroom with the LST "taking over" the class for that period.

Scheduling booktalks takes a lot more work. You need to do a thorough interview with any teachers who are using your service for the first time. If you don't have any ideas about this class going in, you will probably not do well. Part of scheduling is also considering the time of day. Since booktalking requires more of your and the class's energy, the end of the week is not a good time, nor are classes first thing in the morning or late in the afternoon. Classes right after lunch are the most fun and challenging, as the Twinkie rush kicks in during the middle of the presentation. Darting in and out of rooms every ten minutes is too confusing for the teachers, provides too little interaction with YAs and finally too herky-jerky on you to get into a good pace.

After you have written your individual booktalks, you need to structure them into a presentation. If you have seen the group before, either for booktalks or for a tour, you don't need to go through the whole "introduction" section and can jump right into books. If it is your first time, however, then introductions are necessary. You need to decide how many books you cover given the time you have. When a band puts together a concert, they break it up into sets. In that set, they structure the songs to a particular effect. Lots of bands begin with an "old favorite" to get immediate recognition, then play new material, and encore with more old favorites. That's a good model to keep in mind when putting together booktalk presentations.

WHAT ARE ELEMENTS OF A SUCCESSFUL BOOKTALK PRESENTATION?

- **Always prepare more than you need.** You don't want to run through all of your titles in twenty minutes and utter, "Any questions?" Have long and short versions of presentations for titles so you can stretch or shorten depending on the time factor and audience reactions.

- **Booktalk in teams.** This means that LSTs have to prepare less material, but is also has other advantages. It allows both people to utilize their booktalking strengths and keeps a higher energy level. It also provides an opportunity to learn new techniques and gain inspiration from other people's material. Finally, you can have a lot of fun playing off each other.

- **Check out books.** If possible, bring multiple copies of titles with you on the visit that you can check out in the classroom. It will answer that immediate need the YA has for the book that might cool before they can get to the library. There is the risk that you will lose a title, but the idea is to get the books into YAs hands. You might get a kid that's delinquent, but think of the YAs who got the hot book now. If you cannot bring books with you, take names and place reserves.

- **Consider AV.** Some people use PowerPoint to display the book jackets or illustrations from nonfiction titles. Some LSTs do booktalks over the PA system or the in-school cable channel. You could use AV to complement the booktalk, or you could make a videotape to replace your visit. Background music or even sound effect tapes could be effective if not overdone or played too loudly.

- **Don't start with books.** Introduce the library by connecting with the something they may already like: your magazine titles.

- **End with a bang.** Save your best talk for last. Be careful of the timing, though; you don't want your best talk cut off by the bell.

- **Give something away.** End the booktalk presentation by putting something in their hands. It could be a book list, a flyer about a program, an evaluation form for your talk, a reading interest survey, or even posters from magazines.

- **Go next to AV.** Again, speak to your audience's interest in order to get it. Show them some of the recent AV acquisitions in your library, especially videos. Give away movie posters if you have them on hand.

Once you have been doing this for a while, you can put together a list of books you know cold. Pass out this list and ask the audience to tell you based on the title and a one sentence tagline which book they want to hear.

- **Keep notes handy.** Some people bring a written book-talk with them, while others speak entirely from memory. A good compromise is a "cheat sheet" listing the names of the major characters and one- or two-word reminders of the outline of your talk so you can get from point A to B even with sudden memory loss.

- **Make a list.** No matter how hard you try to work in the title of a book, many kids just are not going to remember. List the titles you are going to talk about, then also list similar titles. You could also hold up those books as part of the presentation. Make sure you distribute a copy of the list to the school librarian and within your own library system so when a YA comes looking for a title, but he or she forgets the list, someone can still help him or her.

- **Find movie tie-ins.** For a first booktalk, consider a title they recognize, one with a movie tie-in or one that a movie was based upon.

- **Relate inside information.** If you can relate any personal information about the author, it makes the book more real to the audience.

- **Relate personal experiences.** No, don't bore them with the story of your prom, but you probably can dig into other experiences they can relate to. That personal anecdote makes you more of a person to them and speaks to common YA emotions.

- **Talk with the teacher first.** Not only do they need on introduce you, but they will also help (or hinder) you in setting the mood for the class. If you want the YAs excited and even talkative, tell the teacher this. If not, the teacher may feel the need to settle them down when you are trying to "get them up."

- **Craft smooth transitions.** The transitions between your talks need to be smooth to give the impression the "act" fits together, rather than being a random selection of books. Try to make the last word of one book-talk be the first word of the next. If doing horror stories, a basic transition is, "If you thought that one was scary, then..."

- **Use a known author.** At this point, you are establishing credibility and making them listen to you. Choosing a Stephen King book establishes the common ground between their interests and your resources. You don't need to sell Stephen King, but you do need to sell the idea that your library has "good stuff."

- **Use your captive audience.** Give them a short survey to solicit responses about whatever topic will help you plan better services. Ask them about their music or programming interests, or any other kind of information you would like to collect. If you are trying to start a YA advisory group, give people a place to write down their names, e-mail addresses, and phone numbers.

- **Bring your calendar.** If you've only arranged to visit one teacher, ask that teacher to invite others to your booktalk. Chances are you'll land some more visits.

It seems simple enough: read a book and tell someone about it. Booktalking involves so much more planning, preparing and evaluating. Because booktalking is a performing art, practice improves your performance. You can practice, write down talks, and try them out on your friends, but eventually it is getting in front of that classroom of YAs that makes you better. Despite all of the help offered in this chapter, there are many things not covered. If your barrier to booktalking is stage fright or fear of public speaking, there are books out there to help overcome those barriers. If your barrier is fear of YAs, then that is something you need to get over if you plan on serving this age group. If your barrier is your administration, refer to the discussion of the advantages of booktalking at the beginning of this chapter. If your barrier is a lack of booktalk experience, that is an easy one to get over, because you only have to break through it once.

SO, WHAT DOES A BOOKTALK ACTUALLY LOOK LIKE?

Here are sample booktalks, which illustrate many of the hooks described earlier. Some of these are variations of talks which first appeared in the Novelist database.

Thirsty. ANDERSON, M.T.

Chris is a pretty normal teenager. He's got a couple of good friends who take turns insulting one another. There's Rachel, the girl of his dreams who sits near him in English class. There are his parents, who fight all the time. There are all the trappings of teen years, including Chris' passion for McDonald's, which he notices grows stronger by the day. It must be just a growth spurt, he thinks as he tries to figure out why he is hungry all the time.

Chris is a pretty normal teenager. He's got these friends who he hangs out with. One day they are walking down by the lake that is a landmark in their town. They start up with each other again, but the teasing gets too personal and Chris gets angry. He pushes his pal Tom down on the ground near the lake. A violent urge overtakes Chris. His mouth begins to water. He looks down at Tom, and then glances at the water. That is when Chris finds that he has no reflection.

Chris is a pretty normal teenager, except for two things: he's a vampire and he's very, very thirsty.

Baby on the Car Roof and 222 More Urban Legends. CRAUGHWELL, THOMAS.

You've all heard the one about the baby on the car roof, right? You see, there's this young couple driving across the country, and strapped in the car seat between them is their nine-month-old baby. After a while, the husband starts to get tired and wants the wife to drive, so they pull over to the side of the road—but it's not as easy as switching sides. They put the baby on the car roof, and then pull all the stuff out of the front seat. The husband scoots over, the wife walks around and gets herself settled, and then off they go. Only one thing is missing: the baby who is still in the car seat on the roof of the car.

Did this really happen? That's the pull of urban legends. There was a whole movie called *Urban Legends* about these things that supposedly really happened. This book is loaded with urban legends like that. The book is organized by subject, so there are urban legends about cars, animals, celebrities, technology, crime, strange deaths, supernatural encounters, and tales of revenge.

You know in most states there are laws that let just about anybody over the age of eighteen carry a handgun if they want to for personal protection. Lots of people think it is a good idea, but one woman does not. It was a busy day at the shopping mall. This woman was tired from a long day of shopping and carrying around heavy bags. She was a little light-headed when she saw the man opening the door and getting into her white SUV. She got closer to the car and screamed at the man. When the man merely looked at her, she dropped the bags and pulled a gun from her purse. Again, she told the man to get out of the SUV, but the main just told her, "You're crazy, lady." The woman fired the pistol and shot the man in the leg. He screamed in pain and lay next to the car. The woman quickly threw her shopping bags in the back seat, put the gun away, and took her keys out. As she heard the man moaning in pain and agony, she tried putting the key in the ignition but it wouldn't fit. Why? Because it wasn't her SUV. Did it really happen? Does it really matter?

Getting Away with Murder. CROWE, CHRIS.

A lot people think the civil rights movement began with a courageous act of nonviolent resistance by Rosa Parks on a bus in the big city of Montgomery, Alabama in December of 1955—and that's true, to some degree. But in many ways, it was a cowardly act of violence in a little-known town in Mississippi in August of 1955 that was the start of the long march for civil rights. Maybe the Supreme Court said that black and white children should go to school together in Brown vs. the Board of Education, but things like that didn't matter much in rural Mississippi, where the drinking fountains were still labeled "white" and "colored."

That was the world that fourteen-year-old Emmett Till entered in August of 1955 when he ventured down from Chicago to spend the summer with his cousins in this little backwater town. This was the world that fourteen-year-old Emmett Till came face to face with when he entered the store owned by a white couple named Roy and Carolyn Bryant. Roy was away for the day, working a second job. Emmett Till walked into the store and something was said. Did Emmett Till "whistle" at Carolyn Bryant, did he say something suggestive, or did he merely say "bye, baby," when he left the store on August 24, 1955, in rural Mississippi? News spread throughout both the black and white community that something had happened at the store, and all hell was about to break loose.

A couple of days later, on August 28, Roy Bryant and his pal J.W. Milam showed up at the door of Emmett Till's uncle and asked for the "boy who did the talking." They took Emmett from the house and drove him to the boondocks. And they beat him. And they shot him. And they killed him. And then they buried his clothes. And then they strapped his body to a piece of scrap metal and let it sink into the Tallahatchie River.

But the murder is really just the beginning of the story. Emmett Till's body was fished out of the river and returned to Chicago. His mother demanded that the funeral be held with an open casket so the world could see "what they done to my boy." The black newspaper *The Chicago Defender* ran a photo of Emmett Till's bashed-in face lying in the coffin. In the court of public opinion, Bryant and Milam were guilty. But in a courthouse in Mississippi in 1955, things were different when the case went to an all-white jury. Do you want to bet on the outcome? Do you want to know how easy it was for people like Bryant and Milam to get away with murder?

Money Hungry. FLAKE, SHARON.

Greed is very, very good. That's what Raspberry thinks. And it is money that she thinks about almost twenty-four seven. She thinks about it not because she has a lot of it, but because she's been poor most of her life. At least now she's got a place to live. It's not that nice, and it's in the projects, but it's not the street. She remembers after she and mother ran away from home, ran away from her father, ran away from his abuse, ran away from his drugs, ran away from the horror of that house, how life was better on the streets.

Raspberry wants the green stuff and she'll do just about anything to get it: as long as it's legal and as long as it doesn't hurt anybody else. And that is what Raspberry really wants. It's not money for the sake of money. She wants something else: she doesn't want to get hurt again. She says: "If you got money, people can't take stuff from you—not your house, or your ride, not your family. They can't do nothing much to you."

So Raspberry sells pencils and candy. She hatches schemes and involves her friends. Nobody around her has much; the people in the projects are just like her: they are money hungry. They want never to be hurt again.

They say money can't buy happiness; well, Raspberry wants to prove them all wrong. Her stomach is empty and so is her wallet, but she's plenty money hungry.

America. FRANK, E.R.

This is the story of America. This is the story of Now and Then.

Then: America was born to a drug-addicted mother. In the past fifteen years he's never had a real home for long. He is caught in the system; sometimes he is lost within it.

Now: America is in a residential program, listening to Dr. B. trying to get him to talk. Dr. B. wants to know why America tried to take his own life. What's wrong with America?

Then: Is America white? Is he black? Does it even matter? Yes, to the rich white family who adopted him as a baby but who turned him away when he started turning his color.

Now: In his file, it probably says something like "America is a lot of trouble." "America might be crazy." It might even say that America might be a murderer.

Then: His mother gave birth to America and rejected him. Then she took him back, and she left him behind again.

Now: America lies in his bed at night, trying not to cry, trying not to hear other kids screaming. America wants to fly, let his spirit soar, even if he's locked in his room.

Then: So another family comes along and says they love America. Mrs. Harper adopts him and teaches him to read. But if Mrs. Harper is so good, then why is her brother so evil?

Now: He's working in the kitchen, but he's always getting in trouble. America hates carrots and he throws them away. They remind him of the past: of then, of that, of it.

Then: Mrs. Harper's brother showed America the carrot peeler, showed him how it can peel away skin. White skin, black skin. Does it even matter?

This is the story of Now and Then. This is the story of America.

You Don't Know Me. KLASS, DAVID.

"You don't know me." John, who claims his father named him after a toilet, is cut off from the world. He lives most of his life in his head and believes that no one knows him. Not his mother, who is rarely home and spends her time working to make ends meet. To his mother, John would say, "You don't know me." Not his father, who left home when John was four, never to return. To his father, John would say, "You don't know me." And certainly not the man who John calls "the man who is not my father." That is his mother's boyfriend; that is his mother's future husband. That is the man who terrorizes John on a daily basis. Hard slaps to the head; harder and more brutal verbal abuse. To this man, John would say, "You don't know me." At school, well, teachers try, but they are too busy. There are friends, but sometimes friends fight. And then there is Violet, the girl he longs for, but certainly she does not know him.

John doesn't know all that much about life, but he is learning. He is learning the hard way. He learns that, "Your real enemy is someone who knows you, knows all about you. That person who knows you best is the person who can harm you the most."

So, if no one knows him, John figures, he can't be hurt.

John is wrong—very tragically wrong. Because more than sticks and stones can break bones. What John is going to know most about is simple: pain.

John lives most of his life in his head, which is a safe place to be, because in the real world, he's about to get his ass kicked.

Letters From the Inside. MARSDEN, JOHN.

Before the Internet, before e-mail, before chat, people actually used to write letters. A pretty common thing was the concept of a pen pal. You would find the name of a person who lived in a different city, state, or sometimes country, and start writing to them.

This book is set in a different country (Australia) and a different time (before the Internet). It is about two girls who strike up a friendship as pen pals. The book starts off with a series of letters between Tracey and Mandy.

Like all friendships, their communication starts off with common stuff. Friends, families, school, and the rest of the daily grind. On the surface, it seems like Mandy is the one with the hard life: a violent brother, parents who seem too busy, and friends who seem not to care enough. Mandy has a hard life, of this there is no doubt. On the surface, it seems like Tracey's life is wonderful as she tells Mandy about her wonderful parents, her wonderful house, and even her horse.

But as the letters grow more intense, they increase in intimacy. Secrets are revealed, lies are told, and truth is separated from fiction. These two girls are separated by more than miles; something else separates them. Something else separates Tracey from the rest of the world as she writes these *Letters From the Inside.*

Remember Me. PIKE, CHRISTOPHER.

She didn't know that she was dead.

When Shari Cooper awoke at home after being at her friend's birthday party, her family acted like she wasn't there. They didn't hear a thing she said. They wouldn't even look at her. She didn't know that she was dead. Then the call came from the hospital. Her mother started to cry. Her father's and her brother's faces went pale. But Shari didn't know what was wrong until she followed them to the hospital. She did not know that she was dead. There she saw the body lying on the cold slab in the morgue. She saw her parents and her brother looking at the body lying on the cold slab. She was the body lying on the cold slab. That's when Shari knew she was dead.

The police ruled it a suicide, but she knew the truth. She had been murdered. Since the police won't investigate, she will—from beyond the grave. She will find her killer; she will get justice; she will seek vengeance; she will learn the truth. She spies on her friends, listens to their conversations. She knows what they are thinking; she can even enter their dreams. And it is there in a dream that she finds the truth. She finds the Shadow—pure evil that kills the living and the dead.

This time, will she know? This time, will Shari know she is dead? Will she have time to find the killer and to whisper two final words to her friends and family: "Remember me?"

Shayla's Double Brown Baby Blues. WILLIAMS, LORI AURELIA.

Here is something you might hear your parents or grandparents talk about—how life was so much harder when they were growing up, how they walked to school uphill in the snow. Was life really harder? That is open to debate, but this is true: life is faster now. A lot faster. When your grandparents were growing up, it took time and effort and energy to make dinner: now it takes a microwave or a drive-through window. Everything is faster, including childhood.

This book is about what happens to teenagers who never got a chance to be children. This book isn't about drama; it is about trauma. This book is not about survival in the wilderness, but living for the city.

Here is what the title means: the main character is an African-American teenager named Shayla. Her father is remarried and his new wife has a baby—on Shayla's birthday. So Shayla's got the baby blues times two. If Shayla's life is full of blues, then that of her friends is full of darker colors. Her best friend Kambia (from the book *When Kambia Elaine Flew in from Neptune*) is putting her life back together day by day. Then there is Lamm, her new friend. Lamm is smart and funny and caring, and also drunk most of the time. This is a book about three young people who are under the age of eighteen, but it seems like they already have lived through a lifetime of hurt. And if life wasn't hard enough, what are you going to do when you got a case of the double brown baby blues?

7 OUTREACH AND PARTNERSHIPS

"The best way to let you know about upcoming library programs or events is at school. We practically live there. Announcements, Assembly, Posting flyers if brightly colored."

—*a teen library volunteer*

Outreach is about partners, new ideas, old scenarios, and endless possibilities. We define outreach services as activities that take place outside of the library setting. Outreach refers either a community relations—promoting services—or to actual service delivery, such as booktalking, in a location outside of the four walls of a library. Sometimes those two prongs of outreach overlap; normally one sets the stage for the other. Community relations also means networking, attending meetings, or other settings which allow you to bring teen library services to a particular forum. The result of this networking is often a partnership. Partnerships are the agreements we make with schools or businesses to make outreach, as well as building based, library services happen. Partnerships can be a real plus for libraries by extending resources, providing easy access to another organization's customer base, and by increasing the library's visibility in the community. Both partnerships and outreach are exciting, difficult, creative, satisfying, and often the best way to spend your time and money. This, while daunting, can be the kind of challenge in which you see the best results for teens.

The term partnership is used generically to describe three very specific types of activities that libraries engage in with other institutions.

- **The first type of partnership is communicative.** This is where the library merely seeks to team up with another organization for the purpose of getting its message out about its services—generally, or sometimes specific programs or projects. A communicative partnership may be as simple as an agreement with a local CD shop to post flyers, a school to make PSA announcements, or a cable station to air PSAs produced for the library by teens. You are asking for very little, often only access to your partner's audience.

- **The second level of partnership is cooperative**. In these partnerships, the library asks for something like coupons from businesses, space in a newspaper, access to the partner's audience, but is expected to provide something as well; perhaps only recognition of the gift. Libraries are good at asking for things, though, not as good in providing something in return to those who work with us. Cooperative might also mean an arrangement to bus in teens from an after-school program, do a project with another youth-serving agency, or develop a booklist with a school librarian. You need to invest a little more, but then again, you are getting more in return.

- **The third level of partnership is collaborative.** The first two normally involve the library advancing its goals and the partner advancing their goals; a true collaboration means that both groups create new goals within the context of the partnership. Collaboratives take a while to get started, as there is a whole process of identifying needs, establishing roles, setting goals, and finding resources. While the other arrangements may simply be handled with a phone call or through e-mail, a collaborative means setting down on paper why, who is going to do what, when, and where. There is an inverse relationship here; collaborations take the most time, but normally have the highest pay-off, while a communicative requires little, and often little return is found.

There has been much literature about the power of partnerships, such as the State Library of California's *Joint Ventures: The Promise, Power, and Performance of Partnering* document, so we'll try to focus here on how partnerships can benefit teen customers, not why libraries should partner.

The types of partnerships LSTs engage in depend upon many factors, but primarily we look to partners to help us reach the teen audience outside of the library setting. Partnerships are the foundation for outreach. Often partnerships are made at a higher level than LSTs, so we'll try to focus on the small stuff, knowing that often the more our libraries can find community partners, the more teens can benefit. The most logical and most used outreach partner for a public library based LST is the local schools, while LSTs in schools know that it is only through partnerships with teachers that the best results for students are obtained.

WHAT IS OUTREACH AND WHO IS THE AUDIENCE?

Outreach is taking the library out, to anyone and anywhere who will have you.

It can be as basic as distributing flyers for your new Web site/programs to the high schools; it can be as formal as speaking to the local Rotary Club about your services to teens in a juvenile detention center. It can be as tricky as coordinating multiple visits with multiple supervisors of teens in group homes to get them all library cards so they can check out books you have brought. Perhaps the most important concept in all of outreach is face time. That is, getting your face—and message—in front of teens, or the people who work with them, that could make use of your services. Sometimes face time means presenting; sometimes it means staffing a booth at a school function, delivering a service, or even just showing up so you have the opportunity to interact one-on-one with teens, or those that serve them. The problem with face time is it's a long-term investment in a library environment consistently concerned with short-term results.

Your imagination, your community, your resources, your administrative support, and your willingness to connect with community partners are the only limits in how your outreach programs will succeed. The possibilities and levels of involvement are endless. School visits are a good place to start with lots of probable nonusers; you have a somewhat captive audience and there are other adults around to reinforce ideas and information after you have gone. Students are all in the same situation; for example, they all have to do science-fiction book reports. What they really need are suggestions for books they might actually like. Assigning a science-fiction book report does not mean that the LST or teacher has a great list of titles for the students to choose from; but if you can provide those services, everyone wins. You get face time with the teens, who probably never see you; they hear about a variety of books that will help them with an assignment and hopefully make them think differently of the library next time around. Finally, the teacher sees the value of you as an educational partner.

We may look at this visit as targeted to middle-school students but you are providing outreach library-services to people other than the teenagers in the room. Often the audience for outreach services isn't quite so obvious. Once you establish a relationship with one group, a juvenile detention center for example, you can begin to look at groups that splinter off from your original contact—teens on probation, teens in foster care or group home, the adults that run those places or provide education, and other services. You can also investigate other groups associated with the detention center, such as mental health, AA/NA, anger management, religious groups, career classes, and GED classes. Then, see if you can be of assistance. Often there are materials the library can provide or offer opinions about that these other groups may find helpful or they may be unaware that the library can provide. One of the most important questions to ask any partner at an outreach activity is "Who else should I see?" While most cities have some sort of youth-services collaborative, it is most often the unofficial networks that achieve the best results. While cold calling a potential partner often works, it is better if you can get a current partner to make the introduction or smooth the way.

WHY SHOULD A LIBRARY ACTIVELY REACH OUT TO THE COMMUNITY?

When you begin to do outreach, your library becomes seen as a viable part of the community. The first thing that happens when staff begin going out into the community on a regular basis is promotion of the library to nonusers and their parents, who may also be nonusers. You will immediately tap into a population that you always knew existed, but never knew quite how to reach. Since we rarely see or hear from these people, this group seems to have the most need. They are unaware of the value and resources the library provides; therefore, they are not able to use or support it.

This is useful regarding circulation statistics, especially at budget time and when we compare the outreach services that take place inside the library. Your use of materials will increase and in turn the circulation statistics will increase, which is important to pay attention to, not only how many items are checked out but what types of materials. The types of materials checked out and requested can give you insights into what types of programming would appeal to those customers. But those are relatively short-term reasons.

We want people to use our materials and resources that we work hard selecting. We want the library to prosper to be important in peoples lives. We want to connect people to ideas and experiences that will make their lives better. You already have the people that come in your door; they get it. It's the people you never see that need you and the library. Whatever the circumstance, there are people in our community that would use the services of the library if it was made a little more convenient. Some have the attitude that if they really wanted to use the library, they would find a way. Also, if they haven't found a way, they say, "Well, we are here, open 10-9 during the week; what more do they want from us?" So our libraries services must realign

If we can't really change when we serve teens—since few libraries ever add hours in the evenings or weekends—then LSTs need to focus on where we serve our customers.

with our customers, where they live and ration their time. And our teen customers, when asked, almost always tell us the main thing they would change about the library is its hours. Thus, they really do want to use our resources, but it just doesn't fit into their schedules.

WHY IS OUTREACH SO IMPORTANT IN TEEN SERVICES?

Teens use products that are marketed to them. The goods and services we are marketing may not be "cool," but they are quality; they are free, will help them in the short- and long-term, and will help them save time. Outreach is direct marketing at the most fundamental level like visiting school is like going door to door, except each door opens to thirty potential customers. Every teen is a potential library customer.

When you are providing outreach to teens, there are many things happening:

- You are reaching teens that aren't aware of the library and the resources available. These teens may already be library users, but you might turn them onto a new service or a hot new title that is outside of their current use and reading habits.

- You are giving positive attention to teens who may only equate adults with bad attention. We are a benevolent people.

- You open a flow of communication between the library and teenagers. Part of face time is just letting teens meet someone on the outside. People like to go where at least someone knows their name.

- You gather opinions and ideas from teenagers regarding the library and your service. Outreach can't be just about telling; it is also about listening. When you give teens a chance to ask questions or offer opinions during a school visit, you'll find them more receptive to information that comes in the form of an answer rather than a speech.

What services are best delivered as outreach?

Just about every service we've talked about throughout this text can happen just as well on the road as in a library's four walls. If our true interest is in the outcomes not on numbers, on making a difference rather than just making a hash mark on a statistics sheet, then where services are delivered is not as important. The taxpayers pay for library services, not just a building. Thus, LSTs can deliver lots of services outside of the library.

- **Collections.** By taking library materials to specific locations. This might involve deposit collections in classroom, juvenile detention centers, group homes, or other locations. It is bringing the materials to the teens rather than expecting them to come to us.

- **Information services.** Even if they are passive such as homework help or Web sites. We need to conceptualize our reference services that are Web based as an outreach service, not less of a technical service. If outreach is bringing library services to people where they live, work, or congregate, then certainly our Web services allow teens to use the library from their bedroom or computer labs.

- **Booktalking.** Anywhere to teens, such as in a classroom or group setting.

- **Programs such as book discussion groups.** It is easier if you try to get ten kids to come to a public library all at the same time for a book discussion group, or for the public librarian to work with a school to do the discussion at the school. What matters is the outcome, not the location.

- **Programming.** This includes cultural, crafts, and entertainment. We'll talk about how to do programming later, but once we focus on outcomes, it is easier to conceive of outreach programs. If we want teens to have a positive library experience, where is it written that it must take place in a library? Given the difficulty of arranging teens' schedule along with access issues, it just makes more sense for one librarian to travel, than expecting ten, twenty, or two hundred teens to do so. For some programs with vast appeal, such as an author or performer visit, a school or recreational-center might be the only venue large enough. Most meeting rooms are too small, and unless we do it during off hours, which you might argue is a form of outreach as well, the commotion caused by such a program is sure to impair normal library operation. Libraries can also sponsor programs at events in the community. The library can sponsor an event at a skate park, a mall, or a movie theater.

• **Summer reading promotion.** The visit to promote summer reading is a staple of public librarians, even if there is virtually not a shred of evidence that it has direct impact on participation. Thus, LSTs need to begin to document the success of these visits, and make them more than just show and tells.

• **Programs to at-risk teens or groups.** These include programs that cover parenting and pregnant teens. Given shrinking resources, we need to justify our outreach efforts. School visits to English classes have historically been where we have conducted this booktalking effort, and have also generally given us the most bang for our buck. But, are those really the kids who most need library services? Many of those teens *do* have access to the library, *do* have computers at home, and *do* have resources—time, money, supportive parents—who will get them to a library. What about teens who are parents? In GED programs? In jails? In alternative schools? Those teens might not have the resources, and also might most need the information or programs we can deliver off-site. The need is greater, but that doesn't mean the results will be as spectacular. If we think outreach is only about numbers, then we'll keep doing the summer reading program show and tell; but if we realize the outreach is about outcomes, then LSTs will look instead at what is best for the most vulnerable teens in the community, not at what is best for the library's statistics.

• **Simple promotional programs.** In September, push library cards with a table at open houses and parent/teacher nights. Also, send library card applications to all the media centers. Students can return completed application to media center, the media center gets them to library, and then staff processes and mails cards to students.

• **Information-literacy instruction.** In the school setting, this is often done in the library, but public libraries need to take the classroom to take this show on the road. The instruction can be with teens, with teachers, or even with parents.

WHAT ARE THE BENEFITS AND DRAW-BACKS OF OUTREACH?

The benefits are twofold. The library benefits from more members of the community being aware of the library and using it. The library, because of connections made throughout the community, has the chance to be seen in a different light—as a proactive entity. The customers who receive outreach services are more informed, read more, and are aware of the possibilities within the library, not only databases to use for homework or the latest Meg Cabot book. When LSTs work with teachers, it creates a laundry list of benefits for teens, such as:

- ability to obtain materials easily,
- better understanding of how libraries work,
- clearer assignments,
- increased access to information,
- increased access to information technology,
- increased access to recreational reading,
- innovative programs to meet their needs,
- library staff with better understanding of their needs,
- reduced frustration when using libraries,
- reduced stress when using libraries, and
- reduced time spent in library after school.

Looking at the research from many states, certain relationships become clear.

- There's a relationship between expenditures for library media centers and test performance.
- The size of the library media center's total staff and the size and variety of its collection matter.
- Students whose library media-specialists played an integral role in education tended to achieve higher average test scores.

The bottom line, of course, for students, teachers, and the community is that kids do better in school. While people will argue endlessly about how money is spent within the educational system, there is probably agreement on one thing: everybody wants kids to do well in school, no matter how doing well is defined.

Outreach from the school library into the classroom makes a difference; especially when it is backed up by funding for staff, collections, and technology. We can only infer, for there is sadly yet no research to document, that students with access to a public library that funds teen services and where the LSTs are involved in collaborative activities with schools will excel. Public librarians do school cooperation because it works for teens, plain and simple. Not because it makes our job easier or because it is fun, but because we know that library partnerships can increase student learning and achievement.

But more than knowing it works, it is what our public wants us to do. Gallup polls have indicated that formal education support is seen by the public as an important role for public libraries to play; the

Lifelong learning, the hallmark of any public library, begins by complementing the formal educational system through informal settings.

assumption being that the purpose of this role is to support student learning and achievement. Education and instruction was seen as the sole province of the schools as part of the school library media program. Technology has made it necessary that public libraries get involved in information literacy; it is not just about educating our customers, but about empowering our teen users. The need for constant training and instruction about new information technology has forced public library LSTs to take another look at their role in supporting student learning and achievement. If public library staff receives the proper instruction and training, then they can become full participants in the education of their customers. Communities no longer see the formal educational institutions as the sole providers of learning, in part because of the recognition of the need for lifelong learning.

So, if outreach and partnerships are so wonderful, why are they not more plentiful? The drawbacks to outreach vary with the types of services you provide—drawbacks that cut across the board are—the more you promote the library the more people come into the library. It might sound odd, but you may have the mindset that is the exact outcome desired, but other library staff may think differently. The type of people coming into your library may change; staff may have to learn to serve customers they would rather not serve at *all*—teenagers. If you are out beating the bushes, you have to have staff back at the branch that are ready to serve them—no matter their needs.

There are other drawbacks as well.

- Once you start providing outreach services, everyone wants a piece of you, and there may not be enough staff to go around. This is almost always objection number one, "We need you on the desk." Yes, but teens in schools and shelters also need the LST. Why is the desk, especially in large systems with telephone, chat, and e-mail reference available to any customer who walks into any library, still the holy land? Is the desk where the action is? Is it where our customers are? We don't think so.

- Staff at facilities and schools change, and a new person may not even understand what type of service you were providing. Schedules, rules, and interests may change the services you provide; they may want more of you, less of you, or things you cannot provide.

- The hours that work for a correctional facility or other community partner may be the exact opposite of your work schedule, and that may include weekends.

- Administration does not see the value; they like to put your picture on the cover of the Annual report, but your funding does not reflect that prominent position.

- Library staff doesn't know or understand what you do; mainly because you are outside of the building; therefore, you must not really be working. You have got to bring back the goods and let your coworkers, who often are carrying a heavier desk schedule, see the results your outreach is bringing. In this case, you might want to tell the story in terms of what it is doing for the library—in other words, what is in it for them.

- Once you start, you see how many people need outreach/library services and it is hard to say "no" to any opportunity.

WHAT ARE THE OBSTACLES AND HOW DO YOU OVERCOME THEM?

Staff and money are the two biggest obstacles. Lack of support from your boss or administration can also be tough to overcome; money and staff may be easier. A community that does not see the value of the library and is not open to the idea of the library trying new and innovative ideas, can be a challenge that may take time to change. When you first begin outreach you may encounter people who are not opposed to working with the library but they are genuinely surprised that the library offers such services. This will surprise you because you are obviously willing to provide the service with the right connections. Part of our job is to educate the public that the library does actually offer such outreach services. And keep educating them because people change jobs and forget.

Even with time and money as an obstacle you can start small but smart.

- Focus on one school, one staff person for four to six hours a month.

- Focus on one activity like doing booktalks.

- Be realistic about the time it takes to put together a good booktalking list.

- Take advantage of the tools that are out there to help you with booktalks and that will make those students remember you and the books.
- Partner with the school librarian—one with whom you already have a personal or professional relationship.
- Have the school librarian look ahead to the assignments she knows are coming, which sadly is not always the case.
- Get the e-mail addresses of the teachers you will be seeing and ask them what types of books his or her students like or don't like.
- Have the school librarian/teacher report any success stories that you aren't around to see.
- Track your progress. Check the circulation on titles of books before you go out and talk about them; then monitor the status of those titles for the next several months.
- Compile numbers of how many students you were able to see in two hours—at least fifty if you only see two classes—and how many teenagers were served in the library while you were gone by the staff person "on the desk."
- Invite your supervisor and anyone else to come and observe; dispel whatever notions they had in their head of what outreach is. Let them see it and you in action. In the worst case, tape it. Have people write letters on your behalf—administrators listen to the public, especially parents whose teen picked up a book because you told them about it and this was a first.

There are ways to help with changing the mindset of your community. For the most part it has to come directly from the library and eventually from talkative people who have enjoyed your services. Once you have figured out who your target audience is—let's say a middle school—then you need to be at meetings, in-services, new teacher orientation, luncheons, and anywhere else you can be promoting your service of booktalking. You'll want to visit the school you want to provide outreach to in the late spring, two weeks before school is out and introduce yourself to the school LST. They will be packing up their library most likely and students won't be checking out books, so they may have a minute to talk if they aren't helping with Field Day. Give them a flyer, sample booklist, and your card; tell them you would love to come and do free booktalks for their students once they get settled into the school year. Underline the word free. Be sensitive to the fact that the first few weeks are chaos. You might mention the booktalks work great if a class has a book report due during the first quarter. Mention that you will use a mix of titles owned by the school and public library. Also mention you will give the school librarian a list beforehand in case they want to pull the books for check out. Think like they think, what will help them do their job better. The worst thing to do is come on too strong with too many ideas and projects; most school based LSTs are already too busy, and this will put them off. Instead of telling the school everything you can do right from the get-go, focus on a small project that proves you can work together. From that success, all other things flow.

One of the best ways into a school is if you have a personal relationship with someone who works at the school and can vouch for you. After hitting a school district hard with promotions and getting nowhere, it was a school librarian moonlighting at the public library that took a chance with having the library come and give booktalks to her sixth graders. She spread the word in an e-mail and at a meeting soon after the visits. Then the library had several calls from other middle schools interested in having booktalks at their schools. A personal recommendation was all it took. A mistake that many LSTs make in working with schools is trying to work with every teacher. We put together those back to school packets, send newsletters, and speak at meetings trying to tell every teacher our message, when perhaps we should focus on these personal relationships with teachers, who tell their peers.

> The best thing you can do in any partnership is, when your partner thanks you for your participation, to thank them for the opportunity and then say, "Who else do you know that might be interested in this service?" Outreach is all about building relationships.

HOW DO WE MOVE FROM OUTREACH IN THE COMMUNITY TO COMMUNITY PARTNERSHIPS?

This takes a little longer, but it comes from consistent good work at various outreach sites. It comes from taking the initiative and showing up at meetings for projects, ideas and planning in which the library should be involved—face time. People in other agencies have to start thinking about the library as part of the team, the solution; as an agency with something to offer. Another program requires first-time teen offenders to attend a drug and alcohol film discussion group with their parents. The library is included to do a Web page presentation to both groups about information the library has to offer. Information presented about local laws, the corrections system in your area, resources for drug and alcohol counseling, resources at the local schools, lists of activities for teenagers, and other services the library offers. The corrections system is not the expert in gathering information, the library is; and so, they called the experts to let us do what we do best.

WHO ARE OUR POTENTIAL PARTNERS IN THE COMMUNITY?

Every community that is big enough to have a library is normally also big enough to have one or two possible partners. The roadmap for partnership is a Rolodex or address book, but it begins by looking at what is in the community. It begins by asking the question, "Who else in this community touches the lives of teens?" The follow-up question then is what can the LST offer these potential partners and what will the partners offer them. Every community is different, but every community is also all the same in that there are several groupings of potential partners:

FORMAL EDUCATION
_ Public schools
_ Private schools
_ Charter schools
_ Alternative schools
_ Home schools
_ Special programs
_ Adult education
_ GED
_ Adult literacy classes
_ Community colleges
_ Colleges and universities
_ Parent/Teacher groups
_ Teacher's professional associations

GOVERNMENT DEPARTMENTS
_ Police
_ Anti-Gang Task Force
_ DARE
_ Fire
_ EMS
_ Health
_ Parks and Recreation
_ Housing
_ Community Development
_ Elected officials
_ Jails/Juvenile detention center
_ Juvenile court/community service

YOUTH SERVING AGENCIES
_ Boy/Girl Scouts
_ Church or Temple youth groups
_ 4-H
_ Junior Achievement
_ Boys/Girls Clubs

CULTURAL/RECREATIONAL
_ Art museum
_ Science museum
_ Theater groups
_ Dance companies
_ Music groups

Figure 7-1. Potential partners in the community

YOUTH SERVING AGENCIES
_ YMCA/ YWCA
_ Explorers
_ Summer programs
_ After school programs
_ Homeless youth programs
_ Drop out programs
_ ROTC

OTHER
_ Political clubs
_ Social clubs
_ Adult service clubs
_ Professional associations
_ United Way
_ Health Communities Project
_ Voluntary Action Agency
_ Ethnic clubs
_ Neighborhood associations

CULTURAL/RECREATIONAL
_ Young audiences/youth performers
_ Arts Council
_ Local historical society
_ Improv comedy groups

COMMERCIAL/MEDIA
_ Sports teams
_ Martial arts
_ Fast food/ pizzeria
_ Hobby shops
_ Radio stations
_ Television stations
_ Cable access
_ Newspapers
_ Beauty shops
_ User car lots
_ Music stores
_ Video stores
_ Coffee shops
_ Bookstores
_ Sporting goods
_ Supermarkets
_ Department stores
_ Gap and other youth clothing
_ Malls
_ Formal shops
_ Skating rinks
_ Putt-Putt
_ Entertainment centers
_ Arcades

Figure 7-1. Continued

Certainly every community is different, but almost all have one other thing in common—the yellow pages. It is still the best community directory available to the LST. The other common element in every community of teens is just that—the teens themselves. Ask where they go, who they listen to, and how they spend their time. A key to outreach and partnerships is to find avenues of opportunity to interact with teens outside of the four walls of the library; in order to do that, you need to know where to find them.

WHY SHOULD ALL LSTS WORK WITH TEACHERS?

Often teachers and the LST have the same goals. Both want to get the library, books, and reading into the lives of their students. Students are one of the best recipients of outreach visits for reasons mentioned previously. The LSTs at the school can do their part, and be the intermediary, but it can be easier and more reliable to work directly with a teacher. They know what assignments they are planning for the year; they know their students and they see them every day. The combination can be very powerful for all parties involved. You get access to a variety of teens to spread the good library word, the teacher is able to hear about important resources at the library and the students make a connection with the public library, get great information, hear about books they might enjoy, and a temporary break from listening to their teacher. It's a win all the way around.

The obvious benefit is getting inside the school to see what really goes on as far as assignments are concerned. Because that is what it is really all about right? No! That is only part of it, a nice part that may make a difference to the people who always complain about "Had we known about the assignment…" The more you are a presence at a school, the more you will find out, but only if you do your part and ask. Talking to the teachers and the LSTs at the school about everything, their collection, students, their budget, what they struggle with, Internet, and anything else you can think of.

From consistently booktalking—twice a year—at a middle school for the past four years, a public librarian was involved in the following things strictly by nature of being a person from the outside that was interested in their lives: judging science fairs, poetry workshop, catalog instruction, author visits, writing workshops, helping a student who was suffering abuse at home that attended the school, the public library's teen advisory council, talent show, career day, staff jewelry party, many staff lunches, and received a fleece vest with the school name and logo.

WHAT ARE OBSTACLES TO WORKING WITH TEACHERS AND HOW DO YOU OVERCOME THEM?

Working with teachers is, for most LSTs, one of the single most frustrating experiences in the profession. In a perfect world, teachers would

Teachers are very, very, busy people, and we've yet to make a convincing case that they should change their work to incorporate ours. Moreover, it is not the job of teachers to tell librarians what they are doing; it is the job of LSTs to learn what teachers are doing.

open their arms to librarians, but the truth everyone knows is far from that. Despite the massive work done by school librarians and AASL, in many schools, librarians are not always in the loop when planning assignments.

You might need to start by educating teachers regarding what the library provides and what you do as an LST. You need to be flexible and accepting of the limits of what a classroom teacher can do. Meeting teachers half-way can remove most of the obstacles; if you want them to give up class time for you, then you need to be prepared to be flexible enough to meet their needs. One LST was trying to get into a middle school but the teachers only wanted to free up class time for formal library instruction pertaining to an upcoming research project. So the LST struck a deal; one outreach visit of catalog instruction/Internet searching for the research paper and then one outreach visit of booktalking on the day after research papers were handed in. This is a break for the teachers, the students, and a follow up visit for the LST with the students. The teacher and students received the research help they needed, and the LST got to connect twice with the same group of teens, showing them the homework side of the library and the fun side of reading.

HOW DOES THE LST IN A PUBLIC LIBRARY BEST WORK WITH TEACHERS?

- **Colleague.** Start with the librarian in the school or media coordinator for the school system. This seems easy enough; but even this first simple step, contains some pitfalls. Librarians in schools, however, are no different from most teachers; they feel they have too little time and resources. Work around their schedule and share resources with them—professional magazines for instance. The message you want to send is, "We can help each other," but sometimes that looks like a turf grab and is thus resisted. They have their own problems, even if they are also yours. They know all about teachers not notifying them about assignments. They will be amazed that you expect a teacher to pick up the phone to call you or write you a letter when that same teacher will not even walk down the hall to tell them. Their problems are your problems, and, hopefully, both of you will be willing to help each other find solutions. If you look good, they can look bad. If you work with a teacher and make visits to booktalk, that school librarian might look bad because they don't offer the service. If teachers begin to take you up on offers for library instruction or other services, then the question arises, "Why is this not being handled in the school." All activities need planning; not only with the full knowledge of the school librarian, but also by involving them on the planning stages and inviting their participation in all aspects. They can also feel underappreciated. You should look for ways to provide them with recognition because it's a smart bet they are not getting much in their school. Every time they help you, write a thank you note or a letter to the principal is a nice touch. Because they feel overwhelmed, even as much as they might agree on the principle of cooperation, the reality of making it work seems time consuming. The best road to cooperation is to work cooperatively. Instead of your laundry list of cooperation opportunities, pick one small project the two of you can work on together. Maybe it could be a union list or reference book rotation plan, or maybe customizing some of the documents in this manual, but choose one project that needs both sides working on it. After planting the seed, larger projects involving more cooperative planning become possible. The relationship might be stronger and, as allies, you can work toward ending some of your mutual frustration with teachers.

- **Expect some resistance.** While many school librarians know all of this, that doesn't mean the doors will always open for them. Some school librarians may feel they have absolutely nothing to gain by working with you; they know their teachers and what they need. If they tell you about those teachers, then maybe those teachers will take their business elsewhere. There is a subtle competition between libraries, just like there is competition between branches in a library system. You have to find what you have to exchange in order to get the school librarian to help you. It really needs to become a win-win situation. Sometimes you can figure it out, but sometimes you just have to put the question to them, "Now, what can I do to help you?"

- **Navigating the school maze.** Every school is different on what is the proper protocol, and libraries are different as well. It seems often the first official contact comes at an administrative level with a library director contacting a school superintendent. Best case scenario is your director writes the superintendent and expresses ideas for working with the schools; and then, asks for permission to make contacts. This next contact again might vary depending upon the school. You might have to work through another layer and work with a curriculum supervisor such as the English department, or maybe the coordinator for media services. Depending upon the size of the school, after talking with the school librarian, you can contact teachers directly or work through a department chairperson. If you can invite yourself, or better yet get invited, to a department meeting, you have finally reached teachers. After you have formally met them at these department meetings, you can begin making individual contacts. Who you contact depends not only on the culture of the school and library, but also on what your objectives are at first. If you want to publish and distribute an e-newsletter for teachers, that will be an administrative decision for sure.

- **School planning document.** Located in the Core Documents at the end of this book is a document which can assist you in obtaining and organizing information about schools—the school planning document. When completed, the document serves as a planning tool and, at the end of year, as a vehicle to evaluate cooperative activities. The document takes you step-by-step through the kinds of information you will need to work with schools. Once you obtain it, you can use the information from it to put together a mailing list. This list will be invaluable. To compile it, either stop in or, better yet, call and ask to speak to the school secretary. Make sure to call in what would be slow periods for a school office so they will have time to talk with you. Once you have a list of contacts, you want to tell teachers whom they can contact. Such a list should also tell teachers what services you have available. Distribute poster-size copies of this document to school librarians and administrators. Another variation is to shrink the services section onto a blank pre-addressed post card and print one out for each teacher.

> If you have put together a successful program with a teacher and school librarian, write that up as a press release filled with quotations from the teachers and distribute it widely. Let teachers put you over with other teachers.

Like much of young adult service, school-library cooperation presents a contradiction. Nothing would help YAs more than for these two institutions, which both strive to meet their needs, really to work together; yet, for many reasons, sometimes it seems nothing is harder to do. Almost every librarian could tell a story about a teacher marveling at a database product amazed at what is available. Unless they have gone back for retraining or the school has been proactive, most teachers; research notions stem from pre-high tech times. They are still thinking books and magazines, instead of full text articles and Internet documents. And it is not because they are Luddites, but because their experience is not with technology. Like most of us, they would prefer to stay where they are comfortable.

Libraries are sold on cooperation. Our history shows the advantages; the development of library systems, the creation of automation networks, the daily proof-in-the-pudding known as interlibrary loan, libraries know it works. Teachers, however, have different mind-sets and different values. The key to success is for LSTs to learn those values, ask good questions of our educational colleagues, and let them tell us how we can best support student learning and achievement rather than merely telling them how wonderful we are.

WHAT ARE SOME OUTREACH SUCCESS STORIES/BEST PRACTICES?

Not enough? Here are some best practices of libraries who realize that library service is about delivering the service, not about the physical space. The following are some outreach and partnership success stories of LSTs who have been creative in the past:

- Attended and presented at district in-service for school librarians or teachers. This gives the LST a chance to explain your outreach services and how they can add value to the school day. The key to these presentations is to stay on a couple of themes and push just a couple of services. Don't overwhelm your audience with the quantity of services you can offer; impress them instead with the quality of a few services and how it can help their students.

- Attended literacy nights at schools where teens, young children, parents, and grandparents have different stations or tables to visit. Also use incentives.

- Attended family nights at schools with a reading booth created by school and public librarian working together. Family night was funded by the Title I program.

- Born to Read, Reach, and Read, Raising a Reader, or other programs aimed at working with teen mothers; often supported through contacts with hospitals and health clinics.

- Celebrated Banned Book Week and other celebrations with programs held at both the school and public library

- Created a cooperative literary-magazine involving the school, the public library, and local chapter of the National Writer's Union.

- Created cooperative employment programs between school based interns and libraries.

- Developed a partnership with probation officers to have community service done at the library by juvenile offenders.

- Developed a tutoring program held in the public library in conjunction with a local fraternity.

- Developed full blown programs like the School Corps at the Multnomah County Library in Portland, Oregon, where staff take library programs and services directly to schools. The CLASP program in New York was a great example of this type of dedicated commitment of library resources to outreach.

- Developed, in cooperation with a sexuality education program that works in the schools, a booklist of fiction and nonfiction about teen health issues, focusing on STD prevention.

- Hosted information-literacy programs with home-school associations, GED classes, or other "nontraditional" students.

- Hosted, in conjunction with high school and a local college, a college fair in the public library including speakers, Q & A, and handouts about getting into school.

- Joined forces with local middle school to develop a grant for after-school programming. The grant, from 21st Century schools, was funneled through the schools, but the public library subcontracted to hire staff to provide programming.

- Met on a regular basis with librarians from schools, community colleges, and other institutions to discuss issues, brainstorm problem solving, and share resources.

- Organized a mentoring or homework help programs held in the library but sponsored by another organization such as a high school Honor Society or maybe a college fraternity/sorority.

- Partnered with assisted living centers, where members of TAG made visits to drop off books.

- Partnered with District Attorney's office where the library offers at-risk teens, ages sixteen to nineteen career counseling, workshops, library cards cleared of fines, computer training, book discussions, college scholarship information, and armed forces information.

- Partnered with social service agencies/programs, such as Meals on Wheels, to provide a project for teen library volunteers.

- Set up a cooperative materials delivery-system with middle schools and high schools. Students are able to go into school library and place reserves within public library that were delivered to the school. Kids returned the items at school.

- Set up a library-card outreach in September and pushed library cards with a table at open houses and parent/teacher nights. Also, sent library card applications to all the media centers. Students could return completed application to media center. The media center then brought them to the library, and staff processed and mailed cards to students.

- Send newsletter to high school librarians announcing events, programs, and resources.

- Set up deposit and collection services at group homes, foster care placement centers, hospitals, rehab centers, alternative high schools, and homeless shelters.

- Shared parts of the YA Fiction collection. Once school was over, teens chose books to take from the school library to be used in the public library during the summer.

- Shared the Accelerated Reader program. During the summer time, the school library housed the AR computer at the public library who then used it as their teen summer reading program. (Note: check with your AR or similar representative about your ability to do this based on the site license, but several libraries report doing this.)
- Spoke at career day to inform teens about careers in library and information science.
- Teamed with community-access cable station to produce Teen Talk, a cable television show. The teens that participate in this teen issues program decided on the topics that would be discussed. They built the set and did all of the taping and editing as well.
- Teamed with newspapers during Teen Read Week, where papers provided full coverage of events, booklists, and even members of staff to appear at library events.
- Teamed with newspapers to jointly sponsor a creative writing magazine.
- Teamed with newspaper for members of TAG to provide book reviews.
- Teamed with local social service agency to provide programming as part of summer free lunch program, including heavy use of teen volunteers to provide programming/crafts for younger children.
- Worked with a high school that has a teen parenting center, aimed at teen moms and their babies. Child care program was started by instituting a deposit collection of materials for moms. Did preschool programming. Librarians from public, school, and college libraries met to discuss issues, share books, bring back info from other meetings, and also share Web sites.
- Worked with library's TAG. Had an information booth complete with giveaways and chances to win other prizes in the school cafeteria once a month, and all week during Teen Read Week.
- Worked with local sports teams to provide guest readers in schools and public libraries during Teen Read Week.

If you examine the award-winning programs in the Excellence in Library Services project, a large majority of them are built on successful outreach and partnerships. If you look at the book *Running A Successful*

Communities must join together in networks of all shapes and sizes to create an environment which provides teens with the opportunity to thrive.

Library Card Campaign, the number one success factor for most every campaign was a commitment to taking the library out into the community and establishing partnerships within that community to provide financial support, access to customers, and share resources. The success of so many of the PLPYD projects was directly due to outreach and partnerships. Finally, one of the clear messages of the youth development movement is no one can do this work alone.

WHAT ARE THE ELEMENTS OF SUCCESSFUL PARTNERSHIPS WITH SCHOOLS?

Let's look at the elements of success for successful school and public library cooperation using a mnemonic called FASTING.

- **Fitting in.** Curriculums dominate school planning; there is so much material that needs to be covered in so little time. Teachers want to cover as much as possible and many resent an interruption to that schedule, whether it be assemblies or library activities. For example, when booktalking promote titles tied to the unit the teacher is doing. We need to tie our work to the state standards and achievement tests. With fewer resources and less time, our work must directly complement student achievement and student learning if we hope to succeed.

- **Asking.** It seems obvious, but the need to gather information is paramount. You need to know what schools are in your service area, who works there, and a myriad of other data. It won't fall in your lap; you need to go out and get it using the form provided.

- **Scheduling.** Many public libraries spend time preparing extensive "back to school" flyers for teachers during the summer and drop them off in at the beginning of the school year. They are dismayed when the document produces no results, oblivious that the start of the school is the worst time to give teachers anything because they are doing daily triage to keep their heads about water. Learn from the school librarian the rhythms of a school and when are the best times to intercede.

- **Teaching.** The process of cooperation is really one of teaching and educating. Teaching teachers about libraries, teaching administrators about YAs, and often teaching other staff about how to teach students.
- **Intervening.** Look for teachable moments, that is situations where you can educate a teacher to what libraries have to offer.
- **Networking.** Make yourself available to attend department meetings; better yet try to attend and speak at PTA/PTO meetings to get your message out. It is much better to have teachers and parents promoting cooperation, rather than just you.
- **Goal setting.** As mentioned, do one small thing with one teacher. When it succeeds, that teacher will sing your praises. Our experience in working with teachers has been that once a teacher buys in, they are willing to shill for you.

Teachers are, however, merely a means to the end of reaching YAs. They are a distribution channel to YAs. Many YAs cannot go to public libraries, or are not allowed; but by using teachers, public libraries can make connection through programs services and materials with teens who never even cross our threshold. You can't create raving fans or satisfied customers until that moment. Cooperation among public librarians, school librarians, and teachers has many rewards for the participants, but even more for the young adult, who is the real customer.

WHAT ARE THE ELEMENTS OF SUCCESSFUL PARTNERSHIPS WITHIN THE COMMUNITY?

- **Champions.** Look for people in high places that will tell your story for you. Try to get them at community meetings to be the one to suggest bringing the library to the table. Use their credibility, but then you had better deliver.
- **Core values sharing.** Early on, lay out the five core values mentioned here, or other professional values,

and learn what matters to your partner. Once you share a common set of values, then you can go more easily and move in the right/same direction.

- **Celebrate successes.** Nothing brings a team together, in the short-term, like wining. Nothing tears in apart, in the long-term, like everyone reaching for their slice of the credit pie. Focus on the first; develop good relationships and documentation to avoid the latter.

- **Collaboratives.** A wonderful way to get started in networking is by joining and attending meetings of various collaboratives. Even if the work of the collaborative itself is not directly related to what LSTs do day-to-day, chances are the larger goals are ones we share. But just as important, the collaborative meeting brings forth numerous opportunities for the LST to meet, greet, and tell our story.

CONCLUSION

If we want to connect young adults and libraries, we must do it on their turf, not just ours. Through partnerships with schools and other agencies, LSTs can get access to those captive audiences to not only tell our story, but also to deliver our services to teens who, for one reason or another, are unable to visit libraries. Outreach, however, isn't just about making presentations, but it is also building bridges in the community for support. If we want to be seen as a player, then we need to get ourselves to the tables of educational, cultural, recreational, and governmental institutions that share our values and our concerns for reaching the teen audience.

Outreach provides LSTs with not only a chance to tell our story, but also to listen to teens tell their stories about why they do or don't use libraries. Every visit to a classroom for booktalking, programs, information literacy, career day, or whatever other reason is an opportunity to get ideas from teens about what we could do better. Sometimes the conversation is on paper in the form of a survey; other times simply asking questions. No, it is not a focus group; but at the same time it is, because the teens we meet in the classroom, in the shelter, or behind bars are ones that need us most to do what we can, despite the obstacles; to connect them with libraries.

Outreach is a continuum, from things as basic as making a booktalking visit, to as complex as making a million dollar plus deal to develop a library card campaign. There is a value in just about every kind of outreach; so as in all things, you must find the opportunities that are local, that have support, that can be reached within your resources, and that have a payoff for teens in the long or short-term. We can do face times at a back to school night and we can get media sponsorships for summer reading programs, but both embrace our core values, meet our audience, and allow us to extend our reach.

8 PROGRAMMING

"If I could run the library for one day I would have bands in to entertain us, workshops like creative writing programs, game days so kids could play Magic: The Gathering, or D&D [Dungeons and Dragons], and events for parents and teens about college and financial aid."

—a teen in a focus group in Minnesota

Do the words "teen programming" strike fear in your heart? The good news is that many, if not most, of the LSTs who have attempted programming for teens have survived. You may feel out of your element. You may know about story times and preschool "make and takes." You may be new to libraries, and those older kids leave you weak in the knees. Be assured that programming for teens may have a different feel than a story time, but at its heart you will see similarities. Some will describe it as controlled chaos; others will be amazed at the positive response from teens. Programming can help your library go from merely supplying a YA collection and responding reactively to information requests, to proactively developing events to meet the needs of teens. A program is defined as a library-sponsored activity that takes place outside of the context of reference services and is designed to inform, entertain, or enrich users, as well as promote the use of the library and its collection. With teen users, put the accent on entertain and add the word "fun."

Rosemary Honnold's book, *101 Teen Programs that Work,* and Kirsten Edward's work, *Teen Library Events,* are both full-length texts that provide lots of practical information about planning all types of teen programs. We'll do some of that too, but in addition to *giving* you "fish" (lists of program ideas and models to beg, borrow, and steal), we also want to *teach* you to fish by providing you with a way of planning teen programs. The most frequently asked question about teen programs at training workshops is "what is a good program?" but in reality that is probably the last question that needs to be asked. If you have followed a planning process that involves youth and uses information derived from surveying your community and your collections, then the answer to that question becomes obvious: it depends. It depends upon the resources available to you and those already in the community. It depends on what your teens want, but also on what the library wants to achieve. Therefore, the way to offer the best product is to use the following question and answer process that, while not foolproof, should do the best job of helping you connect teens with library programs.

WHAT IS PROGRAMMING FOR TEENS?

There are no 100 percent guaranteed successful teen programs, not even if you offer food.

You may have so many ideas rolling around in your head that each book you read is an inspiration, and each teen you talk to gives you a new idea for a program. But how do you separate the pipe dreams from potential teen programs and get the most out of your ideas, energy, and budget? You may feel pushed into programming for teens for several reasons: other libraries may be doing it; your director may want the middle school crowd to be a little bit more "directed" or "controlled" when they are in the library; or you may keep hearing about teen programming at workshops.

Teen programming can take many shapes and have several levels of involvement.

- **Involve staff members.** Recruit staff to help "put on" the program by splitting up the majority of the work before, during, and after the program, including the planning, implementation and evaluation.
- **Hire a presenter.** Hire an adult who will present information or perform an activity that would appeal to teens. You may even be able to find someone who will volunteer their skills.
- **Use a teen presenter.** Ask a teen who has knowledge or expertise that would appeal to other teens to give a presentation.
- **Ask teens to pitch in.** Ask teens to plan, implement, and evaluate the programs.
- **Be available.** Interact with teens on their time, be available, and make activities that are—at least on the surface—without adult involvement.
- **Be almost spontaneous.** Not every teen program needs to get on your library's "master program schedule" six months in advance. Sometimes, like with craft programs, it just happens because you've noticed a teen interest in a certain subject or activity.

The main thing that all programs have in common is they allow teens to connect to the library in a different way and to see the LST in a different way.

We talked earlier about how teen programs differ from children's programs, but there are also many similarities:

- **Enjoyment.** Everyone, no matter their age, wants to spend their time doing something they enjoy—they want to have a good time, be relaxed, laugh, and smile. Enjoyment comes easy to children, but teens are becoming aware of the challenges of adulthood and they face activities that may not always be enjoyable, such as homework or after-school jobs. They are aware of their time and must balance and choose activities based on the perceived enjoyment level.

- **Atmosphere.** Children, teens, and adults all gravitate toward a warm, inviting, relaxed atmosphere. Libraries need to extend that type of welcoming atmosphere to teens in conjunction with programming. Recall that one of the things that California teens said they liked about libraries was "story times for children," which seems to suggest that they recall fondly that atmosphere and experience.

- **Ages.** Generally, for their programming purposes libraries define teens as sixth graders (twelve-year-olds) through high schoolers (seventeen-year-olds). This definition may vary with the educational setup; for example, if sixth grade is in the elementary building, it may make sense to start your teen programming at seventh grade or the middle school/junior high school level. With children, certain tasks become easier as coordination and understanding develop. This also applies to teenagers. Many teen programs require higher levels of physical, emotional, and intellectual development. Teen programs are appropriate to teen development, and that may leave out an eleven-year-old or it may include them—it depends on the program. Similarly, a preschool story time may leave out a eighteen-month-old or include them depending on the program.

But while there are some similarities, there are plenty of differences, which make teen programming—no matter how well-planned—a challenge:

- **Mobility.** Preschoolers are put in the car and taken to a story time; teenagers make the choice to come to the library and attend your program, and they have to get a ride or walk. By the time they are old enough to drive, most teens have active social or work lives that make a library program just one of many options available to them.

- **Parent involvement.** Parents are "programmed" to bring their young children to the library—not so with teenagers. For their teenagers, parents are more likely to pay for "enrichment programs" or to take teenagers to school for events and activities. We have to "reprogram" parents to think of the library as an option for their teens. So many children's programs are built to allow parents and children to interact, but teens—especially young teens—want to avoid being seen with their parents at all costs.

- **Choices.** Younger children just don't have the choices for free time that teens do. From sports, to volunteering, to after-school activities, teens have a lot of time dedicated to other pursuits. A key to programming is to complement those activities rather than compete with them.

- **Teen attitudes.** While some teens do view the library as a place for information *and* fun, that is not the popular view. Add to that the attitude that anything "studious" is uncool, and you have a lot of peer inertia pulling teens away from library-sponsored events.

- **Staff attitudes.** A child's opposition to authority can be short-lived or cute, so most children are greeted with acceptance by library staff. However, many adults perceive that teens have an "attitude." This can be the case, but it may also be that teens feel a little out of their element and don't mask it well. Generally, the attitude given out by staff at the front door is the attitude that can be expected from the participants. If you think teens are stupid and don't listen, then that is what you will probably get. If you think teens are interesting people with value who can follow directions and be creative, then that is what you will probably get.

Programs that do everything right still are not slam-dunk, guaranteed successes. There are a lot of obstacles that come hand in hand with the teen audience. Let's acknowledge we won't top the numbers of the people doing children's programs; more importantly, we don't want to do so. Instead, we want to find programs that provide teens with an expectation of quality so that the obstacles come tumbling down.

Programming for teens is *not* the exclusive property of public libraries. Lots of people in the community do teen programming, but sometimes school-based LSTs will be the leaders in programming. After all, the hardest part of most any library program is getting people to attend, but school libraries have access to a captive audience. That said, the best school library programming is normally not that which is required for teens to participate in, but rather an optional activity held after or before school, or during lunch. School library teen programming is often more focused on literacy and information literacy rather than a lot of craft programs. But for teens, these programs can still be a great deal of fun and may earn them extra credit.

WHY EVEN DO TEEN PROGRAMMING?

Given everything else that is on our plate, that is a fair question to ask. Let's lay out six possible goals for teen programming.

Teen programming will:

- Increase use of the collection and other core services;
- Inform, entertain, and enrich teens;
- Attract new users or convince current users to use the library differently;
- Promote the library in a positive light in the community;
- Increase youth involvement opportunities; and
- Support healthy youth development.

Notice that attendance is not, of itself, a goal. Attendance is a means to achieve these goals. The more people, the more people who meet the goals, right? Wrong. One of the unique things about teen programming is that quantity does *not* always equal quality. For example, a teen book discussion group with fifty kids in attendance is, on the stat sheet, a huge success. For the forty or so kids who read the book and never got a chance to speak, it is a total failure.

Perhaps one of the best and most familiar models for teen programming takes place in the children's room at toddler times. Most toddler programs are limited, highly interactive, and focused on the child having a positive experience. We don't follow the same model for toddler times as we do for preschool programming because it is not developmentally appropriate. Now, that said, how do we justify programs we spend hundreds of dollars on when only five kids show? It may be true that those five attendees enjoyed the program. But the five teens would have enjoyed it as much, and probably more, if they were surrounded by a hundred of their peers.

We can determine the program's likely outcome by looking at the scope of the program. While there is certainly a place in libraries for big, blow-out performances in front of a passive, yet enthusiastic audience, there is just as much value in the small, highly interactive programs. Most of the research about programming tells us that it needs to be intense and extended. One-shot deals don't really make a big difference in people's lives. Thus, the smaller, more intense programs, like book discussion groups, youth advisory councils, or literary magazines, will help us, and teens, meet more of our goals.

Programs should be fun, but they can also be fundamental in building assets for teens. Youth involvement in programming shouldn't be limited to setting up chairs or passing out pencils, but should consist of real opportunities. We need to focus on how to get teens to attend programs and, as this chapter outlines in detail, how to plan programs that will do just that. But we also need to think about what happens to teens after they leave the program. We continually need to ask ourselves, "How did that program build the forty developmental assets?" "How did the library contribute to healthy youth development?" "How did the library contribute to making the community better?" We need to ask these questions for our own evaluation and for our community, our directors, and our funders.

Perhaps, then, the first step in planning teen programs is to look inward and adjust the expectations. The clown show organized for hundreds of preschool- and elementary-age kids is not analogous to the small book discussion group for teens. If anything, those huge summer children's programs are the exception, not the rule. Classes that help seniors learn to surf the net, show parents how to read to their babies, or teach genealogists how to use the library's collection are the "norm" for public library programming. Our bosses want numbers, but LSTs need to work with administration (and for that matter, other staff) to advocate a different measurement for teen programs. In a sense, the main number we need to focus on is always the same: forty. How did the program build one or more of the forty assets in young people?

> We need to plan programs that focus mainly on the benefit to teens, not programs that merely improve library program attendance.

WHAT ARE THE REAL NEEDS OF TEENS?

If planning programs to build these forty assets seems too formidable, let's narrow the list and the audience. While there are many library programs that appeal to older teens, the fact is that older teens are very busy. It is not that they reject using the library; it is just that there are so many other options. There are successful programs for older teens, but libraries report the most success and enjoyment in their programming for younger teens.

If you read the professional literature or listservs, chances are that all the successful programming for young teens meets all seven of the basic needs of young adolescents. Now, no thirteen-year-old will come

> Young adolescents find value in programs that speak to their desire for:
> - Physical activity;
> - Competence and achievement;
> - Self-definition;
> - Creative expression;
> - Positive social interaction with peers and adults;
> - Structure and clear limits; and
> - Meaningful participation.

to the desk and ask, "Do you have an event that will allow me to exert myself physically in a structured environment with clear limits, while providing me with opportunities for creative expression or meaningful participation with peers and adults?" But when you read about poetry slams, role-playing game nights, library lock-ins, tie-dye programs, or talent shows, then you realize that these seven basic needs, as well as the notion that "teens just want to have fun," are the building blocks for successful teen programs.

WHAT TYPES OF PROGRAMS APPEAL TO TEENS?

- **Opinion.** Programs that allow teens to give their input and offer open dialogue about community issues, as well as library services and collections, can appeal to teens. This can provide an avenue for teens to express their opinion through a book review notebook with review sheets that can be filled in on the teens timetable and at their comfort level. You can take a weekly or monthly poll on a world issue that is essentially a drop-by ongoing program. This provides teens with a way to state their stance on the particular issue and allows other teens to observe the responses of their peers.
- **Cultural.** These programs gives teens the opportunity to explore artistic or intellectual pursuits. Consider a pottery demonstration or a poetry open mic night.
- **Informational.** Teens may show interest in programs that offer direct information about issues or matters that affect them. Try a "first job" or "car care" program.
- **Educational.** An educational program about vegetarianism or a book discussion group can be an enriching experience for teens.
- **Recreational.** A chocolate program or a skateboarding demonstration combines enjoyment with the potential of learning something.

The type of programming you choose depends not only upon the interests of your teens, but also on the resources available. It's not just money, but also space, time, support, and your own internal resources, that must be considered. While there are many types of teen programs, there is really only one type of LST to do programming: one who has a high threshold for rejection. While these categories hold potential for all kinds of library programs, in most libraries, the tradition of story times and other preschool programs runs deep. While children's librarians create lots of innovative programs, they also have plenty of staples. LSTs focusing on teen programming are usually making it up as they go along, with little history of programming success or failure.

That said, there *are* a few teen programming staples worth exploring, such as craft programs and book discussion groups. In addition to these topic-based programs, teen summer reading programs and "Teen Read Week" programs are growing in popularity and serve as important models for all teen programs. Finally, many public libraries have created after-school programs to provide a little bit of everything: tutoring, activities, and reading promotion.

> The most important traits for LSTs involved in programming are the ability to take risks and to be persistent.

CRAFT PROGRAMS

Craft programs can be a big initial draw and a gateway to other types of programs. One LST used crafts as the draw, and added her interest in history to make the program more meaningful. She combined quilting and the history of the Underground Railroad, booktalked several historical fiction YA titles, told them a bit of history, and taught them the basics of hand quilting. You may not have experience as a quilter, but you can booktalk while a quilter from the community provides a demonstration. Another LST had older teen girls demonstrate their hobby of knitting to their peers while he provided the snacks and yarn. Yet another LST hired the high school girl he bought coffee from every morning at the local coffee shop to teach other teens how to make the jewelry he saw her wearing.

Craft programs can fall into two categories—process oriented or product oriented. Figure out which category your activity belongs to and you will save everyone some stress. If you want the teens to take the lead and use their creativity, an open-ended program in picture frame decorating will fit the bill. You supply the decorative items—glue guns and the picture frames (or ask the teens bring their own)—then step back and let them be creative. If you want the teens to come away with a specific product, choose the materials and colors, prepackage everything, teach them the details, and let them follow the preprinted directions.

Often teens are attracted to activities that are unlike school, and this is where the library fits in—we are a bridge between school and free-time activities and interests. You may get comments about these craft programs not being library-related. People may not understand that teens, like adults, are interested in learning new skills, ideas, or activities. No matter what the craft, there are books in the library that relate to and support the program. However, for some programs you may have to think about your program and your collection in a different way. For a duct tape program, there are a few duct tape craft books that may be available. But consider adding nonfiction titles such as Piven's *The Worst-Case Scenario Survival Handbook*, Read's *Alive,* or Krakauer's *Into Thin Air*, or fiction survival titles such as Marsden's *When the War Began*. There is a college scholarship offered for the best duct tape prom outfit, so pull the prom issue of several teen magazines, college scholarship books, fiction about college experiences, titles about ordinary people coming up with inventions, and *Inventors' Digest* magazine. As always, put out your new books and booktalk them whether they relate to the program or not.

The great thing about YA craft programs is that, more times than not, teens have the manual dexterity, creativity, and independence to tackle new things on their own. Many times giving them the supplies and some initial instructions is all that is required. One LST was concerned because he had never scrapbooked, but he knew it might be a popular program. He read several books, asked questions of several people he knew who did scrapbooking, bought the supplies they recommended, and was prepared to scrapbook—though he wasn't quite sure what to do. He laid out the supplies, scissors, paper, and glue and several books with tips on how to scrapbook. Once the program got started, he realized these teens knew way more than he did, and it did not really matter what he knew, because there was no right way to scrapbook. Afterward, he mentioned it was the most relaxed program he had done in a while—mainly because there wasn't a lot of handholding. He had a chance to talk with some of the teens he knew from other programs and meet some new teens for the first time. If you are doing a craft program that is fairly involved and has many specific steps, it will be to your advantage to practice the craft at least once. Be sure to think through how you will teach a group of ten- to fourteen-year-olds to master the steps and if each person needs supplies or if they can share.

BOOK DISCUSSION GROUPS

Book discussion groups are a natural, but they may take time. To get a core group of teens to attend, start with teens who show an interest in participating and let them guide the group. Book discussion groups break down into two types: either everybody reads the same book or everybody reads what they want and discusses the story or the genre their books share. One group is relaxed and everyone talks about what they are reading—almost always something different. The LST offers suggestions—new books or books she has recently read—and the teens offer their suggestions. The only constant is when they meet. Another group always reads fantasy, and they choose their books three months at a time so they can be advertised. Also, if one of the members misses a month, he or she still knows what the book is for the next month. One group is sponsored by the Friends of the Library; the LST gets a list of popular books that are in paperback for the group to choose from, she booktalks each title, and she gives the teens time to examine each title and make their decisions. They choose a title and the Friends group purchases paperback copies for each participant to read and keep. The more choice you can give teens, the better the group experience. It may take a month or two for the group to settle down to a consistent group of readers, but your group will constantly be changing. Friends, siblings, and girlfriends will come and go and add their unique flavor to the group.

TEEN READ WEEK

Teen Read Week (TRW) is an annual, week-long national literacy initiative sponsored by YALSA to help build connections between teens and libraries. The TRW Web site (www.ala.org/yalsa) provides a description of the current year's theme, advice for librarians who are new to TRW, theme-specific programming ideas, and resources that include informational Web sites and books about the year's topic, promotional materials created by ALA specifically for TRW, a sample press release, a public service announcement (PSA), a proclamation, official logos with graphics, and a place for participating librarians to register, share ideas, and provide feedback.

Whether you do thematic programming for TRW based on the annual theme selected by YALSA or not, special programs and events during this week will allow you to get the word out to local teens that the library really is a teen-friendly zone. Use this week to shine a spotlight on what your library has to offer young people by highlighting the teen advisory board, ongoing classes and events, and materials that teens might not know exist in the library collection, such as graphic novels and manga, teen magazines and comic books, new release videos and anime, and computer and video games.

If you choose not to do thematic programming, the following programs are a great way to promote reading and the library during TRW.

What Are You READ!ing? Contest

This program idea, based on the celebrity READ! posters published by ALA Graphics each year, can be a great kick-off for Teen Read Week. Hold a contest a few weeks before the start of TRW asking teens to

> YALSA's Teen Read Week, started in 1998, has grown into a nationally-recognized program on a mission to encourage teens to read both for pleasure and for educational purposes.

submit the name of their favorite book along with a short write-up explaining why they like the book. Select some of the best entries and photograph these teen winners with their favorite books.

Read-In

Since finding a time to read can often be a problem for busy YAs, set up a "Read-In" at your library and invite local teen readers to bring their pillows, blankets, and sleeping bags and fall into a book for an hour or two. Provide refreshments, hand out reading incentives, and give away reading-related prizes like gift certificates to a local bookstore or comic-book store. This kind of program is always more fun if you can do it after hours, so, if possible, hijack your library one evening and turn it into the ultimate teen-friendly zone for some uninterrupted, quality time with the books.

Scavenger Hunt @ the Library

Place a handful of "special" bookmarks in books throughout the library. If a teen patron checks out one of these books during TRW, he or she is an instant winner. A prize can be as simple as a nice bookmark or a small denomination gift certificate to a bookstore. This simple event can take place throughout the week and does not require much money or a major investment of time. It is also a great idea to do this in addition to several specific programs, since it is ongoing and promotes the use of the collection.

Get Carded @ Your Library!

This idea, taken from ALA's "Get Carded @ Your Library" campaign to promote national Library Card Sign-up Month, could be a week-long event during TRW where a teen can get an incentive prize simply by showing up at the library and flashing his or her library card. These prizes, which should be simple and promote library use, might include a free print card, a free copy card, or a "get out of library card debt free" card (if this is legal within your library system). For teens without a library card, this is the perfect opportunity for them to get signed up.

Coffeehouse for Teens

Invite teens to drop by and share a caffè latte or an iced coffee one afternoon or evening at the library during Teen Read Week. Create a friendly

The "Get Carded" poster from the ALA online store (item 5065–0202 at www.alastore.ala.org) is a great promotional item for Teen Read Week in October or Library Card Sign-up Month in September.

environment, play some music, and have a few icebreakers ready to get the group talking. This is also a great time to ask participants to share their favorite books, authors, movies, and music.

SUMMER READING PROGRAMS FOR TEENS

Although a majority of libraries around the country creates and carries out traditional summer reading programs, the intended audience is usually children, occasionally addressing the developmental and recreational needs of preteens and teens. For libraries that have made an effort to create a place for YAs within the library community, it is imperative that there be some segment of a library's summer reading program that speaks directly to the needs of teens. In addition, a summer reading program for YAs should allow participating teens to be directly involved in the creation of the program, providing an opportunity for teens to provide input during the developmental phase as well as during the program itself.

The following three library systems recognized the need for this autonomous summer reading program for YAs and went about creating individualized programs that incorporated reading activities, contests, and special events specifically for participating teens. In addition to teen oriented programming, each library took into account the importance of using age-appropriate marketing materials—from "cool" logos, to emoticons, to the use of the Internet—when attracting a young adult audience.

Although each library developed and carried out their teen-oriented summer reading programs in different ways, the outcome was the same: teen-friendly programs that were not only successful, but developmentally appropriate, fun, and flexible. Each of the highlighted programs required different things from participants, but they also had a few things in common: they kept it simple, they made it possible for teens to get involved on many levels, they allowed free choice when it came to selecting reading materials, they incorporated the Internet in some way, and they all had great prizes that teens would enjoy.

Train Your Brain
Public Library of Charlotte and Mecklenburg County Library, Charlotte, North Carolina

"Train Your Brain" (TYB) was an online summer reading program for rising sixth graders through rising twelfth graders who live in Mecklenburg County, North Carolina. A program that took place completely via the Internet, TYB allowed teen participants to get involved by simply signing up, reading, and keeping track of total hours read on a personal online reading log. Participants were eligible for prizes for every ten, twenty, thirty, and forty hours of reading they completed. Participants could also enter to win a fifteen-dollar Borders gift certificate by answering the TYB poll question each week. Although the reading component was not unique to a teen program, the online format and the prizes were teen-friendly and developmentally appropriate. Each teen who registered online for TYB was able to print out a ten-dollar fine waiver that allowed each participant to waive up to that amount in library card fines. Then, for every ten hours of reading completed (or programs attended, as one program equaled one hour of reading), participants were eligible for drawings for great prizes that included a home stereo, a football jersey and autographed football from the local professional football team along with a twenty-dollar gift card, an expandable Palmtop Computer, and a complete Dell computer system.

LOL :) Laugh Out Loud
Johnson County Library System, Johnson County, Kansas

A summer reading program for preteens and teens in sixth grade through twelfth grade, "LOL :)" was simple and easy, allowing a participant either to pick up a reading log or to print one out from the library's Web site. On this log the preteen or teen would choose his or her own summer reading goals, document each title read, and then turn in the completed log to receive a free paperback book and completion packet. "LOL :)" ended with a literal bang—an after-hours "Battle of the Bands" for participating teens. In addition to this grand finale, special programs especially for teens were planned all summer, such as "Bicycle Maintenance Repair," "Duct Tape Crafts," "Mehndi Henna Painting," "Babysitting Workshop with CPR," and more.

TRP '03
Denver Public Library, Denver, Colorado

As a direct result of teen feedback that a thematic summer reading program for young adults was "uncool," Emily Dagg, Teen Library Coordinator for the Denver Public Library, came up with a new plan for 2003: base the program around a logo, not a theme, and hold a contest to find the winning logo submitted by local teens. Open to any resident of Denver between the ages of twelve and eighteen with a valid library card, TRP '03 was also simple and had great prizes. Once registered, a participant had to read four books. For each book read, the teen won a prize: a food coupon for the first book, a free book for the second, a Colorado Rockies keychain and a Colorado Rapids ticket for the third, and a blank book (with a "cool" logo on the cover) for journaling, reader's diary, or sketching for the fourth.

Upon the completion of four books, each participant was also eligible for the end-of-program grand prize drawing for one of four Dell desktop computer systems. In addition, each branch had a drawing for a portable CD player for local participants.

AFTER-SCHOOL PROGRAMS

Some of the most successful programs for serving teens are the ones directed to those classified as "at risk." While this term has different meanings, generally it speaks to teens who, due to socioeconomic circumstances, are likely to engage in risk-taking behavior and/or drop out of school. Many of the most innovative programs described in the volumes of *Excellence in Library Services to Young Adults* target this market. In doing so, the programs not only focus on specific needs of at-risk teens, but also attempt to overcome the obstacles that prevent these young adults from succeeding. All such programs are built on the premise that "information is empowering." The idea is that the way out of poverty and the path away from destructive behavior is through education, information, and knowledge. Although many such programs were built without knowledge of the development assets model, the success of most of them can be directly related to how well and how often they do help teens in their transition to adulthood.

One such program, named as one of five in the 2000 edition of *Excellence in Library Services to Young Adults,* was the ASPIRE program. ASPIRE (After-School Programs Inspire Reading Enrichment) was the Houston (Texas) Public Library's after-school homework assistance program for at-risk middle school students. ASPIRE represented, in many ways, a typical public library after-school program. The goal was for the public library to make a positive impact on the life of middle schoolers by giving them the opportunity to improve their grades in an alternative educational setting. Programs like ASPIRE are not typical after-school programs filled with crafts and basketball; they combine the best that libraries can offer middle school students with solid research provided by other successful programs for young adolescents.

The program consisted of four essential elements: tutoring and reference assistance; Internet access and instruction; educational activities and software; and reading enrichment programs. ASPIRE ran throughout the year, Monday through Friday, from three to six p.m. Gathering in a meeting room or on the public floor around the computers, ASPIRE served an average of twenty to twenty-five students a day. Some were regulars and came every day, while others showed up only on days when there were special events. By providing a positive after-school alternative, the library helped reduce risk-taking behavior among middle school students. By focusing on tutoring and technology, ASPIRE helped increase student achievement and prepared students for the twenty-first century. Finally, by encouraging reading and library use, ASPIRE helped create better students and lifelong learners, and contributes to positive youth development.

ASPIRE targeted at-risk students in grades five through nine. ASPIRE centers were placed in branches in low-income neighborhoods, which often lack other after-school programs. Many of the schools served by ASPIRE were considered "low performing" by the Texas Educational Association, with many students who score low in the state's standardized test. ASPIRE offered at-risk teens an after-school alternative in a learning environment. The library was a natural place to reach at-risk teens between three and six p.m. since it has always been a "hangout" for middle schoolers with time on their hands.

Aspiring is what middle school teens do. They aspire to learn to be adults, they aspire to be older, and they aspire to better themselves. Young adolescents deal with four main issues: independence, excitement, identity, and acceptance. Every aspect of the ASPIRE program grew around these roots. Middle schoolers were given the tools to be independent. By teaching teens how to search the Internet and how to locate information, and by encouraging independent reading, ASPIRE helped create teens who succeed in learning independence and responsibility. ASPIRE taught teens how to study, how to build a Web page, and how to succeed in the new information culture. ASPIRE wanted teens to identify themselves not only as library users, readers, and Internet searchers, but most of all as youth who aspire to improve themselves. As they do, ASPIRE provided acceptance. From posting A+ assignments on each site's "Wall of Fame," to posting student written poetry and student created Web sites on the ASPIRE homepage, the ASPIRE librarians gave teens a place to celebrate their achievements and encourage their healthy development.

WHICH TEENS ARE YOU TRYING TO REACH WITH PROGRAMS?

The audience for your teen programming may start with "library teens," but it will soon expand to include a variety of teens. Be aware of the developmental stages of the age groups you are targeting. If you want the high school crowd (fifteen- to seventeen-year-olds), Readers Theatre may not appeal to them; but having the high school drama club or forensic club help you with an improv comedy night featuring other high schoolers and their friends might do the trick. Obviously certain programs will appeal to certain ages of teens but you can be aware of the other activities that are being offered or not being offered to specific age groups and what about the activity appeals to a certain age range.

- **Twelve- to thirteen-years-old.** This group is interested in being teenagers in every possible way. Their opinions are unfiltered, are coming off of a regular art class or creative expression opportunity, they will go where they are invited because they are too young for things they deem "cool." Try craft programs such as making soap or locker magnets, organize game nights, or help them write letters to pop stars.

- **Fourteen- to fifteen-years-old.** This groups is able to remember topics and discussions from one month to the next. While they don't always get a regular opportunity to be creative, they have the ability to express their emotions through writing or acting. They can assist with crafts as well as participate. Try a poetry night, readers' theatre, improv, a book discussion group, and higher-level crafts.

- **Sixteen- to seventeen-years-old.** This group is able to give opinions while taking multiple factors into consideration and craves the practical application of information. They have developed niche interests. Try holding a teen-made film contest; a Magic: the Gathering card game; programs about "vegetarian life," a first job, or car care; or issue forums that pertain to their lives.

While teens may share age-related interests, to assume what topics or programs will interest the teens in your area is risky. You must be willing to listen, observe, and react. Just because you are not personally interested in a topic or subject does not excuse you from providing that subject through a program or activity. You do not have to do it alone; find partners in your library or community who do have an interest in such topics and assist them in providing an opportunity for teens to learn and enjoy. Sharing your interest or skill with teens can be a great opportunity not only for you, but also for the teens, who will get to see an adult learning something new and struggling with new things just as they do.

HOW DO YOU PLAN TEEN PROGRAMMING?

If planning is your strong suit, plan away; but remember to keep your audience in mind. When planning for teens, don't set everything in stone; instead, be flexible and allow others to have input—especially the teenagers. If you are the spontaneous type, great. But don't forget you are planning for teens, and if they have to get a ride or they must choose between your program and another activity, they may need a little advance warning. Plan out large events like a Battle of the Bands many months in advance, but keep some board games around for an impromptu and unadvertised game afternoon.

Some people get stuck here: the planning process seems overwhelming so it gets put off—for a long time. Look at what other libraries are doing and copy, study, and borrow their programs. Start small; it can be incorporated into the other programming at your library. Plan one program a quarter as you begin, then gather input and keep your ears open for suggestions and feedback. As you become more comfortable with teens and programming, teens will begin to look to the library as an option. As you experience success with programs, not only will you gain confidence, but you will also gain further interest in programming as teens start to look forward to happenings at the library. Success breeds success.

That is, of course, only true if the funds are available for more teen programming. The most common statistical argument is that if 25 percent of the bodies that walk in the library are between the ages of twelve and eighteen, shouldn't that equal 25 percent of the budget allocated to teen services? That should be the case, but it usually isn't—or if it is, that librarian is keeping it quiet! However, most LSTs providing teen programming are experienced at making the most of their budgets. LSTs become resourceful and inventive, which can often result in some very interesting programs. You can also try to tap the usual sources of fundraising: soliciting donations, finding corporate sponsors, and asking the "Friends of the Library" to financially underwrite programs. However, these sources can make for shaky services and a tense LST. The optimum situation would be to have a specific budget for teen services or teen programming that is not dependent on donations, but could certainly be enhanced by them. This may take time to set up, and it may mean working with your business office, director, or manager. It may take explaining—or even proving—the value of teen programming (see assets for ammo in Chapter 1) to your community. But working toward a stable budget is worth the effort for you and the teens in your community.

> Each program is not an end; it is also a means to gather more input from teens about future programs.

WHEN AND WHERE DO YOU DO TEEN PROGRAMS?

You need to find what works for your teens, your library, and your community. Good old trial and error, teen involvement, and planning can give you many answers.

Look at your programming from different points of view. There's the school year point of view, which focuses on days off, early dismissal days, holiday breaks, and the sports schedule; and the community point of view, with church youth nights and other church activities, as well as any other events aimed at teens in your community. You will go crazy if you try to pick a day or time when nothing else is going on, but it doesn't hurt to be aware of other activities. You may be able to add onto or partner with what another organization is doing, or you may schedule around it. You may also realize the conflicting activity is aimed at a small group of teens, and there really won't be a conflict. Ask teens for preferred times or for days that are typically bad for them. During the school year, a good bet is Friday, when high school teens are heading to sporting events; everyone is happy to be out of school, and the library is the last thing on their minds. During the summer, the opposite may be true. Try the same program in several different time slots; you may hit on one that works better than the other. Don't get discouraged if the secret to the perfect time slot for programming eludes you. Do the best you can while taking all those factors into consideration.

Just as important a question as when a program should start is when it should end. In most cases the answer rests on the length of time it will take a teen to accomplish the activity or task provided. A common time for a program is an hour. Be sure to factor in a little socializing time at the beginning of the program to act as an ice breaker; find out where everyone goes to school, or talk about the newest movie. Have a food and drink time, and follow it with a little more socializing time, which could include talking about books, new music, or what they liked about the program. If you are practicing a craft, keep track of the time it takes you to learn the new skill, and then factor in time for five to ten teens doing the same, with you assisting a few of them.

When you are planning, promoting, and implementing your teen programs, you should be mindful of the habits of parents. Most parents automatically take their young children to the library for story time because their parents took them to story time. But if the library was not on a parent's radar for programs or activities when they were between twelve and seventeen, then probably they may not automatically think of taking their teenagers to the library for programs. Educating or training parents to connect the library with teenagers is our job. That connection happens at the reference desk, during checkout, during adult programs, on the Web page, while speaking to the PTA, on back-to-school nights, and any other time or place you encounter parents. This education of adults can include teachers, youth group leaders, counselors, coaches, and, of course, other library staff—adults who are in a position to disseminate information to teens and their parents.

If you have multiple locations offering teen programs during the same three-month period, try to allow several weeks between the same program, if possible. This provides options for anyone promoting the program. When they are talking to teenagers about attending, it gives the teens multiple access points depending on where they live, their schedule, and how willing parents are to drive them to a specific location. Providing the same program at multiple locations also allows teens who really enjoyed the craft to return and be your experts. Repeat programming can be beneficial to you; you only need to prepare once, and you have the chance to refine your program by changing what didn't work, adding whatever you forgot or needed more of, and getting different ideas and reactions from the teens who attended.

HOW DO YOU DETERMINE PROGRAMMING TOPICS?

You start, of course, by figuring out what teens need and want. Teen involvement has been mentioned as part of the planning process, but gaining that involvement may take some time, especially if your library is new to teen programming. Teen involvement is important because it will make your programs better; teens are more likely to participate in something they had a hand in planning, and the program will have more of a "teen flavor" than if a forty-two-year-old had planned it. When you are involving teens in planning, ask all the questions, have the teens talk it through, and hit some of the details to help them understand the process you go through every month. Let them know up front the budget, time limitations (if any), and library rules that are nonnegotiable. Discuss the time and supplies the program will require.

Another excellent way to come up with program ideas is by looking at how teens are already using your library. What Web sites are they visiting? What magazines are they looking at? Most importantly, what books are they checking out? While not every program needs to have a clear and direct collection connection, materials still matter. Chances are, if kids are interested in reading about a topic, they might be interested in learning more through some sort of program.

The answer to where programs can take place is easy: anywhere. If you don't believe us, take a look at Chapter 7 to learn how outreach can mean not just promoting services, but delivering them as well.

Ask yourself this question: "Dewey" or don't we know the best topics for teen programs? Brainstorm through the Dewey areas, listing every possible subject matter that might make for an interesting program. Or if you don't want to brainstorm on your own, race ahead to "What are examples of successful teen programs?" (see Figure 8-1) to read over one hundred program ideas classed by Dewey decimal numbers.

HOW DO YOU IMPLEMENT A TEEN PROGRAM?

So you did your planning, and now the day has come for the program. Teen volunteers are yet another avenue for promoting and assisting with programs. Think back to a party you attended in high school or college. If there was no one in the room, house, or gym, did you have a strong desire to go in? No. You did another loop around the block, hit the "Quiki-mart," and made another pass to see if anyone else showed up. Not much has changed; not many teens want to be the first one at a program.

So what can you do to make this transition a little easier? If you have teen volunteers who know you and are comfortable in the library, ask one or two to come early and help "set up." They can actually help set up, and they can act as teens who were the first to arrive. If you are already talking to them and things seem normal, other teens might not fear walking in and joining the party. If you can't manufacturer "first arrivers," have a task for the first teens to help with in some way: separating, unloading, rearranging—anything—and talk to them while this is going on. Asking them to find a radio station that they like. The music will fill the empty space and up the "cool" factor. One LST schedules teen programs on Saturday afternoons following her Teen Advisory Council. This works for several reasons: the teens picked the time of the Advisory Council, they are more likely to stay longer for something than come back at a different day and time, and parents are more likely to want to drop off teens for two to three hours than for one hour. What errands can you do in one hour? That parent or older sibling usually ends up waiting around the library, and after about forty-five minutes they give their teen the "we-have-to-go" look. But two to three hours, depending on the program, means a stop for groceries, time spent at another siblings soccer game, or another adult on their way home. For the non-driving teen crowd, these are realities.

The perfect setting for teen programming has an accessible, teen-oriented collection and an area where teens can be themselves without stares and comments from curmudgeonly adults. Everyone who works in a perfect library is set, but the rest of you have work to do! See what you already have on your side, and make it work for you. Most libraries have a separate meeting room that you use for programming and community meetings, so bring in carts of new books and magazines from the collection, play music, bring food, and, if possible, employ teens to decorate. Other libraries have no separate room, and the teen collection is surrounded by a seating area of its own. During business hours, hold teen programs that lend themselves to the space, but schedule more animated programs for after-hours so teens can be themselves, and you don't have to worry about complaints.

HOW DO YOU PROMOTE A TEEN PROGRAM?

See Chapter 9 for promotion ideas.

WE HAD A YA PROGRAM AND NO ONE CAME, WHAT HAPPENED?

Tenacity and persistence—you gotta have 'em. There may be a hundred reasons why a program was not as successful as you had hoped. But you must try them again, give them another shot—nothing bad is going to happen. In fact, you might figure out the factor that got in the way last time. Ask the teens who do show up to a program what else they might like to do at the library, and you might be surprised at their answers.

Numbers—we collect numbers or statistics on everything. But with teen programming, you have to change the way you think about the numbers game. Realize that teens are choosing to come to your program. Let's go over that again—teens are *choosing* to come to your program. So what does that really mean for your numbers? It means when you look at the seventy-five children who came to the Father's Day craft for two- to eight-year-olds, you must remember that every one of those children were put into the car and brought to the library by an adult. Those children may have had a great time at the program, but was it an independent choice? Probably not. Teenagers make the choice to come to the library and attend your program. Now, you may have the younger eleven-year-old brother who is forced to come to a soap-making program because his older sister wants to come, but he will come around! If you have a fantasy book discussion group and five teens show up, think for a minute—five is not a lot, but would you really want more? How would a discussion go with ten, fifteen, or twenty teens? It probably wouldn't go—the discussion would get out of control, not everyone would get the chance to talk or have their opinion heard, and the next time they might be less likely to come back.

Compare that to story time for four- to five-year-olds with twenty kids in attendance; the goal is a little socialization, singing, parent/child interaction, and listening and interacting with a story. Most of these objectives can be accomplished with twenty four- and five-year-olds, but would ten or fifteen be better? It depends on your point of view. Are numbers all that matter, or does the experience have any value? Go back to the fantasy book discussion group—what are the objectives?

Promoting fantasy books, giving teens a chance to talk with other teens about the books they love, helping teens express their thoughts and views on books and other issues, providing a little socialization, building decision-making skills, and practicing listening and interacting with others. For teens, these objectives are best met in a smaller group: teens will comfortable expressing their opinions among people they know and the LST will be better able to facilitate the group and get to know each teen. Do small numbers at teen programs mean it was unsuccessful? Probably not, but be prepared for people to use numbers as the measure of success.

HOW DO YOU EVALUATE A TEEN PROGRAM?

Surveys and written evaluations can get you the raw data you might need for a report, but it can miss the heart of the program and what the teens who attended thought. Teens will answer the questions put in front of them, but you don't ask the right questions, you may never receive the most useful comments. Adults don't want to answer hundred-question evaluations, and teens don't either. Teens may not be as tolerant or polite as adults, and you will get the silly answers much quicker. With each paper evaluation, figure out two pieces of information you really want to know. How did they find out about the program, and do they have other suggestions for programs? An adult could answer these questions with no problem, but you may get many "I dunno" and "no" answers from teens. Tweak the questions a bit. How did they find out about the program—friends, a parent, school, a Web page, the newspaper, a flyer? Leave a blank space, and give them options. Which teen activities would they attend—soap making, a fantasy book club, a game night, a pizza taste-off? Again, leave a blank space for their suggestions. At the very least, you will find out what advertising avenues are working (or not working), and the level of interest in four different programs; at the most, you may get suggestions for other programs you haven't thought of.

Some teens are more comfortable talking about what they experienced than writing about it. Again, have a few pieces of information in mind when you ask your questions. Note the following exchange:

LST: What did you like about the poetry coffee house? [Don't stop here; follow up based on their answers.]

Teen: The poetry.

LST: What else?

Teen: I thought all the different people were cool.

LST: Did you like being able to read your own poetry or listening to other people's poetry?

Teen: Listening to other people's.

LST: Would you come to a poetry workshop where teenagers could share their poetry and get feedback?

Teen: No, I don't write poetry.

LST: Would you come back for a poetry slam that was a competition?

Teen: Yeah, maybe; could we rap?

This teen isn't interested in a workshop-type poetry program, does not think rapping is considered poetry, is comfortable with the idea of performing in public, wouldn't be scared off by a competition, but is content listening to others perform. Other programs that might appeal to this teen are a poetry slam, open mic night/karaoke, battle of the bands, comedy improv, or a gathering of local musicians talking about songwriting. Give examples or scenarios and ask their opinions in order to narrow down what their answers mean for you and the library. It may take a little longer than a paper survey, but giving teens a chance to follow up on their answers will result in a better evaluation.

The other anecdotal type of evaluation is not as invasive; it involves eavesdropping and watching body language. If teens are having a truly rotten time, it will be hard to hide, and most teens wouldn't go to the trouble to hide it—they would leave or disengage from the activity. Watch how the teens interact with each other, the activity, and the LST. Do they stick around after the program is technically over? Do they ask for it to continue? Do they ask when they can do it again? When parents come to collect them, do they want to go? Does the teen explain what he or she did, give the play-by-play? Do they mention the program to other staff at any point? Do they remember you because of the program the next time they are in the library? Do they come back to other programs or to the library in general?

Evaluation can be the hardest part, even with a strong desire to improve. Who can be completely objective? Make a list of things you want to cover or incorporate into a program, booktalk nonfiction and fiction, highlight upcoming programs, talk to each teen at least once, laugh a little, and relax. You will remember to do a few of these things, and every time after that you will remember another. Get feedback from another staff person who can be honest and whom you trust to help you with a program. Ask a teen you have known for a while for his or her opinion. Is there anything that you could do to make the program better?

One LST uses a staff evaluation after programs that affect staff beyond those who helped with the program. For example, a "Battle of the Bands" may affect circulation staff, information staff, and branch managers, not to mention the maintenance staff—especially if you blow the power grid. Other staff members may not have much knowledge of the program, but you can get a feel for the level of disruption in the building. This can go a long way toward good staff relations and staff members may see some ways to make your program better. They may even be willing to help!

WHAT ARE EXAMPLES OF SUCCESSFUL TEEN PROGRAMS?

At workshops, we always allow the audience to share successful program ideas. There isn't enough time to get the entire rundown—sometimes there is time for nothing more than a *TV Guide*-style summary. With that in mind, here are some two hundred plus programs based on what we've heard on the road, read about on listservs, or learned about in the professional literature. In some cases, there is really nothing more than an idea or subject area; in others, we've provided a little more detail.

These programs represent a sample of programs being done in libraries other than our own. We've arranged them in broad Dewey order, but we are public service folks, not catalogers, so please be patient with us.

Call #	Programs
000	Banned book quiz and display
000	"Chew and Chat": informal advisory board with snacks
000	Computer art: demonstration and interactive workshop
000	Computer breakdown: teens explore the inside of an old computer to see what is inside these machines they use every day
000	Computer shopper: demonstration and interactive workshop on how to purchase a new or used computer
000	Crossword puzzles or word searches: tutorial on how to make your own
000	Desktop publishing with Microsoft Publisher: general introduction to desktop publishing using Publisher; students create projects, including flyers to promote other library programs
000	Geek U: basic technological training that lets teens learn a new application or sharpen old technology skills with a new project each week (calendars, greeting cards, digital photos); includes Web challenges and prizes for participation
000	*Guinness Book of World Records* contest/quiz
000	Trivial Pursuit Junior: questions to answer each week; teens write down an answer, you pull out a winner and offer a prize
000	Newspapers in education: teens use the paper to learn library skills

Figure 8-1. Teen library programs organized in Dewey subject order

000	Read-to-me buddies: teens volunteer to read to small groups of children
000	Storytelling program: high school and middle school drama and English classes learn how to tell stories; include visits to teen mothers
000	Technology teen volunteers: teens volunteer to be responsible for troubleshooting computers and printers, providing one-on-one instruction for library patrons, and more
000	Teen monthly contest: teens enter a drawing for a chance to win; advertise at high school library and other places
000	Trivia contest during Teen Read Week: contest follows TRW theme; teens earn an incentive each time they come in; get name announced
000	Web design workshop: teens learn the basics of creating their own Web pages using Microsoft FrontPage; can teach how Web pages work, how to insert images and text, and how to publish a site to the Internet
000	Zines: teens create zines featuring drawings, writing, and reviews
100	Astrology: demonstration and interactive workshop
100	Chinese horoscopes: demonstration and interactive workshop
100	Dream on: interactive dream interpretation workshop
100	Fortune-telling: demonstration and interactive workshop
100	Ghost stories and local legends
100	Handwriting analysis: demonstration and interactive workshop
100	Hypnosis: demonstration and interactive workshop
100	Stress reduction: workshop on coping with stress from school, activities, and work
100	Tarot card class: teens learn the basics of tarot and have a reading done
300	After high school 101: workshop where teens learn about resources at the library that will help them find a job, select a college, buy a car, etc.
300	ASVAB (Armed Services Vocational Aptitude Battery) study workshop
300	Boy Scout badge programs
300	College admission workshop: teens learn the ins and outs of the process and how to write the essay
300	College search quick tour: teens (and parents) learn about library resources related to college information
300	Fashion show: program held in collaboration with a store like "Hot Topic"; library provides models and holds musical sets in between
300	Forensic science: demonstration and interactive workshop
300	Free practice test for PSAT, SAT, etc.
300	Gay teens: presentation and discussion
300	GED workshop
300	Get a REEL job: workshop about media careers
300	Girl Scout badge program
300	Haunted library tour: good for a Friday night; Friends serve refreshments; recommended for children seven and older; teens organize it, plan it, and implement it

Figure 8-1. Continued

300	"I Think I Can": a partnership with courts/schools; teens in trouble are assigned to read a certain number of books, get a library card, and write book reports
300	Legal rights: demonstration and interactive workshop
300	Mehndi (henna tattoos): presentation and workshop
300	Military careers: presentation and discussion
300	Money 101: finance and investing for teens.
300	Money management: teens learn how to manage their money, balance checkbooks, open up a checking account, and make smart, well-informed financial choices
300	Police/detective work: demonstration and interactive workshop
300	Practice pal program: teens work with younger kids using educational games and drills
300	Prom fashions/plan your prom
300	PSAT study night: tips on how to take the PSAT
300	SAT preparation workshop: teens learn time management and test strategy techniques
300	Scary stories and urban legends: performance by a storyteller followed by a chance for teens to tell their own stories and talk about the truth behind various urban legends
300	Sports as a career
300	Study hall: teens can use the meeting room for studying just before/during final exams
300	Study night after hours
300	Summer jobs workshop: basic tips on interviewing for a summer job and filling out an application; could be held in conjunction with a job fair featuring employers who hire teens in the summer
300	"Surviving the College Application Process": teens learn the ins and outs of the college application, financial aid, and decision-making process
300	Tattoo demonstration: learn about tattoos (pro and con) and get a temporary tattoo
300	Victorian tea for mother and daughter
300	"Where the Jobs Are: Present and Future Opportunities": workshop with a job counselor to help teens learn current and future employment trends
400	Asian calligraphy: demonstration and interactive workshop
400	Cooperative cultural programming with high school language classes
400	Dictionary game: teens create fake definitions or words, then have contest to fool others
400	Hieroglyphics: demonstration and interactive workshop
400	"Rhyme Time": a contest to come up with the most words that rhyme in the shortest period of time

Figure 8-1. Continued

400	Sign language: demonstration and interactive workshop
500	Astronomy: demonstration and interactive workshop
500	Birds of prey: demonstration and interactive workshop
500	Chemistry magic: demonstration and interactive workshop
500	Fairly scientific: a science fair in reverse; teens learn about various fields of science, talk to professional scientists about their work, and learn what science fair judges look for when they judge student entries
500	Math tutoring: high school honor students tutor middle school students
500	Nature programs: presentation by a naturalist, followed by chance for teens to interact with animals; especially popular: snakes, bats, and anything else creepy, crawly, or slimy
600	Auto repair 101: local mechanic shows how to change tires, etc.; can market this to young women who think auto repair is a "guy thing"
600	Babysitting clinic: workshop conducted by the Red Cross; provides teens with basic information and a certificate of completion
600	Beauty makeover
600	Bicycles: demonstration and interactive workshop
600	Books for babies: workshop conducted with other agencies; targeted to pregnant and parenting teens
600	Buying used cars: demonstration and interactive workshop
600	Candy making: demonstration and interactive workshop
600	"Chocolate Fest": snacks and library-based activities related to finding information; includes contests, quizzes, and scavenger hunts
600	Codes: demonstration and interactive workshop
600	Cooking around the world: demonstration and interactive workshop with snacks
600	Cooking quick: demonstration and interactive workshop on how to prepare quick and healthy snacks
600	"Face Forward": a Mary Kay (or other) beauty representative shows teens basic skin care
600	Teen parent workshop: teens learn the importance of reading to their young children and receive information about medical, housing, and financial services available to them
600	"Ice Cream Social": homemade ice cream workshop
600	Low-rider cars: demonstration and interactive workshop
600	Model cars, planes, and rockets: demonstration and interactive workshop
600	Motorcycles: demonstration and interactive workshop
600	Parenting workshops held by organizations that serve teen parents
600	Pizza-tasting contest: teens rate the best pizza in town
600	Scooters: demonstration and interactive workshop
600	Slot car racing: demonstration and interactive workshop

Figure 8-1. Continued

600	SPCA: animal shelter employees show pets, talk about volunteer opportunities, and answer questions
600	Teen café: once-a-week meeting to read, play games, solve puzzles, eat, and make crafts; Thursdays recommended
600	Teen health issues: presentation on topics like depression, stress, and eating disorders
600	UN table: teens sample meals/snacks from around the world
600	Weird pets: demonstration and interactive workshop about nontraditional pets such as ferrets or snakes
600	Yoga workshop
600	Yuck night: outdoor games and activities involving gross stuff
700	Acting 101: teens learn the basic techniques of theater arts and improvisation (selecting props and costumes, staging, imitating mannerisms, and delivering lines with dramatic impact)
700	Acting workshop, held in conjunction with a visit to the library by a theater troupe
700	African drumming and storytelling: performance and interactive event
700	After-hours programs: programs held at night, especially on Fridays without football games (pizza taste-off, book cart races and "forbidden" activities called "You Can't Do That in the Library," etc.)
700	Air brushing: demonstration and interactive workshop
700	Animation contest: teens draw their favorite animated characters
700	Anime workshop: teach teens how to draw Japanese animation
700	Art exhibit of work from middle school teens
700	Art workshops: topics such as jewelry-making, kaleidoscope construction, and collage creation
700	ATVs (all-terrain vehicles): demonstration and interactive workshop on selection and repair
700	"Bang the Drum": teens make their own traditional drum
700	Basketball slam dunk contest: held in conjunction with a poetry slam
700	Beading workshop: teens create necklaces, bracelets, and other accessories
700	Birthday bash: monthly party to celebrate birthdays; tied to a library activity such as using Chase's Calendar of Events or using microfilm
700	"Bookworm Bookmarks": craft program to make bookmarks at the beginning of the school year
700	Bow hunting: demonstration and interactive workshop
700	Boxing: demonstration and interactive workshop
700	Camping: demonstration and interactive workshop
700	Candle making: demonstration and interactive workshop
700	Card and comic book club: held on Saturday afternoons; teens trade with each other and with the library; play card games such as Magic: The Gathering

Figure 8-1. Continued

700	Chess program: the senior high school chess club plays every Thursday afternoon
700	Clay molding
700	"Clowning Around": workshop to teach teens basic clown techniques, gags, and makeup; teens can volunteer to perform for children's programs at the library
700	Comic book contest
700	Comic book illustration workshop
700	Dance demonstration: features hip-hop dancers; consider renting a dance machine
700	Decorate your locker contest: teens decorate their lockers to promote a favorite book as part of Teen Read Week
700	Drawing cartoons and comics
700	"Duct Day!": tweens and teens are invited to create cool stuff out of duct tape
700	Extreme sports: demonstration and interactive workshop
700	Game night: weekly program with board games and computer games
700	"Have You Seen This Scene?": match the movie scene to its title and win a prize
700	Hemp jewelry-making
700	Hip-hop symposium: a panel of record company representatives, song writers, attorneys, librarians, and other community members
700	Holiday craft making
700	Improv night: older kids put on an improv show
700	Juggling workshop
700	Karate/martial arts workshop
700	"Library of Terror": teens write a script, use zombie costumes, and decorate the library for a children's program
700	Live music from local teen bands
700	"Magic: The Gathering Open Play": teens can bring their own cards and test their skills against others
700	"Magnificent Murals": local artist guides teens on the creation of a large-scale masterpiece at the library
700	"Manga Maniacs": regular club to meet and discuss new manga publications
700	Mask making: demonstration and interactive workshop
700	Monopoly, Scrabble, and other board came tournaments
700	Native American crafts
700	Origami: interactive workshop that teaches the history and the art of Japanese paper folding
700	Paper airplanes: demonstration and interactive workshop
700	Photography contest: winning photos are posted both in the library and on the library's Web page
700	Pictionary and other active games

Figure 8-1. Continued

700	Picture frame art: teens learn how to make their own photo frames
700	"PlayStation Mania": a chance to trade tips and codes, as well as swap games
700	Puppet building workshop: teens work with a local artist to create large scale puppets; student can use the puppet during the summer to put on programs at library and in the community
700	Radio personalities: demonstration and interactive workshop
700	Remote-control car racing
700	Sand painting: demonstration and interactive workshop
700	"Scary Movie Quiz": teens test their knowledge of scary movies (or books) at Halloween
700	"Scrapbooking Club": regular club to learn about different techniques and share scrapbooks
700	Screen printing: a local artist teaches teens techniques of screen printing used to make stunning prints of original artwork
700	Skateboarding: demonstration and interactive workshop
700	Skiing: demonstration and interactive workshop
700	Snowboarding: demonstration and interactive workshop
700	Sound systems for home and car: demonstration and interactive workshop
700	Sports card collecting: demonstration and interactive workshop
700	Stage makeup workshop: a workshop on how makeup is used in theater, TV, and movies; perfect for Halloween
700	"Sweet Dreams": teens learn the history of the dream catcher and make one to take home
700	Teen band performance: an after-hours Summer Reading Program party; good for the end of the year
700	Teen-created booktalk videos: booktalks performed as skits or interviews
700	Teen drama club: teens pick and then present a play based on a children's book; held over the summer on weekly basis
700	Teen movie night: screening of a movie based on book; includes food and book discussion
700	"Teen Open Mic Night": teens perform for other teens
700	"Teen Reading Raffle": teens fill out a raffle ticket for every book they read; everybody wins something, and the more you put in, the better the chance of winning
700	"Teen Talent Show": teens show off their talents and win a prize
700	Teens script and perform in a video about the library's collections, computers, etc.
700	Tie-die: teens dye t-shirts outside; attracts attention to the library
700	T-shirt decoration: teens create their own t-shirts to wear when they volunteer

Figure 8-1. Continued

700	"Video Stars": PTA purchases video cameras; teens do book commercials with a tag line about getting it free at the library; teens suggest books for teachers to use in classrooms.
700	Yo-yo tricks
700	"Yu-Gi-Oh!": teens bring their own cards or borrow the library's deck and challenge each other
800	"Calling All Guys": an all-male book discussion group
800	"Who Said That?": features famous quotes, movie lines, song lyrics, and popular culture phrases; teens have to match the person who said it to the quote itself; the teen with the most correct answers gets a prize
800	"All-School Read-In": an idea from a principal; a list of titles is circulated and each student gets to keep a book out of three titles they choose; a local vendor provides books and gives a booktalk
800	Accelerated Reader software/hardware loaned to public library during summer
800	"Battle of the Books": librarians select titles for fifth and sixth grade (or seventh, eighth, and beyond); the public library buys several copies; librarians make up questions and act as timers and scorekeepers.
800	Book club based on the state book award: teens submit their local vote for the award
800	Book swap program: the library pulls books from their book sale and allows teens to exchange books
800	"Breakfast Club": held during breakfast break; students provide the librarian with input on which books to buy and then get the first chance to check them out
800	Harry Potter party: includes costume contest, food, and movie theater passes
800	Journaling: workshop teaching teens to create journals and use writing as a way of knowing
800	Lock-In: held from six p.m. Friday to six a.m. Saturday for Teen Read Week; teens aged thirteen to seventeen make crafts, burn CDs, paint masks, have a pumpkin-decorating contest, and eat lots of food
800	"Lunch Bunch": book discussion group; teens bring a sack lunch and the library furnishes chips, soda, and—of course—books
800	"Mad Libs Poetry": teens fill in the blanks and create their own version of famous poems
800	"Magnetic Poetry Fun!": teens create their own magnetic poetry kits and spend some time composing poems
800	"Middle Earth Madness": Lord of the Rings trilogy tie-in that tests a teen's knowledge of hobbits, elves, wizards, etc.
800	Mother-daughter (or father/son) book group
800	Murder mystery at the library: can use a kit from Highsmith (www.highsmith.com)

Figure 8-1. Continued

800	"Order of the Fantasy Fanatics Challenge": contest testing teens' knowledge of fantasy novels
800	Poetry café: held in conjunction with National Poetry week in April; Friday evening program allowing teens to read favorite poetry or poetry they wrote; free food and drinks
800	Poetry contest: held every in the spring; teens can submit two poems; program is capped off by an open mic night to announce winners; success of program lead to the publication of the compiled poems and a follow-up short story contest
800	"Poetry in the Dark": poetry reading outside by candlelight in an area with benches
800	"Power of the Pen": creative writing contest; partner with school boards and the newspaper; program leads to publishing a book or poems on the Web page
800	"Readers' Theater Troupe": teens become their favorite characters from stories using different hats or props for each character
800	"SF&F Fans Group": Science fiction and fantasy fans group that meets each month to discuss featured themes and books and to enjoy activities and light refreshments
800	Spoken word performance: demonstrations, live performance, discussion, and poetry slamming
800	"Tales of Terror Writing Contest": teens compete to write the best scary short story
800	"Teen Book Reviews": reviews written by teens that appear in the local newspaper
800	"Teen Graffiti Board": teens leave poetry, messages, riddles, titles of good books they've read—whatever they wish to write or draw on a large sheets of paper
800	"Teen Playreaders": regular group of teens who read plays aloud
800	"Teen Read Week Hard Cover Café": teens bring a book, listen to live music, and booktalk
800	Teen story hour: runs four to eight weeks; teens read together and then discuss what they have read
800	Writing workshop: feature a local author as kick-off for a literary magazine
900	Oral history: demonstration and interactive workshop
900	Visit from the Society for Creative Anachronism or another historical reenactment organization
900	Local history programs involving teens using technology (video, digital cameras, etc.) to record the community's past
900	Finding hidden treasure: demonstration and interactive workshop
900	Programs, quizzes, or other activities to celebrate, commemorate, or explore various historical events (Juneteenth, Holocaust, 9/11, etc.)
900	"History Day": information-literacy session aimed at teens and their parents
900	"Name Game": program where teens find out meaning of their names
900	"Rooting into Your Past": genealogy demonstration and interactive workshop

Figure 8-1. Continued

WHAT ARE THE KEYS TO DEVELOPING SUCCESSFUL TEEN PROGRAMS?

- **Choose a popular topic.** While trying to guess what is popular with teens is no easy trick, an LST should be able to determine which topics have broad popularity by asking, by looking at the collection, and by observing what teens are surfing on the Internet. But just as important are topics that enjoy deep rather than broad popularity. For example, the majority of teens are not interested in subjects like scrapbooking, anime, and role-playing games—but those who are interested are usually fanatics who look for any opportunity to pursue their interests.

- **Partner with schools, school groups, and youth service organizations.** Whether the partner provides information or an audience, those programs will succeed in terms of attendance, and you may be able to capture the partner groups' audience for other library programs.

- **Promote; don't just publicize.** This is subject of the next chapter. Simply put, the role of your library's community relations department is to provide you with publicity materials; it is your job to use those materials to promote your programs.

- **Make connections to what is happening in the lives of teenagers.** This means looking for topics that are not so much popular as necessary—study nights, SAT classes, etc. You can also make connections to the calendar, to the curriculum, and to the state education standards.

- **Think "high-touch."** The best model for teen programs is not story time, in which we perform and the audience watches, but toddler time, in which we provide an interactive experience consistent with the developmental needs of the child. The developmental needs of teens and toddlers are more similar (the need for attention and independence, etc.) than not.

- **Youth involvement.** We've devoted an entire chapter to this practice, but the key is involving the right number of youth in the right ways. Teens can be involved in so many ways, from coming up with ideas, to preparing promotional materials, to actually doing the program themselves.

> Too often, we use the children's performer/audience model and that doesn't work as well for teens. Most teens want to do, not just watch.

- **Define success and tailor expectations based on the needs of your library and teens.** A teen book discussion group with eight teens in attendance might be a "success" on the stat sheet, but it won't be for the teens who attended but didn't get a chance to speak. While there are some exceptions, remember that in many teen programs there is an inverse relationship between the quantity of attendees and the quality of the experience. At the same time, we must define our expectations. To say "well, the three kids that were here enjoyed it," works for the first meeting of a book discussion group because you want and need a small group; to say that for a performance by an author or band that allows for no interaction doesn't work. We need to be honest with ourselves, but we also need to be honest with our superiors to help them understand that teen programming is not as simple (in every sense of the word) as children's programs. It is not just a matter of booking a performer, putting out some flyers, and waiting for the parents to bring the kids. Moreover, while there is nothing wrong with enjoyment being the only "outcome" of a children's program featuring a clown, teens need more than that. If we are to focus on the outcomes for teens, we must stop focusing so strongly on the output for the library.

CONCLUSION

This is a little more difficult than story time, isn't it? Yet, the rewards are greater. Sometimes teens will value a program because they learned a skill, sometimes because they created a craft. While crafts don't directly tie into the larger mission of a most libraries, they do tie into something just as important: providing teens with an opportunity to engage in meaningful activities. Are crafts meaningful? Are book discussion groups meaningful? The fact that a teen chooses to participate gives that activity meaning. Programming allows LSTs to turn our core values into activities that teens will value.

9 SPACES AND PROMOTION

"I think it's a good idea to have the high interest nonfiction in the teen section because it is a lot easier to find. I know that I won't browse the nonfiction in the adult section just because it's so big (unless it's for a project or something), but in the teen section all I have to do is walk by and I usually see something that pertains to me or my interests. And yeah, I'll admit it, the flashy titles and things that look like they are directed at teenagers (and therefore should be easier for a teen to read and relate to) are usually what catch my interest."

—*an Indiana high school student*

Collections and programs are products, but if you want teens to use them, you'll need to promote them effectively. Promoting programs, not to mention core services, is something most libraries struggle with, not just the LST. We put out the flyer and then hope that people come. That's not promotion or marketing; that is wishful thinking. Similarly, we build a collection and believe just having it is enough. Maybe it was enough before there was Borders and Amazon, but books on shelves isn't enough anymore. Thus, the past few years have seen a renaissance in young adult spaces, especially in large urban libraries. Whether it is a new building (Phoenix, Arizona and Salt Lake City, Utah) or a renovated one (Austin, Texas), or just carving out new space in an old building (Houston, Texas), public libraries are making a commitment to teens. We get teens to attend our programs through promotion; we get them to use our collection through creating attractive spaces.

> We get more money every year, more books, more programs, and sometimes more staff, but rarely more space; thus, space is perhaps the single most valuable commodity available to LSTs.

WHAT ARE THE ELEMENTS OF SUCCESSFUL TEEN SPACES?

We must first realize that every library already has a young adult space—the entire library. Teens use libraries holistically and even the best, "coolest," and newest teen space isn't going to serve all teens. While in many ways a secondary school library is, in and of itself, a young adult space, there is still work to be done. Many of the design elements found in the public library teen spaces will work just as well in a school. Teen readers in school libraries needs to find a place to find the new stuff, rather than looking through the classics on the shelves, more for the teachers support, than for student use. In the public library, teens are all over the place; the purpose of a teen space is to centralize the recreational and perhaps informational resources for teens. And that means more than just a rack of paperbacks; and it means more than just fiction.

In large libraries, teen areas must have nonfiction, as the high school junior from Carmal Clay (Indiana) Public Library noted. A YA section of YA novels shows we are responding to tradition, publishers, and perhaps our library's own needs, but not that of customers. Perhaps eighth grader Sarah Hughes, also from the Carmal Clay Public Library (Indiana) says it best, "If the teen sections only had young adults fiction books it could not be considered a teen section, it would be young adult fiction. The teen area of the library makes teens feel comfortable, welcome, and a part of the library and it would not be complete without the nonfiction books that teen library users have requested. It would be a lot more complicated to find a nonfiction teen book and uncomfortable for some to go in the adult section to learn about teen problems and find books written for teens." A teen space without nonfiction isn't really one.

Once you've decided on the scope of the collection, then comes the fun part—the sequences. Deciding what goes where and always asking the question "why?" before moving or buying a single piece of furniture is part of sequencing. Teen spaces will vary library to library, but every library needs one, just like every teen wants their own room. It's about identity, which is the most basic teen developmental need. But for the library, there are other benefits. A teen space will help reduce challenges as it means that Francesca Lia Block's mature musing in books like *Weeetize Bat* are not shelved in a youth area next to Michael Bond's *Paddington*. A teen space can become a focal point for services, programs, and recruiting volunteers.

The elements to remember when creating a teen space are numerous but important.

> A teen space sends a message, if done right, that "this is not your father's library" by blowing away the stereotypes of libraries, and librarians, by presenting a fresh, fun, and flexible environment.

- **ADA.** Make sure when planning your teen area that you understand the ADA requirements regarding accessibility. Aim to build access into the design of the area as integral, not an afterthought. ADA regulations provide merely the minimum requirement, so these guidelines should be the starting, not the ending, point.
- **Ambiance.** Colors matter, of the floor, the walls, and the ceiling. Too much overwhelms and too little is visually unexciting.

- **Collection development.** You can build the most beautiful teen area in the world, but if your collection development isn't just as responsive, kids might come to hang out; but they won't find anything to hang onto to make them want to return.

- **Comfort.** Teens report they enjoy the atmosphere at Barnes & Noble because, as one California teen focus group participant said, "They have coffee, music, comfortable furniture, and you can talk as much as you want. It's way better than a library." Libraries, for good reasons, don't pipe in music or allow for unlimited conversation; some have taken the coffee route, but the comfortable furniture is obtainable.

- **Community space.** In addition to the young adult area, LSTs need to be advocates for community space within the library. Not only can this space be used for programming and youth involvement, but it could also be used to display teen artwork, literary efforts, and other visual arts.

- **Computers.** There is not always room for this, but computers are certainly desired. If there is not room for wires for Internet connected computers, then consider either laptops or stand-alone units with word processing software.

- **Displays.** There is an array of subliterature about library displays, so there is little to add other than these words. Don't do it yourself. Unless you are a creative dynamo with artistic talent, visual merchandising background, and a lot of free time, let teen volunteers take over this task. They can do it just as well as you, and then you can spend time developing programs, doing outreach, and building the collection rather than making signs, and a big mess, out of glitter. Here's one to do on your own: a display of books, which feature faces on the covers. It doesn't fit around any holiday, but the responses as the books fly off the shelf is cause for celebration.

- **Food and drink.** The bookstore and coffee shop experience is one many teens like and would like to replicate in the library. At home, most teens manage to read, use a computer, listen to music, and snack and sip without spilling a drop. Libraries, however, have had long standing prohibitions against this, and both sides

One of the California kids said while explaining the preference for Barnes & Noble, that "it's all not just boring and dry like a library."

of the argument have valid points. While some of these rules were designed and directed at teens, other libraries use them as a way to control the activity of the homeless population that frequents most urban libraries. There has to be a middle ground between being the Snack Gestapo and allowing Domino's to make a delivery of pizza to the study area.

- **Freshness and maintenance.** If you are doing all the right things, the YA area should be a mess everyday. It should be messy, as well, before teens show up as you "seed" it with new books that just happen to be lying around on the tables that teens use to study, or sitting next to the computers. However, if it looks like the room of a typical teenager, no one can find anything. While that may work for one teen, it doesn't work when serving a lot of them.

- **Fun.** Perhaps the most compelling reason to do any, or all, of these things is simply to try to make the teen part of the library "fun."

- **Library promotion.** Walls and kiosk space, the end of shelves and the shelves themselves, and maybe even the floor could be used to promote library programs and services. Try to get your Friends group to purchase a good multipurpose display fixture, preferably with a slat wall.

- **Light.** The lighting in most libraries is pretty substandard; in the young adult areas, which often get tucked in an alcove, it is even worse. You can build it; but if they don't see, they won't come. Putting the YA area near a window will allow natural light to enter, and it will provide the opportunity to see and be seen. The Phoenix teen space's fiber-optic ceiling effects is the ideal and maybe unattainable, but it does remind us that ceiling space is perhaps the most overlooked and underused part of most libraries, especially teen areas.

- **Location.** It is easier to name the locations in a library where a young adult area does not belong: next to the children's room, circulation desk, reference area, or quiet study/reading area. In addition to a location with traffic, the location must afford some privacy; yet, at the same time, allow staff to observe the area, for safety and customer service.

- **Magazines.** A face-out shelving unit filled with the covers of young adult magazines is as good, if not better, than any sign. This shelf tells teens this area is for them.

- **Merchandising.** Displays are not merchandising; they are tools of merchandising. Merchandising is as much a philosophy as it is a practice. Paperbacks are the cornerstones of merchandising because of their size; you can cram more of them attractively into a small area, and their covers are often more attractive than their hardback relatives. If you look at the vast literature on merchandising, you will realize that most YAs seek out books, rather than a book. Admit it, most YAs find books because of covers, not reviews, or because of recommendations from friends, not from you. If you weed your hardbacks, you now have room to display the ones remaining, and their circulation will increase.

- **Not everything belongs on a shelf.** Comics can go in bins, paperbacks in book dumps, and magazines in boxes. By mixing up how materials are shelved, we may create some confusion to the minority of teens seeking a certain book; but make it easier and more attractive for the majority of teens browsing for something to read.

- **Passive youth involvement.** In addition to involving youth directly in focus groups or advisory boards to gather information to build, and maintain, in a successful young adult area, there has to be a place for passive youth involvement. It could be as simple as a suggestion box, although there is no sense providing such a vehicle, if teens won't know if you really are listening. Next to any suggestion board, or graffiti wall, needs to be a space for the library staff to reply that tells teens we listen to their opinion.

- **Photo wall.** Showing off your past successes, is a great way to promote your programs. Have a wall, photo album, or scrapbook that is highly visible to document in pictures what is happening for teens in your library. A mural done by a local high school might present a more permanent photo wall and is a great example of youth involvement.

- **Plugs and power.** With more teens bringing their own computers, handheld or laptop, it is just as important as providing hookups, wireless if possible, to let teens surf away while relaxing in a comfy chair.

- **Post the house rules.** Consider having the teens who help put together the space; also put together the rules for the area. Clearly spell out the expectations of those using the area, focusing more on what teens should/could do rather than a laundry list of prohibitions.

- **Privacy.** Most teens, upon getting their own room in their parents' house, put up the "do not disturb" sign. Teens like and need privacy, but the ability for staff to monitor the area, as well as the desire to have it in a visible place so teens can find it, has to be balanced.

- **Put the books with the teens.** When teens enter a library, particularly boys, they make a beeline for the computers. Some go to chat rooms, others send e-mails, while many surf the Web, gathering information; not for school, but for themselves. In other words, teens use computers either to build their personal cultures or to explore their interests, or even both. But while they are on the computers, where are the titles that might help them in their quest? On a shelf half a room away. Place books near the computers, printers, and copiers. Place them on tables and chairs where teens gather. Place books by the phone, checkout desk, and other high teen-traffic areas. The worst that can happen is that the books don't get checked out and need to be reshelved.

- **Quiet space.** It is not in the teen room and certainly not near any service desk, but there also needs to be a quiet place for teens to study. Everything about kids multitasking and being able to talk is true, but never 100 percent of the time. Sometimes, especially around exams for high schoolers, what is needed more than anything is a quiet place to study. So many teens don't have that at home, and libraries are their only option. Libraries with meeting rooms just sitting unoccupied, need to look at engaging volunteers to consider making this great space available for quiet study.

- **Reading promotion.** From reading-promotion posters—please, take down the ALA read posters from the 1980s—to movie posters, to booklists, to bulletin boards, wall or kiosk space is crucial in order to use the environment to promote the product.

Ask for respect, and you just might get it in return.

In the focus groups in California, they asked over and over again for the library to provide them a space to be teenagers.

- **Relaxed rules.** Perhaps the most important part of a successful young adult area isn't the TV and technology, but a tolerance level. A YA area isn't just about the physical space, but about an "emotional space," where teens can behave like teens.

- **Rules plus.** Many libraries have adopted for their teen space the following rules with signage to boot: "ADULTS NOT ACCOMPANIED BY A TEEN SHOULD LIMIT THEIR VISIT TO 15 MINUTES!" If challenged, this restriction would probably need to be rescinded, but the idea of keeping the teen space, in particular the computers, for teens is the right idea.

- **Shelving fixtures.** There are better systems out there than the book shelves we've been using in libraries since Melville Dewey. Try to enter the twentieth century at least and look at slat wall shelving, trifold displays features, zigzag shelving, book display units, and even cardboard book dumps to think of ways we can store and display books that allow people to get intrigued by looking at the covers rather than a stiff neck from staring side ways at the call numbers.

- **Signage.** It has to be big, bright, and bilingual. It should be devoid of library jargon and teen slang. Neon is nice. The signage, however, can't just be in the YA space alone; there needs to be ways to direct kids who don't know about the space to get there. It might be signs by the front door, footsteps painted on the floor, or maybe lots of small flyers by the heavily trafficked areas and collections. Putting up a sign in a YA area is great to tell people where they are, but doesn't help them get there.

- **Space that works.** A true young adult space isn't just a rack of paperbacks or a couple of bookshelves, but a real space that has room for hanging out, programming, displays, and computers.

- **Study space.** The pedagogy of teaching has changed dramatically in the past decade. From teacher as guru, to guide by the side. Move away from lecture and memorization, except for those standardized tests, and more toward group work. If you want teens to congregate in the young adult area, they need space to spread out and do their work, both schoolwork and social work.

A name, like Teen Zone, Wired for Teens, or ConnecTeen does establish the space as a "brand" that can be leveraged in other promotions.

- **The name.** the big question is always do you call it the teen area or the young adult area, or something else. It depends. If you have done all of these things, especially youth involvement, then the name is irrelevant. The space will have an identity based on how you plan it rather than what you call it. Lots of libraries spend time developing names, often involving contests among teens.

- **Think like 7-11.** When you go into a convenience store in order to get to the milk you need to go past the candy, chips, and soda. Use that retail mindset when thinking of what belongs in a young adult area. Consider housing Cliffs notes and classics in the YA area. This provides a "reason" for teens who may not normally find the young adult area, perhaps because they are not regular library users or avid readers, to visit the young adult collection and be exposed to all that a strong young adult collection can offer.

- **Traffic.** Start by looking at the traffic patterns of your library; where do young adults travel to and from? While there is a lot to be said for the privacy that a "back area" location might offer teens, they need a reason to go there, and they need to know it exists. By putting a YA area outside of the main traffic areas, you are limiting use.

- **Tunes.** The teen space at the Phoenix Public Library is known for many things, but perhaps the most unique feature is the "jukebox" room. The importance of music in teen life is well documented, but the idea of music playing in a library is unheard of. Headphones for computers, a CD player, maybe MP3 player, or an Apple computer to download I-tunes, need to be part of the mix. Needless to say, a CD-burner with the appropriate copyright notices pasted all over it should be included.

- **TV/Video/DVD/gaming equipment.** Many libraries also recognize the heavy visual teen culture; and at the same time, the uncanny ability of so many young adults to multitask and make cable TV and video/DVD available to watch in house. Many teens would certainly enjoy a gaming environment, although this stretches the recreational mission of a public library pretty far and would be seen by many, including many teens, as more distraction than attraction.

• **Youth involvement.** While this is last on the list, it is first and foremost as an element of success for planning great YA spaces. Many of these ideas listed above about young adult areas are illustrated time and time again in the "YA Dream Spaces" articles which have been running in almost every issue of *VOYA* since Cathi MacRae assumed editorship. These are "how I done it good pieces" from big and small libraries, public and school, who created a successful YA space. While each is different; almost all are the same in that there was youth involvement. From choosing the furniture to naming the space and even keeping in maintained, getting teens to feel ownership of the space is the primary key to success. Teens can certainly help with almost all of the above elements as well. It's last on this list, but needs to be first and foremost in your thinking, especially when designing a new area. It is not helpful to just say "What do you want?" to a group of teens that have no experience in picking fixtures for a library; instead, it is your job to facilitate and guide teens on the choices available. Allow them to dream, but if you don't provide some guidance, then you'll get disappointment rather than excitement.

Whether you are planning a new space or designing an old one, these elements of success should enable you, and your teens, to find a place of their own in any school or public library.

WHAT ARE SOME OF THE BEST PRACTICES FOR PROMOTING LIBRARY SERVICES TO TEENS?

A key part of a successful young adult area is having space allocated to promote library programs. That is important, but also short-term thinking. Libraries don't generally do well communicating to the public about exactly what it is we do. This is even truer with teens, because most libraries have not figured out how to crack the market. While lessons from Peter Zollo are helpful, much of his insight is aimed at using media to promote goods to teens for purchase produced by companies with million-dollar-plus ad budgets. It is good stuff, but that is not the situation that most libraries find for themselves. Normally, libraries don't have access to media and don't have a lot money to spend on promotion. We are not selling one product or brand name; instead, we sell events (programs) and ideas (libraries as helpful places). An attractive space is a nonverbal message to teens, but to get teens to attend programs and use services, the messages need to be very verbal, and very visible. There are plenty of books on library marketing, but the key to marketing to teens is the same as building a collection, doing reference, and just about everything else.

The word "promote" is used often and it has many meanings. For the best output from your promotion efforts, you and your staff need to be excited about the program. This does not mean wearing clown makeup and doing cartwheels every time you mention the program. But it does mean have enthusiasm, whatever shape that takes. If you are not excited or enthused about the program, why would anyone take time to come to the program, especially teenagers who most certainly have other things they could be doing. Promoting the program does not mean putting flyers on a table and calling it a day. Do you pick up flyers from tables? An evaluation rarely comes back from a teenager with "picked up a flyer" circled as the way they found out about a program. As with most people, word of mouth works the best; flyers don't hurt and they are great to give to adults, the newspaper, radio, or cable access station to use in promoting the program; but flyers on a table is the beginning, not the end, of promotion.

If you have ever shopped at a retail store or been through the drive-through at fast food restaurant, you know they always ask you if you want to "add on" an item. You probably didn't go in with that particular item on your mind; but, by mentioning it, they make you think twice. One store offers socks, another a triple burrito, why don't we offer a free, cool program? If you are embarrassed to sell/promote your own programs to teens, or parents of teens, you need to go back to the planning stage. You should have an "add on" phrase for your programs that you can work into all exchanges with teens. In a perfect world your entire staff would be doing this, but part of it is leading by example. If you are excited and informed about your YA programming, then mentioning it at staff meetings, an e-mail the week before a program, or putting a flyer in everyone's box is way to market your produce. Adults might read those flyers, then other staff will catch your enthusiasm; and, if they don't, at least they will be informed enough to answer questions. Another part of promotion is your library Web site. This is a great place to promote your programs as well as ask for feedback about your other YA services.

If you are a one-person department, what Renee Vaillancourt dubbed "a YA lone ranger," you may be responsible for creating the advertising materials for your programs. There are many computer programs that can make this easy work, but even easier work might be having a teen volunteer help with the design and layout of advertising. If getting the teen on the computer is not possible, let teens choose

> Don't waste time printing flyers; instead, spend time building relationships with teens.

graphic, colors, and fonts; anything that will give your promotional items a teen touch instead of an adult touch. One LST asked the art department in her library system for a sign to help carve out a teen area in her branch. They were helpful but the sign that arrived had a graphic of young kids on bikes eating ice cream. Several adults even thought it looked childish, so the lesson there may be twofold. Be specific about your intent and what the end product should be; have teen input and possibly stay away from graphics featuring "teens" or an artist's interpretation of "teens." It may become dated quickly. Whereas a graphic of a shape, lines, or an object may last longer; think about certain companies or brands and the symbols they use. It is not often a person but an object or shape, such as Sprint and the pin dropping, Microsoft and the wavy four-color flag, the Nike swoosh, or the WWE's scratchy logo.

Zollo and others involved in teen marketing are light-years ahead of the curve of where most libraries are. Most libraries still believe the *only* way to promote a program is to print a flyer. Little thought is given to the flyer's design, its placement in the library or the community, or even the information that will "grab" a person's attention; instead, by printing the flyer, we believe we are promoting the program. We are asking, in effect, for a young person with many choices of how to spend their time to come to our event. A plethora of messages come to them through all sorts of media making their pitch, and we think that teens will pick up flyers on a library table and that will persuade them to return. It does happen, but it is not the only way. There are lots and lots (and lots) of other ways to promote programs, services, and collections.

- **Be a good host.** Encourage community organizations that to cater teens but lack meeting space to hold events at the library, and ask, in return, that they pass out literature about the library, or allow someone from the staff to speak briefly.
- **Be bilingual.** Whenever possible and applicable, make sure that programs are promoted to Spanish language or other media.
- **Billboards.** Very expensive, but doable and very effective; especially if placed near teen locations such as skate parks, schools, and malls.
- **Book reviews.** Work with the local paper to do reviews of books by teens in the teen section. If you are in a small market and have trouble getting the newspaper to cover your events, there is a solution. Invite one of the editors to get involved in a teen activity, such as judging a writing contest. Now, they have a vested interest

- **Bookstore look.** Post new book covers using color copies from Amazon.

- **Build transportation money into grants.** If you can't convince teens to come to programs on their own, then have money to bring them to the event via public transportation.

- **Buy.** Purchase ads in yearbooks, student newspapers, and school district newsletters to promote teen services to students, parents, and teachers.

- **Cable access TV.** Every community with cable has it, but few take advantage. While it is true that hardly anyone deliberately sits down to watch a cable access show, teens flipping through the remote might stop if they saw a show featuring other teens. You could videotape just about anything as long as you have permission—programs, booktalks, book discussion groups, and author visits. End the program, or better yet a crawler at the bottom of the screen, listing upcoming teen events at the library. Also, many schools have their own cable access stations.

- **Date due slips.** We are not sophisticated enough to do this in a really directed way, but if your circulation system issues a receipt, then wish every one a Happy Teen Read Week in October. Let teens, and the community know that your library does teen.

- **E-mail lists of teens.** When teens attend an event, get their e-mail address in order to build a mailing list. Or, given how teens change e-mail addresses quickly, get them to address a postcard to themselves that you can use to invite them to your next program.

- **Fast food.** Work with one local fast food chain, and perhaps a pizza chain as well, to market library services through signs, special placemats, etc.

- **Flyers redux.** There are so many variations. Some libraries make them look very unprofessional, like something a punk band would do to promote a gig. Others put all the information on the flyer, including the address, but leave out the fact the event is at the library. Flyers can be stuffed in books being checked out or on display, hung up all over the library, handed out at the every reference transaction, posted at schools, posted in the community, and posted on the library shelves. Anywhere but lying buried in a pile of other flyers.

SPACES AND PROMOTION **265**

Link Web sites. School and public library teen Web sites need easy to find direct links on each other's Web pages.

- **Give away.** Have a raffle or drawing connected with every program, or just have one weekly. This will generate food traffic as word of mouth spreads.
- **Homegrown "read" posters and bookmarks.** Hire a photographer, or use one of your teens with skills, to take pictures of teens in various locations around the library, and then post them. This is easier now thanks to do-it-yourself materials available from ALA Graphics.
- **Lists.** Put reading lists everywhere and change them often. Download them, make your own, and borrow them.
- **Loyalty.** Provide teens with a customer loyalty program where they can earn "points" by attending events, volunteering, and writing online reviews.
- **Mailing lists and e-mail lists.** Develop these to promote teen programs that include schools, school groups, faith-based organizations, youth organization, as well as local media.
- **Mouse pads.** Design mouse pads with your library's teen Web site address. They are cheap and they work. Get one for every computer lab, every teacher, and every school library.
- **Parades.** Participate in community events, including parades. This is not only a great promotional opportunity, but a magnificent youth involvement one as well. Some libraries train teens to be a "book cart drill team."
- **Parks and recreation departments.** These, and other government agencies, could sign on as promotional partners. In their promotional materials listing summer events and classes, they could also advertise library programs. You could do something do the same with community education promotional materials.
- **PowerPoint presentation.** Put together a nice, not too long, PowerPoint, and provide one for every teacher about the library. You could also have ones, complete with handouts, that could be used to do information-literacy sessions. Or, for the teachers among us, maybe a flash based Web site.
- **PTAs and other connectors.** Parents still have a big influence over the life and times of their teenagers, so don't write them off. Parents who are involved in

school organizations are good resources to spread the message to, not only because they need the information themselves, but PTA parents are usually connected to people in other groups.

- **Radio remote.** An on-site radio broadcast normally costs a great deal, unless you are involved in some sort of partnership agreement. A local radio station, however, might be willing to mention an upcoming program or special event, especially if offer to put the station's logo on your flyers or teen Web site.

- **Rap.** Work with a local hip-hop group to produce a public service announcement and/or video about using libraries. Remember, one of Tupac's first big public successes was performing as part of a rap contest to celebrate the Enoch Pratt Library's hundredth anniversary.

- **Regular open house or program.** Make it very low key, but with free food. You use this event as a way to get people in the door to inform them about other programs and services.

- **School announcements.** Especially effective if they are "live" on in-school cable.

- **School bus ads.** While public transportation ads might work, they cast too wide a net. Since many teens, especially in junior high, ride a school bus, why not work with schools to put ads in those buses? Or simply put a flyer for an upcoming program at local bus stops that teens frequent.

- **School newspaper.** Pitch stories about library programs, new resources, and any changes in service.

- **School visits.** This is harder and harder to do with class time sucked up by studying for standardized test, so a school visit needs to be connected to the teacher's goals, not your agenda. There are plenty of other ways to do school visits outside of the normal and formal way of moving from class to class. How about a booth at the school open house to sign-up teens for library cards? How about a table in the cafeteria to promote a big program, or in the school library?

- **Sell and show.** Have every staff member "selling" to teens; proactive and friendly customer service is the best promotion of all.

Reward teachers, other librarians, and library staff who promote your programs. Praise them and encourage them to get others involved.

- **Signs in front of schools**. These often just sit empty during the summer. Ask schools to put a positive message about summer reading or programs.
- **Student ambassadors.** If there is not enough staff to get the word out to teens, recruit student ambassadors who could earn community service credits by being the school and library go-between.
- **Student clubs.** Clubs provide a great vehicle for cooperation program planning, but also to promote library programs, services, and collections.
- **Sun days.** Hold programs outside if possible and applicable. Talk about a way to attract attention.
- **Teens as spokespeople.** Always let teens tell their stories about why libraries matter to them, and should matter to their peers. In writing, on video, or over the radio, aim for maximum teen involvement. Partner with school drama, speech, or related clubs to find hams ready to carry out the message.
- **Use the calendar.** Plan programs for those special weeks—Banned Book Week, Teen Read Week, and the like—that come with "canned" promotional materials to download and/or purchase.
- **User guide.** Create a user guide that provides hours, information of technology, and, for larger libraries, where and how to find books. It should be informative, yet entertaining; perhaps done as a comic created by a teen artist. Think like customers. Don't do a user guide about "remote access databases"; instead do one called "How to use the library when the library is closed." It is the same information, but you are telling the story in a way that interests the user.
- **Video promotion.** There are plenty of best practices for teens doing video production to promote libraries. From cutting thirty second "spots" promoting their favorite books to full blown booktalk reenactments, turn teens with interest, time, and talent on a project on using the library.
- **Web sites.** In addition to promoting events on teen Web sites, how about a pop-up ad every now and then? Also, put digital photos of past events to show those teens who did not attend exactly what they missed.

- **Youth group and youth serving organizations.** You should be approached about communicate partnerships so that you promote their programs and they do the same for you.

- **Youth involvement (again).** Let your local teens tell us the best methods for reaching them. The ideas probably won't be much different than the ones you've read here, but it will validate them for you; and also, if they suggest it, they just might carry it out. For example, hold a contest, in larger system, among libraries for best teen areas. Make sure to includes prizes for the best use of teen volunteers, best use of space, and then best overall display.

CONCLUSION

Most libraries focus on promoting the special, not the everyday. That makes sense, except so many of our teen customers, and noncustomers, don't know what we do everyday. Yet, all these good ideas to draw teens into libraries mean nothing if the staff is not friendly, if the collection is not in shape, if there is no YA space, and if the experience is negative. The best promotion isn't flyers, but instead having all staff ensuring that teens have a positive library experience and making that easier by having a separate but equal young adult area. If teens have a good experience, they will spread the word. You can't buy word of mouth advertising; you can only earn it.

10   TECHNOLOGY

"If I ever go when I need a book, I'm scared to ask them where it is, because I don't want them to think I'm stupid for not knowing how to use the computer."

—*a California teen speaking about his library experience*

One of the most challenging things about providing library services to young adults is getting them to view the library as a teen-friendly zone. With the proliferation of technology in libraries across the country, more and more young people are viewing the library today as a home away from home—one with state-of-the-art hardware, top-of-the-line software, cutting-edge computer peripherals, and that oh-so-important high speed Internet connection. No longer the silent repository of old books and outdated information, today's libraries are a teen's portal to the world.

According to a 2001 national survey conducted by the National School Boards Foundation, 75 percent of teenagers had access to the Internet either at home or at school, and 49 percent of households had Internet access. In a similar study conducted by the Pew Internet and American Life Project in 2002, researchers estimated that 78 percent, or approximately eighteen million, preteens and teens between the ages of twelve and seventeen use the Internet on a regular basis. These studies prove what those of us who work with teenagers already know—young people use the Internet; they use it for recreation, they use it for research, and they use it for communication. More than ever, libraries can offer young people something they may not be able to get at home or in school—unlimited, predominantly unrestricted access to the Internet. Rather than protest this inevitable use of the library, celebrate it. Take advantage of this opportunity and use it to begin developing a relationship with each and every teen who walks through that door looking to sign up for a computer.

HOW DO WE SERVE TECHNO-SAVVY TEENS?

Although teens today have grown up with the Internet, this does not mean that they know exactly what it is, how it works, or why it is important to evaluate all that information that can be found at the click of a button. The World Wide Web is a labyrinth of information consisting of millions of sites (perhaps billions by the time this book reaches you). Just because a teen knows how to listen to music on the Web or search for computer or videogame cheat codes using Google does not mean he or she knows how to use the Internet.

Surfing the Net for fun and using it as a research tool are two completely different activities with two very different goals. While there is nothing wrong with a teen browsing the Web looking for the newest game or online adventure, the problem occurs when we, as information professionals, assume that because a young person knows how to sit down at a computer and log on to the Internet, he or she knows how to navigate the Web effectively and efficiently using search tools. As an LST, this often falls under the "other duties as assigned" category of your job. Fear not. Whether you graduated from library school a few months ago or a few decades ago, the information in this chapter is meant to serve as a foundation, providing you with some basic information about the role of technology and how it impacts young adult services today. By the end of this chapter, you should be much closer to talking the techno talk and walking the techno walk with your teen patrons.

WHY IS IT IMPORTANT FOR THE PUBLIC LIBRARY TO PROVIDE INTERNET ACCESS TO TEENS?

Over the last ten years, the Internet has become a vital part of the informational world, dramatically changing the way people interact both socially and professionally. Whether young people use the Internet for education, communication, or recreation, it is vital that they have the opportunity to learn, through hands-on experience, the information-literacy skills necessary for future success. Research has shown that the public library is the number one place for teens without Internet access to get online who do not have Internet access at home or school; therefore, it is imperative for public libraries to remain a place of equitable access in order to continue helping bridge the "digital divide." In addition, the Internet can be a portal to the world and a place where teens can expand their social circles and develop a community of like-minded individuals outside of their immediate surroundings. For teens who feel ostracized by their peers, cyberspace is often a safe haven, a place where young people can find support and affirmation. For some teens, the Internet is the sole means

The digital divide is the disparity between people who have access to computers and the Internet, and people who do not. Although the existence of this division has been, and continues to be, controversial, many studies have been conducted that provide quantifiable evidence that it does exist, both nationally and globally. For more information about the digital divide, check out the Digital Divide Network (www.digitaldividenetwork.org).

of finding information about topics like sexuality and sex education—subjects that might be considered controversial in some communities. If they have access, for the most controversial aspect of all things Internet is, in our opinion, the gap between those who have access and those who do not.

HOW CAN I HELP MY TEEN PATRONS TO SEARCH THE INTERNET SUCCESSFULLY?

You need to teach them about the different kinds of search tools, including search engines, portals, directories, indexes, and meta-searchers. There are three basic types of search tools: search engines, subject directories, and meta-search engines. The tool most people are most familiar with is the search engine, an automatic indexing program that uses a computer program (a crawler, spider, or wanderer) to create an original database of keywords through browsing Web pages on the Internet. When you go to the search engine interface, for example, the Google homepage, you enter one or more keywords, and the search engine searches its preexisting database, matching keywords and creating a list of "hits," or sites, for you that contain your specified keywords. Although Google (www.google.com) is currently considered the best, there are a number of search engines that work quite well, including All the Web (www.alltheweb.com) and Teoma (www.teoma.com). Subject directories like Yahoo! Search directory (http://dir.yahoo.com) and the Librarians' Index to the Internet (www.lii.com) are searchable databases of Web sites that have been selected by humans and classified by subject. A meta-search engine, such as Vivisimo (www.vivisimo.com) or Ixquick (www.ixquick.com), simultaneously searches a number of subject directories and search engines, creating a list of the most relevant "hits" from all available sources.

For more information about search tools, including new sites, updates to existing tools, and the tips, tricks, and tutorials for more productive online searching, check out these online resources: Search Engine Watch (www.searchenginewatch.com) and the Search Engine Showdown (www.searchengineshowdown.com).

It's important to teach your preteen and teen patrons about the various search tools because they need to know how and when to use a particular tool for a specific kind of search. It is also important to teach them when to use quotation marks, Boolean strings, or keywords, depending on the type of search tool they are using. Remember when you were in library school and you first heard the term boolean? As you teach young people to navigate the Internet, remember that feeling and be patient as they learn these new rules for online searching.

AS A REFERENCE LIBRARIAN AND AN LST, HOW CAN I HELP TEENS WITHOUT DOING ALL OF THE WORK FOR THEM?

There is a huge difference between handing teens the information and teaching them how to find it on their own. It's a new take on an old proverb: "Give a teen the answer, and he has the answer for the day. Teach a teen to find the answer, and he'll have the answers for a lifetime." If you are trained as a reference librarian, you have been taught how to conduct a reference interview, distill the information need, and then return the answer. You're not teaching the user to be self-sufficient. When you work with young people, one of your primary goals is to empower them and encourage information literacy and independent thinking. This requires you, as an LST, to temper a natural inclination to provide too much esoteric information and detail and to find a balance between providing answers and providing the skills young people will need to find the answers on their own.

DOES MY LIBRARY NEED AN ACCEPTABLE USE POLICY?

Ideally, the best time to create policies and procedures that address computer and Internet use in the library is before computer access is made available to the public. However, this is a luxury most libraries will not have because Internet access has been a central component of library services for years. In spite of this, your library can still be proactive by either creating an Internet-specific acceptable use policy, or updating your current policies and procedures to reflect the continually changing role of technology in the library.

A written acceptable use policy (AUP) is an agreement created by your library and approved by its governing structure. The policy serves three basic purposes:

- To delineate publicly all rules that apply to computer/Internet use within the library;
- To define publicly boundaries of acceptable behavior regarding Internet use within the library; and
- To specify publicly the consequences of violating those boundaries.

If your library does not use filters, this policy is especially important because it will serve as a disclaimer releasing the library from all liabilities associated with the viewing of, use of, or exposure to any information that might be considered harmful. If your library already has an AUP, it is important that this document be reviewed periodically in order to keep it up-to-date in the event of a complaint or question about what is considered acceptable. In general, this policy should be written by your library's administration and library board and then approved by your governing organization's legal department.

IF I DISAGREE WITH MY LIBRARY'S FILTERS, IS IT ILLEGAL FOR ME TO TURN OFF A FILTER ON A COMPUTER THAT I KNOW IS GOING TO BE USED BY A MINOR?

Yes. Your job as a librarian requires you to distinguish between your personal and your professional values and beliefs. Filtering is required by law if your library is the recipient of government funding; therefore you are required to uphold this law or risk punishment for defying a decision made by your library system in accordance with a national statute.

DO I HAVE TO LET TEENS CHAT IN THE LIBRARY IF I'M CONCERNED ABOUT THEIR SAFETY?

If your library does not have a written policy prohibiting chat for all users, then yes—a teenager is free to chat online so long as he or she is not breaking any law or defying any library policy. Unless you are that child's parent, you have no say as to whether or not he or she can participate in an online chat. What you can do is provide classes for all library patrons addressing online safety.

WHAT ARE THE MAIN AREAS I SHOULD COVER IN A CLASS ON ONLINE SAFETY FOR TEENS?

- Begin any class on online safety with an overview of the Internet—what it is and how it works.

- Explain how anyone, anywhere, can access the Internet at any time. Stress that what you see on the Internet is not always what you get; remind preteens and teens that just because someone says they are a fourteen-year-old girl living in the town next to yours does not mean it is true.

- Talk about the pros and cons of identity role playing. Explaining that a large number of people in chat rooms create a role to play while online, testing boundaries of age, gender, and sexual orientation. Let your students know that, while this is not always the case, it is always a possibility; therefore, all chatters should take any information exchanged with a grain of salt.

- Point out that it is never a good idea to share personal information (last names, phone numbers, e-mail addresses, home addresses, etc.) with someone in a chat room, on a blog, on an online bulletin board, or via an instant message (IM), because while you may think you are only sharing this information with the intended recipient, it is possible that there are any numbers of lurkers (people who "sit" in chat rooms as observers and not participants) watching and writing down this information. Think of a chat room as a crowded hallway in school—you never know who's listening, so don't share information that you don't want others to receive. Encourage teens who participate in chat to create a user name that does not divulge personal information like a first and a last name.

- Encourage young people to ignore any unsolicited response in a chat room and to not respond in kind. If a young person receives any kind of suggestive, obscene, or threatening response via IM or e-mail that makes him or her feel uncomfortable and/or afraid for his or her safety, encourage that person to contact someone of authority who can report the offending party.

For more information about online safety, check out SafeTeens.com (www.safekids.com/safeteens/). SafeTeen.com's "Teen Safety on the Information Highway" is intended for a young adult audience and includes basic rules about staying safe online, information about what constitutes harassment, and several in-depth "Did you know?" sections that address safety in chat rooms, e-mail, bulletin boards, newsgroups, and forums.

TECHNOLOGY, LIBRARY, AND THE LAW: A BRIEF HISTORY OF INTERNET FILTERING

Congress Passes the Communications Decency Act (CDA)—February 1, 1996

The CDA was the first national attempt by Congress to protect children from obscene or indecent content on the Internet by criminalizing the online transmission of such materials to a person eighteen years of age or under.

Supreme Court Rules that the CDA Is Unconstitutional—June 26, 1997

The CDA, opposed by the American Library Association (ALA) for its threat to undermine Freedom of Speech, and brought to court by the American Civil Liberties Union (Reno v. American Civil Liberties Union), was declared unconstitutional with a 7–2 ruling by the Supreme Court.

ALA Adopts the "Resolution on the Use of Filtering Software in Libraries"—July 2, 1997

Written and adopted by the ALA, this declaration affirmed that the use of filtering software to block patron access to constitutionally protected speech was in direct opposition to the Library Bill of Rights (www.ala.org/Content/NavigationMenu/Our_Association/Offices/Intellectual_Freedom3/Statements_and_Policies/Intellectual_Freedom2/librarybillofrights.pdf).

Congress Passes the Children's Online Privacy Protection Act (COPPA)—October 1998

This law, passed by Congress in October of 1998 and put into effect April 21, 2001, required commercial Web sites to obtain parental consent before soliciting or disseminating personal information (e-mail address, home phone number, address, etc.) from a child under the age of thirteen.

ALA Releases the "Statement on Library Use of Filtering Software"—November 17, 2000

Issued by ALA's Intellectual Freedom Committee, this document provided an explanation of filtering software, in addition to a laundry list of reasons why filtering/blocking software in the library was unconstitutional. This statement also contained examples of how libraries could promote access to the Internet.

Congress Passes the Children's Internet Protection Act (CIPA) and the Neighborhood Children's Internet Protection Act (NCIPA)—December 21, 2000

Passed by the U.S. Congress as part of a major spending bill (H.R. 4577) and put into effect April 20, 2001, CIPA placed restrictions on government funding and required that all school and public libraries that received some form of federal money install filtering software on all computers that provided Internet access. NCIPA specified what had to be included on a library's Internet safety policy.

ALA Votes to Initiate Legal Action Challenging CIPA—January 2001

Again, ALA claimed that this law was unconstitutional and an infringement on First Amendment rights.

Philadelphia District Court Overturns CIPA—May 2002

A district court in Philadelphia unanimously ruled that CIPA violated the first amendment rights of library patrons.

Supreme Court Upholds CIPA—June 23, 2003

In United States v. American Library Association (No. 02–361), the U.S. Supreme Court reversed the lower court's ruling, deciding to uphold CIPA. However, a stipulation was made to the existing law that states that a mandated filter should be voluntarily disabled upon the request of an adult library patron.

WHAT IS A FILTER?

Basically, a filter is a computer application that can be specifically programmed to block particular Web sites due to their objectionable content. CyberSitter, Cyber Snoop, Internet Guard Dog, and N2H2, Net Nanny, and SurfControl are all examples of filtering software packages that have been utilized in libraries throughout the country.

HOW DOES FILTERING SOFTWARE WORK?

Filters block Web sites that contain supposedly inappropriate or obscene content using two methods:

1. By blocking Web site Uniform Resource Locators (URLs) that have been preselected and entered into a database by the programmer; and/or
2. By blocking sites that include one or more preset keywords, phrases, or letter patterns that have been deemed inappropriate or considered problematic by

the programmer. These words, phrases, or patterns might appear in the Web site's URL, within the contents of the Web page, and/or be listed on the Web site's meta (search) tags.

Although some filtering software packages do block sites using a combination of the two methods, no filter has yet been created that is one hundred percent reliable and accurate. Until such a filter is created, it will remain possible for a user to access a site on a filtered computer that contains obscene material, while at the same time disallowing access to legitimate sites such as those that address health issues, politically sensitive topics, sex education, and sexuality.

DOES EVERY LIBRARY LEGALLY HAVE TO FILTER EVERY COMPUTER WITH INTERNET ACCESS?

No. The only libraries that are legally required to install filtering software on every Internet accessible computer are those who receive federal funding via discounted rates and grants for Internet access, Internet service, or internal connections (for example, e-rate program funding or money provided through the Library Services and Technology Act). However, all libraries required by law to install filtering software have until July 1, 2004 to do so, thereby complying with CIPA and the Federal Communication Commission (FCC).

DO I HAVE ANY CONTROL OVER WHAT WEB SITES ARE BLOCKED ON THE COMPUTERS IN MY LIBRARY?

Yes and no. Most companies that create filtering software will not allow you to access their list of blocked sites, but they will allow you to make local changes to this list in order to tailor the filter to your library's community of users.

CAN I DISABLE A FILTER ON A COMPUTER IN MY LIBRARY?

If you are in a position of authority in your library, you most likely have the capability to disable a filter. However, depending on the software and the technological configuration your library system has chosen to employ with regard to filters, it may be necessary to contact a supervisor or a member of your technology department to do so. Note that while a filter can be disabled for an adult patron for legal purposes, there is no legal provision for disabling a filter in a computer that is being used by a patron who is under eighteen years of age.

IF MY PUBLIC LIBRARY CHOOSES NOT TO INSTALL FILTERING SOFTWARE, IS IT MY JOB TO MAKE SURE THAT YOUNG PEOPLE ARE NOT VIEWING ILLEGAL CONTENT ON THE COMPUTERS?

This is a tricky question because, while there is not a national statute decreeing that a librarian can be held legally responsible for what a child is looking at on a computer in the library, there are antiobscenity statutes that differ by state. Therefore, it is important that you know what is and what is not considered legally "obscene" in your state in order to protect yourself. Unlike a school, a public library does not act *in loco parentis* (in the place of the parent); therefore a youth services librarian cannot be held legally responsible for what a child looks at while in the public library.

IS THE VIEWING OF PORNOGRAPHY ILLEGAL IN THE LIBRARY?

No. While it is illegal for young people under the age of eighteen to view any type of pornography, it is not illegal for a consenting adult to view pornography on a public Internet terminal, so long as the adult patron is not viewing child pornography, as that it is a criminal offense. However, if an adult patron looking at pornography is in direct violation of your particular library's acceptable use policy, he or she may be asked to the leave the library.

IS IT TRUE THAT FILTERS BLOCK VALID SITES, IN ADDITION TO PORNOGRAPHY?

Yes, it is true that a perfect filter has not yet been created. However, vast advancements in technology have been made in the past few years. The hope is that one day the progress in technology will ultimately produce an "ideal filter" that will block sexually graphic images, while at the same time granting users access to legitimate content. However, it can be argued that the perfect filter will never be possible due to the dynamic, or ever-changing, nature of the Internet. This is a question that can only be answered with the passage of time. Currently, individual filters can be set to restrict certain types and levels of inappropriate material. Although not ideal, having the freedom to select the level of restriction does allow the library administration to have some control over the amount of filtering deemed appropriate for a given community. Most filtering software applications use a pop-up message to let the user know that he or she is trying to access a site that has been deemed inappropriate.

HOW DO I DEVELOP MY LIBRARY'S TEEN WEB SITE?

- Remember that simplicity is key to creating a developmentally appropriate library Web page for YAs that is both useful and teen-friendly. Do not get caught up in the "more is better" trap, as information overload is the quickest way to turn a young person off from your Web site. Remember that the goal of a library Web page is to provide information, not entertainment. Leave the flash to the game designers and focus on the mission of the library—to provide relative, accurate information for your target audience.

- Do not overload your page with graphics and image maps that do not contribute in some way to the information on the page.

- Organize the material on your page into logical categories, clearly marking sections such as homework help, recommended reading, entertainment, teen health, and college and careers.

- Include Web sites on your page that address sexuality, sex education and teen pregnancy, teen violence, and suicide, and add links to local shelters and crisis hotlines. Once you have selected and evaluated these sites, test them on a filtered computer to be sure that your patrons will be able to access them when they need them. This will be some of the most pertinent information you can provide online, especially considering that these topics are most likely the ones that teens will search for without asking for adult assistance.

- Annotate all of the sites you include on the page, describing exactly what a patron will find when he or she clicks on any given link. Include the URL in addition to the name and description of each recommended site so that a patron has the option of printing the page of links without having to visit each one.

- Link to your library's subscription databases and provide an extensive annotation of each source so that your teen patrons have an idea of how they might use these databases for research. If possible, call them "Magazines and Newspaper Articles" rather than "Databases," as this is a much more descriptive, teen-friendly label.

- Include local resources that a young person might not find anywhere else, including information about local schools, clubs, camps, and job and volunteer opportunities.

- Create a place for teens to submit their own writing, including reviews of books, Web sites, video games, and computer games.

- Include information on your Web site about upcoming programs for teens along with information about how they can get involved by volunteering or serving as a member of the Teen Advisory Board.

- Update your site regularly, adding new links of interest and removing out-of-date links and information.

- Include your library's name and address in a visible place on the site's home page, in addition to contact information.

If you want to know if your library's teen Web page is meeting the needs of your young adult patrons, ask them. Teens are notoriously honest, and it is unlikely that this will be an exception. Provide a questionnaire, and ask broad questions.

- What do you like best about this site?
- What do you like least about this site?
- What do you find most useful about the site?
- What area would you like to see covered in more depth on this site?

You can also ask more specific questions.

- What do you think of the colors used in the Web site design?
- What do you think of the images used throughout this site?
- Do you think the suggested links were good choices for music? Teen health? Book reviews? Entertainment?
- What links do you think we should add to this site to make it more useful?

It is incredibly important to keep your library's teen Web page up-to-date. To do this, ask for input from your teen patrons. Give them a voice, and then listen when they talk about what they would like to see on the site. Chances are good that they will know about the newest and hottest stuff on the Net before you do, so use this to your benefit. You can also surf other library YA Web pages for new sites that focus on both education and entertainment for teens. Focus on larger library systems that have dedicated programs that focus on teens and technology—see "What are some best practices in connecting teens with technology?"

> Professional journals like *School Library Journal* include columns in each issue that highlight some of the best new library Web sites on the Internet.

WHY IS ONLINE COMMUNICATION SO IMPORTANT TO TEENS?

Today's teens have grown up with e-mail as a primary means of communicating with friends, relatives, classmates, and teachers. Over the past few years, as more young people have gained access to computers, a number of other vehicles for communication have risen to the forefront, including chat rooms, IM, online journals ("blogs"), and virtual spaces to self-publish writing and art.

Communication is often cited as one of the top reasons teens go online. The Internet offers a wide variety of communication alternatives that are not only immediate, but also free of long-distance charges. With online communication becoming more widespread among the young and Internet-savvy, today's teens are broadening their communication circles, expanding their horizons, and often creating an online support network of peers who share their interests.

WHAT IS A "CHAT ROOM?"

Some of the best places for teens to chat include Teen Chat (www.teenchat.com) or Yahoo! Chat (http://chat.yahoo.com).

A chat room is exactly what it sounds like—a "room" online where people from all over the world can meet and discuss anything from the latest Eminem video to who dumped who on last night's reality TV show. Most chat rooms are thematic, from general themes based on age or location (for example, "Teens in the Midwest"), to more specific themes focused on a particular topic (for example, "Fans of *Buffy the Vampire Slayer*") to very unambiguous themes with set limitations (for example, sixteen-year-old boy fans of *Lone Wolf and Cub*). A majority of chat rooms allow chatters to talk to the group as a whole or to send a private message to one or more parties within the same chat room.

IS THERE SUCH A THING AS CHAT ETIQUETTE?

Chat 101 (www.ker95.com/chat101) is a great introduction to the world of chat, with tips on "chattiquette," chat terms, and other chat room basics.

Yes. Often referred to as "chattiquette," online etiquette is something most chatters learn as they go. Considering that online chat is a subculture in and of itself, those new to this form of real-time communication can easily be overwhelmed by the slang, abbreviations, and phrases that permeate a chat-in-progress. The best way for a novice chatter to get a feel for how a chat room works is to "lurk" (or watch) and learn. There are also Web sites that provide chat basics such as terminology, abbreviations that can be used as a type of shorthand when conversing in real-time, and rules of etiquette such as not using uppercase letters unless your intention is to "scream" your message.

WHAT IS AN "INSTANT MESSAGE," AND WHO PROVIDES THIS SERVICE?

Instant messaging (or IMing) is a way for people to engage in a real-time conversation on the Internet by exchanging written dialogue on a split-level screen. IMing differs from chat in that participants are able to decide who they want to talk to, and when; chatters are limited to those who happens to be in a given chat room at a given time. IM users are able to establish a "buddy list," or an IM address book, to keep track of people with whom they wish to converse. When a buddy is online at the same time as a user, he or she can contact this person and engage in a written conversation. America Online (AOL) Instant Messenger, or AIM (www.aim.com), and Yahoo! Messenger (http://messenger. yahoo.com) are the two most common tools teens use to IM. Although a teen does not have to be a member of AOL to use AIM, he or she does have to create an AIM account, which is free of charge. If a teen chooses to use Yahoo! Messenger, he or she must first sign up for a free Yahoo! e-mail account, if he or she does not already have one. Once the teen signs up, he or she is ready to IM another person, as long as both people are using the same software, have created IM identities, and are signed on at the same time.

DOES A YOUNG PERSON HAVE TO BE A CERTAIN AGE TO GET A FREE E-MAIL ADDRESS?

Yes and no. The major providers of free e-mail (Hotmail and Yahoo!) do require a potential e-mailer to be at least thirteen years of age if he or she wishes to get an e-mail address without parental consent. Users under the age of thirteen can still get an e-mail address, but they will need a parent or guardian to provide the okay and sit with them through the registration process.

WHAT IS A BLOG?

Essentially, a blog is a Web site with daily, dated entries. A journal for the Internet generation, blogs are available online and are often accessible by the general public. Blogs are a great way for teens to share their thoughts and receive feedback from readers, as most of these online journals have a place to solicit commentary from readers. Originally called a Web log (conjugated to "weblog," dissected to "we blog," and shortened to "blog") this online form of communication has been around since the mid-1990s but has only recently gained widespread popularity with young people.

ARE THERE SITES WHERE TEENS CAN GO ONLINE TO CREATE A BLOG FOR FREE?

Yes, there are several. Both Teen Open Diary (www.teenopendiary .com) and Blog Spot (www.blogspot.com) allow a young person to sign up for a free blog, assuming the user is willing to provide basic registration information. Bloggers usually do not need any previous experience with HTML, scripting, Web editing, or any other kind of programming, as most of these sites allow a user to push a few buttons, make a few selections, and be on their way to online journaldom.

HOW CAN I START AN ONLINE BOOK DISCUSSION GROUP?

An online book discussion group is a great way to utilize a tool that young people already know and enjoy: the Internet. The discussion can be as simple or as complex as you wish, depending on your level of experience and the resources available at your library.

The simplest way to provide an online book club for teens at your library is to join Chapter-a-Day (www.dearreaders.com), a prearranged online book club that provides participating libraries with a section from a book (approximately five minutes worth of reading) via e-mail each weekday; the library can then forward the section via e-mail to participating patrons. At the end of the week, a patron who has read all of the sections they receive via e-mail will have finished two to three chapters of a book. If they like the book, they can check it out from your library. Through Chapter-a-Day, participating teens can share their thoughts on an online forum with people all over the country who are reading the same books.

The next option for creating a more localized online book club for teens is to create a Yahoo! Group page where you can set up a book club chat forum for readers to meet at a set time to discuss a particular book, or post their thoughts to a forum where any member of the book club can read and reply when it fits into their schedule.

The last option is for your library to purchase discussion board software whereby your home institution's Web server would host a Web board where book club members could post to the board and read and respond to fellow members' posts. Although this option is slightly more difficult and could require some external funding, it will also give you more local control over the administration of the board, allowing you to edit, delete, or rearrange posted material, while monitoring the security of the board. In addition, a library-sponsored Web board could serve other purposes. A public library might hold online book discussion groups for adult patrons and staff members. For schools, this software is even more versatile, providing a forum for teachers and students to engage in online discussions about anything from class projects to extracurricular activities.

> Some examples of discussion board software include Discusware (www.discusware.com), VBulletin (www.vbulletin.com), and Chatterbox (www .acromediainc.com /chatterbox.htm).

HOW CAN I GET AN AUTHOR TO DO AN ONLINE CHAT WITH THE TEEN PATRONS AT MY LIBRARY?

Online author chats are a great opportunity for libraries on a budget to unite well-known authors with their core audience. Utilizing chat room technology and instant messaging—online communication tools that teens already know how to use—librarians can easily provide a forum for an enlightening author-patron discussion.

There are two ways to offer an online chat at your library:

1. Sign up with an established company that provides libraries and schools with forums for online virtual visits. For example, Author Chats (www.author chats.com) offers one or more chats each month with authors such as Chris Crutcher, Walter Dean Myers, Garth Nix, and Louis Sachar. A third party from Author Chat's Administrative Team already contacts the author, sets up a date and time for the chat, and provides the forum (chat room) where your patrons will be able to ask questions and receive answers in realtime. All you have to do is sign up to participate, log on at the appropriate time, and submit questions to a moderator who then posts the questions to the author. The teens will be able watch on their computers, but only one person in the room—most likely the

librarian—will be able to enter questions. Most chats last half an hour to an hour, and the number of participating school classes or groups from libraries can vary from one to several.

2. Go out and find an author with whom your young patrons would like to chat. Contact this author and negotiate a fee for a half hour or hour of the author's time. Even if this amount is relatively high, you will still save money by foregoing the usual travel and accommodation fees that are required when bringing in an author for a face-to-face library program. With the author, select a set date and time for the chat. Let the author know what software you will be using to conduct the real-time chat (AIM is a good option, as it is easy for anyone to sign up for a free account). Be sure the computers in your library have AIM installed so that all chat participants will have an opportunity to take part actively in the chat. Before the day of the scheduled chat session, it is a good idea to set up a trial chat between you and the author. This test chat will only take a few minutes, and it will give both you and the author a chance to test the software and work out any glitches.

IS IT POSSIBLE FOR MY TALENTED TEEN PATRONS TO SELF-PUBLISH THEIR WRITING AND ART ON THE INTERNET?

Yes, one of the great things about the Internet is that anyone can publish anything, at any time. In the past few years a number of quality of Web Sites have surfaced whose mission is to provide a virtual gallery for young writers and artists, including:

- **Teen Ink (www.teenink.com).** Teen Ink offers YAs an opportunity to post original prose, poetry, nonfiction, and art in a teen-friendly, supportive environment that fosters creativity and individualism.
- **Teen Voices Online (www.teenvoices.com).** Although Teen Voices is predominantly a print magazine for young women, it does have an online presence where

young women under eighteen can publish original poetry, prose, and artwork.

- **Kids-Space (www.kids-space.org).** Kids Space is an art-hosting site specifically for young people. Although this site is geared more toward younger children, it would be a suitable place for preteens to display their original work.

CAN I CREATE A PRIVATE AREA WHERE MY TEEN ADVISORY GROUP CAN COMMUNICATE ON THE WEB?

Yes. The easiest way to create a "private" place where your teen advisory group can meet online is to set up a Yahoo! Group. This virtual meeting space can be created by anyone who has a Yahoo! account. Within this group page, or virtual home, members of your group can share files and photos, plan group events, share a calendar, post to a group bulletin board, bookmark links of interest, take polls, and chat in realtime. To take part in a Yahoo! Group chat, you will need a personal computer running Microsoft Windows 95, 98, NT, or 2000, and Microsoft Internet Explorer (version 4.0 or later) or Netscape Navigator (version 4.08 or later).

WHAT IS STREAMING VIDEO, AND HOW IS IT DIFFERENT FROM STREAMING MEDIA?

Streaming video is video transmitted to the Internet in a continuous, or streaming, fashion. Rather than require you to download an entire file before the video can be opened and played, streaming video plays from a Web site into a viewer while the rest of the video continues to download in the background. Streaming video also allows you to watch a video and immediately discard the file when done, saving huge amounts of disk space. Streaming media is a streaming video with sound. Both streaming video and streaming media require the use of a "plug-in" or viewer. These helper software applications, including QuickTime, Real Player, and Windows Media, are free to download.

WHAT IS VIDEOSTREAMING, AND HOW I CAN I INCORPORATE IT INTO MY YA PROGRAMMING?

Videostreaming, also knows as Webcasting, allows online users to watch live or archived video programming via the Internet. This is especially useful when you want to make a previous or current video-conference available to Internet users in any location. If your library does not have the capability to conduct a videoconferencing program, you can still take advantage of a Webcast. For example, Video Author Visits (www.videoauthorvisit.com) often videotape their programs and then make the highlights of the program available on their Web site for all interested parties. Although this does not allow real-time participation, it does indirectly bring the authors into your library.

WHAT IS VIDEOCONFERENCING, AND HOW DOES IT WORK?

For more information about videoconferencing, check out "Videoconferencing Resources" at About.com: http://netconference.about.com /cs/videoconfresource/ index.htm.

Interactive videoconferencing technology uses TV monitors, cameras, microphones, and high speed Internet connections to connect two or more locations, allowing people in each locations to both see and hear what is going on at all other locations. Videoconferencing is a great way to conduct virtual field trips, engage in multi-school or library projects, and to support public events like town hall meetings. Unless your library or school is already set up with the required technology, this can be an expensive undertaking. However, many large library systems and school districts have this capability.

WHAT ARE THE BEST DATABASES FOR TEENS?

Although it can be difficult to ascertain the "best," or most authoritative, online databases and Web sites for teens, the following resources and information have been provided to help you establish a solid foundation upon which to build an informational network for teens.

Unlike research books that sit on the shelves of your library, Web-based subscription databases are constantly evolving to provide users with the most accurate, up-to-date information available anywhere.

From online encyclopedias, to television and radio transcripts, to databases of biographies, subscription databases are some of the most under-appreciated and under-used resources for teenagers in the library. It is our job to bring these informational resources out into the open not only by making them available, but also by marketing them to the young people who use Google for any given homework assignment. In addition to well-known databases like Ebsco, InfoTrac, and NewsBank, the following databases provide a wealth of information largely untapped by our young patrons. As the Internet becomes more fee-based than free, it is especially important that we let teens know that they can find full-text magazine and newspaper articles without paying for anything more than the cost of printing at their local public or school library.

- **Bigchalk Multimedia.** This relatively new database houses an archive of audio and video clips, including hard-to-find television and radio transcripts and a large assortment of photographs for grades six through twelve.

- **CQ Researcher.** This database of the Congressional Quarterly (CQ) offers in-depth analysis and reporting on current and controversial issues of the day such as social and teen issues, the environment, health, education, science, and technology.

- **CollegeSource Online.** Two-year, four-year, graduate, and professional schools are included in his database featuring over 24,000 U.S. and international college course catalogs in complete cover-to-cover format.

- **Facts.com.** This archive of information provides the user with newspaper editorials, historic documents, photographs, and statistical data going back to the 1940s. The Facts.com Reference Suite also allows the user to search Reuters On-Line News Services, the World Almanac and Book of Facts, and the World Almanac Encyclopedia.

- **Gale Resource Centers.** This comprehensive database contains a wealth of resources, including the Biography Resource Center, which provides biographical reference tools and magazine profiles, in addition to the nearly one million biographies from the complete *Marquis Who's Who*; the Literature Resource Center, which provides literary criticism, biographies, and bibliographies covering more than

90,000 novelists, poets, journalists, and other writers, in addition to the *Merriam-Webster's Encyclopedia of Literature*; the Student Resource Gold, which provides a vast array of original reference material, primary source documents, and full-text periodical articles; and the Opposing Viewpoints Center, which provides a combination of magazine and newspaper articles on current topics in the news.

• **Grolier Multimedia Encyclopedia.** Based on the *Academic American Encyclopedia*, this database provides a large assortment of journal and magazine articles, tables, maps, and pictures.

• **LearningExpressLibrary.com.** This is a database of online academic, civil service, GED, military, and professional licensing and certification practice tests.

• **NetLibrary.** This is a comprehensive collection of online books (including Cliff's Notes) and research materials.

• **NoveList.** This bibliographic database provides reader's advisory, individual book records, reviews from sources such as *Booklist*, *Library Journal*, *School Library Journal*, and *Publishers Weekly*, and preconstructed booklists, book discussion guides, and relative Web links.

• **ProQuest Historical Newspapers.** This is an archive of the country's leading news authority, the *New York Times*, from 1851 to 1999.

• **World Book Encyclopedia Online.** This database, which received the highest rating in *School Library Journal*'s "2002 Ratings of Digital Encyclopedias" (4.8 out of a maximum of 5.0), provides every piece of information available in the twenty-two-volume print edition, in addition to pictures, maps, animations, and sounds.

WHAT ARE THE BEST WEB SITES FOR TEENS?

Amidst the millions of Web sites currently accessible on the Internet, there are hundreds of thousands of sites that could possibly appeal to

For a list of core sites you should consider for your public library teen Web site, see www.connectingya.com/core.html. For a list of links to an assortment of YA library Web sites around the country, check out the Virtual YA Index at http://yahelp.suffolk.lib.ny.us/virtual.html.

a teenage audience. Of these sites, there are a fair number that are both valid and appropriate for this audience. However, if we were to include a list of these sites in this book, the list would be outdated the minute it was created. There are plenty of excellent articles, books, and peer library Web sites from which to cull a specialized list for your teen user group. Once you have compiled and annotated your list of selected sites, it will be most accessible to your teens if you place it on your library's Web site. While printed handouts of this list will be useful and should be available in your library, it should not be considered the primary document format because you will need to update this list regularly in order for it to remain current and relevant.

WHAT THINGS SHOULD I TAKE INTO CONSIDERATION WHEN I EVALUATE A WEB SITE FOR MY LIBRARY'S TEEN WEB PAGE?

When you begin searching for Web sites to include on your YA Web Site, consider each site's interface, content level, intended audience, reading level, incorporation or absence of graphics and images, currency, and source (validity). Include sites relevant to your community's entertainment, history, and politics.

MEASURING SUCCESS

Although it can be difficult to obtain a quantitative measure of success with regard to technology in the library, it is possible. The most important thing to take into consideration when measuring the success of any given program or class that incorporates technology is how well a user can utilize the technology at the completion of the training. As with any subject that relies on external factors such as the availability or quality of the educational tool, the use of technology requires a learning curve that takes into consideration previous knowledge and the amount of time a user has to apply the technology in an unstructured environment.

WHAT ARE SOME BEST PRACTICES IN CONNECTING TEENS WITH TECHNOLOGY?

The following examples represent the range of comprehensive and specialized programs available for young people in libraries across the country. While this list is in no way definitive of all young adult library programs in libraries today, these programs do an excellent job of providing traditional library services coupled with cutting edge technology.

COMPREHENSIVE YA LIBRARY PROGRAMS THAT FEATURE TECHNOLOGY

Freedom Regional, a Hybrid Public Library/School Library Media Center

Public Library of Charlotte and Mecklenburg County (PLCMC), Charlotte, North Carolina

www.plcmc.org/libLoc/branchFreedom.asp

A combination of a public library and a school library media center for the Philip O. Berry Academy of Technology, this 20,000-square-foot library is a joint venture of the PLCMC and the Charlotte Mecklenberg Schools. The Freedom Regional, the first hybrid library in Charlotte, North Carolina, opened in August of 2003 and serves both the students of the school and members of the community at large. The library has more than 100 computers, plus materials, special services, and activities for teens and families.

Teen Central

Phoenix Public Library, Phoenix, Arizona

www.phoenixteencentral.org

When the powers that be came together in September 2000 to create a state-of-the-art teen area for the Phoenix Public Library, they took an online survey of teens to find out what they wanted from their local library. In April of 2001 they opened the doors of "Teen Central," a 5,000-square-foot space that features not only books, but also surround-sound music, cable TV, a concrete dance floor, a café area with vending machines, and more than twenty computers with Internet access.

Teen'Scape

Los Angeles Public Library (LAPL), Los Angeles, California

www.lapl.org/teenscape/library/teenscape.html

Introduced in 1994, Teen'Scape offers young adult patrons a combination of traditional library services and technology situated within a teen space of approximately 1,200 square feet, separate from the rest of the library, where young people can read, work on computers, study, listen to music, or just hang out with friends. In March of 2000, Teen'Scape was enlarged as part of a grant-funded expansion project financed by the private community through the efforts of the Los Angeles Public Library Foundation. The new location is a little less than 4,000 square feet—the size of a small neighborhood branch within LAPL's Central Library.

The name "Teen'Scape" was chosen to convey that this is a sanctuary owned by teens. It has been a model library program for teens throughout the past decade and is often considered a pioneer in the development of a dream library space for teens.

WIRED FOR YOUTH (WFY)

Austin Public Library, Austin, Texas

www.wiredforyouth.com

Launched in 2000, the Wired for Youth Program at the Austin Public Library, which has served approximately 150,000 young people between the ages of eight and eighteen in its first two years, has more than exceeded the library's expectations. Comprised of ten individual technology centers in libraries throughout the city, each WFY Program is equipped with cutting edge technology, including computers, scanners, digital cameras, and CD burners, and is headed by a professional youth services librarian who has a high level of expertise in both technology and traditional library services for preteens and teens. This program's mission is to provide enrichment opportunities that promote electronic information literacy and contribute to personal and intellectual growth, while providing a welcoming place for Austin's young people within the library community.

INDIVIDUAL YA LIBRARY PROGRAMS THAT INCORPORATE TECHNOLOGY

Geek U @ Austin Public Library

Southeast Austin Community Branch, Austin, Texas

www.wiredforyouth.com

In the fall of 2001, "Wired for Youth" librarian Beth Solomon kicked off a new program called "Geek U" at the Southeast Austin Community Branch of the Austin Public Library. A weekly hour of structured technology classes, this program was especially challenging because Solomon had to create a regularly scheduled learning time that didn't feel like school or an unattractive requirement to be avoided. The classes covered information-literacy skills, library skills, Internet skills, and skills associated with specific software packages such as Macromedia Fireworks, Dreamweaver, Adobe Photoshop, and Microsoft Publisher. Each class focused on one well-defined project:

- create a school semester calendar; make a September 11 condolence card in Publisher to send to a child at the Brooklyn Public Library
- take a photo of yourself and use Photoshop to transpose yourself onto a rock concert stage; paint an alien landscape using Fireworks
- use the Internet to answer ten questions about a given topic on the weekly Web Challenge (with subjects ranging from the

serious, such as National Poetry Month or Hispanic Heritage Month, to the frivolous, but popular, Yu-Gi-Oh! or National Pizza Week Web challenge).

While Solomon started with a very large goal, she found that focusing on small projects and tasks with a limited number of new ideas each time she was most successful at increasing kids' abilities exponentially. Since this program began a few years ago, the attendees of Geek U have amassed an impressive catalog of learned skills, but the best part for Solomon has been watching the teens express the desire to teach skills to their friends.

Virtual Visits @ Haverhill Public Library

Haverhill, Massachusetts

www.teencybercenter.org/pizza/pizza.htm

In 2003 Beth Gallaway, Young Adult Librarian at the Haverhill Public Library (HPL) implemented an idea for chatting online used by author/librarian Toni Buzzeo, who presented a workshop that used free, real-time instant messaging software as a medium to "talk" with an author. Such "virtual visits" eliminate travel time and expenses, accommodate an author's schedule, take only one hour and ten minutes, and are very affordable. However, unlike traditional author visits that have taken place at HPL in the past, the Virtual Visits program uses simple technology to promote reading while it allows young people to interact one-on-one with an author using a favorite pastime of teens—chatting on the Internet. Additionally, Gallaway feels these virtual visits contribute greatly to meeting the developmental needs of teens, while also incorporating fundamental Internet safety and "chattiquette." It challenges teens' reading and writing skills because they are using a specific chat program with an agenda, unlike the random chats that take place online daily between teens across the country. Although this program is still in its infancy, Gallaway has seen great results and believes that the best part of the Virtual Visits program has been watching teens use chat to make meaningful and safe connections.

South Shore Video Contest @ Duxbury Free Library

Duxbury, Massachusetts

www.duxburyfreelibrary.org/videocontest.html

Since 2000, the Young Adult Department of the Duxbury Free Library has hosted a video contest for teens each summer. Open to all teens in grades seven through twelve in southeastern Massachusetts, this contest involves the creation of an original video either by individual teens or by teens in collaboration with public librarians, teachers, school media specialists, teen youth leaders, or church group leaders. The submissions have included videos created for school assignments, performances captured by skateboard enthusiasts, artistic videos using elaborate equipment, documentaries of church group service projects, and videos created by inner-city peer mentoring groups that address decision-making with regard to sex and drugs. Many of the participants enjoy the camaraderie of being part of a group event in which they can be a "ham" in front of the camera or a "techie" behind the camera. For the most part, submissions have been short, clever videos featuring poetry, dance, music, claymation, sports, and crazy reality situations.

The Tycoon Platoon @ Public Library of Charlotte and Mecklenburg County

Charlotte, North Carolina

www.commerceconnection.org

The Tycoon Platoon is an online, serialized comic sponsored by the Library Initiative for Youth in Business (LIYIB), a library program that connects children and teens in Charlotte with the world of commerce, finance, and money management. Centered around four teenagers, each of whom embody an idea about commerce and finance, the Tycoon Platoon is created each month by the PLCMC Graphics Club for Teens, a group of young people who are not only interested in drawing, writing, and graphic design, but also the business world. Officially launched in April 2002, the comic pairs conventional library programming with technology to create a one-of-a-kind publication that embodies the new generation of library services to young people.

YAzine @ Cleveland Heights-University Heights Public Library

Cleveland Heights, Ohio

www.clickthis.ws

A combination of a YA Web page and an online zine, the Cleveland Heights-University Heights Public Library's (CH-UHPL) YAzine is a cache of useful information, quirky factoids, weird links, opinion polls, and teen-submitted poetry, prose, and artwork. According to library Webmaster Laura Solomon, the design was chosen based on the input of focus groups of teens who use the library, and, although the HTML was coded by Solomon, the content for YAzine is provided by local teens. In addition to information about entertainment, the local teen scene, books, health and schoolwork, YAzine also serves as a venue for teen reviews, poll results, and photos of past events. According to Nancy Levin, Young Adult Services Coordinator for CH-UHPL, this is only the beginning for YAzine. As the library's technological capabilities increase and more young people view the site as a gateway, YAzine will expand to include teen forums and digital streaming video.

CONCLUSION

In the first edition of *Connecting Young Adults and Libraries* from 1992, the words "computer" and "technology," let alone "Internet," never appeared in the index, although they may have slipped into the text. The exciting—and scary—thing is that today's LST needs to be as much a "geek" as a "bookworm." But remember—we all do our best work when we are, like our teen users, learning rather than always knowing. While the skill set has changed, the core values that drive our work have not. If anything, technology provides the LST with endless opportunities to develop technology programs that meet—and respect—the unique needs of teens and allow for young people to participate, collaborate, and use technology as a tool to build assets. Our continuing challenge is to defend, and often to define, "equal access" as we work within the context of the laws and community standards that conflict with our advocacy for the free access rights of teens.

11 YOUTH INVOLVEMENT

"For me, volunteering is a wonderful way to make new friends and help the community at the same time. I have found that I feel much better about spending a day volunteering than I do when I stay at home sleeping in. It has been, and continues to be, one of the most gratifying activities I am involved in."

—a Minnesota teen about her experience as a library volunteer

It is easy to blame society for the failure of its young people. It is much harder to be a part of the solution and to be an ally when a young person needs it most during adolescence. By creating worthwhile youth involvement programs that encourage, inspire, and give a voice to young people, you are not only contributing to the future, but also making a difference in the present by helping teens develop feelings of pride and ownership for their community.

If your library is a visible part of your community, then it is a perfect place for teens to get involved. From serving as members of the teen advisory board to volunteering with the summer reading program, teens can offer a fresh perspective, in addition to the energy and age diversity that is often missing in libraries. Teens can also get involved in areas you might not have considered, including serving as members of the library advisory board, as part of the "Friends of the Library" group, as interns, and even as employees. By becoming actively involved in the library, and by serving in leadership roles like the ones mentioned above, teens not only give back to their community, but also they develop confidence and skills, such as communication and teamwork, that will serve them throughout their personal lives and professional careers.

Libraries are for everyone. Libraries that successfully embrace this idea understand that "everyone" means young, old, and every person in between. If your library is a youth-serving organization (and if you have any person under eighteen years of age who walks through your library's door, then you are), it is your responsibility to provide the most complete range of services possible for young people. While this is often easier to do for young children, who are usually escorted to the library by a parent; it can be tricky, though, when it comes to teens. Teens travel in packs, which can be a little

According to the National Commission on Resources for Youth, youth involvement is defined as "the involving of youth in responsible, challenging, action that meets genuine needs, with opportunities for planning, and/or decision-making affecting others in an activity whose impact or consequence is extended to others."

overwhelming to librarians. Teens also tend to be brutally honest, just as likely to tell you exactly what they think about a program or display, as to tell you what's missing from the collection. Embrace these things about teenagers, and use them to your benefit. Introduce yourself to the crowd, and invite them to get involved in making the library a more teen-friendly place. Ask them what *they* want, and then listen to what they have to say.

Youth participation is defined by YALSA (Young Adult Library Services Association) as the involvement of young adults in responsible action and significant decision making, which affects the design and delivery of library and information services for their peers and the community. Youth can participate on many levels, for again it is as much a philosophy as it is a practice. A teen advisory group (TAG) is one type of involvement, one level, but it is not the only vehicle for turning practice into reality. Youth participation can entail small things, like suggestion boxes and surveys; it can also mean bigger things, like a TAG or a selection committee; or it can be the biggest things of all, such as creating opportunities for teens to sit on the library board, or make significant decisions about the day-to-day routine of library services. The level depends upon many things, such as the skills of the LST, but it hinges a great deal on the work environment. A library where the director makes all decisions, from the top down without input from staff, is probably not open to putting teens on the library board. A key to turning youth participation into action, then, is to understand when, where, and how to begin.

WHAT ARE THE GOALS AND OBJECTIVES FOR TEEN INVOLVEMENT WITH THE LIBRARY?

The answer to this question lies largely in how you envision teens getting involved with your library. If you are considering having teens join an existing governing body, such as a library board, a foundation, or a staff council, you need to decide how these teens can best serve as representatives for the library's teen demographic. If you are thinking about creating a new organization, such as a teen advisory board that will consist solely of young people, you need to make decisions about how this group can take on a leadership role within the library, how you can get this group actively involved in the decision-making process, and how this group can provide input to the library's primary governing body, whether this is the staff, board, or foundation. Any good partnership requires clear goals and objectives. Once you establish these, both the library administration and participating teens will know what to expect (and just as importantly, what not to expect) from this joint venture.

Since youth participation is a partnership, the goals and objectives must benefit everyone concerned. Also, a true collaboration often creates new goals, rather than merely allowing each group to forward and foster its own agenda. The partnership card is one to play with the administration, as most people with financial accountability, especially in tight economic times, more often look outside the library for partners to help with resources. Youth participation activities actually look inside the library to make partners with our own customers, by providing opportunities to move teens from passive customers to active contributors. In doing so, youth participation is a means of achieving more responsive services for teens while providing teens with the opportunity to build both external and internal assets.

So the library might relate the goals of youth participation to improving service, but the goals for teens are about improving themselves. Teens are likely to engage in a youth participation activity for fun, for a school project, and just because they like libraries, so it meets some very practical needs. Yet, the work itself and the relationship that youth participation allows teens to develop with the LST and other adults, are meeting other goals, such as the goal of healthy youth development. In fact, you could easily demonstrate that an intensive youth participation activity builds and cultivates external assets, such as the following:

- Other supportive adult relationships
- Community values youth
- Youth as resources
- Service to others
- Safety
- Adult role models
- Positive peer influence
- High expectations
- Creative activities
- Time at home/constructive use of time

Youth involvement can also build internal assets, some of which include these:

- Achievement motivation
- Caring

- Integrity
- Honesty
- Responsibility
- Planning and decision making
- Interpersonal competence (which is often what home-schooled teens are looking for in volunteer position)
- Personal power
- Self-esteem
- Sense of purpose

Oh, and also the need to eat pizza, drink pop, and laugh. Not an asset in and of itself, but pretty important stuff to your average fourteen-year-old.

WHO BENEFITS FROM TEEN INVOLVEMENT?

Involved teens are likely to bring a new audience to the library. Once teens begin having positive experiences at the library, they will most probably spread the good news among their friends that the library is not so bad a place after all. So, when done well, everybody benefits, including participating teens, the teenage population served by your library as well as their families, the library staff, and the community as a whole. Not only will teens bring a new perspective to the library, they will also bring an authentic voice, helping you develop relevant, meaningful programs for people their age, which will reflect both what teens want and what they need from the library. Involved teens create a better library environment for those who cannot or do not choose to be involved.

That is important to remember: many teens, like other library customers, have no interest whatsoever is getting involved. They want to come in, check out their books, and go home. That is the model most of them are accustomed to in both public and private sector. Let's use an example from the teen world: hamburgers. McDonald's does it for you (you don't have it your way) and consequently can give it to you fast. Burger King lets you decide what goes on your burger, which takes a little longer, but they are still fixing the burger. Fuddruckers lets you not just choose the condiments, but also lets you put them on the burger yourself. So which is the better burger? It depends: if you want it cheap and quick, go to McDonald's; if you want it your way and have the time, go to Fuddruckers. Youth participation, like Fuddruckers, maximizes customer input, produces the highest quality meal, but also costs the most. As with hamburger restaurants, there are multiple levels of youth participation, and not all burgers, or teen advisory boards, are created equal. Also, Fuddruckers takes the most time, which requires the most patience. Youth participation takes not just involved teens, but teens and staff with time, patience, and persistence.

Youth participation begins not with teens, but with adults in the library recognizing that teens can make a positive contribution, and respecting the right of young adults to participate in decisions regarding matters that affect them. An LST must first be a youth advocate before he or she can facilitate youth participation. LSTs know the value of youth participation, even if they have not involved youth in their library, for it is the centerpiece of our profession. Getting youth to participate in libraries is one of the core values identified in *New Directions for Library Services to Young Adults*. Turning that value into practice is one of the twelve goals outlined in the same document. That document built greatly on the literature from the youth development field where most of the models, going back to the work of the Carnegie Council over a decade ago, emphasize the importance of youth participation. The level of youth participation is one of the key success factors in the "coolness" youth development based model used by the Urban Library Council in the PLPYD project. Youth participation serves as the foundation for most of the programs that YALSA has identified as "excellent" since 1994.

Understanding youth participation is a core competency for an LST, as defined by YALSA, and certainly we've demonstrated throughout this book how youth participation can be used to connect young adults and libraries. Just because we have only given it one stand-alone chapter does not mean that youth participation is not important to success in all these areas. But perhaps the simplest reason to pursue youth participation is because it works. It works for you the LST, for the library, and for the teens themselves. Here is the formula: teen input to the LST creates successful outputs (e.g., circulation, program attendance) for the library, which equals outstanding outcomes (asset building) for teens.

> YALSA practices what it preaches by creating vehicles for allowing youth participation in its own work, such as having teens sit on panels in programs and most drastically (and successfully) in giving over a day of the Best Book committee meetings to let teens have their say.

WHAT IS THE ROLE OF THE LST IN YOUTH INVOLVEMENT?

In this chapter, we focus a great deal on what teens do when involved and how to get them involved, but first we focus on your role as the LST. Your job is to guide, not direct; to empower, not to exploit. To empower teens means to provide them with an opportunity to be valued by their community and have opportunities to contribute to others. Empowerment is a big word in the library workplace, but it means different things to different people. Up front with youth participation, you need to establish how much you are really willing to empower teens, demonstrated by giving over—that is, giving up—real responsibility. This is not easy: most library professionals have "control issues," to put it nicely. We would rather do it ourselves (and then complain how busy we are) than give it over to someone else, let alone a teen, because they can't "do it right." But they can, and they will, if we actually empower them.

The best definition of the role of the adult comes from YALSA's *Youth Participation in School and Public Library: It Works*, which states "the key is to give teens enough structure so they are not overwhelmed, yet enough freedom to be creative and learn from their mistakes." Most of the traits it takes to involve youth successfully are, not surprisingly, the same one required to be a great LST:

- Dedication
- Flexibility
- Good listener
- Good time manager
- Independence
- Patience
- Persistence
- Problem solver
- Reliability
- Risk taker
- Sense of humor
- Trusting

Perhaps the most important trait of all is to be respectful of teens, both their ideas and their actions.

WHAT ARE THE GUIDELINES FOR YOUTH PARTICIPATION?

YALSA has developed guidelines stipulating that projects involving youth should have the following characteristics:

- Be centered on issues of real interest and concern to youth.
- Have the potential to benefit people other than those directly involved.
- Allow for youth input from the planning stage forward.
- Focus on some specific, doable tasks.
- Receive adult support and guidance, but avoid adult domination.
- Allow for learning and development of leadership and group work skills.
- Contain opportunities for training and for discussion of progress made and problems encountered.
- Give evidence of youth decisions being implemented.
- Avoid exploitation of youth for work that benefits the agency rather than the young adults.
- Seek to recruit new participants on a regular basis.
- Plan for staff time, funds, administrative support, transportation, before launching a project.
- Show promise of becoming an ongoing, long-term activity.

WHAT ARE THE DIFFERENT WAYS I CAN GET TEENS INVOLVED IN MY LIBRARY?

There are numerous ways to get teens involved:

- Community service volunteer
- Focus groups
- Friends of the Library board member
- Fund-raiser
- Homework tutor
- Interactive opportunities on a library Web page
- Intern
- Library board member
- Library long-range planning team member

- Materials selection committee
- Part-time employee
- Program assistant
- Programmer
- Reading tutor/book buddy
- Substitute employee
- Suggestion box
- Surveys
- Technology tutor
- Teen Advisory Group (TAG)
- Teen Friends Group
- Teen Read Week program committee member
- Teen Summer Reading program committee member
- Volunteer (see the list of 100 possible tasks later in this chapter)
- Web page developer
- Zines, newsletters, and other communication tools

Whatever you decide, the most important thing to remember is that youth involvement requires trust on the part of both you and the teen. Once you have invited a teen to be a part of the organization, let him or her contribute in a meaningful way, including taking on jobs that require leadership and responsibility. In addition, make it a point to empower participating teens, by involving them in the decisions that directly affect them, including programming and collection development.

HOW DO YOU WORK WITH TEENS AS ADVISORY BOARD/LIBRARY BOARD MEMBERS?

Participation in a library's YA advisory group or on a city council appointed library board is a great opportunity for a young adult to participate actively in the planning and management of the library's services and programs for its teen population. Additionally, both of these opportunities provide young people with a chance to make positive civic contributions, develop leadership skills, and acquire a sense of responsibility for the community in which they reside.

A teen advisory board can get teens directly involved in the decision-making process. Similar to their school's student council, a TAB is a select group of teens who will help you make decisions about all things related to YA programming in the library. Comprised of a group of young adults, who offer both advice and feedback about everything from programming special events to material selection, your library should count the TAB as part of the organization's governing body, meeting regularly, helping you make decisions, and providing input about policies and procedures that directly impact the library's teen population. It is also helpful to create a mission statement for the TAB that represents the philosophy of the group, including the priorities, values, and principles that guide the decisions of the organization. Your TAB's mission statement should provide overall direction and clarify the organization's purpose and meaning. To put it simply, a mission statement is a written description of why an organization does what it does, in fifty words or less. Keep in mind that a mission statement should be simple, giving an overview of the group's responsibility. This simplicity allows for flexibility, which you will need as the TAB, and the mission of the group, evolves over time. If you want to define the goals and the objectives for the group, create this as a separate document.

Most public libraries around the country have a library board, appointed by the city council, which has the responsibility of listening to the needs of the community and reporting back to the council about library development, policies and procedures, and management. Although it is rare for a library board to include a teen member, libraries that view young adult library services as a priority would greatly benefit from having a young adult representative on the board. This would be someone who could offer a unique teen perspective on issues that directly affect this demographic, including the development of teen-friendly facilities, services, and policies, while at the same time serving as an advocate for issues of importance to teens, such as extended library hours and Web site filtering policies.

HOW DO YOU RECRUIT YOUNG ADULTS TO SERVE ON THE TEEN ADVISORY BOARD?

First, take a look around you. Make a note of the teens you see frequently in the library and make it a point to introduce yourself and to let them know that you are establishing a teen advisory group, of which you would like them to be a part. Be sure to get their contact information, and then follow through with a call or an e-mail letting them know you are excited about the possibility of working together. Next, encourage them to invite any friends they think might be interested, as word of mouth is the best form of marketing when it comes to teens. Also, be sure to introduce yourself to any teen you see in the library, making it a point to let them know you are around if they need help. Once your interaction, hand them a comment card that asks for feedback about their library experience. On this card create a place for a teen to leave a name and an e-mail address or phone number if he or she is interested in becoming involved with the teen advisory group. Also, around the library where teens congregate, next to the magazines, the computers, or wherever you keep the CDs and DVDs, you can post flyers about how a young adult can get involved with the teen advisory board. Another great way to spread the word to teen readers is to put bookmarks in the most frequently checked out YA titles, including graphic novels, required reading for school, Cliffs Notes, and serials. After you have exhausted places to post the news inside the library, go out into your community and post flyers in places frequented by teens, such as neighborhood recreation centers, churches and synagogues, bus stops, schools, and so forth. Also, contact local community groups and ask them to spread the word or post a flyer; try the YMCA, 4-H, local homeschool organizations, the Girl Scouts, the Boy Scouts, church and synagogue youth groups, and boys and girls clubs.

Once you have done the footwork, sit down and create a simple press release, including details about the library, how the library is embracing the teen demographic, information about how an interested person can get involved with the teen advisory board, and your contact information. Send this out to the local newspaper, smaller community newspapers, and school newspapers. Finally, be sure to include this information on your library's Web site, perhaps linking to an online (or printable) application for interested teens. While you may want to establish a base number for membership of the teen advisory board, it is probably best to remain flexible, because many teens will only be able to participate occasionally, and possible new members will surface all the time.

ONCE YOU HAVE RECRUITED TEENS FOR YOUR LIBRARY'S TAB, WHAT'S THE NEXT STEP?

The first thing you need to do is have interested teens fill out an application form for TAB membership. Both for statistical documentation and handy reference, your application should include a place for the teen to provide his or her name, mailing address, e-mail address, phone number, school, grade level, birth date, and a place for a signature from the parent or guardian. The application is also a great place to list the required time commitment, including a place for a teen to acknowledge this commitment formally.

WHAT ORIENTATION AND TRAINING DO YOU PROVIDE FOR YOUR LIBRARY'S TAB MEMBERS?

Whether you call it an orientation, or simply the first meeting, make it fun. Provide food, play music, prepare a few icebreakers, and a give everybody a chance to talk and get to know one another. This first meeting is also a great time to talk about the goals and objectives for the group. Once you have talked about how the group is going to contribute to the library community, it is a good time to have the teens help you develop the TAB's mission statement. Again, you need to establish ownership at the onset, so the teens know that you are facilitating their activities, not running the show. Allowing the teens to contribute to the mission statement not only helps establish ownership, it provides an opportunity for all the teens to think about how they can contribute individually to the group's mission.

This first meeting is also a great time to confirm everybody's contact information (including names, mailing addresses, e-mail addresses, and phone numbers), to set a schedule for future meetings, and to brainstorm ideas for future projects. Any required training will most likely happen "on the job," allowing you to teach and meet the developmental needs of the group as you go. However, you might want to arrange training for any staff members who will be working with members of the teen advisory group, especially for those who have never worked directly with young people. Expect challenges. Expect setbacks. Expect prejudice. Know going in to it that it will not always be easy. However, it will be worthwhile, it will make your library a more diverse and teen-friendly space, and it will, in the long run, contribute to the development of a new generation of lifelong library users.

WHERE CAN YOU FIND OUT MORE INFORMATION ABOUT TAB IN LIBRARIES?

In addition to the numerous articles in professional journals and books addressing the development and existence of teen advisory groups in libraries, you can join two really great listservs for LSTs involved with teen advisory boards. Here you can post questions and read responses from other librarians who are dealing with a large number of the same issues and problems that you might be experiencing. In addition, this is a great forum for collective brainstorming, problem solving, solution seeking, and support and encouragement from other LSTs, who share your mission of having a successful TAB.

- **TAGAD-L**. Teen Advisory Groups—Advisory Discussion. This listserv, hosted by topica.com, is a discussion forum for the advisors of any public library teen advisory group or board. To subscribe, send an e-mail to tagad-l-subscribe@topica.com.
- **YA-YAAC**. Young Adult Advocate Discussion List. The goal of this YALSA listserv is to allow teen library advisory groups and the librarians who coordinate them in school and public libraries to share information and ideas. To subscribe, send an e-mail message to listproc@ala.org. Leave the subject line blank, and in the body of the message type "Subscribe YA-YAAC [first name last name]."
- Our professional literature is filled with information about doing youth participation. Two of the best recent books on the subject are Linda Braun's *Technically Involved: Technology Based Youth Participation Activities for Your Library* (ALA Editions, 2003) and Diane Tuccillo's forthcoming book Library Teen Advisory Groups (Scarecrow Press, 2004).
- Literature dedicated to other professions is just as important, for youth participation is not just a library concern. A great number of the listservs and journals about youth development, youth and technology, and asset building stress youth participation, such as Deb Fisher's *Assets in Action: A Handbook for Making Communities Better Places to Grow Up* (Search Institute, 2003).

HOW DO YOU GET A TEEN APPOINTED TO THE LIBRARY BOARD?

The first thing you need to do is set up a meeting with your library director to ascertain his or her position about the possibility of electing a teen to the library board. Beware of one critical caveat: without the support of your library director, it will very difficult to proceed. Once you have the support of your library director, you need to read the library bylaws that govern the library board's operation. If the bylaws contain an age requirement for participating board members, first you need to arrange a meeting with the library board to discuss the possibility of changing the organization's governing bylaws, specifically the age requirement for appointees. Even if no age requirement exists, you still need to set up an appointment with the library board to evaluate their response to the possibility of appointing a teen board member. Again, this will be an uphill battle, if you do not have the support of the community leaders, including library administration and officers of the library board. Finally, once you have the support of the board, you need to contact a local city councilman or councilwoman to propose the idea of a teen board member. Be prepared to argue the case for having a young adult serve on the board, including statistical information about the number of people between the ages of twelve and eighteen who reside in your community, number of teens who have library cards, number of teens who patronize the library, success stories about teen programming in your library system. Also, take along information about your library's teen advisory board, including tangible examples that highlight how this group has contributed overall to the library, focusing on how youth participation has helped the library achieve effective library services for this age group. In addition, it will be helpful to arm yourself with case studies/success stories about teen board members in other areas of the country, including not only stories about teens who have successfully served on library boards, but also on other civic and community-based boards, and on special task forces that have included teen representatives. You cannot over-emphasize this last point, for while people say they want facts, often they just want to hear good stories and youth participation is loaded with success stories.

WHAT ARE THE STEPS TO CREATING A SUCCESSFUL TEEN VOLUNTEER PROGRAM?

As with everything on the LST's plate, the first step is to rally support from administrators. You might need to sell them on the benefits of using volunteers, in particular teen volunteers. You will also have to manage, in particular in a union environment, the concerns of other staff members that volunteers are a good thing. Finally, you will need to train yourself, and others, to trust teen volunteers whom often have

THINGS TO HAVE READY WHEN YOU ARE RECRUITING VOLUNTEERS:

- Sample task/project list
- Day and times of volunteer opportunities (e.g., Tuesday and Thursday, 10 a.m. to 4 p.m.)
- A calendar of the summer volunteer session (e.g., June 1–August 10)
- Your business card with the address of library
- A volunteer application

little, if no experience, in the workplace. Once you have things in order at the library, it is time to start building a teen volunteer program.

Teen volunteers in the library are a win-win opportunity for the library, the community, and most importantly the teens. The library gains teen input, interaction and perspective, the community benefits from teens that have had valuable work experience, and teens profit from their involvement in activities that increase their work experience and opportunities that help build assets. Most libraries use teen volunteers in the summer when the need is most obvious and teens are available. While this is the norm, don't forget about using teens as volunteers during the school year for ongoing volunteer tasks, special projects, and other areas of teen involvement.

You can recruit teens from your community in a number of ways: spread the word among library staff, post advertisements inside the library, during school visits, raise awareness among your school librarian connections, attend volunteer fairs and nights at local schools, and promote the opportunity at teen programs, or by personally recruiting teens as you interact with them on a daily basis. You should have an idea of the best age range for the teens you want to recruit. Be sure to keep the tasks or duties they will be involved in during the summer in mind. If you use twelve- to fourteen-year-olds they may be reliant on parents or others for transportation, and while fifteen- to eighteen-year-old volunteers may not have as many transportation issues, their numerous commitments may limit their availability. If possible, begin to keep a list of tasks that you have in mind for your teen volunteers, tasks you need to tend to daily and weekly, as well as any special projects you only tackle every so often. This will give you a realistic idea of what tasks teens can help you with, as well as identify any projects that are more involved and may require direct adult/staff participation. While you will find some projects or tasks better suited to older teens, others will suit younger teens quite well. When you recruit teens at a school volunteer fair, have a list of tasks available—a list on paper or real-life examples in pictures—for teens and parents to look at, so they can get an idea of what the summer will hold for them. Volunteering at the library is not for every teen or adult; if you can show teens examples of what you might ask them to do you can use everyone's time wisely. If teens, parents, and the library, have the same expectation, then you end up with better volunteers. Many libraries offer incentives or a little bonus for volunteers such as exempting them from fines. While this should not be the single draw for teens to volunteer it may be a nice gesture.

After you have recruited a number of teens, the next step is to interview them to get a better sense of each teen. You need not subject recruits to a long and exhaustive interview, but it is important to find out pertinent details, such as how often they plan to volunteer, would they like a regular schedule or will it vary depending on other activities and vacation and what other demands they have on their time. You may find some teens are suited to volunteer, but are really already booked solid for the summer. A regular day and time can work to your advantage so you can plan projects and have any materials ready for certain tasks. Mapping out any children's programs that teen volunteers can assist with is another way of scheduling. These one-time programs may be a better fit for teens who want to volunteer, but have a busy schedule.

Having a list of tasks can also help teens understand what the library expects of them during their volunteer time. Teens enjoy hanging out with other teens, and often, younger teens will feel more comfortable volunteering with another teen. This can work for you, because two teens can accomplish a lot together: run a drop-in program, inventory supplies, or organize a paperback shelf quicker than one can. At the same time, any task, it is easier to get off track with two of anybody. You will need to handle friends volunteering together on an individual basis, and you can revisit the decision throughout the summer if need be. The goal is to volunteer; if you can enjoy your friends while doing this, without it getting in the way of volunteering, everyone will come away happy. You will also be able to get a sense of each teen's personality, how comfortable they are with adults, and their previous experience in job situations—paid or unpaid.

Each teen is different, but generally teens want to do something they consider valuable and interesting—if it is interesting the fun will usually follow. Teens want experience doing a variety of tasks, they want to feel important, that their input and time has made a difference, that they have helped someone. You will have teens that want to volunteer because their parents are making them; this situation can go sour quickly if there is no motivation to be productive, but there are ways to engage the teen and use their strengths to your advantage. The high school requirement of community service hours may motivate older teens, which usually makes them show up consistently, but they still need to be put to good use. Of course you may have a teen who is not motivated to be a volunteer, no matter the circumstances, and as the adult you will recognize the symptoms. Be prepared to suggest that maybe the library is not the best volunteer opportunity for them, maybe next summer, maybe never. Offer other possibilities or at least provide direction in finding other volunteer possibilities, and in the long run everyone will be better off. As a teen volunteer there is nothing worse than realizing that you and the volunteer opportunity are not a match, that you are not useful in this particular role, or that there really is nothing for you to do. As the LST, it truly is about matching tasks with teens' interests, it can make your summer go smoothly and you will end up with teens who have a great work experience, being productive, valued, using their strengths, and learning new skills.

So how do you select the best teens for the task? Part of this will come from your interview with each teen and the other part will come with experience and common sense. If you are not sure about a task match, give the teen a choice; most teens will pick a task they enjoy, can accomplish, or think is interesting. The more teens volunteer the better you and they will become at assessing a task and knowing what best fits their skills. Of course, you will have tasks that never seem to find a match, which is simply a marketing challenge. You need to find a way to market that task differently, pair it with another task or find the right teen for the task. Everyone has something that does not interest her or him, and teens are no different.

In general, certain characteristics lend themselves to certain library tasks.

- **Outgoing/talkative teens**—handing out programs, flyers, evaluations, welcoming patrons to a program, helping patrons with computer questions, book sale assistant
- **Creative or artistic teens**—creating bulletin boards, reading to children one-on-one, assisting with story time, assisting with the library Web page, photographing programs/displays
- **Quiet/shy teens**—making name tags, developing scavenger hunt, word puzzles, and so forth, for younger children, maintaining displays, making flannel boards
- **Detail-oriented teens**—inventory supplies, checking collection for Accelerated Reader books and labeling, making sure newspapers/magazines are in order, preparing summer reading packets
- **Active teens**—helping with children's program, interacting with grade school children, crowd control, exit interviewing program attendees, assisting with book sale, story time, program set up and clean up

WHAT ARE SOME POTENTIAL TASKS FOR VOLUNTEERS?

Below is a list of volunteer tasks that might be generic to most any library. School libraries might have different tasks, and certainly smaller public libraries might not have this wide a range of things to do.

All of these tasks, of course, need to complement the work of paid staff members, and not replace it. Before engaging teens in these tasks, or others that you may think of, make sure you work with your library's volunteer coordinator and union representative, if applicable, to ensure that teens are seen as assets to the organization, not threats. Some tasks that teens might do include:

- Adopt a shelf in the teen area
- Ask customers if they need assistance on the computers
- Assist in collection-development projects (checking lists against catalog)
- Assist in computer classes
- Assist with an outreach activity in the community
- Assist with bilingual story time (Spanish class students)
- Assist with book sale set up, actual sale, and take down
- Assist with crowd control and taking attendance for summer programs
- Assist with program set up and clean up
- Assist with story time
- Attend community parade as reps for library
- Check collection for Accelerated Reader books and labeling
- Check in materials
- Check YA collection vs. standard lists
- Clear drop boxes
- Collect reviews
- Compile databases of programs, customers, volunteers, school contacts
- Conduct inventories of supplies
- Create a book review newsletter
- Create a suggestion box
- Create book displays, including making props and signs, for summer and beyond
- Create bulletin boards for summer and beyond
- Create materials for fall, winter, and spring programs
- Create props for displays

- Decorate magazine boxes
- Design and maintain a story time database
- Design covers for periodical boxes
- Develop activities to support story time
- Develop booklists: top ten lists (Amazon model)
- Develop branch library Web page
- Develop scavenger hunt, word puzzles, and other activities, for younger children
- Distribute flyers and lists at programs and in the community
- Distribute posters/flyers to promote summer reading
- Do a magic trick or other skill as a way of introducing a program
- Do exit interviews with program attendees
- Do word-processing projects on the computer, such as compiling mailing lists
- Do work outside of the building to keep the library beautiful; e.g., planting
- Document programs
- Document their volunteer work
- Dust/clean shelves
- Greet customers as they enter the library
- Help with outreach events
- Help youth utilize computers in a role such as CD-ROM/links volunteer (help children with CD-ROM programs, bring computers back to main screen, assist people as trained)
- Hold a fund-raising bake sale at the book sale
- Keep stats for summer programs
- Locate fun Web pages for kids
- Look through book sale items for materials to add to collection
- Maintain display case
- Maintain displays in the library by refreshing with new titles, replacing booklists, and so forth.
- Maintain/update Web page, in particular teen sites
- Make flannel boards

- Make name tags
- Make sure newspapers and magazines are in order
- Make sure the computers have paper and sharpened pencils near them
- Make up questions for scavenger hunts
- Manage computer sign-ups
- Manage mass-mailing projects
- Move and shift books to create shelf space in congested areas
- Organize supply areas
- Page reserve books
- Photocopy documents
- Photograph programs
- Plan, develop, and manage craft programs
- Prepare back-to-school packets
- Prepare materials for forthcoming programs (September–May)
- Prepare PowerPoint presentations
- Prepare summer reading packets
- Process and reenforce library materials, such as paperbacks and magazines, using tape or Plastikleer.
- Produce a mini-carnival
- Produce a program for parents on "books they should read"
- Produce original programming
- Promote summer reading at the schools through theater groups
- Pull materials from the Weeding Report Lists
- Put barcodes and stickers on new materials
- Put on a performance: teen talent show
- Read one-on-one to children in the library
- Recruit other teen volunteers
- Repair books and other materials
- Review books for VOYA
- Run the video projector for summer video programs
- Search Amazon.com for materials to fill collection gaps

- Search the Web for homework sites
- Select and purchase refreshments for programs
- Send mail/e-mail requesting publications
- Serve as an ambassador for the library in the classroom
- Shelf read
- Shelve Easies and Easy Readers
- Sign up and manage summer reading prize program
- Straighten the children's area
- Straighten the holiday books/make sure they're in order
- Stuff envelopes
- Suggest music, magazines, and other media for library purchase
- Teens run Internet sign-up sheets
- Test out problem videos and tapes
- Train teens to be clowns, puppeteers, musicians, jugglers, and entertainers
- Use computer to see how many times certain materials have been checked out
- Use the library catalog to determine number of copies of specific titles
- Vacuum out the easy bins
- Weed and organize the vertical file
- Weed magazines, newspapers, dated materials
- Weed the young adult collection for condition
- Withdraw materials
- Work one-on-one with adults who need help using computers
- Work with YMCA after-school program, as a source for teen summer help: various tasks
- Write an article for school paper about the library
- Write and produce a skit to promote summer reading to children
- Write reviews of materials that might be of interest to kids or teens
- Write thank you notes to teachers, librarians, and others

HOW DO YOU RUN A SUCCESSFUL TEEN VOLUNTEER PROGRAM?

Once you have a core of volunteers it is important to orient them to the library. In the orientation, teens can meet each other, since they will probably work together at some point; you can give the same information to everyone at one time and answer questions that apply to the whole group. Important things to cover with your teen volunteers:

- Check-in/sign-in location or procedure
- Contact/emergency information
- Everyday tasks to do when they arrive
- Length of shifts
- Name tags
- Procedure if they are unable to volunteer for their assigned shift
- Staff break room, restrooms, drinking fountain and first aid kit
- Tour of the library including where they can keep backpack, purse, and personal items
- What they should wear

It is important to introduce teen volunteers to other staff members, as well. Make sure that volunteers wear name tags so that staff can easily identify teen volunteers.

A big task for the LST is to help library staff learn teen volunteers' names by reintroducing teens throughout the summer, take photos of your teen volunteers and post in staff room. Teens will see that they are part of the staff and begin to understand the true experience of working with adults. In addition to daily repetitive tasks that require attention, some projects may take special training. You should treat such projects like any other project and clearly lay out the goal, plan of action, examples, and the time line for the volunteer working on the project. At first, it may be best to partner a seasoned volunteer with yourself or a seasoned volunteer with a new volunteer depending on the project. Be realistic about the special projects you give to volunteers; it is good to have expectations that are laid out for the volunteer, but if you would struggle with the project as an adult, be sure it is something a teen volunteer can handle given the length of their shift, skills and type of project. Check in periodically to see if there are questions, and be ready to offer suggestions and other resources if needed. If things are cooking along as planned, express your thanks and acknowledge their accomplishment. Be prepared to lend a hand with library details or jargon that the teen may not understand, or step in completely if the frustration level gets too high. As much as teen volunteers help out the library, they themselves are a program, an ongoing, summer long, one day a week program. We are building trust and relationships with these teens over time, as well as growing developmental assets.

We cannot overlook the vital role that libraries can play in teens' lives. Libraries can gain as much from having teens work and volunteer in libraries as teen can gain from volunteering at libraries. For many teens this is the first opportunity they have to work with adults who are not family members, whether or not the work is paid. Helping teens navigate the workplace, volunteering, interaction with adults, and meaningful participation and achievement can be the most valuable service the library provides.

Whether you are working with teen or adult volunteers, it is important to communicate with other staff—regarding volunteer work opportunities. There will be a time when you are not at the library, you are busy, and a volunteer is done with a task. From the volunteer point of view, there is a sense of security in knowing their next task. Similarly, the library staff do not want to supervise another person; volunteers are here to help, not to become a task for someone else. The best solution is to create a dedicated space for your volunteers: a notebook for checking in, a list of tasks for the day, posted schedules, upcoming programs or special projects, and volunteer contact information. The volunteers will always know where to go for their next task, as will library staff if there is a question.

During your summer as you experience teens doing good work, it is important to reward teens for their exceptional work on several levels. Most libraries that have a core of teen summer volunteers throw some type of recognition at the end of the summer—a pizza party, ice cream party, or some celebration to thank teens for their hard work, but also to offer a social setting for teens who have gotten to know each other during the summer. While this final recognition is great, it is not without some drawbacks. Not every teen volunteer may be able to attend due to scheduling conflicts, and the group party setting may not allow you to celebrate or praise individual strengths. For teens to realize their strengths and weaknesses, often individual attention is the best solution.

The perfect situation is to "catch" each volunteer demonstrating a positive skill or strength while they are volunteering. Praise them in the act and explain the details of the skill or strength they have exhibited. Enthusiastically say, "Thanks for working on the paperbacks, you did a good job," so the teen knows he or she did something right. Then explain what you mean by good job and how that relates to the work

> Working with teen volunteers develops the "empowerment" assets of service to others, youth as resources, and community values youth.

and mission of the library as a whole, "I appreciate the way you organized the series paperbacks, you really had to think through how you were going to organize the variety of series, look at the space you had in the shelf, and figure out how to make it work. I think other teenagers will be able to find the books they want a lot easier. You also paid attention to the details—the labels you made for each series are spelled correctly, which will help other people who shelve the paperbacks. I also wanted to thank you for pulling out the books that looked beat up or had torn covers, the collection looks a lot nicer now and there is a little more space." Four sentences and the teen is aware of specific things they did well, why it was an important task, and how it will help other patrons. They have an understanding of the value of their task and how the library is working toward better customer service.

By the same token, just as you praise a teen for doing a good job, so also a teen that has misunderstood or did not read directions requires your attention. You are not doing this teen any favors by glossing over a mistake made or a project that was done incorrectly. This may embarrass the teen, but by explaining where things went wrong and offering a chance to right the wrong, both of you may come away with better skills. You may improve your ability to explain a project with better details, or you may realize that a certain task is not volunteer-ready. The teen will benefit from listening better, asking questions and learning to interact with an adult in a give and take situation. Will you be able to have this level of interaction with each teen volunteer? Maybe not everyday, for every task, but hopefully during their summer, over six, eight, or ten weeks, you will have the chance to observe each teen and give constructive feedback and praise on his or her work. It may take extra time, but the benefits are worth it. Ask other staff to help you out if they see teen volunteers doing good things, you can't be around every volunteer all the time. While this type of verbal praise can be effective, you can also use a variety of other perks for praise. If everyone is eager to do a special task, use it to your advantage, have a drawing each week for a soda pop, candy bar, or other small item. A teen who works hard, overcomes a challenge, or exhibits a positive attitude, gets first pick at the new books, or magazines that week, or becomes the highlighted teen volunteer of the week. Ask teens what would be a good incentive or "you did great" item; you may be quite surprised at the library perks that a teen considers special.

All of this attention begs the question of supervising. Who has the time to supervise all these teen volunteers? Most adult volunteers have a staff person they can go to if they have questions or concerns and teen volunteers should be treated in the same manner. If you have a large team of volunteers you may need or want to share the supervising duties with another staff member, preferably a teen-friendly staff member whose schedule does not overlap with yours. This shared duty will give teens yet another positive adult relationship; it will lighten your load and give another staff member the experience of working with teens in a positive light. Depending on your volunteer load you may divide teens up by schedule or give your partner half of the teens to supervise. As stated early, it is important for all staff to be aware of teen volunteers and their tasks, especially if a question about a task arises. By having a mix of daily tasks for volunteers to do (such as, reshelving series paperbacks, straightening the children's area, or maintaining displays and projects, like making flannel boards, pulling book reviews, or creating bulletin boards), you can be better prepared for times you are unavailable.

As with any volunteer or work situation you may run across teens who are not suited for the task or project you have planned. The teen may have an interest in the project, but not the skills, and retraining may be the solution. Again this may seem like a time-consuming activity, but you do not have to retrain the teen volunteer. Other experienced teen volunteers, ones who have worked on similar projects in the past, can take on the responsibility of training; the same applies to teens who are working in your libraries as a page, as well as various staff members, a number of people other than you may be able to share or teach certain skills to a teen volunteer. Unlike adult volunteers, who have had job or other volunteer experience, teens are looking for that type of experience. The time that it takes to teach a teen to use a computer program, laminator, or copy machine, is small compared to the impact of the learning experience on a teen.

As your summer winds down and your teen volunteers head back to school, it is important to send them a note of thanks and appreciation for their time and effort over the summer. Again highlight the difference they made to you, the library and other patrons if possible, and if they fit the bill, be sure to invite them back next summer, if not for any special projects you might have during the school year. During winter and spring break you may also need volunteers, so put a bug in their ear now and when you contact them in a few months it won't be a surprise. Keep a database of teen volunteers, those available during the summer and those who express interested in helping throughout the year. As the library may be the first work experience many teen volunteers have you may be called upon to write letters of reference or recommendation. Use available form letters to make this task quick and easy, but be sure to get all the details from the teen concerning where to send the letter and the deadline. If you have gotten to know your teens during the summer highlighting specific traits or strengths will come easily.

By the time August rolls around, you will have weathered another summer of programs and teen volunteers. The best way to end your summer is to wrap things up so that next spring this process will go even smoother. Have the teen volunteers fill out an evaluation about tasks they did and did not enjoy, what was difficult or hard to understand, and what they would change for next summer. Talk with them in small groups and listen, really listen to their feedback, do not try to defend your actions. If you were unorganized and lost the schedule a few times, sit back and take it, their feedback has tremendous valuable for you and for them. The skill of analyzing your actions and the actions of others is valuable. Give teens the chance to evaluate themselves, on paper or verbally; an opportunity to look back at what they did well, where they struggled and what they learned is important. When you attach no grade, teens may be able to focus on the process more than the product.

Every summer you will have teen volunteers you want to clone, you secretly hope they will fall in love with the library and spend every spare minute they have volunteering. They are efficient, creative, personable, and helpful. Usually these teens are involved in a variety of other activities and projects, but if you have special projects that occur during the school year approach these stellar volunteers and see if they are interested or need community service hours. Usually teens are willing to return to a place they are comfortable with and have knowledge about, it makes their lives that much easier. You may have to work around their schedules but their continued help may be worth it.

> Volunteers are also ripe for entry-level paid positions, so when you talk up working at the library, point out different duties they would be involved with as a page or shelver, and maybe one day as an LST

WHAT ARE SOME TEEN VOLUNTEER SUCCESS STORIES?

One of the features of the Hennepin County Library Teen Links Web site is a section called "Get Involved," which focuses on youth involvement activities at the library and in the community. As part of this section, LSTs document volunteer success stories (Available: www.hclib.org/teens/involved.html). Here are just a few to give you an idea that it is not what volunteers can do for you, but what volunteering does for them, in their own words:

- **Abbi.** "I've been volunteering at the Excelsior Library for about two months. The library was my choice of volunteer work for the High School Service Learning Project; hopefully I can continue to volunteer after my SLP ends. Volunteering at the library is really fun for me, because the librarians have a sense of humor. Two teens volunteer the same day I do, so we get to chat while we work. Despite their reputation as quiet, boring places, libraries are actually interesting and fun places to be!"

- **Lauren.** "For me, volunteering is a wonderful way to make new friends and help the community at the same time. I have found that I feel much better about spending a day volunteering than I do when I stay at home sleeping in. It has been, and continues to be, one of the most gratifying activities I am involved in."

- **Marassi.** "As an admitted bookworm since my days as a toddler, I've spent many an hour roaming the library in search of a good book. Then, it was *George and Martha*, and now *The Hobbit*. But regardless of my age, there is always the perfect book waiting. Last summer, I started volunteering at the library, almost as a way to give something back to those who made my years of reading possible. Now, after five months, I love doing things around the library—shelving projects or setting up displays—and I still get a kick out of going through the 'staff only' door. Yes, it's the little things that bring me joy. So, thanks to the library for being my second home for my 15 years!"

- **Matte.** "I have volunteered at the library for over a year. It has become a normal part of my Saturday afternoon and I rarely miss it. I really like volunteering at the library because the librarians are friendly and really appreciative of my help. I have learned a lot about the library system and the people in it. Volunteering at the library has really exposed me to great books and opportunities. Most importantly, it's fun!"

- **Meredith.** "I began to volunteer at the library two years ago. I work two hours on Saturdays and it has been a pleasant experience. The librarians are very kind and appreciative of me volunteering. One time they even bought us pizza! There is never a dull moment in the library despite what you might think! By volunteering, I get to give back to the community and hang out with my friends and the really nice librarians. I encourage anyone who's reading this to come and volunteer!"

- **Shalene.** "Volunteering at the library has been a wonderful experience for us both. For me, a social klutz, bookworm, and mud pie master, joining the library was eye opening. Other volunteers accepted me for who I am, and didn't seem to mind my lack of

Abercrombie and Fitch clothing. Personally I think there's some sort of magical little creature at the library because projects that fall apart at school, or at home, seem to function beautifully, and look attractive. Also I get to spend my time in a place filled to the brim with books. And lastly, the subtle pleasures of walking through a door marked, 'Staff Only.' Who, I ask, could resist that?"

HOW DO YOU CREATE PROGRAMMING WITH TEENS AS PERFORMERS?

Quite often, the best resources we have for programs and special events are the teens who frequent the library. Who better to lead a program on skateboard safety than an accomplished teen skater? Who better to paint faces at the library grand opening than a local teen artist? Who better to present a special costumed story hour than members of the local high school's drama club? Getting teens actively involved with library programming is a great way to make use of a natural resource, while contributing to the diversity of the library by giving teens an opportunity to program for all ages, including young children, fellow teens, adults and senior citizens.

> Getting involved in actual library programming, when a teen moves from helping with a program to being the program, is to bring youth involvement full circle in the library.

Teen programmers not only have the opportunity to contribute actively to the library community, but to provide services and programs that are completely out of our scope, as adults. These services and programs might include anything from a hands-on demonstration teaching the latest moves in hip-hop to a class on finding the best cheat codes on the Internet for computer games.

Volunteering in the library provides a teen with the opportunity to give back to the library community. Serving on a teen advisory board gives a young person the opportunity to have a voice in the development of library services to teens.

HOW DO YOU GET TEENS TO WORK IN THE LIBRARY?

Whether it is an internship or an actual staff position, real-life work experience within the library is a great way for a teen to learn about how a library works from the inside out. Stories and statistics abound highlighting how the librarian workforce is aging, with major articles in leading professional journals reporting that an unprecedented number of professional librarians will retire in the next ten to twenty years, leaving a huge gap in the library workforce. According to census data, more than 25 percent of librarians will reach the retirement age of sixty-five by 2009, increasing to 59 percent by 2019. On top of those astounding statistics, the library profession has done very little in the last decade to recruit young people actively into librarianship, contributing to only 12 percent of current librarians falling into the twenty-five- to thirty-four-year-old age range. This number, which is less than half the statistical average for this age bracket in other professions, is due in large part to the low salaries compared to other professions that require an advanced degree, the negative image perception of librarians, and MLIS graduates choosing to enter information-related professions outside of the library. For those of us who work with teens, it is imperative that we provide them with an opportunity to experience, firsthand, the dynamic field of library sciences as a discipline that is continually evolving to meet the needs of an ever-changing information technology environment.

HOW DO YOU BEGIN GETTING TEENS INVOLVED AS MEMBERS OF THE LIBRARY STAFF?

Whether you choose to create an intern position for a teen or open up the job market to allow teens to apply as pages and assistants, you need to create a job description for the position that includes a description of responsibilities, the time commitment, requirements if there are any, and a list of special skills that might be useful. Once you have created this job description, get the word out to the community, both inside and outside of the library, that you are looking for a few good young men and women to represent the teen demographic in the library: attend school and community job fairs for teens; place an ad in the local newspaper and in school papers throughout the city; post a message on both your library's Web site and the city or county Web site; let the local high school counselors know about the available positions; contact local government organizations who provide job resources for teens (for example, the Youth Services Division of the Texas Workforce Commission). Once you have hired interns or employees, hold an orientation. During this informational session, provide each new employee or intern with a letter documenting the expectations and responsibilities of each position. Also, use this time to let the young people ask questions, and get answers, about how they can best serve the library. Remember to let the teens know that you have an open-door policy, encouraging them to come talk to you if they have any problems or concerns about their job responsibilities during their period of service to the library.

WHERE DO YOU BEGIN EVALUATING YOUTH INVOLVEMENT AT YOUR LIBRARY?

Evaluating youth involvement is an ongoing process. Keep records of all activities and provide multiple opportunities for both formal and informal feedback from participating youth and adults.

Evaluation is an essential component of youth participation in libraries, whether teens are serving on governing bodies or contributing to library services as volunteers and programmers. To evaluate a program is to examine its worth, and to compare the goals and objectives that were established at the onset of the program to the actual accomplishments since the program's inception. Continual evaluation of youth involvement not only improves the program, but also helps both you and your library assess the effectiveness of established procedures.

The first thing you need to do before undertaking an evaluation of any program is to identify the specific purpose of the program. Then, you need to establish realistic parameters, unambiguously defining goals and objectives for the group. Next, monitor and document progress toward the group's set goals and objectives. You can use both informal and formal methods to do this, such as collecting oral and written feedback via follow-up interviews and written surveys, or by keeping track of statistical data over a set period of time, including how many youth participate each time the group meets. The final thing you will want to do is set a date for reviewing the evaluative material in order to assess the program; i.e., did the group reach the predetermined goals and objectives?

WHAT IS THE BEST WAY TO EVALUATE YOUTH INVOLVEMENT IN YOUR LIBRARY?

There is no "best" way to evaluate youth involvement. Whether quantitative or qualitative, the evaluation method you choose to measure the success of teen participation should fit your need and help you adapt any future programming to fit the needs of contributing teens and the library as a whole, while at the same time meeting the goals and objectives of the program. Look at both outcomes and outputs.

Quantitative research methods involve assigning numbers to things (e.g., gathering statistics about the number of youth in attendance at any given program). Qualitative research methods involve gathering empirical data about the opinions, attitudes, and feelings of participants and observers about a particular program. Generally considered more subjective, a qualitative evaluation can take the form of an interview, focus group, informal survey, or comment card. Sometimes, the best method for evaluating a program is a mix, combining both numbers and testimonials to document whether or not a program is meeting the goals and objectives outlined at the onset of a project or program requiring teen involvement.

WHAT ARE SOME BEST PRACTICES IN YOUTH INVOLVEMENT?

TEENS AS ADVISORY BOARD MEMBERS/LIBRARY BOARD MEMBERS

The First Colony Library Youth Advisory Council
First Colony Branch Library
Fort Bend County Libraries (FBCL)
2121 Austin Parkway
Sugar Land, TX 77479
www.fortbend.lib.tx.us
The First Colony Branch Library, in Sugar Land, Texas, formed its Youth Advisory Council as a result of receiving a DeWitt Wallace-Reader's Digest Fund grant to work with teens in low-income areas. Although the group, which formed in 2002, only meets once per month, they have accomplished quite a lot in a relatively brief period of time. The produced a three-minute promotional video for the YA summer reading program, which was written, taped, and edited by TAG members. The video, which was distributed to area middle schools and played over the closed-circuit classroom monitors during morning announcements in the month before school let out, was a huge success, contributing to tremendous participation in that summer's reading program for teens. Future plans for this group include using the library's distance learning equipment to collaborate with teen advisory groups at other branches to plan collectively for upcoming summer reading programs for teens.

Library Youth Volunteers
Marion County Public Library
201 East Main Street
Lebanon, KY 40033-1133
The teen advisory group at the Marion County Public Library is more than a sounding board for teens at the library. As their name implies, this group

spends time each month helping Children and Youth Services Librarian Amy Morgan with programs, special events, and more. Taking advantage of her teen participants' willingness to help out and get directly involved, as both an advisory group and a group of action, Amy shares the work with her teens, having them help plan special programs for the younger children that they coordinate and perform. This group also spends time doing things like cutting out crafts for future children's programs, designing book displays for the teen and children's areas, decorating for holidays and special events, helping set up the large meeting room and seating for library events, and even pitching in and shelving returned books occasionally.

Wired @ Carver! Teen Advisory Committee

Carver Branch of the Austin Public Library
1161 Angelina
Austin, TX 78702
www.wiredforyouth.com/acb/acb.cfm
Members of the Wired @ Carver! Teen Advisory Committee do more than help select books and CDs for the library. This group of teens between the ages of twelve and sixteen plan and teach computer-related classes, help with Wired 1-on-1 Sessions, and help plan and carry out special events for the library and community. Over the past three years, some of these special events have included a Wired for Youth (WFY) Patio Sale to earn money for state-of-the-art headphones for the Carver WFY Center, a "Celebration of Women" in honor of women leaders in the community during Women's History Month, a Holiday Nacho Party to bring the community together in celebration of Hanukkah, Christmas, and Kwanzaa, and a city-wide Yu-Gi-Oh Tournament for teens throughout Austin. This group also spends several hours each month writing article and book reviews, taking photos of special events, and laying out copy on the computer for *Wired @ Carver!*, a monthly newsletter available both in print and online at the WFY @ Carver Web site.

Teen Library Board Member

Virginia Beach Public Library (VBPL)
4100 Virginia Beach Boulevard
Virginia Beach, VA 23452
www.vbgov.com/dept/library
In Virginia Beach, Virginia, the library board reflects the demographics of the town, with approximately seven to eleven members, one of whom must be a high school junior or senior, serving this population of approximately half a million people, of whom a little less than fifty thousand are between the ages of thirteen and nineteen. Both innovative and reflective of VBPL's commitment to their teen patrons, the library's inclusion of a teen on the library board is a model for all libraries that wish to provide teens an opportunity to be actively involved in how government affects community services.

Teen Advisory Board

Arlington County Public Library
1015 North Quincy St.
Arlington, VA 22201
www.co.arlington.va.us/lib
This is a joint school and public library venture where the TAB members have engaged in a wide variety of activities. They have reviewed best books,

attended ALA meetings and author talks, testified at county board budget hearings on behalf of the library, contributed to the monthly TAB newsletter, and spoken at an open house for teens and their parents about "Books I'd Like My Parents to Read."

TEEN PROGRAMMERS

As you saw in the programming section, there are plenty of ways to transform teens as program attendees to program performers. Here is more information on some great models:

Dascaloja Puppeteers
Clearwater Public Library
100 North Osceola Avenue
Clearwater, FL 33755
www.clearwater-fl.com/cpl
Teens learn and practice the art of puppetry and performance through weekly presentations during the summer program at the library as well as at other sites throughout the community, such as recreation centers, churches, and camps. The teens "prepare and present a puppet show seven times a week during the summer, including plays, skits, and other live-action activities." Family attendance at performances has ranged from fifteen to two hundred. The name of the group was taken from letters of the names of the original five members.

YA Drama Group
East Islip Public Library
381 East Main Street
East Islip, NY 11730
http://eipl.suffolk.lib.ny.us
Each and every summer and fall, Jo-Ann Carhart, head of young adult library services for the East Islip Public Library, in New York, transforms the teens who frequent her library into a YA drama group. The group, which creates, produces, and performs, original dramatizations of children's books, poems, and songs, not only promotes literacy and the library, but provides hours of entertainment for younger library patrons.

Teen Zine
Minneapolis Public Library
250 Marquette Ave.
Minneapolis, MN 55401
www.mplib.org/wft/wft_zine.asp
Teens at Minneapolis Public Library put out *Dreams of Ours: A 'Zine by Teens for Teens*. This magazine is published three times a year and serves as a vehicle for self-expression, mostly art, poetry, book reviews, and music reviews. Over two thousand copies are distributed through the library, as well as through all media specialists and English departments at middle and high schools in Minneapolis, plus any school not covered but attended by one of the group's editors. The library's public affairs budget picks up the production cost and about $500 per issue, although the zine has an online home (www.mplib.org/webforteens.asp). While online e-zines are fine, for many teens, there is still something very important about seeing their name, or the

names of their friends, in print. *Dreams of Ours* involves about fifteen to twenty students who attend the monthly editorial meetings (weekly during the summer), although others participate by sending in their work. Most of the founding members (the zine started in the 1990s) have moved on, staff constantly recruits new members. Finally, the library also sends copies to the library board members, the city council, and the mayor. In one of the library's annual reports, the success of the zine was not described in terms of numbers of copies, but rather the number of developmental assets the project was building within teens. In particular, the project focuses on the empowerment external assets and social competencies internal assets as the LST running the zine offers guidance, but leaves much of the work and decision-making to the teens.

Magic By Alex
Oakland Public Library
125 14th Street
Oakland, CA 94612
Teen magician extraordinaire Alex Gonzalez was named "San Francisco Bay Area's Best Stage Magician" in 2002. A year later he added the public libraries in Oakland to his growing list of performance venues, including public libraries throughout northern California. Alex, who began performing in libraries when he was sixteen, is now eighteen and a regular performer for summer reading programs around the state.

Second Saturday Coffee House
Williamson County Public Library
1314 Columbia Ave.
Franklin, TN 37064
On the second Saturday of every month, from 8 p.m. to 11 p.m., at the Williamson County Public Library, you will find hundreds of teenagers hanging out and listening to local bands. The monthly event, which is open to all high schoolers, has become known in town as a great venue for local teen talent who want to play for their peers, with more than thirty-five local teen bands playing the library since the program began in 1998.

Intergenerational Programming with Teens
Johnson County Library System
9875 West 87th Street
Overland Park, KS 66212
Teens who frequent the Johnson County Library in Kansas have an opportunity to expand their horizons by participating in intergenerational programming, dedicating a set period of time each month to visit and share stories at a local senior center. The program encourages meaningful interaction between young adults and senior citizens.

TEENS AS INTERNS/LIBRARY STAFF

Urban Libraries Council
Public Libraries as Partners in Youth Development (PLPYD)
1603 Orrington Ave., Ste. 1080
Evanston, IL 60201
www.urbanlibraries.org/plpydhome.html

The entire PLPYD initiative, sponsored by the DeWitt Wallace-Reader's Digest Funds, provided nine preselected public libraries with resources to develop innovative programs for low-income youth during nonschool hours. This project produced plenty of youth development models, but many of the best involved teens taking on temporary paid positions to do everything from running a copy center to providing homework help.

Job Shadow Day
Cleveland Heights-University Heights Public Library
2345 Lee Road
Cleveland Heights, OH 44118
www.heightslibrary.org
Encouraged by both ALA and the Public Library Association (PLA), the Cleveland Heights-University Heights Public Library, in Cleveland Heights, Ohio, hosted a Job Shadow Day for high school students in mid-2003. "The program took place during National Library Week, following the Ohio Library Council's 'Ohio Loves Libraries' initiative and coinciding with PLA's 'Ask Me Why I Love My Job' recruitment initiative. The program was a response to the Cleveland Heights City's Visioning Statement recommendation for youth leadership development and to our library's Strategic Plan recommendation for a recruitment plan that addresses diversity." Designed to introduce teens to the field of librarianship, the four-hour program included a showing of "Me! A Librarian!" (an energetic recruitment video created by the Ohio Library Council), a presentation about various library jobs, required education, possible salary range, a panel discussion led by young librarians (under forty years of age), and an opportunity for participating teens to "shadow" a professional librarian in one of six departments. For more information about Job Shadow Day, visit www.jobshadowday.org.

Library Page Fellows Program, a Librarian Career Mentoring Program
Queens Borough Public Library
89-11 Merrick Blvd.
Jamaica, NY 11432
www.queenslibrary.org
The Page Fellows Program is a fifteen-week course that encourages library pages to explore librarianship as a possible career choice. The program, which has been extremely successful since its inception in 1998, is unique with respect to recruitment for the library profession. The long-range goals of the program include recruiting people into librarianship, increasing diversity in the staff, creating a base of library advocates, and raising an awareness of the importance of libraries for the community. The short-term goals include introducing librarianship to young people between the ages of seventeen and twenty-one, giving young people a better understanding of the library, and providing participants with skills and resources they can use in school and in future professional careers.

The Beatties Ford Road Teens Succeed Program
Beatties Ford Road Branch Library
Public Library of Charlotte and Mecklenburg County
310 North Tryon Street
Charlotte, NC 28202

www.plcmc.lib.nc.us/teenSucceed/about.htm
Teens Succeed! is a program that targets inner-city youth, ages twelve to sixteen, from the Westside area of Charlotte, North Carolina. The program, designed to encourage development in teen leadership, employability and life skills, focuses on introducing teens to the library as a viable career choice by implementing weekly hands-on training opportunities, where the teens see behind the scenes of the library. The areas covered include shelving, shelf reading and organizing. The teens are also exposed to the programming. They create and facilitate programs for the public specially geared toward the young adult patrons.

TEENS AS WEB PAGE BUILDERS AND CONSULTANTS

Teens Online

Hennepin County Public Library
12601 Ridgedale Dr.
Minnetonka, MN 55305
www.hclib.org/teens
This nine-member team supports the library's award-winning Teen Links Web site. Teen Links is created and maintained by staff of the library with the help of the Teens Online Board. Members of this team do everything from reviewing the current links and look of the Web page, to developing their own Web content. While the teens cannot "write" directly to the library's server, they do prepare Web pages, some loaded with graphics and others that are merely an annotated list of links, about topics in the "free time" section. Teens have created Web pages for the library on subjects such as local teen events, computer game reviews, Anime, martial arts, and online quizzes. One of the teens designed the board's own page, which lists for each teen a short biography, while another contributed an article to VOYA. Teens are asked to participate in monthly meetings and respond promptly to Teens Online e-mail communication. Even though it is a group of techie teens, the kids prefer to meet in person than by using electronic chat boards. The teens are diverse in gender, demographics, and age. The Teens Online board is only one example of the youth involvement on Teen Links. In the "Read On" section, teens can contribute book reviews (earning a chance to win prizes during the summer and Teen Read Week) and even contribute a "top ten" book list of their favorite weeds. There are also plenty of places on the Teen Links page for teens to suggest improvements, request that a site be added, and on occasion participate in an online survey. Another area of Teen Links with youth involvement is the "Life Stuff" section, which deals with various teen lifework subjects. For the section on GLBT, the library enlisted the assistance of a local high school's Gay-Straight Alliance, and two other teen volunteers at the Hennepin County Library. Teen Links is an excellent mode of taking the philosophy of youth involvement and putting it into practice.

Young Adult Advisory Board

Boulder Public Library
1000 Canyon Blvd.
Boulder, CO 80302
www.bplyaab.org
Although this group does many project for the library, one of the most visible is their Web page, which also serves as the library's teen Web page. According

to the site, the page is "created and maintained with the strong input of middle and high school students. [It] may contain creativity, originality, and wit, as well as in-depth discussions of books, music, movies, poetry, creative writing, and catapults as a possible alternative to modern plumbing."

WHAT ARE THE ELEMENTS OF SUCCESS IN YOUTH INVOLVEMENT?

While there are no sure-fire, works every time, formulas for thriving youth participation activities, below are some elements of success.

- **Build relationships.** That is, as Stone Cold would say, the bottom line. Almost any LST engaged in youth involvement activities will tell you about the personal relationships they have built with individual teens. They will tell you how those teens remain in contact after they graduate, how they continue to share their successes, and sometimes even how they became librarians themselves. But, there is the downside, or rather dark side, here, which we will touch on in Chapter 12.

- **Create a variety of tasks.** As mentioned earlier, not every teen is at the same level of responsibility or has the same skills, talents, and interests. So youth participation activities need to provide a variety of ways for teens to participate; not just different tasks, but also different levels of participation and maybe even different venues.

- **Define needs of the project.** If you are doing youth participation, you have to have a reason for both your director and for the teens themselves. Youth participation is an end for teens, but also, in order to garner support, needs to be seen as a means to meet some community need.

- **Define roles and rules.** One youth participation group was asked to help with a library's teen Web page efforts, but were not given any guidance or limitations on what their role was. The very first suggestion was change the logo. A good suggestion, but sadly not practical since they library had recently purchased a thousand mouse pads with the logo. The fault wasn't with the teen for suggesting it, but with the LST running the group who didn't clearly define what the ground rules were. You can, and should, inspire teens to brainstorm, dream, and create, but you also need to define clearly what is possible. If not, then their voices are just blowing in the wind and everyone's time is wasted. Teens realize they do not have a real voice.

- **Encourage diversity.** Teens are drawn from the entire library community, not just one school. This ability for teens to interact outside of their normal circle is a plus for them, but also for the library to establish ties with lots of schools. Some TAGs actively help LSTs in communicating with teachers and school librarians, acting as a go between to ferry documents, materials, and always ideas.

- **Know the limits of youth participation.** The punch line of the above story about the logo is that the logo was "tested" before other sets of teens who loved it. While youth participation certainly can be successful in creating better services, programs, and collections, you cannot listen exclusively to the collective voice of the TAG. There are lots of teens who, for very good reasons, are not and do not want to be involved at this level, and you must take their needs into account.

> TAGs speak for themselves and can be seen as speaking for other teens; but, a TAG is not, and cannot be, the monolithic voice of all teens.

- **Seek balance.** The most crucial success factor is also the hardest. The LST needs to find the balance between getting the work done and letting teens have fun; between empowering teens to do good work and making sure teens are not being exploited to do somebody else's work; between spending a lot of time with a few teens and less time with a lot of teens, even if the TAG is providing the information to make services to all teens better; between wanting to direct the work and knowing that facilitating is favored; between asking for input and enacting all of the input that teens will provide. Finally, successful youth participation means creating a balance between structure and flexibility.

- **Understand your resources.** Recognize not just how much, if any, funding is available for youth participation activities, but how much you can allow. That is only the tip of the iceberg. Do teens involved in youth participation have access to staff computers, phones, areas, and break rooms? Do they get to use the copier for youth participation stuff? The scanner? The digital camera? Can they post things directly on the library's Web site? Pizza, pop, an hour once a month, and a meeting room is a nice start, but these are not the only resources you need, to do youth participation right.

- **Win-win and celebrate.** All these elements and all these ideas really do not mean a great deal if youth participation is not "fun" for teens. Yes, they can learn, grow, get empowered, build assets, have outstanding outcomes, and all those good things. But they also want to laugh and be acknowledged. The work of a TAG is perfect fodder for library annual reports, testimony before funding agencies, and at library volunteer recognition events. Yet, teens who are involved get the certificate and the handshake, but mostly we will need to give them attention, respect, and finally our gratitude.

- **Win-win.** Whatever the project, there is something for both sides. Youth and libraries each benefit *and* contribute in a meaningful way.

CONCLUSION

Youth involvement represents a big shift in professional thinking, moving from services *to* teens and working toward services *with* teens. As discussed, the context from which many LSTs operate does not allow them the opportunity or access to engage in "higher level" youth involvement activities, like many described above or in the work of the Public Library as Partners in Youth Development project. What should be clear, however, is that as YALSA named its publication on the subject: *Youth Participation Works.* This news is nothing groundbreaking: as far back as 1992 when the Carnegie Council on Adolescent Development was studying programs for adolescents, they clearly identified that youth involvement was key success factor. In the last edition of this book, youth involvement was noted as one of the ten trends shaping YA work, and YALSA on the national level has not only preached youth involvement, it has practiced it. Youth involvement at any level is important, so do not be discouraged if you cannot get teens involved in designing your new YA space; instead, seize the opportunities that are available and make the most of them. Nothing succeeds like success.

12 ISSUES IN YOUNG ADULT SERVICES

"Congress shall make no law abridging the freedom of speech."
—*The First Amendment*

"Materials may not be brought into the correctional facility which pose a threat to staff or negatively impact treatment programs."
—*a service agreement between a public library and a youth correctional facility*

One of the defining characteristics of adolescents is that they are persons who no longer want to be considered dependent children, yet are not treated in society as independent adults. From that fundamental contradiction stems most issues related to teens on the large political landscape all the way down to fights with parents inside every home. This push-and-pull of the teen years reveals itself in libraries, as well. While some staff, board members, and administration types want to lump teens into the children's room, others just want to ignore them, figuring there is no reason for a focused effort. Many professional issues revolve around YAs, precisely because it is a time of transition and vulnerability.

Just like teens themselves, the LST is caught in the middle. All LSTs have a boss to whom they need to answer, policies they need to follow, and work rules to obey; what happens when one or more of those items conflict with the legitimate rights of teenagers in a library? Everything is done in the name of protection: filters are put on computers to protect young people from harmful images; filters are taken off computers to protect the first amendment rights of teens. LSTs thus are stuck in the middle, yet for many issues facing YAs in libraries, there is no middle ground, no shades of gray. The problem with most library policies is they are absolutes, which allow no leeway for circumstances, judgment, and even common sense.

Above and beyond all, LSTs are advocates for youth. We want to create the conditions where they can make their own choices: sometimes, we do that by speaking for them, other times by developing access vehicles for teens to voice their opinions directly to decision makers. The decision makers, however, in the post-9/11, post-Columbine, and, most importantly, post-CIPA world, increasingly look to limit youth access, and thus, there is a heightened need for youth advocacy.

> Society and libraries vacillate between allowing YAs to behave responsibly, while at the same time wanting to protect them.

> Good customer service cannot flourish in a straitjacket, and we all know "I was just following orders" is a scary excuse.

In this chapter, we present scenarios that tackle issues often faced by LSTs in school and public libraries. Many of the scenarios are presented as questions at the reference desk, sometimes asked by teens, sometimes not. Each question will identify the speaker; you have to imagine yourself on the other side of the desk. Yes, many of these are fictional questions (few teens would come up to the desk and ask for *Playboy*), but the issues they represent are very real. We will present, as best we can, both "sides" of the issue. The foundation for all these issues begins at home with your own library's policies, which often include the adoption of various ALA policy documents. The ethical foundation of our profession, often spelled out as well in ALA documents, comes into play. The laws of the city, county, state, or nation where you work and live are foundational, as well. Finally, all of us seek to follow Spike Lee's advice and "do the right thing," which results in the best outcome for teens in our libraries. But, as in Lee's movie, the right thing is sometimes ambiguous at best.

The issues faced by LSTs do not just come in the form of questions over the reference desk. Sometimes the trickier queries come not from customers, but from colleagues and the administration. They may come during a job interview, a performance review, a post-"incident report" meeting, or during budget confabs from an administrator asking why support (a.k.a. dollars) should go to young adults. One of the big issues in serving YAs is learning to become a leader, an advocate, but also being a "team player" to garner support from colleagues. LSTs often get very frustrated with other staff and higher-ups who don't get it. You need to turn that energy around, stop beating your head against the wall, and instead learn the methods of influence that will allow us to open doors (and pocket books) to gain the resources to get the best outcomes for teens.

The big issue, of course, arises when these two worlds collide. Consider this hypothetical scenario: your director is approached by a juvenile correctional center to provide library services to the teens who reside there. This is good for your director, because it allows her to show cooperation with another government body, as well as to have access to funding in the areas of juvenile justice, youth development, and crime prevention. Also, both you and the director can agree that this presents a wonderful example to show how reading, libraries, and lifelong learning can have an impact on the lives of troubled young people. So, this is a very good thing. The juvenile correctional center is eager to have the service, but there are a few conditions. They present a list of books and magazines you cannot bring, because, in their opinion, they undercut the mission of their facility. A majority of these materials might be by or about African Americans, in particular resources that speak to the streets. Martial arts books are not allowed due to the potential negative impact they could have on the safety of the correctional officers, and also books with heavy sexual content are prohibited. And also...You get the idea.

You have in your hand your library's policies on free access to materials; you have the Library Bill of Rights, and your own training, which tells you that libraries do not censor: we don't deny patrons, regardless of age, access to certain materials. Your director has the same documents in her hand, but she also has an eye on the bottom line, on the benefits of inter-departmental cooperation, and maybe on winning an award for the service. You can "take the deal" and provide library services which compromise your principles, but does give these young men and women behind bars some library service. Or, you can hold fast, and thus not provide any service and at the same time, not win any points with your director. It would be nice to think a compromise could be reached, but the facility is insistent they get the last word on what books and magazines kids can read. There is no give there. What do you?

That is just one of many difficult issues or decisions LSTs have to face every day. While you work on the answer to this one, here are a few others to mull over.

(TEEN) DO YOU KNOW WHERE I CAN BUY A TERM PAPER?

A collision of values sparks most of the tough issues we face. As with most all of the issues we explore in this chapter, this one is certainly a case of where you stand depends upon where you sit. If you sit in a school librarians' chair, it seems pretty clear that not only would you not help the teen buy the paper, that under your school's policies regarding student conduct, you might be required to report even attempted plagiarism. In a public library, which has no code of student conduct, the answer is less than clear-cut, especially if we think beyond the specific incident and look instead at those core values we identified in Chapter 1 to serve as a foundation for all that we do with teens. If we really believe that we should respect the unique needs of teens, this is a real good example of "giving them what they want." We will respect their information request, not judge it, and do our best to answer it. Also if we truly believe in equal access, most librarians wouldn't think twice about helping an adult patron find this information or something similar. Then there is the other side of our values, for we also believe in the value of collaboration. Would it not be difficult to collaborate with teachers if you enable or even actively assist teens in plagiarism? Of course it would. We support healthy youth development, yet clearly, from the developmental assets approach, helping a teen purchase a term paper, we are not building, but eroding assets such as honesty, integrity, and responsibility. So what is the right answer? What do you do?

(TEEN GIRL) DO YOU HAVE ANY BOOKS ON MARRIAGE?

Gradually through your reference interview the subject changes to wife abuse to dating violence. You begin to notice she seems upset and she has a bruise on her face. Do you refer her to a battered woman's shelter? Do you give her 800-numbers to call or even local hotlines? Do you recommend a YA novel about dating violence as an attempt at bibliotherapy? Would you do more or less for a teenager than another patron, or should you do anything at all? This relates back to privacy as well—would you contact a school counselor about this YA and ask them to intervene? Is that your place or role? What do you do?

(TEEN) DO YOU HAVE A COPY OF *THE ANARCHIST COOKBOOK*?

This is yet another selection issue, but the question takes on heightened significance post-Columbine and post-9/11. It seems to be the perfect example for discussing issues of intellectual freedom, selection verses censorship, and perhaps even social responsibility. A lot of libraries weasel out of this one by purchasing a copy to show their Intellectual Freedom colors, but then not replacing it when it is lost, or not buying more copies to fill the (inevitable) long hold list. Buying one copy isn't really an answer; if anything, it compounds the problem. It is also a lot harder to say that we cannot purchase this title, or similar books whose claim is purely entertainment, but then provide instructions on how to do damage to other human beings, because on-demand publishing makes it virtually impossible to be out of print. Do you support healthy youth development by purchasing a book that will be checked out by teens, who have access thereby to instructions on how to make a bomb? What do you do?

(TEEN) CAN I CHECK OUT THIS COPY OF THIS *FIGHT CLUB* DVD?

Another tough nut. Contrary to popular belief, no law prohibits teens from attending R-rated movies, but rather the movie industry policy does. The same policy often extends to video stores, but libraries that embrace free access ignore the industry standard. Some libraries can do this through technology; they simply block library cards of people under the age of eighteen from checking out certain materials. As good of an idea in some ways as youth or teen library card sign-ups, this is such an obvious drawback since it means your library could easily set up a program to link library card type to item types and thus block access, that is probably best a road not taken. The question is again one where our professional standards and community standards clash—few members of the public will come out for renting R-rated movies to teens. Who wins? What do you do? Would anyone take issue with a teen checking out the book, *Fight Club*? But does *Fight Club* belong in a school library or public library teen area?

(TEEN) WHY DON'T YOU HAVE ANY GOOD CDS?

We touched in the collection section about the opportunities and challenges of purchasing popular music, especially when the genres that are in demand by teens are often those with parental advisory labels. Do you buy both the real version and the "clean" version? Do you place limits on checking out the parental advisory recordings, as a music store would? If you involve teens in music collection development, as you should, do they understand what the rules are, and why? Can you build assets on one hand and purchase materials that celebrate pimping on the other? What do you do?

(SAME TEEN) HEY, I ACTUALLY FOUND A GOOD CD, NOW WHERE CAN I BURN A COPY?

Copyright and the digital age is a marriage made somewhere other than in heaven. People trying to protect their intellectual property don't stand much of a chance, because just about anything can be copied, shipped, stored, and filed in a matter of seconds. At the copy station, we normally tape up a statement about copyright infringement, but do we do the same at every computer terminal with a CD burner? Every printer? Every disk drive? What, if any, role do libraries have in enforcing copyright? If not that, then at least in not creating opportunities for patrons (especially teens) to break copyright laws? What do you do?

(TEEN) WHICH OF THESE COMPUTERS HAVE FILTERS?

We dealt with filters in Chapter 10, Technology, and CIPA seems to be the controlling authority here, so library systems again need to choose between the bottom line (those strings-attached federal funds) and the foundation of the profession. CIPA is a disaster for all libraries, but in particular for youth advocates, because it codifies that children, which includes teens, need protection in libraries. What is next? CIPA for circulation? The problem with all of these issues is the slippery slope: if you give an inch on your core values, does that not hand opponents the chisel and hammer to start chipping away at other values. If you allow filters, then what moral ground is left for you to stand on? CIPA makes the law the worst of all possible worlds: denying teens access to information while allowing access to materials for adults. Filters for all or filters for none are much better alternatives. This is one case where the middle ground isn't a safe place for a youth advocate to live. What do you do?

(TEEN) CAN I RESERVE A MEETING ROOM FOR MY D AND D GROUP?

Why does the idea of free access not extend to the meeting room? If you look at many library policies, you will discover that more than a few impose limitations on service by age, even while the same book of policies will cling to the Library Bill of Rights and all its interpretations. When policies collide, what do you do?

(TEEN) I'M READING ALL THE BOOKS IN THIS FANTASY SERIES, AND YOUR LIBRARY DOESN'T OWN BOOK FIVE. IS THERE ANY WAY I CAN GET IT?

Similarly, most libraries offer interlibrary loan service, but seem to want to keep it secret. We know of few libraries that actively promote ILL at all, let alone to teen customers. But given the intense interest in fantasy, the serial nature of the genre, and the tendency for such books also to disappear over time, we should be more proactive in telling teens about this service. But if you do, can you afford it? What do you do?

(TEEN, OVER THE PHONE) I NEED TO KNOW WHO PLAYED IN EVERY SUPER BOWL, CAN YOU HELP ME WITH THAT?

Many libraries impose limitations on the number of information transactions that staff can answer over the phone, which seems reasonable and the limits hold true for everyone. Libraries that "don't do homework" are even more problematic. On the one hand, we don't do homework: we answer information requests, regardless of the nature, or motive, of the request. Thus, LSTs need to be advocates for fair access, even if it is limited. The rub, however, comes when librarians who don't "get it" rattle off ten addresses for a businessperson, ten best sellers for a regular patrons, or ten video titles for a homebound customer, but then set limits when teens are involved. If you are on the desk when that happens, what do you do?

(TEEN) WHY DON'T YOU HAVE A PROGRAM ON TATTOOS? THAT WOULD BE REALLY COOL.

Indeed, it would be; that is, until the city council, the mayor and the muck-racking local media got involved. The following is a true story. A large urban public library planned a tattoo program for teens complete with a live demonstration, as well as a public health speaker to talk about the "downside" of tattoos. All it took was one parent seeing the flyer, a call to the media and the council, and the library had to batten down the hatches. The stuff that teens want to know about upsets adults; it challenges them. Before you attempt to hold a program like this, or one on safe sex, or who knows what else, that might touch off a firestorm in your library, make sure that you have your director's approval and support. While this may be the time to present "two sides" of the story, that is not what we normally do in a program. A program for/about/by gay teens doesn't need to be balanced with a born-again Christian telling people how to get out of "the lifestyle." Following that logic, do we invite the Ku Klux Klan to every black history program? So, you have kids who want a program on a topic you know is bound to be controversial, landing the library on the front page of the paper for all the wrong reasons. What do you do?

(TEEN) DO YOU HAVE A VENDING MACHINE?

A young teen comes to your library every day in the summer when you open and stays until you close. From what you can tell, he doesn't bring a lunch with him, nor does he seem to leave the building long enough to get something to eat. He doesn't cause any trouble—each day he reads, uses the computers, and sleeps. YA service is so tuned to getting YAs to want to use the library, and here is one that does every day five days a week, eight hours a day, and that is a problem. Is this a neglected child? Should you report this to the child neglect authorities? Should you contact this person's parent or parents? If you do not do anything, in your state you might be committing a crime, and if your inaction is in fact a crime, then are you personally responsible or is the library as an organization responsible? Where do you draw the line between the right to privacy and the need to protect children from harm? What do you do?

(TEEN) DO YOU HAVE A COPY OF *PLAYBOY* I CAN LOOK AT?

That libraries should reflect their community is a given (why else do the community analysis assignment in library school?), but what if the community does not reflect library standards? Not just *Playboy*, but most libraries do not stock any materials (and please, don't bring up the limited release Madonna book from a decade ago) that could be classified as pornographic—not in book form and not in movie form. Why not? We fall back on the "well, it will get stolen excuse," but that does not stop us from purchasing Sunday papers with classified sections, DSMs, Value Line, or nonsecured DVDs and CDs. The "get stolen" excuse is a false excuse and most of us know it. We do not buy pornography because the public would not support it, and because we do not believe it is our role to buy these materials. We draw lines; call it selection or call it censorship, or maybe call it making a decision on how to spend the tax payer's money in a way they can support, but we will give teens what they want, provided everyone is clothed.

This was perhaps the biggest hole in the case against filters: libraries would spend taxpayer dollars on computers, telecommunications costs, IT staff, and so forth, to make pornography available via the Internet, but would not purchase a copy of *Playboy* for the shelves. We would argue that we cannot allow filters, yet it is doubtful that a single library subscribes to, then selects from, the *Adult Video News* (reviews of porn), which is, call it what you will, filtering. Just as Internet filters are not perfect, neither is our selection process. Internet filters are tools created by third parities, which decide what a customer can access; libraries do selection by using selection tools created by third parties in order to decide what a customer can access. Does *Booklist*, used by most libraries, review every single published book? No, it has a criterion for selecting what to include, which sounds a lot like an Internet filter. If we really believe in a "give them what they want" policy, then any library serving teen boys would carry *Playboy*. Actually, that is pretty mild for twenty-first century teen boys: they will want something more hard core, which probably cannot be found in any librarian's guide to magazines. We say we are customer focused, we say we listen to the input of teens, and so the boys in youth advisory groups suggest a subscription for the teen area of *Shaved Pregnant Nazi Lesbian Albino Twins*. What do you do?

(TEEN VOLUNTEER) DO YOU HAVE THE BOOK *DYING WITH DIGNITY: UNDERSTANDING EUTHANASIA?*

You know a YA who has been a patron for years; she has even volunteered on occasion. You notice recently she's been moody, probably depressed. You might say something or try to talk with her, but you never seem to find the time or place. She drops out of sight, next time you see her she is asking you to help her find this suicide self-help book. Now, you've got a ton of questions—you are on record as fighting for access for YAs to all materials. When discussion comes up about buying certain controversial materials, you are on the side of give them what they want regardless. You also would be the first person to discipline a checkout clerk who told a YA they "shouldn't" be checking out a certain item. But you have a real person standing in front of you and that policy, those positions, might not seem so important now. What do you do?

(PARENT OF TEEN) MY SON TELLS ME HE HAS ALL THESE FINES ON HIS CARD. I'LL PAY THEM, BUT I WANT TO KNOW WHAT BOOKS WERE LATE, AND WHAT OTHER BOOKS ARE CHECKED OUT?

This one is very much a local policy matter. It is one of those cases where a well-intentioned necessary policy to protect the rights of young people seems to smack right into the face of common sense. "Yes, since your son is under age, by law you are responsible for these items, but we can't tell you what they are," is our reply. On the receipt we hand the patron for the lost book, do we cross out the title? Teens are beginning to have private lives and they may expect that in a library information will be kept confidential, as they should. While there may be a few exceptions, this might not be one of them. What you don't want to do is what one high school library in Minnesota did: post outside the library the names of everyone who had books checked out (strike one) that were overdue (strike two), and, also let the whole school know the names of the overdue books for each student (strike three). While that is the extreme case, more likely you will encounter the parent who is not really interested in spying on her son, but because she has to pay his fines, would like to find out the titles of the books for which she is paying those fines. What do you do?

(PARENT OF TEEN) AS LONG AS I'M HERE, I WANT TO PICK UP ANY BOOKS THAT MY DAUGHTER HAS ON HOLD. CAN YOU GET THEM FOR ME?

In branches, many times the person picking up the book is not the person who requested it. You can have policies that enforce against this practice, but no one who has ever worked at a branch is going to tell you that if Mr. Smith, who comes in every day, says he will pick up books for his wife, who is at home sick, you would not check those books out to him. To have an "only the person" policy again sounds good on an administrative policy level, but does not really work well in reality. What do you do?

(PARENT OF TEEN, ON THE PHONE) I WANT TO KNOW IF MY SON IS THERE. HE WAS SUPPOSED TO COME THERE AFTER SCHOOL. COULD YOU PAGE HIM?

This seems like a no-brainer. A parent calls, wants to talk to her or his child to arrange the ride home, and asks you to page them. This is a fictional scenario, of course, because this would be the only teen without a cell phone, but nevertheless. We might do this without thinking, but is this not a huge invasion of privacy, as well? Or, they want to know if you could check to see if their son has checked out any books that day, thus proving he has been to the library—they're not asking for the titles of specific books, which almost none of us would give out, but simply for evidence that he was at the library. Do you provide that information? Do you page the teen and when they don't show up tell the caller. By relaying that information have you violated the teen's privacy? What if the mother says it is an emergency? Do you reply, "I'm sorry that your husband was just in a car accident and you would like your son to meet you at the hospital, but our policy is…" So, what do you do?

(PARENT OF TEEN) MY SON HAS TO DO A PAPER ON…

Almost universally, the one type of patron loathed by many librarians, is the parent doing the research for their child. This presents all sorts of potential problems, not the least of which is your own feelings about the situation. Some parents do this willingly, others out of desperation. Helping them is a challenge; you can't do a strong reference interview, because more often than not they do not know about what they need. Since you cannot present them with options to narrow the search, do you broaden the search giving them lots of materials to take home so their child can choose the best ones? Often the parent will come in with the child, but the parent will do all the talking. Focus your eyes on the student and ask her or him the follow-up questions, because that is who will help you complete the reference transaction. Whenever possible, you want to separate the YA from the parent, if you don't you will never learn what the student really needs, only what the parent thinks he or she needs.

(SCHOOL VICE PRINCIPAL) WE KNOW THAT YOU HAVE TRUANT STUDENTS COMING HERE PLAYING ON THE COMPUTER. CAN YOU CALL ME WHEN YOU SEE ANY STUDENTS FROM MY SCHOOL ARE HERE DURING SCHOOL HOURS?

This is a very hard case. Would you expect a school to cooperate with you, which public librarians always clamor for, when we won't cooperate with them? At the same time, we don't call work places to tell them about adults playing hooky from work. There are also some legal issues here: truancy is in almost every jurisdiction against the law. If it is happening, and you know it, but do not report it, what are your personal and your library's legal liability? Are you mandated to be reporters, as with neglect and abuse? If you allow teens to hang out all day instead of going to school, are you supporting truancy or just enabling it; or, is this a right to privacy issue? Some libraries, in particular those in close proximity to schools, have the "no students without a pass" rule, while others adopt more of a "don't ask, don't tell" policy. Our values clash with each other in this case, as well; we want to collaborate with schools, yet we want to respect teen's choices, and yet we also know that a teen spending time out of school is probably not a good sign, inasmuch as truancy is often an indicator of more serious risk taking behavior. What do you do?

(TEEN LIBRARIAN TO ANOTHER TEEN LIBRARIAN) DO WE REALLY WANT TO BUY THIS COMING OF AGE NOVEL *TIETAM BROWN*, BY FORMER WRESTLER MICK FOLEY?

I guess teens would like it, and teens know who he is, but it is just loaded with cursing, sexual content, sexual violence, and graphic violence. Do we want the hassle we are going to get from parents and the director about this? What do you do?

(UNION STEWARD) DON'T YOU REALIZE THAT ALL THIS YOUTH INVOLVEMENT IS THREATENING UNION JOBS?

Unions correctly look with suspicion on volunteer jobs. But youth involvement isn't about taking jobs or replacing people; instead, it is about creating positive outcomes for teens. It is about side benefits like recruiting for the profession, adding new energy and ideas, and making services more effective, because they are more responsive. But the model of services with teens is going to scare some people, with or without unions. If you suggest that teens from a performing arts high school might have a role in programming (or any of the other examples from the Chapter 11), then isn't that undercutting professionalism? We think not. Instead, it is by sharing our expertise that we demonstrate our professional knowledge. We could train a teen to take your temperature and measure your blood pressure, but that doesn't make him or her a nurse, doctor, or health care professional. Youth involvement, especially in programming, should allow for professionals to be more creative. Teen volunteers can often take on the jobs that we probably shouldn't be doing anyway, thus allowing professional more time to be creative. Rather than undercutting professionalism, youth involvement creates the circumstances to allow it to flourish. But your union steward or your children's librarian colleague does not see it that way, so what do you do?

(ADMINISTRATOR) WHY DO YOU HAVE *SPIN* MAGAZINE IN THE YA AREA/SCHOOL LIBRARY?

The objection comes from a concerned adult, but it is not what you first think. The objection is not to the content of the music magazine nor to the covers, which often feature more flesh than a *Penthouse* cover, but to the ads. Your director points out that there are ads for both cigarettes and alcohol. It is not that the adult is arguing a moral point, but a legal one. It is against the law for teenagers to purchase these products. Your director wants it removed from the teen area or the school library. What are your choices? In the public library, you can compromise and allow the magazine to move over with the adult magazines: the magazine is still available, but the access is a little harder for teens. In a school library, the choices are probably to lose the magazine or lose your job. What do you do?

Lots of issues present themselves here. The first, and one that trips us up again and again, is that we believe in free access and we believe in healthy youth development. What do we say when teens use that free access to obtain information about risk taking, or in some cases illegal, activities. Can you support youth development on one hand and purchase CDs with lyrics that glorify every at-risk behavior? Can you make a case for positive outcomes for youth when at the same time you are providing access to books, magazines, and music that celebrate being a gangster, a pimp, or a cop killer? Is it one thing to carry novels that feature fictional teen characters, engaged in smoking and drinking and maybe a little breaking and entering to boot, and another to have ads for smokes in *Spin*? If we move *Spin* from the teen section, then what is next? *Rolling Stone, Source,* and all the other music magazines, which feature similar ads, will follow, and we are back to a rack of *Boys Life* and *Super Teen*. What do you do?

(ADMINISTRATOR) WHY SHOULD WE CONTINUE TO SUPPORT YA WHEN OUR MAIN MEASURE OF SUCCESS IS STILL CIRCULATION AND YA HAS LOWER CIRCULATION THAN CHILDREN'S OR ADULT MATERIALS?

We will skip over the idea that circulation is the only or even primary measure of success in the ideal world, because in this world, it seems to your director, that is what matters. If you look at the numbers every month, the circulation of YA is lower. Or is it? Let us say the budget for children's materials is $20,000 and they circulate 80,000 items; but if your budget is $5,000 and you circulate 30,000 items, then YA has the higher circulation-per-dollar ratio. You can use the same formula for looking at circulation per square feet, or staff hour. Other measures where YA does well are output counts such as turnover rate. If you adopt the ideas here about collection development, another number in your favor will be increase in circulation month to month, and from the year before. Just looking at the hard numbers, services to YAs will come up short. But, when creating ratios using other data, it should be obvious that YA gives the most "bang for the buck."

(ADMINISTRATOR) WHAT SHOULD WE CALL THIS AREA IN THE NEW LIBRARY: YOUNG ADULT OR TEEN?

Depends who you ask. If you ask Peter Zollo, his research from 1992 indicates that people between the ages of twelve and eighteen prefer to be called young men and young women first, then YAs, then teenagers, and then teen. But, when the young people in the focus groups from the State Library of California were split, the younger ones liked the term teen or teenagers, while the older ones preferred to be called young adults. This is best explained by the aspiration of teen life; most teens want to be perceived as older than they are. Thus, the real "teens" in public libraries might really be ten- to fourteen-year-olds (middle school and junior high students), while young adults might be fifteen- to eighteen-year-olds (high schoolers). Some libraries go right to the teens who use the library to come up with names for their teen spaces. A great deal of the naming of the area depends on the teen "market segment" you want to reach. If you want to reach younger teens, then go with teen; older, go with young adult. If you want to reach all, then what do you do?

(ADMINISTRATOR) WHAT ARE THE STANDARDS FOR SERVING YOUNG ADULTS IN LIBRARIES? HOW MUCH OF THE COLLECTION BUDGET SHOULD BE ALLOCATED? HOW MUCH STAFF?

While some states have developed standards for young adult services, most have not. Even state standards, like those of New Jersey, cannot speak to every circumstance. Instead of standards, two core documents provide similar guidance. The first is the chapter entitled "Itinerary for Quality Services to Young Adults" in the *New Directions* document. While every school and public library will have a different complement and arrangement of resources, almost every library has seven action areas (administration, collections, programs, services, electronic resources, facilities and hours, and staff). The document then presents a checklist of resource allocation against which libraries can score themselves. That works on an institutional level; on the professional level, the YALSA Core Competencies document spells out what an LST needs to know/do in order to create positive outcomes for teens. The question then really is not what are you going to do, but what are you going to do first?

(ASKING YOURSELF) WHERE DO I BEGIN?

Good question. It all depends, but a good place is by asking questions of teens, of colleagues, of community contacts, and those interested in the library. Learn what works, what does not, and most of all, learn what programs, services, or collections garner support in your organization. What is the way to your director's or principal's heart, and thus, hopefully pocket book?

(ASKING YOURSELF) AM I EVER GOING TO GET A RAISE? IS MY MANAGER EVER GOING TO RECOGNIZE THE NEED FOR TEEN SERVICES?

These two questions are together because they converge on a single thread: sometimes in order to push the youth advocacy agenda most effectively and do the best for teens, LSTs have to stop being front-line librarians. Library systems that support youth services often have people high in the administration who "get it," because they too were once LSTs. Many of the SUS trainers have gone on to be directors, youth services coordinators, and state youth consultants. This is easier to do than you might imagine. LSTs need to conceptualize their job as being both staff and managers. While they may not manage people, they manage other aspects of their work, and having an LST manage teen volunteers and workers is a good idea. LSTs network in the community, they market services, and they learn how to measure success. In most public libraries, youth librarians are better prepared for management than catalogers or adult service librarians. If you want to see that teens get great service, then are you willing to leave it to someone else to provide while you fight the bigger battles? What are you going to do?

CAN YOU HELP ME?

Yes, the authors of *Connecting Young Adults and Libraries,* 3rd edition (and librarians we have trained) are available to conduct workshops at your library, library system, regional association, or state wide association, about any topic related to connecting young adults and libraries. Our workshops are practical, interactive, and, according to most who attend, "inspirational." For more information, contact us at connecting3rd@yahoo.com or visit our Web site at www.connectingya.com.

CONCLUSION

Wow.

There's a lot of stuff here, isn't there?

So, how do you get started? The customers—teens—are first; the others—your principal or director, sometimes your partners—are second; and you are third. If the programs and services are not planned while thinking about and talking with your customers, then you won't have demand. If its not done with forethought, then you won't have resources. That is you in between; a good place for people to connect young adults and libraries.

This book was structured as a guide for your planning process. Start by understanding why you do this work and be able to articulate that to the powers that be in their terms, values, and goals. Then make sure you understand your customers. There are many ways to do this and we've provided tools, documents, and tips on how to actively engage youth in planning services. By understanding your customers, then you, and your colleagues, can better serve them. The idea is that LSTs don't believe they are the only ones that can serve teens and that all other adults don't like them. The idea is that we must help all staff learn to understand and respect teens; and, by doing so, then staff can better serve them. The work of this book and the SUS project is about expanding the capacity of organizations to serve teens. The third chapter then provided you with the context to understand the broader themes and recent history of services to teens in school and public libraries. While the themes change, the core values do not. Just because there is only one chapter dedicated to a core value like youth involvement, doesn't mean that it is not important as a base for every service response. Similarly, we spend only one chapter on collections, but a strong collection is fundamental to every other aspect of providing services. The remaining chapters provided FAQs and answers to building teen collections, programs, booktalks, spaces, technology, outreach, and addressing vexing issues in the profession, except one.

Some within the field of serving teens and libraries believe that we should only talk about "service with" teens, not "services to," as our paradigm. This is a great theory in a perfect world. It is certainly a goal to aspire to, but the fact is that in our work—a combined experience of thirty plus years in a variety of library settings—has shown us that getting LSTs, let alone administrators, to take this step, is asking a great deal from people who have trouble delegating any decision-making. Youth involvement shouldn't be an end in itself; instead, it is just another means, and one of the best, but not the only one, to help libraries serve teens and build assets within teens.

The "with teens" youth involvement model runs into two central contradictions: teens are customers and most customers want merely to be served, not take part in the process. Also, many youth-advisory groups fail because teens, especially younger ones, don't want to plan; they want to do. Just as we discussed in the section on teen volunteerism, which is one type of youth involvement, not every teen wants to be creative; some, especially those doing community service, want to do their time and leave. The key to youth involvement is finding the right level for the organization and for the youth. This again puts the LST in the middle, right where we belong.

The second contradiction, which we discussed in the programming section as well, is the inverse relationship between involvement and achievement toward positive outcomes for teens. In a perfect world, all activities with teens would allow for an abundance of involvement, but there isn't, in most public libraries, enough resources to provide those intense and ongoing involvement experiences. We need to make those above us understand that what matters most is the quality of the experience, not the quantity. But, if we want support, we also need to put up some numbers. Again, the LST is right in the middle between developing activities that produce outstanding outcomes for a small cadre of teens and those that produce sufficient numbers for the larger audience.

Thus, what connecting young adults and libraries is really all about is finding the right balance between the needs of teens (which differ), the capacity of organizations (which differ), and the goals of the library (which differ). There really isn't one way to go about getting it right; instead there are numerous options based on a set of core values and the individual abilities of LSTs to develop programs, services, and collections. The current "canon" of young adult librarianship is not based on presenting a negative image of teens, but instead, it is built upon the knowledge of LSTs that most organizations lack the capacity to provide a positive holistic experience for most teens in most libraries. What we hope we've done is demonstrate why that experience is important for libraries and teens. We've also provided you with a practical, experience based tips, tools, and techniques not to tell you how to get it right, but rather how to create for your community a response that listens to demand, understands supply, and delivers effective services that connect young adults and libraries.

CORE DOCUMENTS

Following are core documents that we have created and that may be used or adapted for use in your library setting. Rather than reprinting core documents from organizations such as YALSA, ALAN, and ULC, we invite you to visit our Web page at www.connectingya.com to find links to these documents.

CUSTOMER SERVICE: TEEN SECRET SHOPPER BEHAVIOR CHECKLIST

PUT AN X TO INDICATE IF THE LIBRARIAN DID OR DID NOT DO EACH OF THE FOLLOWING.

	DID	DID NOT	PHONE	E-MAIL
Greeted you warmly				NA
Smiled, acted pleasant toward you			NA	NA
Let the desk act as a barrier			NA	NA
Demonstrated welcoming body language			NA	NA
Got up to show you where to find your information			NA	NA
Asked you follow-up questions				
Answered your question completely				
Tried to rush you through				
Offered follow-up help				
Knew right where to find information				
Asked you why you needed information				
Gave you his/her full attention				NA

You may do these reference questions in person, over the phone, or via e-mail. Please check which method you used.

SWIFT PROJECT, CUSTOMER SERVICE: INFORMATION LITERACY PROGRAM PROMOTION

SWIFT

Student Web Instruction for Teachers

❑ Would you like your students to learn techniques to better locate, evaluate, and cite electronic resources for research?

❑ Would you like to strengthen the connection between your school and Hennepin County Libraries?

❑ Would you like to learn more about resources Hennepin County Library can offer to your school?

❑ Would you like us to offer teacher and/or staff trainings at your school?

If you answered "yes" to any of these questions, or if you have other ideas about how Hennepin County Libraries can work with your school, please contact Amy McNally, SWIFT Project Manager, @ 952-847-8503.

Send me updates on the SWIFT Project!

Name:_____School: _____

Grade(s) and subject(s) taught: _____

E-mail address: _____

CUSTOMER SERVICE: INFORMATION LITERACY CHECKLIST

	Done
6 Weeks or More Prior to Training Date: Approve date and time and check for conflicts. Notify supervisor and receive approval. Confirm advanced booking for meeting room or classroom.	
4 Weeks Prior to Training Date: Meet with the school contact to: 1. Discuss the goals and subject area(s) for the session. 2. Complete the "Technical Worksheet for School Visits." Review your trainer's materials, including the PowerPoint show (if there is one). Develop any new handouts or other curriculum materials for the session.	
3 Weeks Prior to Training Date: Practice. Check for currency of links and content. Prepare handouts and resource materials. 1. Order Hennepin County Library items that you intend to use from Library Supply. 2. Send in any duplicating requests to _____ 3. Prepare CD-ROM backup for curriculum materials. Reconfirm time and place for training.	
3–5 Days Prior to Training Date: Check equipment setup on site, including Internet connections and projector. Confirm contact person for technical assistance on the day of the training. Check that you have all the training materials you intend to use.	
Training Date: Check Internet connection and projector. Have handouts and resource materials ready for participants. Welcome guests and make introductions Collect evaluations and record statistics.	

CRITICAL SUCCESS FACTORS

- Schedule sufficient lead time to plan the training session (6–8 weeks).
- Meet with the teacher or media specialist who has requested the training session. Discuss how he or she will participate.
- Test the technology setup on-site. Find out who will provide assistance with the equipment.
- Remember the goal: train the teacher(s), not just the students.

CUSTOMER SERVICE: INFORMATION LITERACY HANDOUT FOR TEENS

Evaluation of Web documents	Interpretation of the basics
1. Accuracy of Web documents Who wrote the page and can you contact him or her? What is the purpose of the document and why was it produced? Is this person qualified to write this document? Does the author provide an e-mail or a contact address/phone number? Is there a distinction between author and Webmaster?	Accuracy:
2. Authority of Web documents Who published the document and is this person different from the Webmaster? What institution publishes this document? (Check the URL domain.) Does the publisher list his or her qualifications? What credentials are listed for the authors? Where is the document published? (Check the URL domain.) Is there a tilde (~) in the Web address, indicating a personal Web site?	Authority:
3. Objectivity of Web documents What goals/objectives does this page meet? How detailed is the information? What opinions (if any) are expressed by the author? Is the page is a mask for advertising? (If so, information might be biased; view any Web page as you would a TV infomercial.) Why was this written and for whom?	Objectivity:
4. Currency of Web documents When was it produced? When was it updated? How up-to-date are the links (if any)? How many dead links are on the page? Are the links current? Are they updated regularly? Is the information on the page outdated?	Currency:

Evaluation of Web documents	Interpretation of the basics
5. Coverage of Web documents Are the links (if any) evaluated and do they complement the document's theme? Is the page all images or a balance of text and images? Is the information cited correctly? If page requires special software to view the information, how much are you missing if you don't have the software? Is the information free or is there a fee to obtain it? Is there an option for frames or for text only or, or is there a suggested browser for better viewing?	Coverage:

PUTTING IT ALL TOGETHER

You may have a Web page that could be of value to your research!

❏ **Accuracy:** Your page lists the author and institution that published the page and provides a way of contacting him or her.

❏ **Authority:** Your page lists the author credentials and its domain is preferred (.edu, .gov, .org, or .net).

❏ **Objectivity:** Your page provides accurate information with limited advertising and it is objective in presenting the information.

❏ **Currency:** Your page is current and updated regularly (as stated on the page) and the links (if any) are also up-to-date.

❏ **Coverage:** You can view the information properly and are not limited by fees, browser technology, or software requirements.

SAMPLE INFORMATION LITERACY LESSON PLAN

INFORMATION LITERACY LESSON PLAN—WEB SITE EVALUATION

Lesson: Learning How to Evaluate a Web Site
Grade Range: 7th–10th grade

Objectives

Enable students to effectively and efficiently evaluate a Web site for accuracy, authenticity, and validity.

Prerequisites

Students should have a general understanding of computers and the Internet.

Materials

- Computer with Internet access
- "Learning How to Evaluate a Web Site" worksheet (see next page)

Lesson Description

By browsing a variety of Web sites and asking a series of relative questions about each site, students will learn to evaluate the content and authorship of any given site in order to determine if the site is a valid reference source with accurate, reliable, and viable information.

Lesson Procedure

Talk about the importance of Web site evaluation and explain how various sites on the Internet can be deceiving in both the provision and presentation of information. Pass out the worksheet and encourage the students to take their time to thoroughly navigate each site in order to fully answer each question.

Conclusion

When the students have completed the assignment, initiate a classroom discussion and encourage the students to talk about what they thought as they navigated their way through the three sites. Ask them if the appearance of each site influenced their opinion as to whether or not a site was an authentic resource. Ask them if this exercise has helped them to realize that it is possible to find bogus information on the Web, passed off as genuine information.

Evaluation

Have the students find alternate Web sites that offer valid information on the same topics as those addressed in the bogus sites on the "Learning How to Evaluate a Web Site" worksheet.

LEARNING HOW TO EVALUATE A WEB SITE

Availability does not equal authenticity when it comes to information on the Internet. These days, anyone can "publish" on the World Wide Web. As the Internet continues to grow, it is even more important that you not rely on Google to select the "best" Web sites for your informational needs, but learn to evaluate the information on each site to determine the Web site author's credibility and the accuracy, reliability, and validity of the information on any given page.

Compare the following Web sites that seem to share a similar topic. As you navigate your way through each site, ask yourself the questions that follow to determine author credibility and the accuracy, reliability, and validity of the information on each page.

AUTHOR CREDIBILITY

Topic: California's Velcro Crop
Web site: http://home.inreach.com/kumbach/velcro.html

As you are navigating your way through the Web site above, ask yourself the following five questions to determine if the author of this Web site is credible:

1. Who is the "author" of this Web site?
2. Is the author's contact information provided somewhere on the site?
3. Is this author affiliated with an organization or institution?
4. Does the author's organization or affiliation bias the content of the site?
5. What are the author's credentials? Does the author experienced/educated in the topic(s) covered on the site?

ACCURACY AND RELIABILITY OF INFORMATION

Topic: Martin Luther King, Jr.
Web site: www.martinlutherking.org

As you are navigating your way through the Web site above, ask yourself the following five questions to determine if the Web site contains accurate and reliable information:

1. Does the content on the site appear to be fact or opinion?
2. Can all of the information on the site be verified by another source?
3. Does this site contain primary or secondary material?
4. Do all of the links work?
5. Is the site's creation date listed? How about a date for when it was last updated?

CUSTOMER SERVICE: SAMPLE TEEN FINE WAIVER DOCUMENT (FOR STAFF)

TEEN READ MONTH FINE WAIVERS @ HENNEPIN COUNTY LIBRARY

Who and What: The Teen Read Month Fine Waivers are an opportunity for teens aged twelve to eighteen to reduce the fines on their library cards by as much as ten dollars. There is a limit of one waiver per teen, and we ask that teens themselves fill out the waivers, not their parents. We want teens to come to the library!

Where and When: The Fine Waivers can be picked up at all twenty-six Hennepin County Libraries, as well as online through our e-library (found on the "Teen Links" page), through the entire month of October. Get the word out!

How: The process is simple. Teens can come to the library or visit our site online, fill out the form, and turn it in to the returns desk. We ask that staff at each library keep a daily or weekly tally of the dollar amounts on the waivers and the total number of waivers received, and then send both the tallies and the waivers to Teen Librarian at the end of the month. Forms can be found in the shared drive.

Why: Teens tend to avoid the library. This program is an attempt to take away an unpaid fine as a roadblock. We want to motivate teens to come back, look around, and see what the library has to offer.

COLLECTIONS: SAMPLE READING INTEREST SURVEY

The Library wants to improve how it serves teens. We are gathering information to learn what we can do better. Please take a minute to help us help you.

Grade:_____ Gender: ❏ Male ❏ Female

Do you have a library card? ❏ Yes ❏ No

What school will you attend this fall? _____

What library do you most often visit? _____

How often do you use the Library? (check one)
❏ Every day ❏ Every week ❏ Every month ❏ Once or twice a year ❏ Never

What do you read most? (check one)
❏ Books ❏ Magazines ❏ Comics

Which type of books do you prefer? (check one)
❏ Fiction ❏ True stories

In fiction, what types of books do you like best? (check three)
❏ Adventure ❏ Historical ❏ Fantasy ❏ Science fiction ❏ Romance ❏ Graphic novels
❏ Humor ❏ Mystery/suspense ❏ Realistic ❏ Horror ❏ Other: _____

In nonfiction, what types of books do you like best? (check three)
❏ Biography ❏ History ❏ Health ❏ True crime ❏ Science ❏ Sports
❏ Humor ❏ Music/TV/movies ❏ Self-help ❏ Poetry ❏ Other: _____

Which best describes how you decide what books to read for pleasure? (check one)
❏ Friend's suggestion ❏ Teacher's suggestion ❏ Browsing in the library ❏ Book display
❏ Librarian's suggestions ❏ Parent's suggestion ❏ Browsing in a bookstore ❏ Book list

What could the library do to improve reading materials for teens? (check one)
❏ School visits to talk about books ❏ More displays in the library
❏ More magazines or comics (which ones?) _____ ❏ Programs to promote reading
❏ More books (what types?) _____ ❏ Book discussion groups

What is the one BEST book you read last year? _____

OPTIONAL: May we contact you to gather more information? Your name, address, and telephone number are private. It is available only to appropriate library staff in support of library service.
Name: _____ Phone: _____ E-mail: _____

PLEASE USE THE BACK OF THIS FORM TO TELL US MORE ABOUT YOUR IDEAS

COLLECTIONS: SAMPLE USER SURVEY

The Library wants to improve how it serves teens. We are gathering information to learn what we can do better. Please take a minute to help us help you.

Grade: _____   Gender: ❑ Male ❑ Female   Do you have a library card? ❑ Yes ❑ No

What school will you attend this fall? _____

What library do you most often visit? _____

How often do you use the library? (check one)
❑ Every day   ❑ Every week   ❑ Every month   ❑ Once or twice a year   ❑ Never

Pick a number from the scale to describe why you use the library to do each of the items listed below. [1=frequently; 2=sometimes; 3=seldom; 4=never]

___ Use the catalog, databases, or teen Web page   ___ Check out materials to use for homework
___ Check out materials to read for fun   ___ Check out materials to read for information
___ Check out music tapes or CDs   ___ Access the Internet
___ Check out videotapes or DVDs   ___ Meet and talk with friends
___ Attend a library event or class   ___ Study
___ Other: _____

If you don't often use the library, what is the primary reason? (check one)
❑ Unable to get to the library   ❑ Not enough time
❑ Nothing at the library interests me   ❑ Don't need it
❑ Do research/find reading material elsewhere   ❑ Not sure what the library has to offer me
❑ Other: _____

What three things could the Library do better in serving teens? (check three)
❑ Set up a youth advisory group   ❑ Offer more magazines
❑ Create after-school tutoring program   ❑ Add more study space for teens
❑ Keep the library open later   ❑ Add more books for school work
❑ Promote what the library offers   ❑ Add more staff to work with teens
❑ Create a teen summer reading program
❑ Offer more books to read for pleasure (what kind?) _____
❑ Have more services available on the Web
❑ Other: _____   ❑ Offer more event (what kind?)
                                        _____
❑ Other: _____   ❑ Other: _____

OPTIONAL: May we contact you to gather more information? Your name, address, and telephone number are private. It is available only to appropriate library staff in support of library service.

Name: _____   Phone: _____   E-mail: _____

COLLECTIONS: GRAPHIC NOVEL BOOKLISTS

TWENTY GRAPHIC NOVELS FOR OLDER TEENS (AGES 15–18)

Busiek, Kurt, and Alex Ross. 2003. *Marvels*. Marvel Comics. Paper (0–785–10049–0).

Clamp. 2001. *Clover, Volume 1*. CLAMP, TOKYOPOP. Paper (1–892–21366–4).

Clowes, Daniel. 2001. *Ghost World*. Fantagraphics. Paper (1–560–97427–3).

Gaiman, Neil, et al. 1994. *Death: The High Cost of Living*. DC Comics. Paper (1–563–89133–6).

———. 1991. *Sandman: The Doll's House*. DC Comics. Paper (0–930–28959–5).

Miller, Frank. 1997. *Batman: The Dark Knight Returns*. DC Comics. Paper (1–563–89342–8).

Moore, Alan. 1995. *Watchmen*. DC Comics. Paper (0–930–28923–4).

Nakazawa, Keiji. 2003. *Barefoot Gen: Volume 1: A Cartoon History of Hiroshima*. Last Gasp. Paper (0–867–19450–2).

Napel, Ted. 2002. *Creature Tech*. Top Shelf Productions. Paper (1–891–83034–1).

Ottavaiani, Jim. 2003. *Dignifying Science: Stories About Women Scientists*. G.T. Labs. Paper (0–966–01064–7).

Sen, Jai. *The Golden Vine*. 2003. Shoto Press. Paper (0–971–75641–4).

Spiegelman, Art. 1997. *The Complete Maus: A Survivor's Tale: My Father Bleeds History/Here My Troubles Began*. Pantheon Books. Hardcover (0–679–40641–7).

Takahashi, Rumiko. 1993. *Ranma 1/2, Volume 1*. Viz Communications, LLC. Paper (0–929–27993–X).

Talbot, Bryan. 1995. *The Tale of One Bad Rat*. Dark Horse Comics. Paper (1–569–71077–5).

Thompson, Craig. 2003. *Blankets*. Top Shelf Productions. Paper (1–891–83043–0).

Tsuda, Masami. 2003. *Kare Kano*. TOKYOPOP. Paper (1–931–51479–8).

Van Meter, Jen, Christine Norrie, and Chyna Clugston-Major. 2002. *Hopeless Savages, Volume 1*. Oni Press. Paper (1–929–99824–4).

Waid, Mark, and Alex Ross. 1997. *Kingdom Come*. DC Comics. Paper (1–563–89330–4).

Watson, Andy. 2003. *The Complete Geisha*. Oni Press. Paper (1–929–99851–1).

Winick, Judd. 2000. *Pedro and Me: Friendship, Loss, and What I Learned*. Henry Holt & Company. Paper (0–805–06403–6).

TWENTY GRAPHIC NOVELS FOR PRETEENS AND YOUNGER TEENS (AGES 11–14)

Bendis, Brian Michael, Mark Bagley, and Bill Jemas. 2001. *Ultimate Spider-Man, Volume 1: Power and Responsibility*. Marvel Comics. Paper (0–785–10786–X).

Crilley, Mark. 2001. *Akiko, Volume 1*. Sirius Entertainment, Inc. Paper (1–579–89042–3).

Dezago, Todd, and Mike Wieringo. 2001. *Tellos, Volume 1: Reluctant Heroes*. Image Comics. Paper (1–582–40186–1).

Gonick, Larry. 1997. *The Cartoon History of the Universe: Volume I: From the Big Bang to Alexander the Great*. Doubleday. Paper (0–385–26520–4).

Hartman, Rachel. 2002. *Amy Unbounded: Belondweg Blossoming*. Pug House Press. Paper (0–971–79000–0).

Hosler, Jay. 2000. *Clan Apis*. Active Synapse. Paper (0–967–72550–X).

Kesel, Barbara, et al. 2001. *Meridian, Volume 1: Flying Solo*. Cross Generation Comics. Paper (1–931–48403–1).

Kunkel, Mike. 2003. *Herobear and the Kid: The Inheritance*. Astonish Comics. Paper (0–972–12591–5).

Marz, Ron, et al. 2002. *Scion, Volume 1: Conflict of Conscience*. Cross Generation Comics. Paper (1–931–48402–3).

Medley, Linda. 2002. *Castle Waiting: The Lucky Road*. Olio Press. Paper (0–965–18523–0).

Miller, Mark, et al. 2001. *Ultimate X-Men: The Tomorrow People*. Marvel Comics. Paper (0–785–10788–6).

Miyazaki, Hayao. 1995. *Nausicaä of the Valley of the Wind: Perfect Collection, Volume 1*. Viz Communications, LLC. Paper (1–569–31096–3).

Naifeh, Ted. 2002. *Courtney Crumrin and the Night Things*. Oni Publishing. Paper (1–929–99842–2).

Nishiyama, Yuriko. 1999. *Harlem Beat, Volume 1*. TOKYOPOP. Paper (1–892–21304–4).

Robbins, Trina, and Anne Timmons. 2002. *Go Girl!* Dark Horse Comics. Paper (1–569–71798–2).

Robinson, James and Paul Smith. 2002. *Leave It to Chance, Volume 1: Shaman's Rain*. Image Comics. Hardcover (1–582–40253–1).

Sakai, Stan. 2000. *Usagi Yojimbo: Grasscutter*. Dark Horse Comics. Paper (1–569–71413–4).

Smith, Jeff. 1996. *Bone, Volume 1: Out from Boneville*. Cartoon Books. Paper (0–963–66094–2).

Tezuka, Osamu. 2002. *Astro Boy*. Dark Horse Comics. Paper (1–569–71676–5).

Torres, J., and J. Bone. 2002. *Alison Dare: Little Miss Adventures*. Oni Press. Paper (1–929–99820–1).

SAMPLE BOOKTALK EVALUATION

Please take a few moments to answer the following questions about today's presentation.

Have you ever seen a booktalking presentation like this before?
❏ Yes ❏ No

How would you describe today's presentation? (check one)
❏ Great ❏ Good ❏ Okay ❏ Not so good ❏ Didn't like it at all

What booktalk did you enjoy most? _____

What did you like most about the presentation? _____

What did you like least? _____

What one thing could we do to improve these presentations? _____

SAMPLE FOCUS GROUP QUESTIONS

The Library wants to improve how it serves teens. Please take a minute to help us help you. We would like to ask you a few questions to get your opinions about what the library is and is not doing well in serving teens. Please be open, honest, and respectful of others' opinions.

DATE: _____ LIBRARY: _____ GROUP: _____ # TEENS: _____

What is the best thing about using the library? Can you give me a specific example of a positive experience?

What is the worst thing? Can you give me a specific example of a negative experience?

If you got to run the library for a day, what is the one thing you would change?

What is the best way to let you know about upcoming library programs or events? Should we be promote events in your school paper, send an e-mail, or is there another way?

Do you find that you are using the library more or less than you used to? If so, what is causing that change?

Have you ever used the library's Web page to find information? If so, did you find it easy to use? What would you change to make it better?

A recent study found that most teens don't have time to read. Do you agree with that? When you do have time, what do you most enjoy reading? Are there any particular kinds of books or magazines that the library should have more of?

Are there any questions that would like to ask me about the library?

GUIDELINES FOR RUNNING TEEN FOCUS GROUPS

1. Go over the ground rules.
   - We want to hear your honest opinions—what you think and feel.
   - What anyone says is confidential—we use the information, but it is not linked to anyone.
   - You don't have to agree with what someone else says—just respect their opinion.
   - We will use this information to help plan better services for teens at the library.
2. Ask teens to take turns being the "recorder."
3. Elicit the most productive responses by:
   - Making the tone of the discussion friendly, open, and fun;
   - Letting the participants do most of the talking—your job is to prompt, not to participate;
   - Making sure no one person dominates by asking direct questions to nonparticipants;
   - Playing devil's advocate on occasion to prevent "group think";
   - Asking teens who are interested to write down additional opinions for you;
   - Asking open-ended follow-up questions if needed; and
   - Allowing the discussion head in a new direction—don't stay bound to the "script."
4. Close the meeting by:
   - Thanking everyone for participating;
   - Handing out business cards or other information;
   - Inviting them to always express their opinions and use the library more; and
   - Inviting them to help start a youth group, become a teen volunteer, or apply for a job.

OUTREACH: SAMPLE SCHOOL PLANNING DOCUMENT

Name of School:			
Address:			
Primary Phone #:			
Fax Number:			
Web Page			
School District:			

Key Contacts

Title	Name	Phone	E-Mail
Art Dept. chair			
Athletic Dept. Chair			
English Dept Chair			
Guidance Dept. Chair			
Head Librarian			
Principal			
PTO Newsletter Editor			
PTO President			
School Newsletter Editor			
School Paper Advisor			
School Secretary			
Security Chief			
Service Learning Chair			
Technology Dept. Chair			
Theater Dept. Chair			
Other			

Key Documents

Document	Contact	Obtain?
AR and other reading lists		
Bell schedule		
Club or organization list		
Curriculum guide		
Library guides, pathfinders, etc.		
PTO newsletter subscription		
School calendar		
School newsletter subscription		
School newspaper subscription		
Student handbook		

Teacher roster
Yearbook
Other

Visit Log

MONTH	DATES	CONTACT	DESCRIPTION
August			Back-to-school open house
August			New student orientation
August			New teacher orientation
September			Library Card Sign-Up Month
October			Teen Read Week
Fall			Teacher in-service
Winter			Library instruction for term papers
April			National Library Week
April			summer programs promotion
Other			

Assignment Log

CLASS	DATES	ASSIGNMENT	FOLLOW-UP

Document Distribution

DOCUMENT	CONTACT	# SENT
Library card applications		

OTHER NOTES

SAMPLE PROGRAMMING SURVEY

In addition to providing books and Internet access, the library wants to provide teens with fun and interesting activities at the library after school and on evenings and weekends. We need your ideas!

1. Did you come to any program, event or special activity at the library anytime this past year?
❑ No ❑ Yes If yes, what program? _____

2. Choose the two types of programs that you would want to attend. (check two)
❑ Art activity (for example: art contest, a craft like beading or scrapbooking)
❑ Book-related activity (for example: book discussion group, author visit)
❑ Drama activity (for example: improv comedy workshop, stage combat, monster makeup)
❑ Health activity (for example: presentation about eating disorders or exercise for teens)
❑ Informational activity (for example: babysitting training, presentation about cool careers)
❑ Music activity (for example: open mic night, how to start a band, visit from a local DJ)
❑ Performing arts activity (for example: dance troupe, storyteller for teens)
❑ Sports activity (for example: skateboarding tricks, tips on canoeing and camping, yo-yo tricks)
❑ Technology activity (for example: building your own Web page, advanced Internet searching)
❑ Volunteer activity (for example: reading to younger children, making displays)
❑ Writing activity (for example: writing contests and workshops, how to write your own poetry)

3. If you don't see something you like listed above, tell us what types of activities the library could present. _____

4. During the school year, when is the best time for you to attend one of these activities?
❑ After school   ❑ Evening   ❑ Saturday morning
❑ Saturday afternoon   ❑ Other: _____

What is one best way to let you know about events at the library?
❑ Posters at school   ❑ From teachers   ❑ From parents
❑ E-mail   ❑ Other: _____

Optional: Tell us a little about yourself:
Grade: _____   Gender: _____
School: _____   Library you use most: _____

Would you like to help us? If so, we'll need your name and your phone number or e-mail address. This information will be used ONLY by library staff to contact you regarding events at the library.
Name: _____   Phone #: _____   E-mail: _____

SAMPLE TEEN PROGRAM EVALUATION

What program did you attend? _____

How did you hear about this program?
- ❑ Flyer in the library   ❑ Program or poster in library
- ❑ Friend or parent   ❑ Teacher at school
- ❑ Library Web page   ❑ E-mail
- ❑ Newspaper   ❑ Other

How did today's program rate with you?
- ❑ Great   ❑ Very Good
- ❑ Average   ❑ Poor

What other types of teen related programs would you be interested in attending?

What is the best time for you to attend programs (after school, nights, or weekends)?

Do you have any general comments about the library and/or its programs for teens?

Have you ever used the library's Web page?
❑ Yes ❑ No

OPTIONAL: May we contact you to gather more information? Your name, address, and telephone number are private. It is available only to appropriate library staff in support of library service.

Name: _____ Phone: _____ E-mail: _____

SAMPLE STAFF PROGRAM EVALUATION/RECORD OF EVENT

Program title: _____

Date: _____ Number of attendees: _____

Intended audience: _____ Actual attendee age range: ____ to ____

Staff members involved: _____

Total staff time required for planning and actual program: _____

Promotion/publicity: _____

Total cost for materials/presentation: _____

Refreshments: ❑ yes ❑ no

If yes, list here: _____

Brief description of program: _____

Feedback from participants (reactions, comments, suggestions): _____

Effectiveness of promotion/publicity: _____

SAMPLE T.A.G. (TEEN ADVISORY GROUP) PARTICIPATION SURVEY AND APPLICATION

Name: _____

Age: _____

How long have you been a member of the library's T.A.G. (Teen Advisory Group)?

Years: _____ Months: _____

Has it been a problem to attend scheduled meetings?

❑ Yes ❑ No

If yes, how can we more fully accommodate your schedule?

What do you enjoy most about serving as a member of the library's T.A.G.?

What do you think has been the biggest challenge serving on the library's T.A.G.?

Do you feel like the librarian supervising the T.A.G. has listened to your suggestions and feedback about providing library services to teens?

❑ Yes ❑ No

If no, how could the Librarian have done a better job implementing your ideas?

Additional comments, ideas, or suggestions:

SAMPLE TEEN VOLUNTEER JOB: WORKING WITH COLLECTIONS

POSITION:

Youth Services Volunteer—Materials Selector

JOB DESCRIPTION:

The library is committed to providing materials that are in demand. Materials Selectors identify high-demand items for addition to their local agency's collection based on their own interests and knowledge of the community. Selectors search beyond traditional "best seller" lists in an effort to tailor the collection to local needs and interests. Suggestions for addition are taken seriously, but final decisions are made at the discretion of the appropriate librarian(s).

DUTIES:

- Work with appropriate librarian to identify scope and goals within areas of collection to be targeted
- Identify methods for collecting information concerning what items are in highest demand by targeted patrons
- Compile orders and/or accompany librarian to retailer/wholesaler to select materials within given budget
- Maintain collection materials as needed (e.g., by pulling low-circulating titles, preparing materials for distribution to another library branch, discarding damaged materials)
- Assist Youth Services librarian in preparing materials for library events and school visits;
- Assist with Friends of the Library's book sales
- Perform other tasks as assigned

QUALIFICATIONS:

- Willingness to make a firm commitment to the assignment for the term

- Experience with (and enjoyment of) working with the library catalog
- Interest in selecting library collection materials that include, but are not limited to, personal interests
- Ability to work independently
- Ability to meet deadlines

SAMPLE TEEN VOLUNTEER JOB: WORKING WITH ONLINE COLLECTIONS

JOB DESCRIPTION:

This nine-member team will support the library's teen Web site, which is created and maintained by staff of the library with the help of a volunteer advisory board.

DUTIES:

- Review library's teen Web pages and suggest improvements
- Suggest links for Web page sections
- Contribute original content such as reviews of books, magazines, computer games, and music
- Develop and maintain subject Web pages
- Offer advice on marketing Web page
- Perform other tasks as assigned

QUALIFICATIONS:

- Age 12–18
- Current e-mail address
- Basic knowledge of Windows and PC environment
- Basic knowledge of locating information on the Web
- Enthusiasm about providing ideas
- Willingness to participate on a creative team
- Web design experience a plus, but not necessary

SAMPLE TEEN VOLUNTEER MANAGEMENT DOCUMENT

TEEN VOLUNTEERS @ HENNEPIN COUNTY LIBRARY

If you are ready to involve more teen volunteers, you may find these tips helpful.

- Identify tasks using the "101 Teen Volunteer Task Ideas" for brainstorming.
- Advertise and recruit for specific positions based on what you need.
- Develop a system for applications, interviewing, and scheduling that doesn't overtax your staff and time.
- Offer a routine orientation on a regular basis to maximize your time.
- Communicate library needs and philosophy during orientation so all volunteers understand how tasks are valued and part of a greater whole.
- Communicate benefits for teens: the potential for a job reference or a letter of recommendation, the benefit to the community, and the acquisition of job skills.
- Have tools in place for communicating tasks, schedules, and other details to staff supervisors.
- Bring the whole staff on board by asking them to identify areas where volunteers could support existing workload and needs. Offer the staff opportunities to supervise volunteers and set and hold high expectations for volunteers as workers, but do not overwhelming staff with too many responsibilities.
- Have a backup list of tasks for volunteers. This frees up staff if they are unable to supervise at the last minute, allows volunteers to work more independently, and assures volunteers that their time is valuable. The list can be generated as a brainstorm or can be posted as they come up on a volunteer task board.
- Give recognition for a job well done.

SAMPLE TEEN VOLUNTEER SUCCESS STORY FORM

Thank for you volunteering at the library. Take a few moments and put in writing the "success story" of your volunteer experience. Thanks for your time!

---

1. What was the best part about volunteering at the library?

2. What did you like least?

3. What skills did you learn?

4. Was there a specific task or project that you are most proud of? Tell us about it.

5. May we use your success story, featuring your first name only, in materials to promote teen volunteering at the library? ❏ Yes ❏ No

Name: _____ Grade: _____ School: _____

TEEN COMMENT CARD

WHAT DO YOU THINK?

Name: _____ Age _____

Name of Library: _____

Is this your first time to visit this library?
Yes ❏ No ❏

Did someone help you find what you need?
Yes ❏ No ❏

Are you interested in serving on our Teen Advisory Board?
Yes ❏ No ❏

If yes, would you rather us call you? ❏ or e-mail you? ❏

(Please provide appropriate information below)

Phone number: _____ E-mail: _____

LIBRARIAN SERVING TEENS
SELF-EVALUATION SURVEY

Institutional Commitment

❏ Yes ❏ No Does your library have an overall plan of services for young adults?

❏ Yes ❏ No Does your library employ a full time LST?

❏ Yes ❏ No Does your library provide a separate and proportionally appropriate budget to fund programs, materials, and services?

❏ Yes ❏ No Does your library measure the success of its services to teens through both quantitative and qualitative measures?

❏ Yes ❏ No Does your library have an unique and identifiable area of the library dedicated to housing materials for teens?

❏ Yes ❏ No Do library policies demonstrate an institutional commitment to upholding the value of equal access to buildings, resources, programs, and services?

❏ Yes ❏ No Does your library annual develop specific goals and objectives to spell out the library's commitment to teen services?

Collections

❏ Yes ❏ No Are teen collections are viewed as an integral part of the library's overall collection-development plan and policy?

❏ Yes ❏ No Does the library collection contain print young adult fiction in hardback and paperbacks (including series books) that reflect teen interests?

❏ Yes ❏ No Does the library collection contain graphic novels?

❏ Yes ❏ No Does the library collection contain adult fiction titles of interest to teens, in particular in the genres of science fiction, fantasy, and horror?

❏ Yes ❏ No Does the library collection contain audio books in both cassette and CD format?

❏ Yes ❏ No Does the library nonfiction collection focus on popular and informational materials?

❏ Yes ❏ No Does the library collection contain a collection of popular music?

❏ Yes ❏ No Does the library collection contain audio visual materials (in VHS and DVD) to meet informational, educational, and recreational needs?

❏ Yes ❏ No Does the library collection contain software or game cartridges to meet informational, educational, and recreational needs?

❏ Yes ❏ No Does the library collection contain comic books?

❏ Yes ❏ No Does the library collection contain magazines of interest to teens?

❏ Yes ❏ No Do you involve youth in the collection-development process?

❏ Yes ❏ No Does the library collection contain nonfiction print materials that support the formal education needs of students?

❏ Yes ❏ No Do you provide access to the teen collection through books by mail, a delivery service to/from schools or youth serving agencies, or by deposit collections in classrooms?

❏ Yes ❏ No Does your library subscribe to the key reviewing journals in the field, in particular *Voice of Youth Advocates*?

❏ Yes	❏ No	Do you help provide access to the collection through booklists, pathfinders, and other tools, either online or in print?
❏ Yes	❏ No	Does your teen collection follow the best practices of merchandising to make the collection more accessible?
❏ Yes	❏ No	Does your library develop collections of materials for young adults in languages other than English (where appropriate)?

Programs and Services

❏ Yes	❏ No	Does your library offer effective methods of internal communication to let staff know about teen issues?
❏ Yes	❏ No	Does your library offer services for young adults based directly on youth involvement in the planning process?
❏ Yes	❏ No	Does your library offer programs that provide young adults with creative outlets?
❏ Yes	❏ No	Does your library offer programs designed to promote use of the collection?
❏ Yes	❏ No	Does your library offer programs to young adults that differ from a "traditional" school setting?
❏ Yes	❏ No	Does your library offer a comprehensive program of information-literacy instruction?
❏ Yes	❏ No	Does your library offer an after-school program that offers tutoring, information-literacy instruction, and other activities?
❏ Yes	❏ No	Does your library offer programs like book discussion groups that allow young adults to respond to what they read?
❏ Yes	❏ No	Does your library offer programs meeting the informational needs of teens in areas such as college and career information?
❏ Yes	❏ No	Does your library offer programs meeting the recreational needs of teens?
❏ Yes	❏ No	Do staff-teen customer service interactions (at all service points) reflect respect, approachability, helpfulness, open-mindedness, a sense of humor, and empathy?
❏ Yes	❏ No	Does your library work with classroom teachers to develop learning activities that enhance the classroom experience, teach information-literacy skills, and engage young adults in the learning process?
❏ Yes	❏ No	Does your library offer programs that feature teens as the presenters?
❏ Yes	❏ No	Does your library offer a formal youth participation program?
❏ Yes	❏ No	Does your library develop programs and services based on the Search Institute developmental assets model?
❏ Yes	❏ No	Does your library offer class visits to the library?
❏ Yes	❏ No	Does your library actively encourage teens to get library cards?

Technology

❏ Yes	❏ No	Does your library host Web pages that support the formal educational needs of students and provide links to the library's catalog, databases, and selected Internet resources?
❏ Yes	❏ No	Does your library host Web pages that support the needs of teens for information on current topics, general information, and lifelong learning, and in areas such as college and career information?
❏ Yes	❏ No	Does your library offer programs, user tools, online tutorials, and Web pages that increase the information literacy of teens?
❏ Yes	❏ No	Does your library involve teens in the planning, implementation, and evaluation of teen Web content?

☐ Yes ☐ No Does your library host Web pages that support interactive methods to gather data from teens, such as surveys and polls?

☐ Yes ☐ No Does your library offer e-mail-based reference?

☐ Yes ☐ No Does your library offer chat-based reference?

☐ Yes ☐ No Does your library develop partnerships with classroom teachers to plan, deliver, and evaluate information-literacy instruction?

☐ Yes ☐ No Does your library offer databases that support student learning and achievement?

Facilities and Hours

☐ Yes ☐ No Is your teen area clearly defined through signage or other means?

☐ Yes ☐ No Does the teen area offer an inviting environment through appropriate lighting, seating, and décor?

☐ Yes ☐ No Are there adequate fixtures and display spaces?

☐ Yes ☐ No Does your library offer multiple computers for Internet access, as well as computers to access the library catalog and databases?

☐ Yes ☐ No Does your library offer multiple computers with access to educational and recreational software, word processing, and other information technology?

☐ Yes ☐ No Does your library offer wireless Internet connections for teens?

☐ Yes ☐ No Does your library offer listening stations or CD players?

☐ Yes ☐ No Does your library offer a viewing station or DVD player?

☐ Yes ☐ No Does your library offer laptop plug-in stations?

☐ Yes ☐ No Does your library offer effective outreach services from the public library to schools, in particular booktalks to promote reading and information-literacy instruction to promote use of the library's resources?

☐ Yes ☐ No Does your library offer after-hours programs allowing young adults to use the library at times such as Friday evenings?

☐ Yes ☐ No Does your library offer facilities to meet the study needs of teens?

Staff

☐ Yes ☐ No Does your library offer work schedules that allow LSTs sufficient off-desk time to plan and develop services, do outreach, and network?

☐ Yes ☐ No Does your library offer training for all staff members working with teens?

☐ Yes ☐ No Does your library provide continuing education training?

☐ Yes ☐ No Does your library recruit and place of teen volunteers?

☐ Yes ☐ No Does your library recruit and place community service workers?

☐ Yes ☐ No Does your library hire teens to work?

BIBLIOGRAPHY

The bibliography lists important articles, books, and government documents related to connecting young adults and libraries published between summer 1996 and summer 2003. There are, however, a few important documents pre-1996 included. The bibliography is arranged by subject headings matching the chapters of the book. The bibliography does not contain Web-based documents or articles: those may be found by visiting www.connectingya.com. If you wish to obtain a copy of this bibliography in a searchable format, please contact us at connecting3rd@yahoo.com.

CHAPTER 1—WHY: THE PHILOSOPHY BEHIND SERVICES TO YOUNG ADULTS

DeMarco, Pat. 2003. "Teens Are a Work in Progress: Finding Our Way in a Construction Zone." *Voice of Youth Advocates* 25, no. 6 (February): 440–442.

Flum, Judith G., and Stan Weisner. 1993. "America's Youth Are at Risk: Developing Models for Action in the Nation's Public Libraries." *Journal of Youth Services in Libraries* 6, no. 3 (Spring): 271–282.

Halsey, Richard Sweeney. 2003. *Lobbying for Public and School Libraries: A History and Political Playbook*. Scarecrow Press.

Higgins, Susan E. 1994. "Should Public Libraries Hire Young Adult Specialists?" *Journal of Youth Services in Libraries* 7, no. 4 (Summer): 382–391.

Jones, Patrick. 2002. "Assets and Outcomes: New Directions in Young Adult Services in Public Libraries." *Public Libraries* 41, no. 4 (July/August): 195–199.

———. 2001. "Why We are Kids' Best Assets." *School Library Journal* 47, no. 11 (November): 44–47.

Jones, Patrick, and Linda Waddle. 2002. *New Directions for Library Service to Young Adults.* American Library Association.

Mathews, Virginia. 1997. "Kids Can't Wait: Library Advocacy Now!" *School Library Journal* 43, no. 3 (March): 97–102.

MacRae, Cathi Dunn. 1999. "Ain't Misbehavin': Doin' What Comes Naturally with Teens in Libraries." *Voice of Youth Advocates* 22, no. 1 (April): 5–7.

———. 1998. "The Secret Lives of Teenagers." *Voice of Youth Advocates* 21, no. 3 (August): 168–170.

————. 2002. "A Quarter Century of VOYA: Visible Acts of Youth Advocacy." *Voice of Youth Advocates* 25, no. 1 (April): 5.

Minudri, Regina U., and Francisca Goldsmith. 1999. "The Top 10 Things You Need to Know About Teens." *School Library Journal* 45, no. 1 (January): 30–31.

Muller, Patricia. 1999. "Come On Down! Your Leadership Role in Advancing the National YA Agenda." *Journal of Youth Services in Libraries* 12, no. 2 (Winter): 13–17.

Sullivan, Edward T. 2001. "Teenagers Are Not Luggage: They Don't Need Handling." *Public Libraries* 40, no. 2 (March/April): 75–77.

Tuccillo, Diane. 2001. "Positive Youth Development: A Positive Move for Libraries." *The Unabashed Librarian* no. 119: 21–23.

"Young Adult Library Services Association Vision Statement." 1994. *Journal of Youth Services in Libraries* 7, no. 1 (Fall): 108–109.

Wemmet, Lisa. 1997. "Librarians as Advocates for Young Adults." *Journal of Youth Services in Libraries* 10, no. 2 (Winter): 168–176.

CHAPTER 2—WHO: UNDERSTANDING THE AUDIENCE

American Psychological Association. 2002. *Developing Adolescents: A Reference for Professionals.* American Psychological Association.

Annie E. Casey Foundation. 1999. *Kids Count: A Pocket Guide on America's Youth.* Annie E. Casey Foundation.

Apter, Terri. 2001. *Myth of Maturity: What Teenagers Need from Parents to Become Adults.* Norton.

Astroth, Kirk. 1994. "Bond Ephebiphobia: Problem Adults or Problem Youths?" *Phi Delta Kappan* 76, no. 5 (January): 28–33.

Austin, Joe, and Michael Willard. 1998. *Generations of Youth: Youth Cultures and History in Twentieth-Century America.* New York University Press.

Barson, Michael, and Stephen Heller. *1997. Teenage Confidential.* Chronicle.

Begley, Sharon. 2000. "A World of Their Own." *Newsweek* May 8: 52–57.

Benson, Peter L. 1999. *A Fragile Foundation: The State of Developmental Assets Among Youth.* The Search Institute.

————. 1997. *All Kids Are Our Kids: What Communities Must Do to Raise Caring and Responsible Children and Adolescents.* Jossey-Bass.

————. 1998. *What Teens Need to Succeed.* Free Spirit Press.

Benson, Peter L., and Karen J. Pittman. 2001. *Trends in Youth Development: Visions, Realities, and Challenges.* Kluwer Academic.

Brownlee, Shannon. 1999. "Inside the Teen Brain." *U.S. News & World Report* 127, no. 6 (August 9): 44–48.

Cannon, Angie. 2000. "Teens Get Real." *U.S. News & World Report* 128, no. 15 (April 17): 46–55.

Carnegie Council on Adolescent Development; Task Force on Youth Development and Community Programs. 1992. *A Matter of Time: Risk and Opportunities in the Nonschool Hours.* Carnegie Corporation.

Corder, Cathy, and Kathryn Brohl. 1999. *It Couldn't Happen Here: Recognizing and Helping Desperate Kids.* Child Welfare League of America.

Csikszentmihalyi, Mihaly, and Reed Larson. 1984. *Being Adolescent: Conflict and Growth in the Teenage Years.* Basic.

Davis, Nannette J. 1999. *Youth Crisis: Growing Up in the High-Risk Society.* Praeger/Greenwood.

DiPrisco, Joseph, and Mike Riera. 2000. *Field Guide to the American Teenager: A Parent's Companion: Appreciating the Teenager You Live With.* Perseus.

Echevarria, Pegine. 1998. *For All Our Daughters: How Mentoring Helps Young Women and Girls Master the Art of Growing Up.* Chandler House.

Edelman, Marion Wright. 1992. *The Measure of Our Success: A Letter to My Children and Yours.* Beacon.

Elkind, David. 2001. *Hurried Child: Growing Up Too Fast Too Soon,* 3rd ed. Perseus.

Federal Interagency Forum on Child and Family Statistics. 2001. *America's Children: Key National Indicators of Well-Being.* Government Printing Office.

Feldman, Shirley, and Glen R. Elffiott. 1990. *At the Threshold: The Developing Adolescent.* Harvard University Press.

Fenwick, Elizabeth, and Tony Smith. 1994. *Adolescence: The Survival Guide for Parents and Teenagers.* Dorling Kindersley.

Ferber, Thaddeus, et al. 1999. *Finding Common Agendas: How Young People Are Being Engaged in Community Change Efforts.* International Youth Foundation.

Hechinger, Fred. 1992. *Fateful Choices: Healthy Youth for the 21st Century.* Carnegie Corporation.

Henderson, Nan. 1999. "Connecting with Today's Youth." *The Education Digest* 64, no. 5 (January): 14–16.

Hernandez, Michele A. 2000. *Middle School Years: Achieving the Best Education for Children, Grades 5–8.* Warner.

Hersch, Patricia. 1998. *A Tribe Apart: A Journey Into the Heart of American Adolescence.* Ballentine.

Hine, Thomas. 1999. *The Rise and Fall of the American Teenager.* Bard/Avon.

Horatio Alger Association of Distinguished Americans, Inc. 2002. *State of Our Nation's Youth: 2002 Horatio Alger Association of Distinguished Americans, Inc.*

Howe, Neil, and William Strauss. 1993. *13th Gen: Abort, Retry, Ignore, Fail?* Vintage.

Howe, Neil, and William Straus. 1999. *Millennials Rising: The Next Great Generation.* Vintage.

Jaffee, Natalie. 1999. *Youth Development: Issues, Challenges, and Directions.* Public/Private Ventures.

Kantrowitz, Barbara. 1999. "The Truth About Tweens." *Newsweek* October 18: 62–71.

Kitwana, Bakari. 2002. *Hip Hop Generation: Young Blacks and the Crisis in African-American Culture.* Basic.

Konopka, Gisela. 1973. "Requirements for Healthy Development of Adolescent Youth." *Adolescence* 8, no. 31 (Fall): 291–316.

Leland, John. 1999. "The Secret Life of Teens." *Newsweek* May 10: 44–52.

Lemonick, Michael. 2000. "Teens Before Their Time." *Time* 156, no. 18 (October 30): 66–74.

Lerner, Jacqueline, and Richard M. Lerner. 2001. *Adolescence in America, an Encyclopedia* (2 vols.). ABC-Clio.

Males, Mike A. 1996. *The Scapegoat Generation: America's War on Adolescents.* Common Courage.

Males, Mike. 2001. "Debunking the 10 Worst Myths about America's Teens." *Teacher Librarian* 28, no. 4 (April): 40–41.

———. 1999. *Framing Youth: 10 Myths About the Next Generation.* Common Courage.

McClaughlin, Milbrey W., Merlita A. Irby, and Juliet Langman. 1994. *Urban Sanctuaries: Neighborhood Organizations in the Lives and Futures of Inner-City Youth.* Jossey-Bass.

McIntyre, Alice. 2000. *Inner City Kids: Adolescents Confront Life and Violence in an Urban Community.* New York University Press.

Nelson, Lynne. 1999. *Helping Youth Thrive: How Youth Organizations Can—And Do—Build Developmental Assets.* The Search Institute.

Patnaik, Gayatri, and Michelle T. Shinseki. 2000. *The Secret Life of Teens: Young People Speak Out about Their Lives.* HarperSan Francisco.

Pittman, K.J., and M. Wright. 1991. *Bridging the Gap: A Rationale for Enhancing the Role of Community Organizations Promoting Youth Development.* Center for Youth Development and Policy Research.

Ponton, Lynn E. 2000. *The Sex Lives of Teenagers: Revealing the Secret World of Adolescent Boys and Girls.* Dutton.

Prothow-Stith, Deborah. 1991. *Deadly Consequences: How Violence is Destroying Our Teenage Population and a Plan to Begin Solving the Problem.* HarperCollins.

Rathbone, Cristina. 1998. "On the Outside Looking In: A Year at an Inner-City High School." *Atlantic Monthly.*

Rollin, Lucy. 1999. *Twentieth-Century Teen Culture by the Decades: A Reference Guide.* Greenwood.

Scales, Peter. 2000. "Building Students' Developmental Assets to Promote Health and School Success." *The Clearing House* 74, no. 2 (November/December): 84–88.

———. 1998. *Developmental Assets: A Synthesis of the Scientific Research on Adolescent Development.* The Search Institute.

———. 2001. "The Public Image of Adolescents." *Society* 38, no. 4 (May/June): 64–71.

Scales, Peter C., and Judy Taccogna. 2000. "Caring to Try: How Building Students' Developmental Assets Can Promote School Engagement and Success." *NASSP Bulletin* 84, no. 619 (November): 69–78.

———. 2001. "Developmental Assets for Success in School and Life." *The Education Digest* 66, no. 6 (February): 34–39.

Scales, Peter, and Nancy Leffert. 1999. *Developmental Assets: A Synthesis of the Scientific Research on Adolescent Development.* The Search Institute.

Schneider, Barbara, and David Stevenson. 2000. *The Ambitious Generation: America's Teenagers, Motivated but Directionless.* Yale University Press.

Somethings DO Make a Difference for Youth: A Compendium of Evaluations of Youth Programs and Practices. 1997. American Policy Forum.

Springhall, John. 1998. *Youth, Popular Culture and Moral Panics: Penny Gifts to Gangsta-Rap.* St. Martin's Press.

Starkman, Neal, Peter Scales, and Clay Roberts. 1999. *Great Places to Learn.* Search Institute.

Stauch, Barbara. 2003. *Primal Teen: What the New Discoveries About the Teenage Brain Tell Us About Our Kids.* Doubleday.

Stepp, Laura Sessons. 2000. *Our Last Best Shot: Guiding Our Children Through Early Adolescence.* Riverhead Books.

Taublieb, Amy Beth. 2000. *A–Z Handbook of Child and Adolescent Issues.* Allyn & Bacon.

U.S. Dept of Health and Human Services, Administration for Children and Families. 2000. *Toward a Blueprint for Youth: Making Positive Youth Development a National Priority.* Government Printing Office.

U.S. Dept. of Health and Human Services, Administration for Children and Families. 1988. *Positive Youth Development in the United States: Research Findings on Evaluations of Positive Youth Development Programs.* Government Printing Office.

Vizzini, Ned. 2000. *Teen Angst? NAAAH...A Quasi-Autobiography.* Free Spirit.

Vollbracht, James R. 2000. *Stopping at Every Lemonade Stand.* Penguin.

W.K. Kellogg Foundation. 1998. "Safe Passage Through Adolescence: Communities Protecting the Health and Hopes of Youth—Lessons Learned for W.K. Kellogg Foundation Programming." *W.K. Kellogg Foundation.*

Wellner, Alison Stein. 2002. "Meet the 'Tweens: Children Between the Ages of 8 and 12 are a Key Market Segment." *Forecast* 22, no. 12 (December): 7.

Wellner, Alison Stein. 2002. "The Teen Scene: As Gen Y Fills the Teen Market, It's Bigger and More Diverse Than Ever." *Forecast* 22, no. 9 (September): 1.

Wingert, Pat, and Barbara Kantrowitz. 2002. "Young and Depressed." *Newsweek* October 7: 52.

Wiseman, Rosalind. 2002. *Queen Bees and Wannabes: Helping Your Daughter Survive Cliques, Gossip, Boyfriends and Other Realities of Adolescence.* Crown.

Wittman, Bob, Rebecca Grothe, and Kathleen Kimball-Baker. 1999. *Taking Asset Building Personally: A Guide for Planning and Facilitating Study Groups.* Search Institute.

CHAPTER 3—WHEN/WHERE: STATE OF THE ART YA SERVICES

Anderson, Sheila B., and John P. Bradford. 2001. "State-level Commitment to Public Library Services for Young Adults: Frances Henne/YALSA/VOYA Research Grant Results." *Journal of Youth Services in Libraries* 14, no. 3 (Spring): 23–27.

Atkinson, Joan. 1986. "Pioneers in Public Library Services to Young Adults." *Top of the News* 43 (Fall): 27–44.

Bishop, Kay, and Patricia Bauer. 2002. "Attracting Young Adults to Public Libraries: Frances Henne/YALSA/VOYA Research Grant Results." *Journal of Youth Services in Libraries* 15, no. 2 (Winter): 36–44.

Bradburn, Frances Bryant. 1999. *Output Measures for School Library Media Programs.* Neal-Schuman.

Broderick, Dorothy M. 1990. *VOYA Reader.* Scarecrow Press.

———. 1998. *VOYA Reader Two.* Scarecrow Press.

Campbell, Patty. 1998. *Two Pioneers of Young Adult Library Services.* Scarecrow Press.

———. 1994. "Reconsidering Margaret Edwards." *Wilson Library Bulletin* June: 20+.

Cart, Michael. 1998. "Young Adult Library Service Redux?—Some Preliminary Findings." *Journal of Youth Services in Libraries* 11, no. 4 (Summer): 391–395.

Carter, Betty. 1997. "Margaret Alexander Edwards: Reaching out to Young Adult Librarians." *Journal of Youth Services in Libraries* 11 (Winter): 175–180.

Chelton, Mary K. 1984. "Developmentally Based Performance Measures for Young Adult Services." *Top of the News* 41 (Fall): 39–52.

———. 1997. "Three in Five Public Library Users Are Youth." *Public Libraries* 36, no. 2 (March/April): 104–108.

Cooke, Eileen D. 1994. "The Political Viability of Youth Services: A Bit of Legislative History." *The Bottom Line* Winter/Spring: 21–25.

Edwards, Margaret. 2002. *The Fair Garden and the Swarm of Beasts: Centennial Edition.* American Library Association.

"First National Survey of Services and Resources for Young Adults in Public Libraries." 1989. *Journal of Youth Services in Libraries* 2, no. 3 (Spring): 224–231.

Gnehm, Kurstin Finch. 2002. *Youth Development and Public Libraries: Tools for Success.* Urban Libraries Council.

Himmel, Ethel, and William James Wilson. 1998. *Planning for Results: A Public Library Transformation Process.* American Library Association.

Holt, Glen E., and Leslie Edmonds Holt. 1999. "What Is It Worth?" *School Library Journal* 45, no. 6 (June): 47.

Howard, Vivian. 2002. *Hot, Hotter, Hottest: The Best of the YA Hotline.* Scarecrow Press.

"In Service to Youth: Reflections on the Past; Goals for the Future." 1994. *School Library Journal* 40, no. 7 (July): 23–29.

Jones, Patrick. 2001. "Showing You the Money: LSTA Funds and Fifty-two Resources to Find Funding for Youth Services in Libraries." *Journal of Youth Services in Libraries* 15, no. 1 (Fall): 33–38.

Loertscher, David, and Blanche Woolls. 2002. "Teenage Users of Libraries: A Brief Overview of the Research." *Knowledge Quest* 30, no. 5 (May/June): 31–36.

Machado, Julie, Barbara Lentz, and Rachel Wallace. 2000. "Survey of Best Practices in Youth Services Around the Country: A View from One Library." *Journal of Youth Services in Libraries* 13, no. 2 (Winter): 30–35.

MacRae, Cathi Dunn. 2000. "The Evidence Is In: How Youth Advocates Must Meet the Millennium." *Voice of Youth Advocates* 22, no. 6 (February): 377.

MacRae, Cathi Dunn. 2000. "YA Radar—Youth Experts Screen the Teen Climate at the Dawn of the Millennium." *Voice of Youth Advocates* 22, no. 6 (February): 384–387.

Massachusetts Library Association. 1997. *Standards for Public Library Service to Young Adults*. Massachusetts Library Association.

Meyers, Elaine. 1999. "The Coolness Factor: Ten Libraries Listen to Youth." *American Libraries* 30, no. 10 (November): 42–45.

———. 2001. "The Road to Coolness: Youth Rock the Public Library." *American Libraries* 32, no. 2 (February): 46–48.

Nelson, Sandra. 2001. *The New Planning for Results: A Streamlined Approach*. ALA Editions.

New Jersey State Library. 2002. *Guidelines for Young Adult Services in Public Libraries of New Jersey*. The Library.

New York Library Association, Youth Services Section. 1998. *Kids Count: Writing Public Library Policies that Promote Use by Young People*. New York Library Association.

Nichols, Mary Anne, and C. Allen Nichols. 1998. *Young Adults and Public Libraries: A Handbook of Materials and Services*. Greenwood Press.

O'Dell, Katie. 2002. *Library Materials and Services for Teen Girls*. Libraries Unlimited.

Ohio Library Council. 2002. "Oh YA: A Manual for Library Staff Who Work with Young Adults." Ohio Library Council.

Sexton, John. 2002. "From Hanging Out to Homework: Teens in the Library." *OLA Quarterly* 8, no. 3 (Fall): 10–12, 19.

Staerkel, Kathleen, Mary Fellows, and Sue McCleaf Nespeca. 1994. *Youth Librarians as Managers*. American Library Association.

Steffen, Nicolle O., and Keith Curry Lance. 2002. "Who's Doing What: Outcome-Based Evaluation and Demographics in the Counting on Results Project." *Public Libraries* 41, no. 5 (September/October): 271–279.

U.S. Dept. of Education, Office of Educational Research and Improvement. 1995. *Services and Resources for Children and Young Adults in Public Libraries*. National Center for Education of Statistics.

Vaillancourt, Renee J. 2000. *Bare Bones Young Adult Services*. American Library Association.

———. 2002. *Managing Young Adult Services: A Self-Help Manual*. Neal-Schuman.

Vaillancourt, Renee, and Jane R. Byczek. 1998. "The Lone Ranger: YA Librarians Alone on the Range." *Voice of Youth Advocates* 21, no. 2 (June): 105–108.

———. 1998. "Homework on the Range: Public Librarians Can't Afford to be Lone Rangers." *Voice of Youth Advocates* 21, no. 3 (August): 183–186.

Walter, Virginia A. 1995. *Output Measures and More: Planning and Evaluating Public Library Services for Young Adults*. American Library Association.

———. 2001. *Children & Libraries: Getting It Right*. American Library Association.

———. 2003. "Public Library Service to Children and Teens: A Research Agenda." *Library Trends* 51, no. 4 (Spring): 571.

Walter, Virginia A., and Elaine E. Meyers. 2003. *Teens and Libraries: Getting It Right*. American Library Association.

Wilson-Lingbloom, Evie. 1994. *Hangin' Out At Rocky Creek: A Melodrama in Basic Young Adult Services in Public Libraries*. Scarecrow Press.

Yesner, Bernice L. 1998. *Operating and Evaluating School Library Media Programs*. Neal-Schuman.

Yohalem, Nicole, and Karen J. Pittman. 2003. *Public Libraries as Partners in Youth Development*. Forum for Youth Investment.

Young Adult Library Services Association. 1998. *Young Adults Deserve the Best: Competencies for Librarians Serving Youth*. YALSA.

Young Adult Library Services Association, Research Committee. 2001. "Current Research Related to Young Adult Services." *Journal of Youth Services in Libraries* 14, no. 2 (Winter): 25–30.

"Young Adult Services in the Public Library." 1968. *Library Trends* October: 115–220.

CHAPTER 4—CUSTOMER SERVICE

Adams, Debra Lynn. 1999. "Where No Young Adult Services Have Gone Before: The Diary of a Startup YA Librarian." *Voice of Youth Advocates* 22, no. 3 (August): 168–171.

Alire, Camila, and Orlando Archibeque. 1998. *Serving Latino Communities: A How-To-Do-It Manual for School and Public Librarians*. Neal-Schuman.

Altman, Ellen, and Peter Hernon. 1998. "Service Quality and Customer Satisfaction Do Matter." *American Libraries* 29, no. 7 (August): 53–54.

American Association of School Librarians. 1999. *A Planning Guide for Information Power: Building Partnerships for Learning with School Library Media Program Assessment Rubric for the 21st Century*. ALA Editions.

Anderson, Shelia B. 2000. "I Stink and My Feet Are Too Big! Training Librarians to Work with Teens." *Voice of Youth Advocates* 22, no. 6 (February): 388–390.

Blanchard, Ken, and Sheldon Bowles. 1992. *Raving Fans: A Revolutionary Approach to Customer Service*. Morrow.

Boatman, William. 2003. "Public Libraries as a Bridge for College-bound Young Adults." *Reference & User Services Quarterly* 42, no. 3 (Spring): 229–234.

Borne, Bobbie. 1999. *100 More Research Topic Guides for Students*. Greenwood.

Broderick, Dorothy. 2000. "YALSA-BK as a Readers' Advisory Tool." *Booklist* 97, no. 1 (September 1): 108.

Buker, Derek M. 2002. *The Science-Fiction and Fantasy Readers' Advisory: The Librarian's Guide to Cyborgs, Aliens, and Sorcerers*. ALA Editions.

Bunge, Charles Albert. 1994. "Responsive Reference Service: Breaking Down Age Barriers." *School Library Journal* 40, no. 3 (March): 142+.

Chelton, Mary K. 1997. *Adult-Adolescent Service Encounters: The Library Context*. University Microfilms.

———. 1993. "Read Any Good Books Lately? Helping Patrons Find What They Want." *Library Journal* May 1: 33–37.

———. 1999. "What We Know and Don't Know About Reading, Readers, and Readers Advisory Services." *Public Libraries* 38, no. 1 (January/February): 42–47.

———. 1999. "Behavior of Librarians in School and Public Libraries with Adolescents: Implications for Practice and LIS Education." *Journal of Education for Library and Information Science* 40, no. 2 (Spring): 99–111.

———. 2002. "The Problem Patron Public Libraries Created." *The Reference Librarian* no. 75/76: 23–32.

———. 2001. "Young Adults as Problems: How the Social Construction of a Marginalized User Category Occurs." *Journal of Education for Library and Information Science* 42, no. 1 (Winter): 4–11.

Cranford, Jessie L. 2000. "Ban This Speech! Customer Service Do's and Don'ts." *Arkansas Libraries* 57, no. 3 (June): 23–24.

Cronin, Blaise. 2000. "Customer Satisfaction." *Library Journal* 125, no. 17 (October 15): 44.

Czopek, Vanessa. 1998. "Using Mystery Shoppers to Evaluate Customer Service in the Public Library." *Public Libraries* 37, no. 6 (November/December): 370–371.

Dame, Melvina Azar. 1993. *Serving Linguistically and Culturally Diverse Students: Strategies for the School Library Media Specialist.* Neal-Schuman.

D'Elia, George, and Eleanor Jo Rodger. 1994. "Public Opinion About the Roles of the Public Library in the Community: The Results of a Recent Gallup Poll." *Public Libraries* January/February: 23–28.

———. 1996. "Customer Satisfaction with Public Libraries." *Public Libraries* September/October: 292–297.

———. 1994. "Public Library Roles and Patron Use: Why Patrons Use the Library." *Public Libraries* May/June: 135–144.

———. 1995. "The Roles of the Public Library in the Community: The Results of a Gallup Poll of Community Opinion Leaders." *Public Libraries* March/April: 94–101.

Durrance, Joan C. 2003. "Determining How Libraries and Librarians Help." *Library Trends* 51, no. 4 (Spring): 541.

Durrance, Joan C. 1995. "Factors That Influence Reference Success: What Makes Questioners Willing to Return?" *The Reference Librarian* no. 49–50: 243–265.

Glick, Andrea. 2000. "The Trouble with Teens: Unruly Teens Target of New Policy at Bedford Park Public Library." *School Library Journal* 46, no. 10 (October): 18–19.

Gross, Melissa. 2000. "The Imposed Query and Information Services for Children." *Journal of Youth Services in Libraries* 13, no. 2 (Winter): 10–17.

Gross, Valerie J. 2001. "The Pinnacle of Customer Service: Partnerships." *Public Libraries* 40, no. 2 (March/April): 85–86.

Hartwell, David G. 2002. "Readers' Advising for the Young SF, Fantasy, and Horror Reader." *Reference & User Services Quarterly* 42, no. 2 (Winter): 133.

Herald, Diana Tixier, and Bonnie Kunzel. 2002. *Strictly Science Fiction: A Guide to Reading Interests.* Libraries Unlimited.

Hernon, Peter, and John R. Whitman. 2001. *Delivering Satisfaction and Service Quality: A Customer-Based Approach for Libraries.* American Library Association.

Hunenberg, David. 2002. "Duh!!! Seven Tips for Improving Customer Service to Teens." *The Unabashed Librarian* no. 125: 10–12.

Johnson, Carol French. 2002. "Union Staff and Customer Service: Do They Collide?" *Public Libraries* 41, no. 3 (May/June): 136–137.

Jones, Patrick, and Joel Shoemaker. 2001. *Do It Right!: Best Practices for Serving Young Adults in School and Public Libraries.* Neal-Schuman.

Labuik, Karen. 2000. "Making the Library Essential: Communications, Marketing and Customer Service." *PNLA Quarterly* 64, no. 4 (Summer): 19.

LeBoeuf, Michael. 1987. *How to Win Customers and Keep Them for Life.* Berkley.

Leonicio, Maggie. 2001. "Going the Extra Mile: Customer Service with a Smile." *The Reference Librarian* no. 72: 51—63.

Lisker, Peter. 2002. "Inspiring Phenomenal Customer Service: Techniques to Sway the Most Reluctant Staff Members." *Public Libraries* 41, no. 6 (November/December): 306–307.

———. 2000. "The Ties that Bind: Creating Great Customer Service." *Public Libraries* 39, no. 4 (July/August): 190–192.

Lubans, John. 2001. "To Save the Time of the User: Customer Service at the Millennium." *Library Administration & Management* 15, no. 3 (Summer): 179–182.

Lugg, Rick. 2003. "I, User—The Unbearable Lightness of Service: Notes on the Customer Experience." *Against the Grain* 15, no. 1 (February): 86–87, 92.

McGuigan, Glenn S. 2002. "The Common Sense of Customer Service: Employing Advice from the Trade and Popular Literature of Business to Interactions with Irate Patrons in Libraries." *The Reference Librarian,* no. 75/76: 197–204.

McLaughlin, Claire S. 1999. "SHINE—Simply Helping Is Not Enough: A Customer Service Campaign that Worked." *Public Libraries* 38, no. 5 (September/October): 316–318.

McNeil, Beth, and Denise Johnson. 1996. *Patron Behavior in Libraries: A Handbook of Positive Approaches to Negative Situations.* American Library Association.

Minkel, Walter, and Roxanne Hsu Feldman. 1998. *Delivering Web Reference Services to Young People.* American Library Association.

Neuman, Delia. 2003. "Research in School Library Media for the Next Decade: Polishing the Diamond." *Library Trends* 51, no. 4 (Spring): 503.

Pinder, Jo Ann. 2003. "Really Looking at Customer Service." *Public Libraries* 42, no. 2 (March/April): 69.

Pritchard, John A. 2001. "Planning for Improved Customer Service at the State Level." *Public Libraries* 40, no. 2 (March/April): 86–87.

"Providing Reference Services for Young Adults: School and Public Librarian Partnerships." 1997. *The Reference Librarian* no. 59: 153–162.

Ransom, Marcia. 2001. "Customer Service and Public Library Building Design and Management." *Public Libraries* 40, no. 2 (March/April): 87–88.

Reilly, Rob. 2003. "Building an Online Reader's Advisory and Getting Good Reads." *Multimedia Schools* 10, no. 4 (September): 61.

Ross, Catherine Sheldrick. 1994. "Best Practices: An Analysis of the Best (and Worst) in Fifty-Two Public Library Reference Transactions." *Public Libraries* September/October: 261–166.

Ross, Catherine Sheldrick, and Mary K. Chelton. 2001. "Reader's Advisory: Matching Mood and Material." *Library Journal* 126, no. 2 (February 1): 52–55.

Sager, Donald J. 2001. "Customer Service and Public Libraries." *Public Libraries* 40, no. 2 (March/April): 85–89.

Saricks, Joyce G. 2001. *The Readers' Advisory Guide to Genre Fiction.* ALA Editions.

Sarkodie-Mensah, Kwasi. 2002. *Helping the Difficult Library Patron: New Approaches to Examining and Resolving a Long-Standing and Ongoing Problem.* Haworth Information Press.

Shearer, Kenneth D., and Robert Burgin. 2001. *The Readers' Advisor's Companion.* Libraries Unlimited.

Smith, Duncan. 1993. *Reconstructing the Reader: Educating Readers' Advisors.* Collection Building 12, no. 3–4: 21–30.

———. 2000. "Talking with Readers: A Competency Based Approach to Readers' Advisory Service." *Reference & User Services Quarterly* 40, no. 2 (Winter): 135.

Smith, Kitty. 1993. *Serving the Difficult Customer: A How-To-Do-It Manual.* Neal-Schuman.

Steinmacher, Michael. 2002. "Inside Pandora's Box: Suggestions for Improving Customer Service Today." *Against the Grain* 14, no. 1 (February): 77–78.

Stevenson-Moudamane, Veronica L.C. 2000. "Online Reference Assistance for Youth Just a Click Away." *Public Libraries* 39, no. 5 (September/October). 260–261.

Talley, Mary, and Joan Axelroth. 2001. "Talking About Customer Service." *Information Outlook*, 5, no. 12 (December): 6–8, 10, 13.

Thompson, Joseph. 2003. "After School and Online: Joseph Thompson Relates the Experiences of One Program that Targeted Chat Reference Service to Children and Teens." *Library Journal* 128, no. 1 (January): 35.

Toch, M. Uri. 2001. "The Yin and Yang of Customer Service." *Public Libraries* 40, no. 2 (March/April): 88–89.

Van Fleet, Connie, and Danny P. Wallace. 2002. "Mr. Green's Axiom: Customer Service or Just Plain Good Service?" *Reference & User Services Quarterly* 42, no. 1 (Fall): 6–8.

Walters, Suzanne. 1994. *Customer Service: A How-To-Do-It Manual.* Neal-Schuman.

Weingand, Darlene. 1996. *Customer Service Excellence: A Concise Guide for Librarians.* American Library Association.

Wilson, Paula. 2001. "Readers' Advisory Services: Taking it All Online." *Public Libraries* 40, no. 6 (November/December): 344–345.

Winston, Mark D., and Kimberly Lione Paone. 2001. "Reference and Information Services for Young Adults: A Research Study of Public Libraries in New Jersey." *Reference & User Services Quarterly* 41, no. 1 (Fall): 45–50.

CHAPTER 4—CUSTOMER SERVICE/ INFORMATION LITERACY

American Association of School Librarians. 1999. *Information Literacy Standards for Student Learning.* ALA Editions.

American Library Association. 1998. *Information Literacy Standards for Student Learning.* ALA/AASL and AECT.

———. 1998. *Information Power: Building Partnerships for Learning.* ALA/AASL and AECT.

Birks, Jane, and Flora Hunt. 2003. *Hands-On Information Literacy Activities.* Neal-Schuman.

Crane, Beverley E. 2000. *Teaching with the Internet: Strategies and Models for K–12 Curricula.* Neal-Schuman.

Doggett, Sandra L., and Paula Kay Montgomery. 2000. *Beyond the Book: Technology Integration into the Secondary School Library Media Curriculum.* Libraries Unlimited.

Ercegovac, Zorana. 2001. *Information Literacy: Search Strategies, Tools & Resources for High School Students.* Linworth Press.

Farmer, Lesley. 1999. "Making Information Literacy a Schoolwide Reform Effort." *Book Report* 18, no. 3 (November/December): 6–8.

Hackman, Mary H., and Paula Kay Montgomery. 1999. *Library Information Skills and the High School English Program.* Libraries Unlimited.

Harris, Frances Jacobson. 2003. "Information Literacy in School Libraries: It Takes a Community." *References & User Services Quarterly* 42, no. 3 (Spring): 215.

Jones, Caryl. 2001. "Infusing Information Literacy and Technology into Your School Library Media Program." *Knowledge Quest* 30, no. 1 (September/October): 22–23.

Lane, Nancy, Margaret Chisholm, and Carolyn Mateer. 2000. *Techniques for Student Research: A Comprehensive Guide to Using the Library.* Neal-Schuman.

Langhorne, Mary Jo. 1998. *Developing an Information Literacy Program K–12: A How-To-Do-It Manual and CD-ROM Package.* Neal-Schuman.

Loertscher, David. 2002. *Information Literacy: A Review of the Research: A Guide for Practitioners and Researchers.* Hi Willow Research and Pub.

Rankin, Virginia. 1999. *The Thoughtful Researcher: Teaching the Research Process to Middle School Students.* Libraries Unlimited.

Riedling, Ann Marlow. 2002. *Learning to Learn: A Guide to Becoming Information Literate.* Neal-Schuman.

Ryan, Jenny, and Steph Capra. 2001. *Information Literacy Toolkit, Grades 7 and Up.* American Library Association.

Spitzer, Kathy, and Michael Eisenberg. 1999. *Information Literacy: Essential Skills for the Information Age.* ERIC Clearinghouse on Information and Technology.

Stanley, Deborah B. 2000. *Practical Steps to the Research Process for Middle School.* Libraries Unlimited.

Stripling, Barbara K. 1999. *Learning and Libraries in an Information Age: Principles and Practice.* Teacher Ideas Press.

Stuhlman, Megan, Bridget Hamre, and Robert Pianta. 2002. "Advancing the Teen/Teacher Connection." *The Education Digest* 68, no. 3 (November): 15–17.

Thompson, Helen M., and Susan Henly. 2000. *Fostering Information Literacy: Connecting National Standards, Goals 2000, and the SCANS Report.* Libraries Unlimited.

Valenza, Joyce Kasman. 2000. "Beware of G(r)eeks Bearing Gifts: Thoughtfully Accepting the Gift of the Internet." *Voice of Youth Advocates* 23, no. 4 (October): 249.

———. 2001. "Imagine—Crossing Library Lines to Achieve Information Literacy." *Voice of Youth Advocates* 24, no. 4 (October): 261.

———. 2003. *Power Research Tools.* ALA Editions.

———. 2003. "Spreading the Gospel of Information Literacy: A Schoolwide Initiative, Year Two." *Knowledge Quest* 32, no. 1 (September/October): 49–50.

Volkman, John D. 1998. Cruising Through Research: Library Skills for Young Adults. Libraries Unlimited.

CHAPTER 5—COLLECTIONS

"A Core Collection of Graphic Novels." 2002. *School Library Journal* 48, no. 8 (August): 44–46.

Abrahamson, Richard F. 1997. "Collected Wisdom: The Best Articles Ever Written on Young Adult Literature and Teen Reading." *English Journal* March: 363–370.

———. 1998. "Back to the Future with Adult Books for the Teenage Reader." *Journal of Youth Services in Libraries* 11, no. 4 (Summer): 378–387.

Abramson, Marla. 2001. "Why Boys Don't Read." *Book* January: 86.

Adams, Lauren. 2001. "Librarians Tell Publishers What They Really Need: A YALSA Survey." *Journal of Youth Services in Libraries* 14, no. 4 (Summer): 32–34.

Adamson, Lynda G. 1999. *American Historical Fiction: An Annotated Guide to Novels for Adults and Young Adults.* Oryx Press.

———. 1998. *Literature Connections to World History: Resources to Enhance and Entice, 7–12.* Libraries Unlimited.

———. 1999. *World Historical Fiction: An Annotated Guide to Novels for Adults and Young Adults.* Oryx Press.

"Adolescent Literacy Research." 2002. *Education Daily* 35, no. 242 (December 24): 4.

"Adolescent Literacy: A Position Statement." 1999. *Journal of Adolescent & Adult Literacy* September: 97–110.

Alford, Jennifer. 2001. "Learning Language and Critical Literacy: Adolescent ESL Students." *Journal of Adolescent & Adult Literacy* November: 238.

Allen, Jane, and Kyle Gonzalez. 1998. *There's Room for Me Here: Literacy Workshop in the Middle School.* Stenhouse Publishers.

Allen, Janet. 2002. *Reimagining Reading: A Literacy Institute.* Stenhouse Publishers.

————. 2002. *Using Literature to Help Troubled Teenagers Cope with End-of-Life Issues.* Greenwood.

Allen, Susan M., and Deborah Regan Howe. 1999. "A Novel Approach: A Teacher-Librarian Collaboration Brings Young Adult Literature into the Classroom." *Voice of Youth Advocates* 22, no. 5 (December): 314–317.

Altmann, Anna E., and Gail DeVos. 2001. *Tales, Then and Now: More Folktales as Literary Fictions for Young Adults.* Libraries Unlimited.

Alvermann, Donna E., et al. 1998. *Reconceptualizing the Literacies in Adolescents' Lives.* Lawrence Erlbaum.

Ammon, Bette, and Gale Sherman. 1998. *More Rip-Roaring Roads for Reluctant Teen Readers.* Libraries Unlimited.

Appleman, Deborah. 2000. *Critical Encounters in High School English: Teaching Literary Theory to Adolescents.* Teachers College Press.

Aronson, Marc. 2003. *Beyond the Pale: New Essays for a New Era.* Scarecrow Press.

————. 2002. "Coming of Age: One Editor's View of How Young Adult Publishing Developed in America." *Publishers Weekly*, 249, no. 6 (February 11): 82–86.

————. 2001. *Exploding the Myths: The Truth About Teens and Reading.* Scarecrow Press.

————. 2000. "Literary Distinction and the Printz Award." *Booklist* January 1: 894.

————. 1999. "Teenagers and Reading: A Generational Neurosis." *Journal of Youth Services in Libraries* 12, no. 2 (Winter): 29–30.

Asselin, Marlene. 2003. "Bridging the Gap Between Learning to be Male and Learning to Read." *Teacher Librarian* 30, no. 3 (February): 53–54.

Baird, Susan G. 2000. *Audiobook Collections and Services.* Highsmith.

Baker, Sharon L., and Karen L. Wallace. 2002. *The Responsive Public Library: How to Develop and Market a Winning Collection.* Libraries Unlimited.

Barron, Neil. 1999. *Fantasy and Horror: A Critical and Historical Guide to Literature, Illustration, Film, TV, Radio, Internet.* Scarecrow Press.

Bean, Joy. 2003. "A Fresh Look at YA Literature." *Publishers Weekly* 250, no. 27 (July 7): 21.

Bean, Thomas W. 2002. "Making Reading Relevant for Adolescents." *Educational Leadership* 60, no. 3 (November): 34–37.

Bean, Thomas W., and Karen Moni. 2003. "Developing Students' Critical Literacy: Exploring Identity Construction in Young Adult Fiction." *Journal of Adolescent & Adult Literacy* 46, no. 8 (May): 638–648.

Bean, Thomas W., and John E. Readence. 2002. "Adolescent Literacy: Charting a Course for Successful Futures as Lifelong Learners." *Reading Research and Instruction* 41, no. 3 (Spring): 203–209.

Beers, G. Kylene. 1996. "No Time, No Interest, No Way! The Three Voices of Aliteracy." *School Library Journal* 42, no. 2 (February): 30–33.

————. 1996. "No Time, No Interest, No Way! Part 2." *School Library Journal* 42, no. 3 (March): 110–113.

————. 2003. "Literacy: What Matters Now?" *Voices from the Middle* 10, no. 3 (March): 4.

Beers, G. Kylene, and Barbara Samuels. 1998. *Into Focus: Understanding and Creating Middle School Readers.* Christopher-Gordon Press.

Beetz, Kirk H. 1991–2002. *Beacham's Guide to Literature for Young Adults* (15 vols.). Gale Group.

Bellafante, Ginia. 2003. "Poor Little Rich Girls, Throbbing to Shop." *New York Times* August 17: 9.1.

Bertin, Joan E. 1998. "Do Teenage Girl Magazines Belong on Middle School Library Shelves?" *SIECUS Report* 27, no. 1 (October/November): 11–12.

Blackburn, Mollie V. 2003. "Boys and Literacies: What Difference Does Gender Make?" *Reading Research Quarterly* 38, no. 2 (April/May/June): 276–287.

Bodart, Joni Richards. 2002. *Radical Reads: 101 YA Novels on the Edge*. Scarecrow Press.

———. 2000. *World's Best Thin Books: Or What to Read When Your Book Report is Due Tomorrow*. Scarecrow Press.

Booth, David. 2002. *Even Hockey Players Read: Boys, Literacy and Learning*. Stenhouse Publishers.

Borwin, Jean E., and Elaine C. Stephens. 1998. *United in Diversity: Using Multicultural Young Adult Literature in the Classroom*. NCTE.

Bowen, Liam. 2002. "Keep Reading Lists Fun." *Voice of Youth Advocates* 24, no. 6 (February): 422.

Bowman, Cynthia Ann. 2000. *Using Literature to Help Troubled Teenagers Cope with Health Issues*. Greenwood.

Bowman-Kruhm, Mary, and Claudine G. Wirths. 1999. "Young Adult Authors Speak Out: Executing a 5Q Manuscript." *Voice of Youth Advocates* 22, no. 2 (June): 103–104.

Boyd-Franklin, Nancy. 2001. *Boys Into Men: Raising Our African American Teenage Sons*. Dutton/Plume.

Broderick, Dorothy. 1995. "Building the Bridge to Adult Literacy." *Voice of Youth Advocates* 18, no. 1 (April): 6.

Brooks, Bruce, Katie O'Dell, and Patrick Jones. 2000. "Will Boys Be Boys? Are You Sure?" *Voice of Youth Advocates* 23, no. 2 (June): 88–92.

Brown, Joanne, and Nancy St. Claire. 2002. *Declarations of Independence: Empowered Girls in Young Adult Literature, 1990–2001*. Scarecrow Press.

Brown, Margie K. 2001. "Silverstein and Seuss to Shakespeare: What is In Between?" *English Journal* 90, no. 5 (May): 150–152.

Brozo, William G. 2002. *To Be a Boy, To Be a Reader: Engaging Teen and Preteen Boys in Active Literacy*. International Reading Association.

Brozo, William G., Patricia Walter, and Teri Placker. 2002. "I Know the Difference Between a Real Man and a TV Man: A Critical Exploration of Violence and Masculinity through Literature in a Junior High School in the 'Hood." *Journal of Adolescent & Adult Literacy* 45, no. 6 (March): 530–538.

Bruggerman, Lora. 1997. "Zap! Whoosh! Kerplow! Build High-Quality Graphic Novel Collections with Impact." *School Library Journal* 43, no. 1 (January): 22–27.

Bushman, John H., and Kay Haas. 2001. *Using Young Adult Literature in the English Classroom*. Merrill Prentice Hall.

Campbell, Patty. 2003. "Prizes and Paradoxes." *The Horn Book Magazine* 79, no. 4 (July/August): 501.

Carlsen, Robert, and Anne Sherrill. 1988. *Voice of Readers: How we Come to Love Books*. National Council for Teachers of English.

Carroll, Pamela S. 1999. *Using Literature to Help Troubled Teenagers Cope with Societal Issues*. Greenwood.

Cart, Michael. 1996. *From Romance to Realism: 50 Years of Growth and Change in Young Adult Literature*. HarperCollins.

————. 1998. "Begetting an Award." *Booklist* 95, no. 1 (September 1): 108–109.

————. 2001. "From Insider to Outsider: the Evolution of Young Adult Literature." *Voices from the Middle* 9, no. 2 (December): 95–97.

————. 1995. "Of Risk and Revelation: The Current State of Young Adult Literature." *Journal of Youth Services in Libraries* 8, no. 2 (Winter): 151–164.

Carter, Betty. 2003. "Alex: The Why and the How (Young Adult Book Award)." *Booklist* 99, no. 15 (April 1): 138–139.

Carter, Betty, Sally Estes, and Linda Waddle. 2000. *Best Books for Young Adults*, 2nd ed. American Library Association.

Chance, Rosemary. 2000. "SmartGirl.com Reading Survey: What are the Messages for Librarians?" *Journal of Youth Services in Libraries* 13, no. 3 (Spring): 20–23.

Channing, Joseph. 2003. "D&Q Explains How to Sell Today's Graphic Novels (Beyond Capes & Masks)." *Publishers Weekly* 250, no. 4 (January 27): 121.

Cooper-Mullin, Alison. 1998. *Once Upon a Heroine: 400 Books for Girls to Love*. NTC/Contemporary.

Cornish, Sarah, and Patrick Jones. 2002. "Retro Mock Printz: The Best of the Best of the Best of Young Adult Literature from the VOYA Years." *Voice of Youth Advocates* 25, no. 5 (December): 353–157.

Cox, Robin Overby. 2002. "Lost Boys." *Voice of Youth Advocates* 25, no. 3 (August): 172–173.

Cox, Ruth E. 2003. "From Boy's Life to Thrasher: Boys and Magazines." *Teacher Librarian* 30, no. 3 (February): 25.

Crawford, Philip. 2002. "Graphic Novels: Selecting Materials that will Appeal to Girls." *Knowledge Quest* 31, no. 2 (November/December): 43–45.

Crew, Hillary. 2000. *Is It Really Mommy Dearest? Daughter-Mother Narratives in Young Adult Fiction*. Scarecrow Press.

Crowe, Chris. 2001. "AP and YA?" *English Journal* 91, no. 1 (September): 123–128.

————. 2003. "Can Reading Help?" *English Journal* 92, no. 4 (March): 102–105.

————. 2002. "Librarians at the Helm of the Frigate." *Young Adult Library Services* 1, no. 1 (Fall): 4.

Crowe, Chris. 2002. "Young Adult Literature: An Antidote for Testosterone Poisoning: YA Books Girls—and Boys—Should Read." *English Journal* 91, no. 3 (January): 135.

Crowley, Stephen. 2003. "We Gave the World New Ways to Dream: Thoughts on Selected Films for Young Adults." *Young Adult Library Services* 1, no. 2 (Winter): 44–45.

Darby, Mary Ann, and Miki Pryne. 2001. *Hearing All the Voices: Multicultural Books for Adolescents*. Scarecrow Press.

Day, Frances Ann. 2000. *Lesbian and Gay Voices: An Annotated Bibliography and Guide to Literature for Children and Young Adults*. Greenwood.

————. 1999. *Multicultural Voices in Contemporary Literature*. Heinemann.

"Defending YA Literature: Voices of Students." 2002. *English Journal* 92, no. 1 (September): 114–118.

Dodson, Shireen. 1998. *100 Books for Girls to Grow On*. HarperCollins.

Doll, Carol A., and Pamela Petrick Barron. 2001. *Managing and Analyzing Your Collection: A Practical Guide for Small Libraries and School Library Media Centers*. American Library Association.

Donelson, Ken. 1997. "Honoring the Best YA Books of the Year: 1964–1995." *English Journal* March: 41–48.

Dresang, Elizabeth T. 1999. *Radical Change: Books for Youth in a Digital Age*. H.W. Wilson.

Dressman, Mark, and Shelby Wolf. 2002. "Young Adult Literature on the Cutting Edge." *New Advocate* 15, no. 3 (Summer): 237–248.

Drew, Bernard A. 2002. *100 More Popular Young Adult Authors: Biographical Sketches and Bibliographies*. Libraries Unlimited.

Dugan, JoAnn R. 1999. *Advancing the World of Literacy: Moving into the 21st Century*. College Reading Association.

Elliott, Joan B., and Mary Dupuis. 2002. *Young Adult Literature in the Classroom: Reading It, Teaching It, Loving It*. International Reading Association.

Fader, Daniel. 1976. *The New Hooked on Books*. Berkley.

Farmer, Lesley. 2001. "Collection Development in Partnership with Youth: Uncovering Best Practices." *Collection Management* 26, no. 2: 67–78.

Flagg, Gordon. 2003. "Not Your Father's Superheroes." Booklist 99, no. 11 (February 1): 988.

Fonseca, Anthony J., and Jun Michele Pulliam. 1999. *Hooked on Horror: A Guide to Reading Interests in Horror Fiction*. Libraries Unlimited.

Furi-Perry, Ursula. 2003. "Dude, That Book was Cool: The Reading Habits of Young Adults." *Reading Today* 20, no. 5 (April–May): 24.

Gallo, Donald R. 2001. "How Classics Create an Aliterate Society." *English Journal* 90, no. 3 (January): 33.

Garbarino, James. 1999. *Lost Boys: Why Our Sons Turn Violent and How We Can Save Them*. Free Press.

Garden, Nancy. 2001. "Gay Books for Teens & Kids: Coming Into Their Own?" *Lambda Book Report* 9, no. 7 (February): 22–23.

————. 2001. "Queer Teens." *Lambda Book Report* 10, no. 4/5 (November): 28–31.

Gates, Pamela S., Susan B. Steffel, and Francis J. Molson. 2003. *Fantasy Literature for Children and Young Adults*. Scarecrow Press.

Gauthier, Gail. 2002. "Whose Community? Where is the YA in YA Literature?" *English Journal* 91, no. 6 (July): 70–76.

George, Marshall A. 2001. "What's the Big Idea? Integrating Young Adult Literature in the Middle School." *English Journal*, 90, no. 3 (January): 74.

Gillespie, John Thomas, ed. 2000. *Best Books for Young Teen Readers, Grades 7 to 10*. Bowker.

Gillespie, John T., and Ralph J. Folcarelli. 1998. *Guides to Collection Development for Children and Young Adults*. Libraries Unlimited.

Givens, Archie. 1998. *Strong Souls Singing: African American Books for Our Daughters and Sisters*. Norton.

Goldsmith, Francisca. 2002. "Earphone English." *School Library Journal* 48, no. 5 (May): 50–53.

———. 2003. "Graphic Novels as Literature (Spotlight on Graphic Novels)." *Booklist* 99, no. 11 (February 1): 986.

———. 2003. "The Emergence of Spoken Word Recordings for YA Audiences." *Young Adult Library Services* 1, no. 2 (Winter): 23–26.

Gorman, Michelle. 2002. "What Teens Want: Thirty Graphic Novels You Can't Live Without." *School Library Journal* 48, no. 8 (August): 18.

Graff, Keir. 2003. "Reference on the Web: Graphic Novels (Spotlight on Graphic Novels)." *Booklist* 99, no. 11 (February 1): 1013.

Greenlee, Adele A. 1996. "The Lure of Series Books: Does It Affect Appreciation for Recommended Literature?" *Reading Teacher* November: 216–225.

Guild, Sandy, and Sandra Hughes-Hassell. 2001. "The Urban Minority Young Adult as Audience: Does Young Adult Literature Pass the Reality Test?" *New Advocate* 14, no. 4 (Fall): 361.

Gurian, Michael. 1998. *A Fine Young Man: What Parents, Mentors, and Educators Can Do to Shape Adolescent Boys into Exceptional Men.* Free Spirit Press.

———. 1999. *Good Son: Shaping the Moral Development of Our Boys and Young Men.* Tarcher/Putnam.

Gutchewsky, Kimberly. 2001. "An Attitude Adjustment: How I Reached My Reluctant Readers." *English Journal* 91, no. 2 (November): 79.

Guth, Nancy. 2001. "Adolescent Literacy: Seven Principles." *Reading Today* 19, no. 1 (August): 23.

Halpern, Julie. 2002. "Ten Geeks, One League of Power, Many Butt-Kicking Comics! Francis W. Parker School Comic Book Club." *Young Adult Library Services* 1, no. 1 (Fall): 41–43.

Halstead, Judith. 2002. *Some of My Best Friends are Books: Guiding Gifted Readers from Preschool to High School.* Great Potential Press.

Hartwell, David. 1996. *Age of Wonders: Exploring the World of Science Fiction*, rev. ed. TOR.

Herald, Diana Tixier. 1999. *Fluent in Fantasy: A Guide to Reading Interests.* Libraries Unlimited.

———. 2003. *Teen Genreflecting: A Guide to Reading Interests*, 2nd ed. Libraries Unlimited.

Herz, Sarah K. 1996. *From Hinton to Hamlet: Building Bridges Between Young Adult Literature and the Classics.* Greenwood Press.

Hipple, Ted. 1997. Writers for Young Adults (3 vols.). Charles Scribner's.

———. 2000. *Writers for Young Adults, Supplement I.* Charles Scribner's.

Hirschfelder, Arlene, and Yvonne Beamer. 2000. *Native Americans Today: Resources and Activities for Educators, Grades 4–9.* Libraries Unlimited.

Hofman, Mary. 2002. "Looking at Language: One Library Media Teacher's Philosophy for Book Selection." *School Library Journal* 48, no. 11 (November): 44.

Hogan, Walter. 2001. *Agony and the Eggplant: Daniel Pinkwater's Heroic Struggles in the Name of YA Literature.* Scarecrow Press.

Horn, Caroline. 2003. "Taming the Teenager: Not a Native of Our Bookshops, that Skittish Creature the Teenager is Nevertheless Developing a Taste for Reading—Given the Right Habitat." *The Bookseller* June 20: 22.

Horn, Caroline. 2002. "Teenage Market in Turnaround: Caroline Horn on How Publishers and Booksellers Plan to Broaden the Market Among Teenage Readers." *The Bookseller* May 17: 14.

Horne, Claire. 2002. "Beautiful, Fresh, Distinguished Books: Teen Readers Take on the 2002 Printz Awards." *Voice of Youth Advocates* 25, no. 5 (December): 348–351.

"How to Keep Boys Interested in Books." 2001. *NEA Today* 19, no. 4 (January): 27.

Huang, Lucia. 1999. *American Young Adult Novels and Their European Fairy-Tale Motifs.* P. Lang.

Hubert, Jennifer, and Patrick Jones. 2001. "Overlooked Books of the 1990s." *Booklist* 97, no. 21 (July): 1998–1999.

Hunt, Gladys M., and Barbara Hampton. 2002. *Honey for a Teen's Heart: Using Books to Communicate with Teens.* Zondervan.

Hurst, Carol Otis, and Rebecca Otis. 1999. *Using Literature in the Middle School Curriculum.* Linworth Press.

"I Cry Through My Poems: Teens Demand Equal Poetry Time." 1999. *Voice of Youth Advocates* 22, no. 1 (April): 22.

International Reading Association. 2002. "IRA Literacy Study Groups Module Focuses on Adolescent Literacy." *Reading Today* 20, no. 3 (December): 34.

Isaac, Megan Lynn. 2000. *Heirs to Shakespeare: Reinventing the Bard in Young Adult Literature.* Heinemann.

Jobe, Ron, and May Dayton-Sakari. 2002. *Info-Kids: How to Use Nonfiction to Turn Reluctant Readers into Enthusiastic Learners.* Stenhouse Publishers.

———. 1999. *Reluctant Readers: Connecting Students for Successful Reading Experiences.* Stenhouse Publishers.

Johns, Jerry L. 2002. "How Do You Make a Difference?" *Reading Today* 20, no. 1 (August/September): 6.

Johnson, Keith. 2001. "Children's Books in a High School Library?" *Book Report* 19, no. 5 (March/April): 6–8.

Jones, Patrick. 2001. "Nonfiction: The Real Stuff." *School Library Journal* 47, no. 4 (April): 44–45.

———. 2001. "Nothing to Fear: R.L. Stine and Young Adult Paperback Thrillers." *Collection Management* 25, no. 4: 3–23.

———. 2001. "The Perfect Tens: The Top Forty Books Reviewed in *Voice of Youth Advocates* 1996–2000." *Voice of Youth Advocates* 24, no. 2 (June): 94–99.

———. 2003. "To the Teen Core." *School Library Journal* 49, no. 3 (March): 48–49.

———. 1998. *What's So Scary about R.L. Stine?* Scarecrow Press.

Jones, Patrick, and Dawn Cartwright Fiorelli. 2003. "Overcoming the Obstacle Course: Teenage Boys and Reading." *Teacher Librarian* 30, no. 3 (February): 9–13.

Jones, Patrick, Patricia Taylor, and Kirsten Edwards. 2003. *A Core Collection for Young Adults.* Neal-Schuman.

Jweid, Rosanne, and Margaret Rizzo. 2001. *Building Character Through Literature: A Guide for Middle School Readers.* Scarecrow Press.

Kan, Kat. 2002. "Really Getting Graphic: A Teen Read Week Art Show Preview." *Voice of Youth Advocates* 25, no. 4 (October): 240–241.

———. 2000. "Teen Life—Manga Style." *Voice of Youth Advocates* 23, no. 2 (June): 108–109.

Kan, Kat, and Kristin Fletcher-Spear. 2002. "Showing Anime in the Library." *Voice of Youth Advocates* 25, no. 1 (April): 20–23.

Kaplan, Elaine Bell, and Leslie Cole. 2003. "'I Want to Read Stuff on Boys : White, Latina, and Black Girls Reading *Seventeen* Magazine and Encountering Adolescence. *Adolescence* 38, no. 149 (Spring): 141–159.

Kaplan, Jeffrey S. 1999. *Using Literature to Help Troubled Teenagers Cope with Identity Issues.* Greenwood.

Kaywell, Joan F. 1999. *Using Literature to Help Troubled Teenagers Cope with Family Issues.* Greenwood.

Kiesling, Angie. 2002. "Tuning in to the Teen Soul: Teen Spirituality Titles." *Publishers Weekly* 249, no. 10 (March 11): 30–32.

———. 2003. "God, Sex and Rock 'N' Roll." *Publishers Weekly* 250, no. 32 (August 11): 130.

Kindlon, Dan, and Michael Thompson. 1999. *Raising Cain: Protecting the Emotional Life of Boys.* Ballantine.

Kirk, Carol A. 2000. "A Response to the Adolescent Literacy Position Statement." *Journal of Adolescent & Adult Literacy* 43, no. 6 (March): 573.

Kivel, Paul. 1999. *Boys Will Be Men: Raising Our Sons for Courage, Caring, and Community.* New Society.

Klause, Annette Curtis. 1998. "A Young Adult Author Speaks Out: Why Vampires?" *Voice of Youth Advocates* 21, no. 1 (April): 28–30.

Klock, Geoff. 2002. *How to Read Superhero Comics and Why.* Continuum.

Knickerbocker, Joan L., and James Rycik. 2002. "Growing into Literature: Adolescents Literary Interpretation and Appreciation." *Journal of Adolescent & Adult Literacy* 46, no. 3 (November): 196–208.

Krahnke, Kitty. 1999. "Teens Test Best Books in Public/School Library Book Groups." *Voice of Youth Advocates* 22, no. 5 (December): 318–319.

Krashen, Stephen. 1993. *The Power of Reading: Insights for the Research.* Libraries Unlimited.

Kunzel, Bonnie, and Suzanne Manczuk. 2001. *First Contact: A Reader's Selection of Science Fiction and Fantasy.* Scarecrow Press.

Leonhardt, Mary. 1996. *Keeping Kids Reading: How to Raise Avid Readers in the Video Age.* Crown.

———. 1993. *Parents Who Love Reading, Kids Who Don't, How It Happens and What You Can Do About It.* Crown.

Lesene, Teri S. 2003. "One Hundred of Our Best Ideas: Young Adult Literature with Staying Power." *Voices from the Middle* 10, no. 4 (May): 54.

Levine, Amy. 2002. "Providing Information on Sexuality: Librarians Can Help Youth Become Sexually Healthy Adults." *Journal of Youth Services in Libraries* 15, no. 2 (Winter): 45–8.

Libretto, Ellen V., and Catherine Barr. 2002. *High/Low Handbook: Best Books and Websites for Reluctant Teen Readers,* 4th ed. Libraries Unlimited.

Lindsay, Jeanne Warren, and Sharon Githens Enright. 1998. *Books, Babies and School-Age Parents.* Morning Glory.

Locke, Deborah. 2001. "Heard Any Good Books Lately?" *Book Links* 11, no. 2 (October/November): 26–28.

Loertscher, David V. 1994. "You Can Count On Reading! Library Media Specialists Make a Difference." *Indiana Media Journal* Fall: 62–70.

MacRae, Cathi Dunn. 1998. *Presenting Young Adult Fantasy Fiction*. Prentice Hall/Twayne.

———. 1998. "The Myth of the Bleak Young Adult Novel." *Voice of Youth Advocates* 21, no. 5 (December): 325–327.

Makowski, Silk. 1998. *Serious about Series: Evaluations and Annotations of Teen Fiction in Paperback Series*. Scarecrow Press.

Martin, Robie. 2003. "Connecting with Boys at Lunch: A Success Story." *Teacher Librarian* 30, no. 3 (February): 27–8.

Maughan, Shannon. 2001. "You Go, Guys." *Publishers Weekly* 248, no. 19 (May 7): 41.

McCaffrey, Laura Hibbets. 1998. *Building an ESL Collection for Young Adults: A Bibliography of Recommended Fiction and Nonfiction for Schools and Public Libraries*. Greenwood Press.

McDonald, Colleen. 2001. "The Hidden Shelf: Teen-to-Adult-to-Teen Book Recommendations." *Voice of Youth Advocates* 23, no. 6 (February): 401–402.

McGillian, Jamie Kyle. 2002. "Get Boys Crazy about Books!" *Creative Classroom* 16, no. 6 (May/June): 30–2.

Mediavilla, Cindy. 1999. *Arthurian Fiction: An Annotated Bibliography*. Scarecrow Press.

Mitchell, Diana. 2001. "Young Adult Literature and the English Teacher." *English Journal* 90, no. 3: 23.

Moje, Elizabeth Birr. 2002. "Re-Framing Adolescent Literacy Research for New Times: Studying Youth as a Resource." *Reading Research and Instruction* 41, no. 3 (Spring): 211–228.

Moje, Elizabeth Birr, et al. 2000. "Reinventing Adolescent Literacy for New Times: Perennial and Millennial Issues." *Journal of Adolescent & Adult Literacy*, 43, no. 5 (February): 400.

Moniuszko, Linda K. 1992. "Motivation: Reaching Reluctant Readers Age 14–17." *Journal of Reading* September: 32–34.

Monseau, Virginia R., and Gary Salvner. 2000. *Reading Their World: The Young Adult Novel in the Classroom*. Boynton/Cook Publishers.

Mooney, Maureen. 2002. "Graphic Novels: How They Can Work in Libraries." *Book Report* 21, no. 3 (November/December): 18–19.

Mort, John. 2001. "Adult Christian Fiction for Young Adults: The Best from the Past Three Years." *Booklist* 98, no. 3 (October 1): 335.

Mueller, Pamela. 1998. *Lifers: Learning from At-Risk Adolescent Readers*. Heinemann.

Murphy, Jendy. 2001. "Boys Will Be Boys." *School Library Journal* 47, no. 1 (January): 31.

National Education Association. 2001. "Reading Remains Popular Among Youth, According to Poll." *Reading Today* 18, no. 6 (June): 13.

Neal, Connie. 2001. *What's a Christian to Do with Harry Potter?: Answers to the Burning Questions Parents, Educators, and Other Concerned Christians Are Asking about Harry Potter*. Random/Waterbrook.

Nel, Philip. 2001. *J.K. Rowling's Harry Potter Novels: A Reader's Guide.* Continuum.

New York Public Library. Annual. *Books for the Teen Age.* New York Public Library.

Nilsen, Alleen Pace. 2001. "It's Déjà Vu All Over Again!" *School Library Journal* 47, no. 3 (March): 49–50.

Nilsen, Alleen Pace, and Kenneth L. Donelson. 2000. *Literature for Today's Young Adults*, 6th ed. Longman.

Norton, Bonny. 2001/2002. "When is a Teen Magazine not a Teen Magazine?" *Journal of Adolescent & Adult Literacy* 45, no. 4 (December/January): 296–299.

November, Sharyn. 1997. "Soap Box: A Young Adult Publisher Speaks Out: We're Not Young Adults—We're Prisoners of Life." *Voice of Youth Advocates* 20, no. 3 (August): 169–172.

Odean, Kathleen. 2001. *Great Books About Things Kids Love: More Than 750 Recommended Books for Children 3 to 14.* Ballantine.

———. 1998. *Great Books for Boys: More than 600 Books for Boys 2 to 14.* Ballantine.

Ott, Bill. 2001. "Outside In and Inside Out (Ruminations on the Role of Outsiders in Fiction for Young Adults)." *Booklist* 98, no. 1 (September 1): 160.

Pawuk, Michael. 2002. "Creating a Graphic Novel Collection at Your Library." *Young Adult Library Services* 1, no. 1 (Fall): 30.

Peck, Richard. 2002. *Invitations to the World: Teaching and Writing for the Young.* Dian.

Pendergast, Tom, and Sara Pendergast. 1999. *St. James Guide to Young Adult Writers.* Gale Group.

Poe, Elizabeth, et al. 1995. "Past Perspectives and Future Directions: An Interim Analysis of Twenty-Five Years of Research on Young Adult Literature." *ALAN Review* Winter: 46–50.

Pollack, William. 1999. *Real Boys: Rescuing Our Sons from the Myths of Boyhood.* Random House.

Pollack, William, and Todd Schuster. 2000. *Real Boys' Voices.* Random House.

Power, Brenda Miller, Jeffrey D. Wilhelm, and Kelly Chandler. 1998. *Reading Stephen King: Issues of Censorship, Student Choice, and Popular Literature.* NCTE.

Printz, Mike. 1992. "A Big Fat Hen; A Couple of Ducks." *Voice of Youth Advocates* 15, no. 2 (June): 85–88.

Programme for International Student Assessment Survey for Adolescent Literacy. 2002. "PISA Survey Accents Role of Teacher." *Reading Today* 19, no. 4 (February/March): 12.

Raiteri, Steve. 2003. "Graphic Novels (Why Libraries Should Collect Graphic Novels, Not Comic Books)." *Library Journal* 128, no. 4 (March 1): 72.

———. 2003. "Graphic Novels." *Library Journal*, 128, no. 12 (July): 66.

———. 2003. "Shelving Graphic Novels." *Library Journal* 128, no. 1 (January): 80.

Reid, Calvin. 2003. "Got Teen Readers? Manga Does." *Publishers Weekly* 250, no. 1 (January 6): 28.

———. 2003. "RH to Start Line of Manga Graphic Novels." *Publishers Weekly* 250, no. 25 (June 23): 15.

Reid, Louann, and Jamie Neufeld. 1999. *Rationales for Teaching Young Adult Literature*. Heinemann.

Reid, Suzanne. 2002. *Book Bridges for ESL Students: Using Young Adults and Children's Literature to Teach ESL*. Scarecrow Press.

———. 1998. *Presenting Young Adult Science Fiction*. Twayne/Prentice Hall.

"Reinventing Adolescent Literacy for New Times: Perennial and Millennial Issues." 2000. *Journal of Adolescent & Adult Literacy* February: 400–420.

Revitzer, Pam. 2002. *Beacham's Guide to Literature for Young Adults* (vols. 10–14). Gale Group.

Rosen, Judith. 2002. "Tapping the Teen Market." *Publishers Weekly* 249, no. 29 (July 22): 84–6.

———. 2003. "Casting a Wider Spell." Publishers Weekly 250, no. 35 (September 1): 38.

Rosen, Julia. 1998. "Mature Young Adult Books are Given a Bad Reputation." *Voice of Youth Advocates* 21, no. 5 (December): 347.

Rosenzweig, Sue. 1996. "Books That Hooked 'Em: Reluctant Readers Shine as Critics." *American Libraries* June/July: 74–6.

Ross, Catherine Sheldrick. 1995. "If They Read Nancy Drew, So What? Series Book Readers Talk Back." *Library & Information Science Research* Summer: 201–236.

Roxburgh, Stephen. 2002. "Young Adult Publisher Speaks Out About Winning the Printz Award." *Voice of Youth Advocates* 25, no. 5 (December): 352.

Safford, Barbara Ripp. 1998. *Guide to Reference Materials for School Library Media Centers*, 5th ed. Libraries Unlimited.

Schon, Isabel. 2000. *Recommended Books in Spanish for Children and Young Adults, 1996–1999*. Scarecrow Press.

Schwartz, Gretchen E. 2002. "Graphic Novels for Multiple Literacies." *Journal of Adolescent & Adult Literacy* 46, no. 3 (November): 262–265.

Scieszka, Jon. 2003. "Guys and Reading." *Teacher Librarian* 30, no. 3 (February): 17–18.

Sinofsky, Esther. 2003. "Young Adult Literature in the Classroom: Reading It, Teaching It, Loving It." *Library Media Connection* 21, no. 4 (January): 119.

Small, Robert. 1992. "The Literary Value of the YA Novel." *Journal of Youth Services in Libraries* 5, no. 3 (Spring): 227–285.

Smith, Carolyn. 2002. "Exploring the History and Controversy of Young Adult Literature." *New Review of Children's Literature and Librarianship* 8: 1–11.

Smith, Karen Patricia. 2002. *African-American Voices in Young Adult Literature: Tradition, Transition, Transformation*. Scarecrow.

Smith, Michael, and Jeffrey Wilhelm. 2002. *Reading Don't Fix No Chevy's: Literacy in the Lives of Young Men*. Heinemann.

Spence, Alex. 1999. "Gay Young Adult Fiction in the Public Library: A Comparative Survey." *Public Libraries* 38, no. 4 (July/August): 224–229.

Squires, Claire. 2003. *Philip Pullman's His Dark Materials Trilogy: A Reader's Guide*. Continuum.

St. Lifer, Evan. 2002. "Graphic Novels, Seriously." *School Library Journal* 48, no. 8 (August): 9.

Stephens, Claire Gatrell. 2000. *Coretta Scott King Award: Using Great Literature with Children and Young Adults.* Libraries Unlimited.

Stephens, Elaine C., and Jean E. Brown. 1998. *Learning About…the Civil War: Literature and Other Resources for Young People.* Shoestring Press.

Stoke, Barrington. 2002. "New Help for Older Reluctant Readers." *The Bookseller* January 18: 43.

Sullivan, Charles William. 1999. *Young Adult Science Fiction.* Greenwood Press.

Sullivan, Edward T. 1999. *Holocaust in Literature for Youth: A Guide and Resource Book.* Scarecrow Press.

Sullivan, Edward T. 2000. "Judging Books by Their Covers, Part II: Hardcover vs. Paperback." *Voice of Youth Advocates* 23, no. 4 (October): 244–248.

———. 1998. "Judging Books by Their Covers: A Cover Art Experiment." *Voice of Youth Advocates* 21, no. 3 (August): 180–182.

———. 2000. "More is Not Always Better: Poor Quality of Many YA Nonfiction Series Books." *School Library Journal* 46, no. 4 (April): 42.

———. 2002. "Race Matters." *School Library Journal* 48, no. 6 (June): 40–41.

———. 2002. *Reaching Reluctant Young Adult Readers: A Handbook for Librarian and Teachers.* Scarecrow Press.

———. 1999. "Solving the Short Story Puzzle." *School Library Journal* 45, no. 1 (January): 38–9.

———. 1997. "To Buy or Not to Buy: The Cases for and Against Hard Cover Young Adult Fiction." *Voice of Youth Advocates* 19, no. 6 (February): 321–322.

Sullivan, Michael. 2003. *Connecting Boys with Books: What Libraries Can Do.* American Library Association.

Swartz, Patti Capel. 2003. "Bridging Multicultural Education: Bringing Sexual Orientation into the Children's and Young Adult Literature Classrooms." *Radical Teacher* no. 66 (Spring): 11–16.

Tacchi, Mary Jane. 2000. "Teens Movin' with Poetry." *Book Links* 9, no. 4 (March): 38–40.

Taylor, Rosemarye. 2002. "Creating a System That Gets Results for Older, Reluctant Readers." *Phi Delta Kappan* 84, no. 1 (September): 85.

"Teen Readers and Adult Books: A Winning Combination: 'The Alex Awards, 1998–2002.'" 2002. *Journal of Youth Services in Libraries* 15, no. 4 (Summer): 50–4.

"Teens Are Reading Plenty, New Survey Finds." 2001. *Publishers Weekly* 248, no. 14 (April 2): 23.

Thompson, Michael. 2000. *Speaking of Boys: Answers to the Most-Asked Questions about Raising Sons.* Ballantine.

Tovani, Cris. 2000. *I Read It, but I Don't Get It: Comprehension Strategies for Adolescent Readers.* Stenhouse Publishers.

Turner, Gwendolyn Y. 1992. "Motivating Reluctant Readers: What Can Educators Do?" *Reading Improvement* Spring: 50–5.

Valenza, Joyce Kasman. 2003. "What About Reading?" *School Library Journal* 49, no. 9 (September): S10.

Versaci, Rocco. 2001. "How Comic Books Can Change the Way Our Students See Literature: One Teacher's Perspective." *English Journal* 91, no. 2 (November): 61.

Wadham, Tim, and Rachel L. Wadham. 1999. *Bringing Fantasy Alive for Children and Young Adults.* Linworth.

Webster, Joan Parker. 2003. *Teaching through Culture: Strategies for Reading and Responding to Young Adult Literature.* Arte Publico Press.

Weiner, Stephen. 2001. *101 Best Graphic Novels.* NBM Publishing.

———. 2002. "Beyond Superheroes: Comics Get Serious." *Library Journal* 127, no. 2 (February 1).

Welch, Rollie. 2001. "What Do Teens Read in One Day? A Teen Read Week Log." *Voice of Youth Advocates* 24, no. 4 (October): 257, 316.

Wilhelm, Jeff. 2002. "Getting Boys to Read: It's the Context! It's Not the Text Type So Much as the Situation that Determines Why and How Boys Engage with Reading." *Instructor* 112, no. 3 (October): 16.

Wilhelm, Jeffrey D. 2001. "It's a Guy Thing." *Voices from the Middle* 9, no. 2 (December): 60–63.

Wilson, Martin. 2002. "Tireless Promoter of Gay-Themed Books for Young Adults." Lambda *Book Report* 10, no. 8 (March): 5.

Winner, Lauren F. 2001. "Nurturing Today's Teen Spirit: New Spirituality Books for Teens." *Publishers Weekly* 248, no. 11 (March 12): 30–2.

Wolk, Douglas, and Calvin Reid. 2003. "Comics Create Big Buzz at BEA: Manga Drives Sales as Graphic Novels Find a Home in Bookstores, Libraries." *Publishers Weekly* 250, no. 24 (June 26): 27.

Wood, Irene. 1999. *Culturally Diverse Videos, Audios, and CD-ROMs for Children and Young Adults.* Neal-Schuman.

Wright, Bradford. 2001. *Comic Book Nation: The Transformation of Youth Culture in America.* Johns Hopkins University Press.

"YA Gallery and Teens Top Ten Books: Teen-Selected Best Booklist to Debut for Teen Read Week 2003." 2002. *Voice of Youth Advocates* 25, no. 5 (December): 334.

Yaakov, Juliette, ed. 2002. *Senior High School Library Catalog.* H.W. Wilson.

———. 2000. *Middle & Junior High School Library Catalog*, 8th ed. H.W. Wilson.

Zitlow, Connie S. 2002. *Lost Masterworks of Young Adult Literature.* Scarecrow Press.

CHAPTER 6—BOOKTALKING

Anderson, Shelia, and Kristin Mahood. 2001. "The Inner Game of Booktalking." *Voice of Youth Advocates* 24, no. 2 (June): 107–110.

Bodart, Joni Richards. 1996. *Booktalking the Award Winners: Young Adult Retrospective Volume.* H.W. Wilson.

———. 1997. *Booktalking the Award Winners 3.* H.W. Wilson.

———. 1998. *Booktalking the Award Winners 4.* H.W. Wilson.

Bromann, Jennifer. 1999. "The Toughest Audience on Earth." *School Library Journal* 45, no. 10 (October): 60–3.

———. 2001. *Booktalking That Works.* Neal-Schuman.

Cox, Ruth E. 2002. *Tantalizing Tidbits for Teens: Quick Booktalks for the Busy High School Library Media Specialist.* Linworth.

Gillespie, John T., and Corinne J. Naden. 2003. *Teenplots: A Booktalk Guide to Use with Readers Ages 12–18.* Libraries Unlimited.

Guevara, Anne, and John Sexton. 2000. "Extreme Booktalking: YA Booktalkers Reach 6,000 Students Each Semester!" *Voice of Youth Advocates* 23, no. 2 (June): 98–101.

Langemack, Chapple. 2003. *The Booktalker's Bible: How to Talk About the Books You Love to Any Audience.* Libraries Unlimited.

Littlejohn, Carol. 1999. *Talk That Book: Booktalks to Promote Reading.* Linworth.

———. 2001. *Keep Talking That Book! Booktalks to Promote Reading* (vol. 2). Linworth.

———. 1998. "Rebels with (and without) a Cause: Booktalks for Grades 7–12." *Book Report* 17, no. 1 (May/June): 27–9.

Littlejohn, Carol, and Cathlyn Thomas. 2001. *Keep Talking That Book!: Booktalks to Promote Reading Grades 2–12.* Libraries Unlimited.

Osborne, Marcia. 2001. "Booktalking: Just Do It!" *Book Report* 19, no. 5 (March/April): 23–4.

Rochman, Hazel. 1993. *Against Borders: Promoting Books for a Multicultural World.* American Library Association.

Schall, Lucy. 2001. *Booktalks Plus: Motivating Teens to Read.* Libraries Unlimited.

CHAPTER 7—OUTREACH AND PARTNERSHIPS

Alessio, Amy. 2002. "Community Teen NETwork." *Public Libraries* 41, no. 4 (July/August): 196–197.

Angier, Naomi, Rebecca Cohen, and Jill Morrison. 2001. "Juvenile Justice Outreach: Library Services at Detention Centers." *PNLA Quarterly* 66, no. 1 (Fall): 16.

Angier, Naomi, and Katie O'Dell. 2000. "The Book Group Behind Bars." *Voice of Youth Advocates* 23, no. 5 (December): 331–333.

Bajjaly, Stephen T. 2003. *The Community Networking Handbook.* American Library Association.

Brown, Margaret, and Pat Muller. 1994. "TAB: A Middle School/Public Library Success Story." *Voice of Youth Advocates* 17, no. 5 (December): 255–258.

Carlson, Pam. 1994. "Books, Books, Books—Let Us Read: A Library Serving Sheltered and Incarcerated Youth." *Voice of Youth Advocates* 17, no. 3 (August): 137–139.

Chonko, Doreen, and Barbara Dirscheri. 2002. "Making Reading Count! A School and Public Library Collaborative Effort." *Florida Media Quarterly* 27, no. 3 (Spring): 9–11.

Farmer, Lesley S. Johnson. 2002. "Encumbering Grants: Managing the Money." *Book Report* 21, no. 1 (May/June): 12–14.

Fitzgibbons, Shirley. 2001. "School and Public Library Relationships: Déjà Vu or New Beginnings." *Journal of Youth Services in Libraries* 14, no. 3 (Spring): 3–7.

Francisco, Grace, and Shelly G. Keller. 2001. *Joint Ventures: The Promise, Power, and Performance of Partnering.* California State Library.

Glunt, Cynthia. 1995. "Guidance To Go." *School Library Journal* 41, no. 10 (October): 56.

Jones, Patrick. 2002. *Running a Successful Library Card Campaign: A How-To-Do-It Manual.* Neal-Schuman.

Jweid, Rosanne, and Margaret Rizzo. 1998. *Library-Classroom Partnership: Library Media Skills for the Middle and Junior High Schools*, 2nd ed. Scarecrow Press.

Kahn, Leslie. 1999. "Pressing the F1 Key—and Retrieving Each Other: Cooperation Between Newark Public Library and Newark Public Schools." *The Reference Librarian* no. 67–68: 99–110.

Kudlay, Robert. 1999. "Orienting Neighborhood Youth to an Academic Library: Creating Campus-Community Connections." *The Reference Librarian* no. 67–68: 111.

Lynch, Sherry, and Shirley Amore. 1999. *The Librarian's Guide to Partnerships.* Highsmith Press.

Madenski, Melissa. 2001. "Books Behind Bars." *School Library Journal* 47, no. 7 (July): 40–2.

McCook, Kathleen de la Pena. 2000. *A Place at the Table: Participating in Community Building.* American Library Association.

McKay, Patricia W., and Janet Baumgardner. 1999. "Teen Read Week Sparks Regional Cooperation in Metropolitan Richmond, Virginia." *Virginia Libraries* 45, no. 3 (July/August/September): 16–17.

Partch, Jackie, and Ruth Foley Metz. 1999. "Multnomah County Library School Corps." *Public Libraries* 38, no. 3 (May/June): 143.

Pitman, Nic, and Nick R. Roberts. 2002. "Building Relationships: Forming Partnerships Between the School and Public Libraries." *The School Librarian* 50, no. 2 (Summer): 69–70.

Pittman, Karen J., Nicole Yohalem, and Joel Tolman. 2003. *When, Where, What, and How Youth Learn: Blurring School and Community Boundaries.* Jossey-Bass.

Ryan, Sara. 2001. "Be Nice to the Secretary and Other Ways to Work Successfully with Schools." *Journal of Youth Services in Libraries* 14, no. 3 (Spring): 15–17.

Sullivan, Edward T. 2001 "Connect with Success: A Few Tips for Public Library-School Cooperation." *Journal of Youth Services in Libraries* 14, no. 3 (Spring): 14.

Vandergrift, Kay. 1994. "Cooperative Dialogue: Using an Instrument to Empower." *Voice of Youth Advocates* 17, no. 2 (June): 73–77.

Vollrath, Elizabeth. 1996. "The Junior High Comes To The Public Library." *Voice of Youth Advocates* 19, no. 4 (October): 197–198.

Woolls, E. Blanche. 2001. "Public Library-School Library Cooperation: A View from the Past with a Prediction for the Future." *Journal of Youth Services in Libraries* 14, no. 3 (Spring): 8–10.

CHAPTER 8—PROGRAMMING

Alessio, Amy, and Kevin Scanlon. 2002. *Teen Read Week: A Manual for Participation.* YALSA.

Ballard, Susan D. 1997. *Count on Reading: Tips for Planning Reading Motivation Programs.* American Association of Youth Librarians.

Bloestein, Fay. 1993. *Invitations, Celebrations: Ideas and Techniques for Promoting Reading in Junior and Senior High School.* Neal-Schuman.

Braxton, Barbara. 2003. "Bait the Boys and Hook Them into Reading." *Teacher Librarian* 30, no. 3 (February): 43–4.

Brouse, Ann. 1999. *Talk It Up! Book Discussion Programs for Young People.* New York Library Association.

Carmichael, Maribeth. 2001. "Creating a Teachers as Readers Group in your School." *Teacher Librarian* 28, no. 5 (June): 22–4.

Charles, John, Joanna Morrison, and Candace Clark. 2002. *Mystery Readers' Advisory: The Librarian's Clues to Murder and Mayhem.* American Library Association.

Chelton, Mary K. 1994/1996/2000. *Excellence in Library Services to Young Adults: The Nation's Top Programs* (3 editions). American Library Association.

Closter, Kathryn, Karen L. Sipes, and Vickie Thomas. 1998. *Fiction, Food, and Fun: The Original Recipe for the Read 'n Feed Program.* Libraries Unlimited.

Cook, Sybilla, Frances Corcoran, and Beverly Fonnesbec. 2001. *Battle of the Books and More: Reading Activities for Middle School Students.* Highsmith.

Daniels, Harvey. 2001. *Literature Circles: Voice and Choice in Book Clubs and Reading Groups,* 2nd ed. Stenhouse.

DeVos, Gail. 1998. *New Tales for Old: Folktales as Literary Fictions for Young Adults.* Libraries Unlimited.

———. 2003. *Storytelling for Young Adults: A Guide to Tales for Teens.* Libraries Unlimited.

Dias-Mitchell, Laurie, and Elizabeth Harris. 2001. "Multicultural Mosaic: A Family Book Club." *Knowledge Quest* 29, no. 4 (March/April): 17–21.

Doll, Carol Ann, Angelina Benedetti, and Barbara A. Carmody. 2001. "Unleashing the Power of Teenage Folklore: Research to Investigate the Power of Storytelling." *Journal of Youth Services in Libraries* 14, no. 4 (Summer): 35–41.

Dorman, Gayle. *3:00 to 6:00 PM: Planning Programs for Young Adolescents.* Center for Early Adolescence.

Dunford, Karen, Kay Walsh Rinella, and Ravi Shenoy. 2002. "Teens Take a Humongous Bite Out of Newly Seasoned Reading Program." *Voice of Youth Advocates* 25, no. 4 (October): 244–245.

Edwards, Kirsten. 2002. *Teen Library Events: A Month-by-Month Guide.* Greenwood Press.

Falck, Kara. 2002. "VOYA's Most Valuable Program 2002: Munching on Books." *Voice of Youth Advocates* 25, no. 4 (October): 238–239.

Fine, Jana. 2002. "From the Field: TRW Follow-Up." *Young Adult Library Services* 1, no. 1 (Fall): 28–9.

Fiore, Carole D. 1998. *Running Summer Library Reading Programs: A How-To-Do-It Manual.* Neal-Schuman.

Fletcher-Spear, Kristin. 2002. "Masquerades and Millionaires: An After-Hours Teen Extravaganza." *Voice of Youth Advocates* 25, no. 4 (October): 242.

Gallucci, Laura. 1999. "A Most Dangerous Game: Mystery-Themed Teen Reading Program." *School Library Journal* 45, no. 1 (January): 47.

Gincley, Leslie. 1998. "Teen Poetry Night." *Voice of Youth Advocates* 21, no. 1 (April): 31+.

Glasgow, Jacqueline. 2002. *Using Young Adult Literature: Thematic Activities Based on Gardner's Multiple Intelligences.* Christopher-Gordon.

Goldfinch, Ellen. 2002. "Reading Aloud to High School Students—What a Pleasure!" *Book Report* 21, no. 3 (November/December): 16–17.

Goldsmith, Francisca. 1999. "A World of Teen Poets at the Public Library." *Voice of Youth Advocates* 22, no. 1 (April): 23.

———. 1998. "Murder, We Wrote…and Played." *Voice of Youth Advocates* 20, no. 6 (February): 367–369.

Haiken, Michele Leigh. 2002. "Sharing Knowledge about Life: Empowering Adolescent Girls through Groups." *Voice of Youth Advocates* 24, no. 6 (February): 411–415.

Haycock, Ken. 2003. "Support Libraries to Improve Teen Reading." *Teacher Librarian* 30, no. 3 (February): 35.

Hetzer, Dawn B. 2003. "Teen Reading: Mission Possible?" *The School Librarian's Workshop* 23, no. 6 (February).

Hill, Nanci Milone. 2002. "You Just Don't Listen! Mother-Daughter Book Groups Fit the Bill." *Public Libraries* 41, no. 4 (July/August): 198–199.

Hoe, Allison. 2000. "Teen Book Chat Program." *School Libraries in Canada* 19, no. 4: 18.

Honnold, RoseMary. 2003. *101+ Teen Programs that Work.* Neal-Schuman.

James, Helen Foster. 2003. *Author Day Adventures: Bringing Literacy to Life with an Author Visit.* Scarecrow Press.

Jay, M. Ellen, and Hilda L. Jay. 1998. *Ready-To-Go Reading Incentive Programs for Schools and Libraries.* Neal-Schuman.

Jones, Jeanne G. 1999. "No Holds Barred at the Teen Poetry Coffeehouse." *Voice of Youth Advocates* 22, no. 1 (April): 19.

Kan, Katherine L. 1998. *Sizzling Summer Reading Programs for Young Adults.* American Library Association.

Kellicker, Patricia, and Jesse Cole Warren. 1998. "Mission Possible: Read! Teens Produce their Own Summer Reading Game." *Voice of Youth Advocates* 21, no. 1 (April): 16–18.

Knowles, Elizabeth, and Martha Smith. 2001. *Reading Rules: Motivating Teens to Read.* Libraries Unlimited.

Kugler, Marianne Russell. 2001. *The Why and How of After-School Programs. The Education Digest* 67, no. 3 (November): 44–50.

Kunzel, Bonnie. 2003. "Shattered by Shattering Glass: A Teen Book Group Forsakes Fantasy for Realism." *Voice of Youth Advocates* 26, no. 1 (April): 19–21.

Kuta, Katherine Wiesolek. 1997. *What a Novel Idea!: Projects and Activities for Young Adult Literature.* Teacher Ideas Press.

Lamberson, Sharon. 2002. "Grow Your Own: Attracting and Keeping Teen Library Users." *Public Libraries* 41, no. 4 (July/August): 198–199.

Lefstein, Leah, and Joan Lipsitz. 1986. *3:00 to 6:00 PM: Programs for Young Adolescents,* 2nd ed. Center for Early Adolescence.

Lesesne, Teri S. 1991. "Developing Lifetime Readers: Suggestions from Fifty Years of Research." *English Journal* October: 61–64.

Leslie, Roger, and Patricia J. Wilson. 2001. *Igniting the Spark: Library Programs that Inspire High School Patrons.* Libraries Unlimited.

Lipsitz, Joan. 1986. *After School: Young Adolescents On Their Own.* Center for Early Adolescence.

Long, Sarah Ann. 2000. "Libraries Can Help Build Sustainable Communities." *American Libraries* June/July: 7.

———. 2000. "Two Afterschool Programs ASPIRE to Take the Initiative." *American Libraries* 31, no. 3 (March): 7.

Maryland Library Association. 1988. *Gambit: Young Adult Programs.* Maryland Library Association.

McCracken, Linda D., and Lynne Zeiher. 2002. *The Library Book Cart Precision Drill Team Manual.* McFarland & Co.

McElmeel, Sharon. 2001. *ABC's of an Author/Illustrator Visit,* 2nd ed. Linworth.

Mediavilla, Cindy. 2001. *Creating Full-Service Homework Center in Your Public Library.* ALA Editions.

———. 2003. "Homework Helpers." *School Library Journal* 49, no. 3 (March): 56–9.

———. 2001. "Why Library Homework Centers Extend Society's Safety Net." *American Libraries* 32, no. 11 (December): 40–2.

Michigan Library Association. 1999. *Yikes! Cool Young Adult Programming Ideas Made Easy.* Michigan Library Association.

Mondowney, JoAnn G. 2001. *Hold Them in Your Heart: Successful Strategies for Library Services to At-Risk Teens.* Neal-Schuman.

Moore, Nancy. 1999. "We Were Reading Geography Books! I Thought We Were Just Reading for Fun: Parents and a Librarian Take on Seventh Grade Book Groups." *Voice of Youth Advocates* 22, no. 5 (December): 310–312.

Moyer, Mary, and Rosalie Baker. 2003. "A Community of Readers." *Library Media Connection* 21, no. 6 (March): 32–33.

Murphy, Jendy. 2001. "Talkin' the Night Away." *School Library Journal* 47, no. 6 (June): 39.

New York Library Association, Youth Services Section. 1998. *Kids Welcome Here!: Writing Public Library Policies that Promote Use by Young People.* New York Library Association.

O'Donnell-Allen, Cindy, and Bud Hunt. 2001. "Reading Adolescents: Book Clubs for YA Readers." *English Journal* 90, no. 3 (January): 82.

Pavonetti, Linda M., Kathryn M. Brimmer, and James F. Cipielewski. 2002. "Accelerated Reader: What are the Lasting Effects on the Reading Habits of Middle School Students Exposed to Accelerated Reader in Elementary Grades?" *Journal of Adolescent & Adult Literacy* 46, no. 4 (December): 34.

Pilger, Mary Ann. 1998. *Multicultural Projects Index: Things to Make and Do to Celebrate Festivals, Cultures, and Holidays Around the World.* Libraries Unlimited.

Ray, Virginia Lawrence. 2003. *School Wide Book Events: How to Make Them Happen.* Libraries Unlimited.

Reid, Rob. 2003. *Something Funny Happened at the Library: How to Create Humorous Programs for Children and Young Adults.* American Library Association.

Rutherford, Deana. 2002. "My Life as a Rodenite." *Young Adult Library Services* 1, no. 1 (Fall).

Sanacore, Joseph. 2002. "Needed: Homework Clubs for Young Adolescents Who Struggle with Learning." *The Clearing House* 76, no. 2 (November–December): 98.

Schwartz, Linda, and Kathy Parks. 1998. *Raising Ravenous Readers: Activities to Create a Lifelong Appetite for Reading.* Learning Works.

Schwedt, Rachel E. 2002. *Young Adult Poetry: A Survey and Theme Guide.* Greenwood Press.

Shoup, Barbara. 2001. "Heart, Mind, and Hands: Creating a Teen Writing Workshop." *Voice of Youth Advocates* 24, no. 3 (August): 174–177.

Singer, Rebecca. 1999. "School-Age Children and the Public Library." *Journal of Youth Services in Libraries* 13, no. 1 (Fall): 36–41.

Smith, Tammy. 1998. "Science Fair Help Day." *Voice of Youth Advocates* 20, no. 6 (February): 373.

Socha, Debbie. 2002. "Celebrating the Day of the Dead." *Voice of Youth Advocates* 25, no. 4 (October): 247.

Sosa, Maria, and Tracy Gath. 2000. *Exploring Science in the Library; Resources and Activities for Young People.* American Library Association.

Sullivan, Edward T. 2001. "Beyond Homework." *School Library Journal* 47, no. 2 (February): 38–9.

Thorson, Coleen. 1998. "Write On: Teen Writing Contest at Hennepin County Library." *School Library Journal* 44, no. 5 (May): 61.

Tice, Margaret. 2001. "Queens Borough Public Library and the Connecting Libraries and Schools Project." *Journal of Youth Services in Libraries* 14, no. 3 (Spring): 11–13.

U.S. Dept. of Health and Human Services, Administration for Children and Families. 2000. *Youth Who Turned Their Lives Around: and the Programs That Helped Them.* Government Printing Office.

Vaillancourt, Renee J., and Julie Gillispie. 2001. "Read Any Good Movies Lately? Conducting YA Book and Movie Discussions." *Voice of Youth Advocates* 24, no. 4 (October): 250–253.

Waddle, Linda. 2002. "Happy Birthday, Teen Read Week!" *Young Adult Library Services* 1, no. 1 (Fall): 26–7.

Wallace, Mildred. 1993. "Tips for Successful Young Adult Programming." *Journal of Youth Services in Libraries* 6, no. 4 (Summer): 387–390.

Ward, Caroline. 1998. "Having Their Say: How to Lead Great Book Discussions with Children." *School Library Journal* 44, no. 4 (April): 24–9.

Warren, Jesse Cole. 2001. "Word is Out: Teen Zine in the Library." *Voice of Youth Advocates* 24, no. 3 (August): 178–181.

Weisner, Stan. 1992. *Information is Empowering: Developing Public Library Services for Youth at Risk*, 2nd ed. Bay Area Library and Information System.

Wemett, Lisa C., and Kimberly Bolan. 1998. "Putting Summer Reading into Action." *Voice of Youth Advocates* 21, no. 1 (April): 19–23.

Youngblood, Lisa, and Christine McNew. 2002. *No Limits—READ!: Young Adult Reading Club and Programming Manual.* Library Development Division, Texas State Library and Archives Commission.

CHAPTER 9—SPACES AND PROMOTION

Abramson, Ilene. 2003. "A Haven for Homeless Kids." *School Library Journal* 49, no. 1 (January): 41.

Anderson, Mary Alice. 2001. "Fighting the Good Fight: Designing a Library Media Center." *Book Report* 20, no. 1 (May/June): 6–9.

Anderson, Sheila B. 2000. "Young Adults' Services, Allen County Public Library, Fort Wayne, Indiana." *Voice of Youth Advocates* 23, no. 4 (October): 254–255.

Baule, Steven M. 1998. "Remodeling the Media Center." *Book Report* 17, no. 1 (May/June): 24–5.

Bernier, Anthony. 2000. "Los Angeles Public Library's TeenS'cape Takes on the New Callousness." *Voice of Youth Advocates* 23, no. 3 (August): 180–181.

———. 1998. "On My Mind: Young Adult Spaces." *American Libraries* 29, no. 9 (October): 52.

———. 1999. "Young Adults, Libraries, and Ritual Space." *Voice of Youth Advocates* 22, no. 6 (February): 391.

"Best Cellar, Waupaca Area Public Library, Waupaca, Wisconsin." 1999. *Voice of Youth Advocates* 22, no. 3 (August): 177–178.

Blount, Patti, and Pam Gardow. 2002. "Double Your Fun with a Combination Public-High School Library." *Public Libraries* 41, no. 5 (September/October): 254–255.

Bolan, Kimberly, and Lisa C. Wemett. 1999. "Makeover Madness: Tips for Revamping Your Young Adult Area." *Voice of Youth Advocates* 22, no. 5 (December): 322–323.

Burton, Elizabeth. 1999. "Like No Other Place on Earth: How Libraries Can Be a Niche for Teens." *Voice of Youth Advocates* 22, no. 1 (April): 20–1.

Bush, Gail. 2003. "Safe Haven." *Voice of Youth Advocates* 25, no. 6 (February): 438–439.

Cox, Robin Overby. 2000. "Do Not Let the Library Be Cool." *Voice of Youth Advocates* 23, no. 4 (October): 240–241.

Davis, Kalisha, and Karolyn Josephson. 2002. *Get the Word Out: Communication Tools and Ideas for Asset Builders Everywhere.* Search Institute.

Dimick, Barbara. 1995. "Marketing Youth Services." *Library Trends* Winter: 463–477.

Erikson, Rolf, and Carolyn A. Markuson. 2001. *Designing a School Library Media Center for the Future.* American Library Association.

Germano, Teri. 2001. "Teen Services Department, Mastics-Moriches-Shirley Community Library, Shirley, New York." *Voice of Youth Advocates* 24, no. 5 (December): 352–354.

Glick, Andrea. 2000. "Making the Library a Cooler Place." *School Library Journal* 46, no. 2 (February): 28.

Hawthorne, Karen, and Jane E. Gibson. 2002. *Bulletin Board Power: Bridges to Lifelong Learning.* Libraries Unlimited.

Knauer, Jan. 2002. "Teen Central: Beamis Public Library, Littleton, Colorado." *Voice of Youth Advocates* 25, no. 1 (April): 30–31.

Lombardo, Cindi. 2002. "Young Adults Area: Orrville Public Library, Orrville, Ohio." *Voice of Youth Advocates* 24, no. 6 (February): 426–427.

Manley, Kathy. 2003. "10 Tips for Surviving a Knock-down, Drag-out Media Center Renovation." *Library Media Connection* 21, no. 4 (January): 50–51.

Mitchell, Lynette. 2002. "Transformation of a School Library Media Center." *Knowledge Quest* 31, no. 1 (September/October): 9–10.

Myerberg, Henry. 2002. "School Libraries: A Design Recipe for the Future." *Knowledge Quest* 31, no. 1 (September/October): 11–13.

Myers, Carolyn M. 1999. "Creating a Shared High School and Public Library." *Public Libraries* 38, no. 6 (November/December): 355–356.

Nichols, Mary Anne. 2002. *Merchandising Library Materials to Young Adults.* Libraries Unlimited.

Oberg, Dianne. 1999. "School Libraries: Inviting Spaces for Learning." *School Libraries in Canada* 19, no. 1: 4–6.

O'Driscoll, Janis. 2000. "A Recipe for Young Adult Spaces and Services." *Voice of Youth Advocates* 23, no. 1 (April): 27.

———. 1999. "A Place of Our Own, Garfield Park Branch, Santa Cruz Public Libraries, Santa Cruz, California." *Voice of Youth Advocates* 22, no. 2 (June): 100–101.

Pratt, Vicky M. 2001. "Teen Area: Swampscott Public Library, Swampscott, Massachusetts: Going a Long Way on a Short Budget." *Voice of Youth Advocates* 24, no. 4 (October): 264–265.

Saunders, Michelle. 2003. "The Young Adult OutPost: A Library Just for Teens." *Public Libraries* 42, no. 2 (March/April): 113–116.

Siess, Judith A. 2003. *The Visible Librarian: Asserting Your Value with Marketing and Advocacy.* American Library Association.

Skaggs, Gayle. 1999. *On Display: 25 Themes to Promote Reading.* McFarland.

Spira, Kirsten Hicks. 2002. "Renovating on a Shoestring: How a Private School Revamped its Library at One-Third the Cost." *School Library Journal* 48, no. 7 (July): 35.

Taney, Kimberly Bolan. 2003. *Teen Spaces: The Step-By-Step Library Makeover.* American Library Association.

"Teen Area: Scott County Public Library, Georgetown, Kentucky." 2003. *Voice of Youth Advocates* 26, no. 1 (April): 32–33.

"Teen Area: Solon Branch, Cuyahoga County Public Library, Solon, Ohio." 2003. *Voice of Youth Advocates* 25, no. 6 (February): 458–459.

"Teen Center: Beachwood branch of Cuyahoga County Public Library, Beachwood, Ohio." 1999. *Voice of Youth Advocates* 22, no. 4 (October): 246–247.

"Teen Center: Shaker Heights Public Library, Shaker Heights, Ohio." 2000. *Voice of Youth Advocates* 23, no. 2 (June): 102–103.

"Teen lounge, Pinellas Park Public Library, Pinellas Park, Florida." 2002. *Voice of Youth Advocates* 25, no. 3 (August): 178–179.

"The New It's Not Totally Dreamland Quiz: Public Library Teen Area Self-Evaluation." 2002. *Voice of Youth Advocates* 25, no. 4 (October): 256–257.

Usalis, Marian D. 1998. "The Power of Paint: Refurbishing School Libraries on a Budget." *School Library Journal* 44, no. 2 (February): 28–33.

Vaillancourt, Renee J. 1998. "Couch Central: High School Students' Area at Carmel Clay Public Library." *School Library Journal* 44, no. 7 (July): 41.

Walter, Virginia A. 1994. "Research You Can Use: Marketing to Children." *Journal of Youth Services in Libraries* 7, no. 3 (Spring): 283–288.

Wilson, Evie. 2001. "Teen Area: Edmonds Library Sno-Isle Regional Library System, Edmonds, Washington." *Voice of Youth Advocates* 24, no. 3 (August): 192–193.

Yutzey, Susan D. 2001. "Promoting Teen Read Week." *Book Report* 20, no. 3 (November/December): 34–5.

Zollo, Peter. 1999. *Wise Up to Teens: Insight into Marketing and Advertising to Teenagers*, 2nd ed. New Strategist Publications.

CHAPTER 10—TECHNOLOGY

"America's Youth Like Playing Games." 2003. *The Online Reporter* March 8.

Anderson, Gregory L. 1999. "Cyberplagiarism: A Look at the Web Term Paper Sites." *College & Research Libraries News* 60, no. 5 (May): 371–373.

Benson, Allen C. 1999. *Connecting Kids and the Internet: A Handbook for Librarians, Teachers, and Parents,* 2nd ed. Neal-Schuman.

Benson, Allen C., and Linda Fodemski. 2003. *Connecting Kids & the Web: A Handbook for Teaching Internet Use and Safety.* Neal-Schuman.

Berger, Pam. 1998. *Internet for Active Learners: Curriculum-Based Strategies for K–12.* American Library Association.

Birkey, Kathleen. 2001. "Diversity and Tolerance in Electronic Sources." *Voice of Youth Advocates* 24, no. 3 (August): 188–189.

———. 2000. "Electrifying the Reference Collection." *Voice of Youth Advocates* 23, no. 25 (December): 340.

———. 2000. "The Challenge of Ever-Changing Online Reference Sources." *Voice of Youth Advocates* 23, no. 4 (October): 250–251.

Brant, Martha. 2003. "Log On and Learn: No More Teachers? No More Books? For Today's Kids, the Internet Has All the Answers." *Newsweek* August 25: 52.

Braun, Linda W. 2003. *Hooking Teens with the Net.* Neal-Schuman.

———. 2001. *Introducing the Internet to Young Learners: Ready-to-Go Activities and Lesson Plans.* Neal-Schuman.

———. 2003. *Technically Involved: Technology Based Youth Participation Activities for Your Library*. American Library Association.

———. 2002. *Teens Library: Developing Internet Services for Young Adults*. American Library Association.

Bryan, Robin. 2002. "Brarydog.net; A Homework Assistance Portal for Students." *Public Libraries* 41, no. 2 (March/April): 101–103.

Buzzeo, Toni, and Jane Kurtz. 1999. *Terrific Connections with Authors, Illustrators and Storytellers: Real Space and Virtual Links*. Libraries Unlimited.

Caplan, Aaron. 2002. "Perspectives: What Rights Do Youths Have in Cyberspace?" *Insights on Law & Society* 3, no. 1 (Fall): 14–15.

Champelli, Lisa. 2002. *The Youth Cybrarian's Guide to Developing Instructional, Curriculum-Related, Summer Reading, and Recreational Programs*. Neal-Schuman.

Committee to Study Tools and Strategies for Protecting Kids from Pornography and Their Applicability to Other Inappropriate Internet Content. 2002. *Youth, Pornography, and the Internet: Can We Provide Sound Choices in a Safe Environment?* National Academy Press.

DiGeorgio, Marvin, and Sylvia Lesage. 2001. *The 21st Century Teachers' Guide to Recommended Internet Sites*. Neal-Schuman.

Diller, Kelly. 2000. "Authors and Teens Online: Enhancing Book Discussions with Technology." *Voice of Youth Advocates* 23, no. 5 (December): 334–335.

Farmer, Lesley S. Johnson. 2002. "Facilities: The Tech Edge." *Book Report* 20, no. 5 (March/April): 26–28.

Farmer, Lesley. 2002. "Issues in Electronic Resource Services in K–12 School Library Settings." *Education Libraries* 25, no. 2 (Winter): 6–12.

Gorman, Michelle. 2002. "Wiring Teens to the Library." *School Library Journal* Net Connect Summer: 18–20.

Gross, Elisheva F., Jaana Juvonen, and Shelly L. Gable. 2002. "Internet Use and Well-Being in Adolescence." *Journal of Social Issues* 58, no. 1 (Spring): 75.

Harmon, Charles. 2000. *Using the Internet, Online Services, and CD-ROMs for Writing Research and Term Papers*, 2nd ed. Neal-Schuman.

Haycock, Ken, Michele Dober, and Barbara Edwards. 2003. *Neal-Schuman's Authoritative Guide to Kids' Search Engines, Subject Directories, and Portals*. Neal-Schuman.

Himma, Kenneth Einar. 2003. "What If Libraries Really Had the Ideal Filter?" *Alki* 19, no. 1 (March).

Hinchliffe, Lisa Janicke. 2001. *Neal-Schuman's Electronic Classroom Handbook*. Neal-Schuman.

Hird, Anne. 2000. *Learning from Cyber-Savvy Students: How Internet-Age Kids Impact Classroom Teaching*. Stylus.

Jacobson, Frances F. 2001. "Online Scenarios for Teaching Internet Ethics to Teens." *Knowledge Quest* 30, no. 1 (September/October): 20–21.

Janes, Joseph. 2003. "Digital Reference for Teens." *Voice of Youth Advocates* 25, no. 6 (February): 451.

Junion-Metz, Gail. 2000. *Coaching Kids for the Internet: A Guide for Librarians, Teachers, and Parents*. Library Solutions.

Junion-Metz, Gail, and Derrek L. Metz. 2002. *Instant Web Forms and Surveys for Children's YA Services and School Libraries.* Neal-Schuman.

Katz, Jon. 2000. *Geeks: How Two Lost Boys Rode the Internet out of Idaho.* Villard.

Kuntz, Jerry. 2001. *KidsClick! Web Searching Skills Guide with CD-ROM.* Neal-Schuman.

La Ferle, Carrie, Steven M. Edwards, and Wei-Na Lee. 2000. "Teens' Use of Traditional Media and the Internet." *Journal of Advertising Research* 40, no. 3 (May): 55.

"Librarians: The Young Adult Heroes of the Web." 2001. *Voice of Youth Advocates* 24, no. 1 (April): 26–7.

MacDonald, Cynthia, et al. 2002. "Digital Encyclopedias." *School Library Journal* 48, no. 11 (November): 58–69.

Mandel, Mimi. 2000. *Teen Resources on the Web: A Guide for Libraries, Parents and Teachers.* Highsmith.

Mangis, Carol A. 2003. "Gen Y Online: Generation Y Has Gone Digital Like No Generation Before It." *PC Magazine* May 6: 25.

Miller, Elizabeth B. 2001. *Internet Resource Directory for K–12 Teachers and Librarians, 2001/2002.* Libraries Unlimited.

Minkel, Walter. 1999. "Five Librarians, One 50-Foot Phone Cord, and a Whole Lot of Chutzpah." *School Library Journal* 45, no. 3 (March): 108–111.

———. 2001. "Pew Study: K–12 Students Prefer Net to Library." *School Library Journal* 47, no. 11 (November).

———. 2002. "Reading (and Teaching) Teens." *School Library Journal* Net Connect Winter: 28–29.

———. 2002. "Seeing the Same Old Sites." *School Library Journal* 48, no. 11 (November): 32.

———. 2002. "Sniffing Out the Cheaters." *School Library Journal* 48, no. 6 (June): 25.

———. 2003. "Teens Get Hip: Health Information Project." *School Library Journal* 49, no. 7 (July): 30.

———. 2002. "The Invisible Web." *School Library Journal* 49, no. 12 (December).

———. 2002. "Web of Deceit." *School Library Journal* 48, no. 4 (April): 50–53.

———. 2003. "Online Access Improves Academics." *School Library Journal* 49, no. 9 (September): 32.

———. 2003. "The Wisdom of Goofing Off." *School Library Journal* 49, no. 8 (August): 35.

———. 2003. "Time to Join the Club." *School Library Journal* 49, no. 7 (July): 37.

Notess, Greg R. 2002. "The Blog Realm: News Sources, Searching with Daypop, and Content Management." *Online* 26, no. 5 (September/October): 70–72.

Patterson, Nancy. 2003. "Becoming Literate in the Ways of the Web: Evaluating Internet Resources." *Voices from the Middle* 10, no. 3 (March): 58.

Polly, Jean Armour. 2001. *NetMom's Internet Kid's and Family Yellow Pages.* Osbourne/McGraw-Hill.

Rodgers, Marie E. 2002. *Multicultural Information Quests: Instant Research Lessons, Grades 5–8.* Libraries Unlimited.

Russell, Carrie. 2002. "A Lesson in Gamesmanship: Should Kids Use Library Computers to Download Games for Their Friends?" *School Library Journal* 48, no. 7 (July): 33.

Ryan, Sara. 2000. "It's Hip to be Square: Designing a Teen-Friendly Library Web Site." *School Library Journal* 46, no. 3 (March): 138–141.

————. 2000. "Wrestling with Teens & Technology: I'm Trying to Learn and Listen and Make Myself Heard: What (Some) Teens Really Do Online." *Voice of Youth Advocates* 23, no. 2 (June): 93.

————. 2003. "Wrestling with Teens & Technology: Why You Need an Intranet." *Voice of Youth Advocates* 26, no. 5 (June): 117.

Semenza, Jenny. 2001. *Librarian's Quick Guide to Internet Resources*, 2nd ed. Highsmith.

Smith, Mark. 1999. *Internet Policy Handbook for Libraries.* Neal-Schuman.

————. 2001. *Managing the Internet Controversy.* Neal-Schuman.

Tapscott, Don. 1997. *Growing Up Digital: The Rise of the Net Generation.* McGraw-Hill.

Trotter, Andrew. 2003. "Study Shows a Thinner 'Digital Divide.'" *Education Week* 22, no. 28 (March 26): 9.

U.S. Dept. of Commerce, National Telecommunications and Information Administration. 2000. *Closing the Digital Divide.* Government Printing Office.

Valenza, Joyce Kasman. 2003. "'Hail, Ranthor!': The Rewards of the Online Gaming World." *Voice of Youth Advocates* 26, no. 1 (April): 29.

————. 2003. "IMing Means Never Having to Say You're Not There." *Voice of Youth Advocates* 26, no. 4 (October): 291.

————. 2001. "Librarians—the Young Adult Heroes of the Web." *Voice of Youth Advocates* 24, no. 1 (April): 26–7.

Verton, Dan. 2002. Hacker Diaries: Confessions of Teenage Hackers. McGraw-Hill/Osborne.

Walther, James H. 1999. "Is Customer Service Now Surf Service?: Working with Library Vendors." *The Bottom Line* 12, no. 2: 85–87.

CHAPTER 11—YOUTH INVOLVEMENT

American Policy Forum. 1999. *Making a Difference for Youth.* Indiana Youth Institute.

Bard, Therese Bissen. 1999. *Student Assistants in the School Library Media Center.* Libraries Unlimited.

Bartlett, Linda. 2001. "Intergenerational Internet: Student Volunteers Conduct Internet Tutorials." *Voice of Youth Advocates* 24, no. 4 (October): 259.

Benedetti, Angelina. 2002. "Tyranny of Teens: The Perils of Teen Participation." *Young Adult Library Services* 1, no. 1 (Fall).

Burton, Dana. 2003. "Bloomington Teen Council: A Community Partnership." *Young Adult Library Services* 1, no. 2 (Winter): 18–21.

Canadee, Amy A. 1999. "Ten Tips for Starting a Teen Advisory Group." *Voice of Youth Advocates* 22, no. 2 (June): 102.

Caplan, Audra. 2003. "Making a Difference: Harford County Public Library's Teen Board Member." *Young Adult Library Services* 1, no. 2 (Winter): 21.

Castro, Cielo V. 2003. "Meetings Focus on Youth Participation in Municipal Government." *Nation's Cities Weekly* 26, no. 22 (June 2): 5.

Caywood, Caroline A. 1995. *Youth Participation in School and Public Libraries: It Works*. American Library Association.

———. 2003. "Giving Back to the Community: Virginia Beach Public Library's Teen Board Member." *Young Adult Library Services* 1, no. 2 (Winter): 16–17.

Chapman, Jan. 2003. "The Care and Feeding of a Teen Advisory Board." *Voice of Youth Advocates* 25, no. 6 (February): 449–450.

Driggers, Preston F., and Eileen Dumas. 2002. *Managing Library Volunteers: A Practical Toolkit*. American Library Association.

Farmer, Lesley. 2003. "Teen Library Volunteers." *Public Libraries* 42, no. 3 (May/June): 141–142.

Hindman, Tom. 2000. "Taming Teen Trainers: Stockton-San Joaquin County Public Library Trains Teens to Become Internet Coaches for Other Patrons." *School Library Journal* 46, no. 7 (July): 31.

Hubert, Jennifer. 2003. "The Young Adult Advisory Board: How to Make It Work." *Voice of Youth Advocates* 25, no. 6 (February): 444–445.

Hundley, Kimberely. 2000. "The Power of Teens." *Today's Librarian* May: 12–16.

Ishizuka, Kathy. 2003. "Preparing Teens for the Future." *School Library Journal* 49, no. 7 (July): 46.

Keating, Lisa M., et al. 2002. "The Effects of a Mentoring Program on At-Risk Youth." *Adolescence* 37, no. 148 (Winter): 717–718.

MacRae, Cathi Dunn. 2001. "Flourishing Forums for Expressive Teens." *Voice of Youth Advocates* 24, no. 1 (April): 5.

National Center for Nonprofit Boards. 2000. *Youth on Board: Why and How to Involve Young People in Organizational Decision-Making*. National Center for Nonprofit Boards.

National Helpers Network. 1996. *Reflection: The Key to Service Learning*, 2nd ed. National Helpers Network.

Nord, Leslie Lea. 1998. "Talking with Young Adults: A Focus Group Experience." *Voice of Youth Advocates* 21, no. 5 (December): 343–346.

Paone, Kimberly Lione. 2002. "Young Adults and Community Service at the Library." *Public Libraries* 41, no. 4 (July/August): 195–196.

Rose, Laurie. 2003. "Teen Library Board Members: Three Perspectives." *Young Adult Library Services* 1, no. 2 (Winter): 14–15.

Rycik, James A., and Judith L. Irvin. 2001. *What Adolescents Deserve: A Commitment to Students' Literacy Learning*. International Reading Association.

Shiflet, Sarah. 2001. "Having Our Say in Best Books for Young Adults: Bethesda Regional Library's Teen Book Reviewers." *Voice of Youth Advocates* 24, no. 1 (April): 24–5.

Shoemaker, Kellie. 1998. "Top Ten Myths and Realities of Working with Teen Volunteers." *Voice of Youth Advocates* 21, no. 1 (April): 24–7.

Slaytorn, Elaine Doremus. 2000. *Empowering Teens: A Guide to Developing a Community Based Youth Organization*. CROYA.

Smallwood, Carol. 1999. "Training Student and Adult Assistants, Interns, and Volunteers: Tips for New Librarians Servicing Small Libraries." *Book Report* 17, no. 4 (January/February): 24–6.

Sprince, Leila J. 1994. "For Young Adults Only: Tried and True Youth Participation Manual." *Voice of Youth Advocates* 17, no. 4 (October): 197–199.

Stilley, Cynthia. 1998. "Newbies No More: Web Training Program for Teens at Flint Public Library." *School Library Journal* 44, no. 7 (July): 39.

Taylor, Jeanine. 2002. "A Young Adult Team, Teen Advisory Council, and Media Specialists: Collaboration in a Community." *Public Libraries* 41, no. 4 (July/August): 197–198.

Tuccillo, Diane. 2000. "YA Boards Work!" *The Unabashed Librarian* no. 115: 7–9.

———. 2004. Library Teen Advisory Groups. Lanham, MD: Scarecrow Press.

Welch, Cindy. 2002. "The Associations: A Commitment to Youth Participation." *American Libraries* 33, no. 11 (December): 10.

Wherry, Allison. 2002. "Techno Teens Give to the Community Through the Library." *Alki* 18, no. 3 (December): 23.

Wilson, Evie. 2003. "The Young Adult Advisory Board: How to Make It Work." *Voice of Youth Advocates* 25, no. 6 (February): 446–448.

Wilson-Lingbloom, Evie. 1999. "Youth Involvement (Especially with Librarians) Saves Lives." *Alki* 15, no. 2 (July): 11.

YALSA. 1989. *Youth Participation in Libraries: A Training Manual*. YALSA.

CHAPTER 12—ISSUES IN YOUNG ADULT SERVICES

Adams, Helen R. 2002. "Privacy & Confidentiality: Now More Than Ever, Youngsters Need to Keep Their Library Use Under Wraps." *American Libraries* 33, no. 10 (November): 44–46, 48.

Allen, Susan M. 1998. "Theft in Libraries and Archives: What to Do During the Aftermath of a Theft." *Journal of Library Administration* 25, no. 1: 3–13.

American Library Association. 2001. *Intellectual Freedom Manual*, 6th ed. American Library Association.

Arrighetti, Julie. 2001. "The Challenge of Unattended Children in the Public Library." *Reference Services Review* 29, no. 1: 65–71.

Auer, Nicole J., and Ellen M. Krupar. 2001. "Mouse Click Plagiarism: The Role of Technology in Plagiarism and the Librarian's Role in Combating It." *Library Trends*, 49, no. 3 (Winter): 415–432.

Austin, M. Jill, and Linda D. Brown. 1999. "Internet Plagiarism: Developing Strategies to Curb Student Academic Dishonesty." *Internet and Higher Education* 2, no. 1: 21.

Barron, Daniel D. 2002. "The Library Media Specialist, Information Power, and Social Responsibility: Part I (Plagiarism)." *Library Media Activities Monthly* 18, no. 6 (February): 48–51.

Barron, Daniel D. 2002. "The Library Media Specialist, Information Power, and Social Responsibility: Part II (Copyright)." *Library Media Activities Monthly* 18, no. 7 (March): 49–51.

Betz-Zall, Jonathan. 2003. "When Intellectual Freedom and Social Responsibility Collide." *Alki* 19, no. 1 (March): 28.

Blume, Judy. 1999. *Places I Never Meant to Be: Original Stories by Censored Writers.* Simon & Schuster.

Brandt, D. Scott. 2002. "Copyright's (Not So) Little Cousin, Plagiarism." *Computers in Libraries* 22, no. 5 (May): 39–41.

Braxton, Barbara. 2000. "A is for Atrocious—E is for Excellent (Plagiarism)." *Knowledge Quest* 29, no. 2 (November/December): 39–41.

Butler, Rebecca P. 2000. "Copyright as a Social Responsibility—Don't Shoot the Messenger." *Knowledge Quest* 29, no. 2 (November/December): 48–49.

———. 2001. "Copyright as a Social Responsibility—Fair Use: I Need It Now!" *Knowledge Quest* 29, no. 3 (January/February): 35–36.

Cheunwattana, Aree, and Pimol Meksawat. 2002. "Small is Beautiful: The Library Train for Homeless Children." *Library Management* 23, no. 1/2: 88–92.

Cialdini, Robert. 2000. *Influence: Science and Practice*, 4th ed. Pearson, Allyn & Bacon.

Clyde, Laurel A. 2001. "Electronic Plagiarism." *Teacher Librarian* 29, no. 1 (October): 32, 58.

Cummings, Kate. 2003. "Pushing Against Plagiarism through Creative Assignments." *Library Media Connection* 21, no. 6 (March): 22–23.

Curry, Ann, Susanna Flodin, and Kelly Matheson. 2000. "Theft and Mutilation of Library Materials: Coping with Biblio-Bandits." *Library & Archival Security* 15, no. 2: 9–26.

Dowd, Frances Smardo. 1996. "Homeless Children in Public Libraries: A National Survey of Large Systems." *Journal of Youth Services in Libraries* 9, no. 2 (Winter): 155–166.

Dresang, Eliza T., and John Simmons. 2001. *School Censorship in the 21st Century: A Guide for Teachers and School Library Media Specialists.* International Reading Association.

Eckert, Janet. 2000. "Plagiarism: As Easy as Cut and Paste." *The Unabashed Librarian* no. 117: 11–12.

Fialkoff, Francine. 2002. "Rampant Plagiarism." *Library Journal* 127, no. 5 (March 15): 70.

———. 1998. "Stand Up for Scholarship." *Library Journal* 123, no. 13 (August): 70.

———. 2002. "Too Sensitized to Plagiarism?" *Library Journal* 127, no. 20 (December): 100.

Garden, Nancy. 1996. "Annie On Trial: How It Feels to Be the Author of a Challenged Book." *Voice of Youth Advocates* 19, no. 2 (June): 79+.

Geloff, Kevin, and Darlene Nordyke. 2002. "Library Services to Homeless Youth." *Alki* 18, no. 2 (July): 16.

Gresham, John. 2002. "Cyber-Plagiarism: Technological and Cultural Background and Suggested Responses." *Catholic Library World* 73, no. 1 (September): 16–19.

Hamilton, Denise. 2003. "Plagiarism: Librarians Help Provide New Solutions to an Old Problem." *Searcher* 11, no. 4 (April): 26–28.

Hannabuss, Stuart. 2001. "Contested Texts: Issues of Plagiarism." *Library Management* 22, no. 6/7: 311–318.

Hannay, William M. 1998. "Term Papers Over the Internet: New Threat to Educational Integrity." *Against the Grain* 10, no. 1 (February): 62.

Hartzell, Gary. 1994. *Building Influence for the School Librarian.* Linworth Press.

Heins, Marjorie. 2001. *Not in Front of the Children: Indecency, Censorship, and the Innocence of Youth.* Hill & Wang.

Holland, Suzann. 2002. "Censorship in Young Adult Fiction: What's Out There and What Should Be." *Voice of Youth Advocates* 25, no. 3 (August): 176–177.

Immroth, Barbara, and Kathleen de la Peña McCook. 2000. *Library Services to Youth of Hispanic Heritage.* McFarland.

Jankowski, Adam. 2002. "Plagiarism: Prevention, Not Prosecution." *Book Report* 21, no. 2 (September/October): 26–28.

Junion-Metz, Gail. 2000. "The E-Plagiarism Plague." *School Library Journal* 46, no. 9 (September): 43.

Karolides, Nicholas J. 2002. *Censored Books II: Critical Viewpoints, 1985–2000.* Scarecrow Press.

Kirkpatrick, Jeffery E. 2002. "Original Thoughts on Plagiarism and Its Consequences." *Book Report* 20, no. 4 (January/February): 30.

Kniffel, Leonard. 1998. "Continuing Education, Social Responsibility Top Agenda." *American Libraries* 29, no. 7 (August): 99.

Lawry, Beth A. 2002. "The Value of a Library Card to a Homeless Person." *Public Libraries* 41, no. 4 (July/August): 200–201.

Lesesne, Teri S., and Rosemary Chance. 2002. *Hit List for Young Adults 2: Frequently Challenged Books.* American Library Association.

Levine, Judith. 2002. *Harmful to Minors: The Perils of Protecting Children from Sex.* University of Minnesota.

MacRae, Cathi. 1995. "Watch Out for Don't Read This! How a Library Youth Participation Group Was Silenced by Schools Yet Made Its Voice Heard." *Voice of Youth Advocates* 18, no. 3 (June): 80–7.

Margolis, Rick. 1999. "Go Ask Alice? Not if Dr. Laura can Help It." *School Library Journal* 45, no. 6 (June): 12.

Martin, Joe. 2002. "The Homeless: Adversity as Diversity." *Alki* 18, no. 1 (March): 12–14.

McCabe, Ronald B. 2001. *Civic Librarianship: Renewing the Social Mission of the Public Library.* Scarecrow Press.

McCarty, Laura. 2000. "Giving Credit Where Credit is Due: Confusing Plagiarism with Copyright Infringement Undermines Principles of Intellectual Freedom." *Alki* 16, no. 1 (March): 16–18.

Minow, Mary, and Tomas Lipinski. 2003. *The Library's Legal Answer Book.* American Library Association.

National Council of Teachers of English. 1998. *Rationales for Challenged Books.* National Council of Teachers of English.

Peck, Richard. 1999. "A Young Adult Author Speaks Out: The Many Faces of Censorship." *Voice of Youth Advocates* 22, no. 4 (October): 242–243.

Peck, Robert S. 2000. *Libraries, the First Amendment, and Cyberspace: What You Need to Know.* American Library Association.

Pipkin, Gloria, Releah Cossett Lent, and Susan Ohanian. 2002. *At the Schoolhouse Gate: Lessons in Intellectual Freedom.* Heinemann.

Reynolds, Tom K. 1999. "A Place to Explore, Think, and Grow: Will Libraries Meet the Intellectual Freedom Needs of Students and Young Adults in the 21st Century?" *Alki* 15, no. 3 (December): 25–26.

Scales, Pat R. 2001. *Teaching Banned Books: 12 Guides for Young Readers.* American Library Association.

Scribner, Mary Ellen. 2003. "An Ounce of Prevention: Defeating Plagiarism in the Information Age." *Library Media Connection* 21, no. 5 (February): 32–4.

St. Lifer, Evan. 2003. "Filtering and Local Control." *School Library Journal* 49, no. 1 (January): 11.

Stebelman, Scott. 1998. "Cybercheating: Dishonesty Goes Digital." *American Libraries* 29, no. 8 (September): 48–50.

Symons, Ann, and Charles Harmon. 1994. *Protecting the Right to Read: A How-To-Do-It Manual.* Neal-Schuman.

Thornburgh, Dick, and Herbert S. Lin. 2002. *Youth, Pornography, and the Internet.* National Academy Press.

Trinkaus-Randall, Gregor. 1998. "Library and Archival Security: Policies and Procedures to Protect Holdings from Theft and Damage." *Journal of Library Administration* 25, no. 1: 91–112.

Troutner, Joanne. 2002. "Plagiarism." *Teacher Librarian* 30, no. 1 (October): 30–31.

Valenza, Joyce Kasman. 2002. "A bad case of the Internet ethics blues." *Voice of Youth Advocates* 25, no. 1 (April): 27.

Wartenberg, Paul. 2000. "The Pros and Cons of Squelching Library Theft." *American Libraries* 31, no. 2 (February): 48–49.

White, Herbert S. 1992. *Ethical Dilemmas in Libraries: A Collection of Case Studies.* GK Hall.

Whitfield, Betty Houchin, and Sandra Davidson. 1998. *Bleep! Censoring Rock 'N' Rap Music.* Greenwood.

Willems, Harry. 2003. "Plagiarism @ Your School Library." *Library Media Connection* 21, no. 5 (February): 28–31.

———. 2002. "Plagiarism—The Library Connection." *The Unabashed Librarian* no. 12: 20–21.

Willis, Dottie J. 2001. "High Tech Cheating: Plagiarism and the Internet." *Kentucky Libraries* 65, no. 4 (Fall): 28–30.

Young Adult Library Services Association. 1996. *Hit List II: Frequently Challenged Books for Young Adults.* American Library Association.

INDEX

Public Libraries as Partners in Youth Development project, 34-35, 51, 65, 301, 329-330, 334
Public Library and the Adolescents, 48
Public Library of Charlotte and Mecklenburg County (NC), 230-231, 292, 295, 330
Public Library Plans for the Teenage, 48

Q

Queens Borough (NY) Public Library, 330
QUICK model for information services, 73-75
Quick Picks (YALSA), 81, 98, 152, 155-156
Quiet space, 67-68, 258

R

Rampant readers, 153
RAP (Remember Accept Project), 25
Readers Advisory Services, 23, 79-82
Read-in, 229
Reading Don't Fix No Chevy (Smith), 108
Reading interests, 100-109, 173
boys, 103, 108-109
teens, 100-108
Reference services, See Information Services
Relationships, importance of, 12, 24, 29-31, 38, 43-44, 171, 204, 332
Reluctant readers, 153-156
Remember Me (Pike), 190-191
Retro Mock Printz, 159-166
Rosinia, James, 82
Rules of behavior, 31-33, 200-204, 258, 259
See also Behavior, redirecting inappropriate
Running a Successful Library Card Campaign (Jones), 215

S

Salt Lake City (UT) Public Library, 253
Scavenger hunts, 229
School Library Cooperation, 207-211, 215-216, 345-344
elements of success, 215-216
teachers, 207-211
School Library Journal (SLJ), 149, 281
School planning form, 210

Search Institute, 4, 37, 43, 308
Search tools, 271
Services and Resources for Young Adults in Public Libraries (1988), 49-50
Services and Resources for Young Adults in Public Libraries (1995), 49, 94
Serving the Underserved (SUS), 4, 63, 94-95
Shayla's Double Brown Baby Blues (Williams), 191
Shelving fixtures, 259
Signage, 259
Simpsons (Television Show), 47
Smartgirl.com, 101, 102-105, 156
Spaces for teens, 6, 7, 22, 56-57, 253-261
Streaming video, 287-288
Student achievement, 15, 40
Study space, 259
Summer Reading Programs, 199, 230-232
SWIFT program (Hennepin County Library), 92-94

T

TAGAD-L (list serv), 308
Technically Involved (Braun), 308
Technology, 61-62, 269-295
elements of success, 283-295
evaluation of, 291-282
Teen advisory boards. See teen advisory groups
Teen advisory groups, 21, 41, 238, 298, 304-308, 326-328, 333-334
Teen Library Events (Edwards), 219
Teen library web sites, 7, 279-282
Teen Read Week, 9, 50, 58-59, 100-101, 102-105, 228-230
Teenage Research Unlimited. See Zollo, Peter
Teens as paid staff, 4, 41, 43, 323-325, 300
Teens as programmers, 9, 24, 59, 60-61, 220, 323
Teens, stereotypes of, 26, 44
Thirsty (Anderson), 185-186
Truancy, 345-346

ABOUT THE AUTHORS

Patrick Jones runs *Connectingya.com*, a firm dedicated to consulting, training, and coaching for youth services. His most recent publication is *A Core Collection for Young Adults* (Neal-Schuman, 2003). In 2002, he published *Running A Library Card Campaign: A How-To-Do-It Manual* (Neal-Schuman, 2002) and wrote *New Directions in Library Service to Young Adults* (ALA Editions, 2002) for the Young Adult Library Services Association. He has also written *Do It Right: Customer Service for Young Adults in School and Public Libraries*, two earlier editions of *Connecting Young Adults and Libraries: A How-To-Do-It Manual* (Neal-Schuman, 1992 and 1998), and *What's So Scary About R.L. Stine* (Scarecrow Press, 1998). He is a frequent speaker at library conferences across the United States, and has written over one hundred articles, reviews, and essays for the professional literature. In spring 2004 he published his first young adult novel entitled *Things Change* (Walker & Company, 2004). He can be found on the Web at www.connectingya.com.

Michele Gorman is the Young Adult/Youth Wired Librarian at the Carver Branch of the Austin (TX) Public Library. She was recently profiled in *School Library Journal* (3/15/2003). Gorman is making a name for herself as an advocate for introducing nontraditional materials such as graphic novels and computer games into library collections. Gorman's charge is making libraries cool enough for today's teenagers to spend time there. Though Gorman does not have a special passion for graphic novels, she understands the importance of giving the patrons what they want. Though she is proud to call her library a "middle-school hangout," she also makes it clear that the library "is not an extension of school." She estimates that between fifty and sixty young adults each day walk through her doors to check on the latest graphic novels, not to do homework.

Tricia Suellentrop is the Teen Services Librarian for the Johnson County (KS) Library. She was the 2002 recipient of the Sagebrush Award for Young Adult Reading or Literature Program for participating in "Read to Succeed," a themed-based literature program for residents of a juvenile detention center. Suellentrop has served two terms on the American Library Association's Young Adult Library Services Association (YALSA) committee Popular Paperbacks for Young Adults. She cowrote and presented the Kansas Statewide Teen Summer

Reading Manual and teaches a Young Adult Services class for Emporia State University. Suellentrop has been a speaker on Young Adult Services and outreach to young adults at many conferences including the YALSA Presidents Program "Key to the Captive Teen," Mountain Plains Library Association, Kansas Library Association, and the Missouri Library Association. Tricia Suellentrop received her B.A. from Benedictine College in Atchison (KS) and her M.L.S. from Emporia State University.